Oklahoma Politics

OKLAHOMA POLITICS: A HISTORY

By

James R. Scales

and Danney Goble

University of Oklahoma Press : Norman

Also by Danney Goble:

Progressive Oklahoma: The Making of a New Kind of State (Norman, 1980)

Library of Congress Cataloging in Publication Data

Scales, James R. (James Ralph), 1918-
  Oklahoma politics.

  Bibliography: p. 351.
  Includes index.
  1. Oklahoma—Politics and government. I. Goble, Danney, 1946- . II. Title.
F694.S28 1982   976.6'05   82-40328

This book is for
Angie Debo .

Contents

Illustrations

MAPS

Preface

N O ONE who has analyzed seriously the evolution of Oklahoma's politics needs an introduction to James R. Scales's "A Political History of Oklahoma, 1907-1949." Completed as a doctoral dissertation at the University of Oklahoma in 1949, that study has stood for more than thirty years as a necessary source for dozens of monographs, regional histories, and state textbooks.

Noting the frequency of citations to it, I borrowed one of the university library's two worn copies to examine as part of my own study of Oklahoma's statehood progressivism. I discovered in it what others had found: an exceedingly thorough, well conceived, and well-executed study that had few competitors for grace and none for comprehensiveness. Clearly, it was a work that deserved publication and a wider audience. That, however, had been delayed by James R. Scales's subsequent academic career, which had taken him into administration and eventually out of his native state to the presidency of Wake Forest University.

When published, my study, *Progressive Oklahoma: The Making of a New Kind of State,* joined a lengthening list of monographs on politics in the Sooner State. Still, none of them nor even the sum of them could equal "A Political History of Oklahoma" for detail and breadth. They did, however, underscore the need for updating, revising, and expanding that work before finally making it available in published form. Under the circumstances, collaboration was both necessary and natural. This book is its product.

Readers familiar with the original dissertation will recognize it as the basis for this book. The differences will also be apparent. New research in primary sources, many only recently available, and in the accumulated secondary literature of the past three decades has provided for a complete revision to bring it up to date. Three entirely new chapters carry the narrative down to 1963, a year that, as we argue, marked a decided change in the nature of state affairs. A fourth new chapter, much more analytical, traces the chief dynamics of contemporary politics through the 1970s.

However uncommon the circumstances of this collaboration, the final work is very much a cooperative product of President Scales and myself. Literally every word has passed the inspection of both of us. Indeed, we have sometimes found ourselves uncertain which of us was originally responsible for the first draft of an idea or a phrase. In the end, we affirm that this joint work has met exactly the test of true collaboration: neither of us could have done it without the contributions of the other.

My own work likewise would have been impossible without the support of time and money made available by a General Research Grant from the National Endowment for the Humanities. Although the Endowment is free from responsibility for the findings and the ideas here, its generosity was indispensable to their formulation in this book. The NEH's support freed me from an onerous teaching schedule that I might give this project the full year that it required and deserved. It also allowed me to finance the research and compensate the services of three typists of exceptional skill and endurance: Donna Duis, Charlotte Bell, and Shirley Anders.

For their support in the award of that grant (and much else), I am indebted to Charles B. Dew of Williams College, H. Wayne Morgan of the University of Oklahoma, Rennard Strickland of the University of Tulsa, and Anne Hodges Morgan of the Robert S. Kerr Foundation.

Very early in our work, President Scales and I reached spontaneous agreement on what is much more than a formality. The dedication page carries the name of Oklahoma's greatest historian. Angie Debo served as a referee for the National Endowment for the Humanities, but she did much more. Her belief in each of us and what we could do brought us together. Her confidence will not go unrewarded if the readers of this work see reflected here something of her devotion to history and her lofty concept of citizenship.

DANNEY GOBLE

Tulsa, Oklahoma

Oklahoma Politics

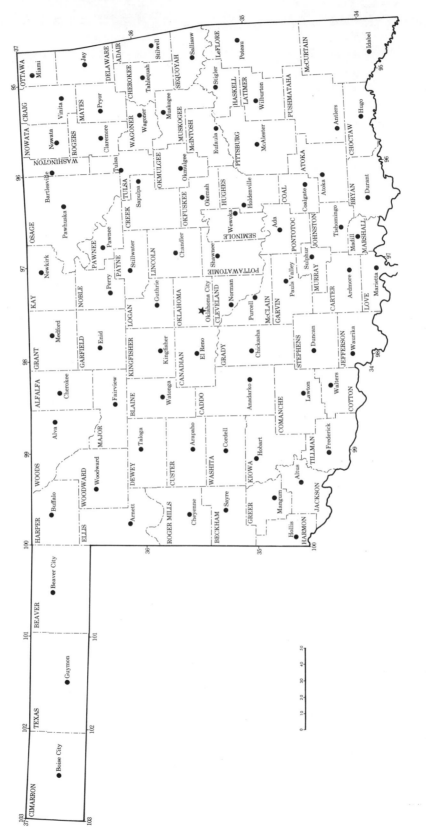

Oklahoma Counties. From Historical Atlas of Oklahoma, Second Edition, by John W. Morris, Charles R. Goins, and Edwin C. McReynolds.

CHAPTER 1

The Party Battle in the Twin Territories

ADMITTED to the Union in 1907 as the forty-sixth state, Oklahoma is one of the nation's youngest commonwealths and its political history one of the briefest. Even at the time of its admission, however, the new state had a heritage of rich political experience—as a regularly organized federal territory in the west and as a network of Indian nations whose members practiced skillful politics in the east.

In the western Oklahoma Territory, county, township, and municipal governments supplemented the territorial government imposed from Washington. In the eastern Indian Territory, the tenuous control of federal authorities overlay five separate Indian republics, each subdivided into legislative, judicial, and recording districts, together with a complex system of town government that varied from one nation to another. All of the era's national political parties—Republican, Democratic, Populist, and Socialist—had local branches and welcomed delegates from the two territories into their councils. Flourishing farms, booming towns, and a burgeoning petroleum industry were attracting new settlers at the rate of a hundred thousand a year. The prizes of politics were worth seeking.

Since its organization by Congress in 1890, Oklahoma Territory had been a proving ground for the new state. Its basic charter of government, the Organic Act, was modeled upon the process in previous territories. Under its authority the president appointed the territorial governor and secretary, together with United States judges, marshals, attorneys, and postmasters.[1] Normally drawn from the ranks of party

---

[1]The territorial governors were: George W. Steele, Republican, 1890-91; Abraham J. Seay, Republican, 1891-93; William C. Renfrow, Democrat, 1893-97; Cassius M. Barnes,

wheelhorses and Union veterans, their presence as "carpetbaggers" was not infrequently resented by politically ambitious residents of every party. Holders of less remunerative posts were in turn appointed by the governor to comprise his cabinet: attorney general, adjutant-general, superintendent of schools, auditor, and treasurer. In later years, as the needs of the territory multiplied, divers boards, examiners, inspectors, agents, and assessors were added to the list of officials, augmenting the governor's considerable patronage authority.

That the most powerful official posts were appointive was no bar to intense partisan activity to fill the jobs left to the electorate. Untouched by federal or territorial appointment were city and county offices and the territory's legislative seats. Election contests to select the thirteen councilmen and twenty-six representatives were particularly partisan. Even more so were the popular elections in which the territory's voters selected their single delegate to Congress. These emissaries, voteless but not voiceless in Washington, became the focal point for political participation. Interest in choosing them was feverish; biennial elections of the delegates were, from the beginning, bruising contests. The size of the vote indicates the intense passions that the races aroused, for a high proportion of qualified electors—averaging perhaps 75 percent of all males over twenty-one—exercised their suffrage during the nineties. Few elections since statehood have even approached that record for voter involvement.

The delegate races provided the surest test of relative party strength for the territory as a whole, and by that measure the Republicans enjoyed the upper hand. In the eight congressional contests between 1890 and 1904, the GOP provided the winner seven times.[2] Presidential referenda showed a similar Republican dominance. Although as a territory Oklahoma cast no votes in the electoral college, Republican nominees triumphed in three of the four preferential contests held before statehood.[3] Finally, the ten campaigns for seats in the territorial legislature yielded Republican majorities in both chambers on three occasions.

Republican, 1897-1901; William M. Jenkins, Republican, 1901; Thompson B. Ferguson, Republican, 1901-1906; Frank Frantz, Republican, 1906-1907. Comprehensive essays covering each executive's administration, as well as those of the acting governors who held interim appointments, are available in LeRoy H. Fischer, ed., *The Territorial Governors of Oklahoma,* The Oklahoma Series, vol. 1 (Oklahoma City: Oklahoma Historical Society, 1975).

[2] The congressional delegates were: David A. Harvey, Republican, elected in 1890; Dennis T. Flynn, Republican, elected in 1892, 1894, 1898, and 1900; James Y. Callahan, Democrat-Populist, elected in 1896; Bird S. McGuire, Republican, elected in 1902 and 1904 to serve until statehood.

[3] The exception was the 1896 campaign, in which the magnetic William Jennings Bryan, running as a joint candidate of the Democrats and the Populists, won the preferential vote. That same year provided the GOP's only setback in the congressional delegate races, when James Y. Callahan was elected by the same coalition.

Only twice did the GOP fail to gain the advantage in at least one house.

The steady success of the territorial Republicans was the consequence of several initial advantages. Political demography may have been the most important. At a time when voter preferences commonly were rooted in older loyalties, the GOP was the beneficiary of the fact that most settlers had been born in the northern or border states, where the party of the Union called up voting habits dating from the Civil War. As the party of Emancipation, it also drew the support of the black migrants from the old Confederacy, who accounted for another 4 or 5 percent of the electorate.[4] In addition, party orators were quick to remind all settlers that a Republican administration, Benjamin Harrison's, had opened the territory to settlement in 1889. It was also a Republican, Congressional Delegate Dennis T. Flynn, whose Free Homes Bill of 1900 had lifted a government mortgage of $15 million from grateful settlers who had claimed land after the initial land run.

Republicans were able to profit from those happy circumstances largely because of one other advantage: they normally occupied the highest appointive political offices. Chosen by the White House, the governor and the other federal officials who surrounded him were certain to be zealous partisans of its occupant. Within the territory, the host of gubernatorially appointed lesser officers were just as certain to be political allies of the governor. Both the federal and the local officials understood that their duties included devoted work to advance their party's cause, particularly on election day, when they labored assiduously to produce a massive partisan turnout. The party that profited most often thereby was the GOP, for Republicans sat in the White House for thirteen of Oklahoma's seventeen years as a territory, and six of Oklahoma's seven territorial governors shared that persuasion. The result was that patronage commonly gave the GOP not only the vital posts of appointed leadership but also the ability to out-campaign its rivals for elective offices as well.

Political affairs in the Indian Territory, if less systematic, were quite as interesting. The elective principle had long been part of the political machinery of the Five Civilized Tribes, the Cherokee, Choctaw, Chickasaw, Creek, and Seminole nations. The choice of chiefs, governors, school superintendents, judges, legislators, and even game wardens in summer elections under the trees was a familiar scene. The suffrage was broad; qualifications varied, but most Indian males over eighteen voted. In their selection of tribal officers, the electors were governed by personality. Family feuds sometimes broadened, however, to embrace factions divided by tradition and principle into something resembling the political parties of the whites.

For all their similarity to white political forms, the Indian govern-

[4]Solon J. Buck, "The Settlement of Oklahoma," *Transactions of the Wisconsin Academy of Sciences, Arts, and Letters* 15 (1907):385-90.

ments regarded the eastern white residents as interlopers—socially, economically, and politically. Town lots, farmland, business franchises, and even education were all Indian monopolies. All lands were held in common by the separate tribes, and political participation was carefully restricted to Indians and a handful of intermarried or adopted citizens. Nonetheless, it was the newcomers who were most active in developing the Indian Territory's bustling towns and thriving agriculture. The more prominent they became, the more their disabilities rankled. Moreover, by the middle of the 1880s, the number of whites in the territory equaled that of the tribesmen; after that date, whites far outdistanced the Indians in the population race. By 1907, both whites and blacks outnumbered the territory's Indian population, the former by nearly nine to one.[5] Pressure to put an end to the Indian monopoly and remove the discrimination against non-Indian settlers inevitably succeeded. The statehood movement itself was both the culmination of that pressure and the occasion of its success.

Although tribal governments were closed to their participation, whites were, nonetheless, active in politics. The federal Indian service long had been embedded in politics. There were hundreds of jobs for politically ambitious whites in the Indian Territory—federal judges, United States commissioners and attorneys, marshals, masters in chancery, Indian agents, superintendents, inspectors, referees in bankruptcy, disbursing agents, court clerks, bailiffs, postmasters, tax collectors, and revenue inspectors, as well as deputies for most of those posts. Field men who came to the territory as government agents stayed on, with or without subsequent appointments, to make their contribution to the development of the new state.

Federal appointments, however, remained the focus of white political activity in the Indian Territory. Because those appointments were patronage selections made during an era of extended Republican national supremacy, it was the GOP that reaped the initial rewards in the east, as it did in the west. Eastern Democrats, whose number was probably greater than that of the Republicans (given the prevalent southern origins of the population) were systematically excluded from the patronage troughs. As a result, their party long lacked purpose, not to mention organization. On the other side, the territory's Republican party existed largely as a distribution center for federal appointments, its activities geared to winning not the voters' approval but the president's favor. For those reasons, both were isolated from the mainstream of the national party battle.

The structures of the rival parties affected their performances less obviously but no less importantly in the Oklahoma Territory.[6] If patronage was the fuel that fired Republican engines, it was also a highly

---

[5] U.S., Department of Commerce and Labor, Bureau of the Census, *Population of Oklahoma and Indian Territory, 1907* (Washington: Government Printing Office, 1907), p. 9.

explosive mixture of personal ambitions that not uncommonly splintered the GOP into warring factions. For at least a full decade before statehood one Republican faction, commanded by the governor and staffed by fellow federal appointees, had done unrelenting battle with a second faction, which was led by the current congressional delegate and embraced most local Republicans. Individuals came and went, but the factions remained durable enemies. At the eve of statehood the rival leaders were Governor Frank Frantz and Congressional Delegate Bird McGuire. As it had since the nineties, the splintered GOP fought over prerogatives and appointments in intraparty battles that often exceeded in passion and bitterness the struggles with the mutual Democratic rivals. In fact, one faction was not above joining with Democratic legislators to further embarrass the executive with investigations that ruined successive gubernatorial careers and animated the most volatile of the biennial sessions.

These unseemly, politically inspired investigations often became the legislatures' chief, if their most dubious, accomplishment. In fact, one of the striking qualities of territorial politics was its lack of more substantive issues. Partisan campaigners found no charge against their rivals too extreme to believe and utter, yet, once in the legislature, they devoted most of their energies to lambasting the "carpetbag" officials and promoting hometown rivalries in furious debates over the location of institutions, including the territorial capital (an issue that led to a near-riot in the first assembly). Otherwise, the territorial legislatures were usually little more than forums for political haymaking. Charges of waste and maladministration, rumors of bribery and corruption, and bickering over minor appointments comprised the agenda of a growing number of assemblies. The programs of successive governors, in turn, were little more than stubborn and futile defenses of their own integrity.

That neither the executive nor the legislative branch was eager to raise more substantive issues testified to another accepted quality of partisan affairs. Both Republicans and Democrats understood that election contests revolved around two fixed poles. First, an abnormally large number of potential voters would actually cast ballots. Second, those ballots would be determined by the voters' traditional loyalties, for most electors returned straight tickets for the same party year after year. For those reasons, the electoral success of either party depended upon its securing a larger turnout than its rival on election day. Both, therefore, had to present united fronts and base their campaigns on long-perfected appeals to the electorate's established allegiances, which usually dated from the Civil War. To the Republicans, this meant "waving the bloody shirt," emphasizing their party's identification with the Union. To the Democrats, it meant summoning up the real or imagined horrors of Reconstruction. For both, it meant that issues of more recent

----

[6]The following argument is more fully developed in Danney Goble, *Progressive Oklahoma: The Making of a New Kind of State* (Norman: University of Oklahoma Press, 1980), chapter 4.

controversy were understated or sacrificed, for to take either side of any currently divisive issue would guarantee a party's defeat. Partisans who agreed would vote for the ticket, as they probably would do anyway, and those who disagreed would make the difference. The disaffected would not vote at all, condemning the entire party to an irretrievable loss; "independent" voters were as rare as those who would switch their ingrained allegiances in moments of crisis. The resulting style of territorial politics approached the heights of irony. The inflamed campaigns of both parties and the persistent record of bitterness at the capital testified not to vigorous clashes over monumental issues of public affairs but to the very avoidance of those issues.

As Oklahoma's statehood approached, however, that style and the politicians who had mastered it gave way to a new mood and new leaders. In company with existing states, the two territories partook of the early twentieth-century reform movement known as progressivism, indeed, of an extremely virulent form of it. In a surprisingly short time the progressive impulse undermined the established order of territorial politics and, eagerly utilized by ambitious men, laid the foundations for the political reformation that accompanied Oklahoma's statehood.

For all its eventual effects upon partisan politics, Oklahoma's progressivism was the outgrowth of experiences unrelated to the maneuverings of parties.[7] It was the political consequence of a series of profound economic and social changes that had ushered in the twentieth century. Central to them was the sudden appearance of massive integrated business corporations, damned by Oklahomans and others with the label of "trusts." At the turn of the century vast new corporate combinations like United States Steel, International Harvester, and American Sugar quickly asserted their dominion over previously chaotic and competitive industries. The most dramatic expression of the resulting transformation was the merger movement, which reached its crest between 1895 and 1905, when some 300 competitive firms disappeared annually. Their places were taken by a relative handful of corporate giants. By 1905 newly organized oligopolistic titans were well on their way to controlling the American economy.[8]

The sudden appearance of these trusts excited a wave of censure that became the most immediate source for political change in the Twin Territories. The provocation was not some irrational resistance to change. Rather, it was the consequence of experiences that this particular change produced, experiences that touched virtually every citizen. One came almost immediately. After a quarter-century of steady decline, industrial prices suddenly began to shoot upward, in company with the trend toward merger. In fact, between 1897 and 1909, industrial

---

[7] See ibid., chapter 7, for a more developed presentation of the following argument.

[8] Alfred D. Chandler, "The Beginnings of 'Big Business' in American Industry," *Business History Review* 33 (1959):1-31; Glenn W. Porter, *The Rise of Big Business, 1860-1910* (New York: Thomas Y. Crowell, 1973).

prices rose by 35 percent. Food and fuel costs, critical to the territories' developing economy, jumped 36 and 53 percent, respectively, over the same years.[9]

Territorial citizens may have lacked the statistics to state the relationship so precisely, but they knew the process intimately. In it they saw direct proof of the dangers that came with combination at the expense of competition. Indeed, they were convinced that there was but one object in trust building, which was "in every case . . . the same — to increase profits by advancing prices."[10] They also detected the ultimate purpose of the trend: to "squeeze the last dollar out of us and have us mortgaged so heavily that our children . . . will be hopelessly bonded and compelled to pay tribute to the trusts which will own all on, above, and below the surface of the earth."[11] The trusts' apparent sovereignty in manipulating retail prices awakened in citizens a consumer consciousness that ignored partisan, class, and occupational differences.

Concern for prices was only one manifestation of that new consciousness. At least as important was anxiety over the safety of products. Upton Sinclair had captured some of that anxiety in *The Jungle,* his famous exposé of one of the most powerful of the new combines, the "meat trust." In 1906 citizens throughout the nation were aroused by the federal investigations that followed—and confirmed—Sinclair's charges. Closer to home, they were watching as Indian Territory railroads shipped carloads of wheat that was contaminated by a decomposed human body and fouled with blood and decay. They learned that a chemist had tested Muskogee's milk and found it adulterated with half a dozen dangerous drugs, as well as chalk, saltpeter, boric acid, and bacteria-infested water. Citizens in both territories were sold foodstuffs declared illegal and hazardous in surrounding states. They protested an unsafe trestle of the Chicago and Rock Island Railroad for eight years, until the span finally collapsed under a fully occupied passenger train, and nearly a hundred persons died. All of this happened in 1906.[12] And all of this could have happened to anyone.

Individuals seemed powerless to discipline the corporate offenders. Having palsied the invisible hand of competition, the trusts had left consumers with little option except to buy their products, whatever their dangers, and to pay their prices, however unfair. When desperate consumers looked to government for relief, they discovered that they were too late. The power of business was pervasive in government. Mass frustration turned to mass rage as citizens saw the Standard Oil Com-

[9] David P. Thelen, *Robert M. LaFollette and the Insurgent Spirit* (Boston: Little, Brown & Co., 1976), p. 71.

[10] *Oklahoma City Daily Oklahoman,* March 7, 1900.

[11] Ibid., March 4, 1906.

[12] *Norman Transcript,* July 26, 1906, January 31, 1907; State of Oklahoma, Pure Food and Drug Commission, *First Annual Report of the State Pure Food and Drug Commission* (Guthrie: Leader Press, 1908), pp. 1-9; *Norman Transcript,* September 20, 1906; *Dover News,* September 20, 1906.

pany twice bribe the territorial legislature to emasculate any attempt to regulate the quality of its kerosene. The experience was repeated when the American Book Company—the "textbook trust"—successively bribed two territorial assemblies and innumerable local school boards to subject helpless parents to outrageous prices for textbooks.[13]

Better than any polemic, these events schooled citizens in the reality of corporate influence in government. As consumers, they observed the irresponsibility of power; as taxpayers, they learned of its inequity. Property taxes gave territorial governments nearly all their revenue, but the powerful proved capable of escaping their share of the common burden. This was particularly true of the major railroads that laced the Twin Territories. The Atchison, Topeka and Santa Fe Railroad, for example, paid taxes on assessments that averaged less than 8 percent of its property's value, whereas individuals in Kiowa County were paying taxes on the basis of 40 percent of market value. Residents of Pottawatomie County also had cause for complaint in 1906, when the same corporation simply refused to pay any taxes at all.[14] In both cases ordinary citizens, the consumers of government, were paying too much because the powerful were paying too little.

A citizenry angered by the arrogant, tax-dodging corporations inevitably generated issues that transcended the narrow agenda of territorial affairs. That anger deepened when the emerging grievances of local producers reinforced those of the aroused consumers.

Small businessmen were particularly vulnerable to the new order. Increasingly, Main-Street dealers found themselves unable to stand up to the new corporate giants, whose artificial price increases threatened ruinous cost squeezes. In 1906, for example, territorial lumber dealers and builders joined to protest that the Southwestern Lumber Manufacturers (the "lumber trust") had raised wholesale prices by an arbitrary one-third, an increment that could neither easily nor justly be passed on to already angry consumers.[15]

Although the concerns of small businessmen were common, they tended to lack organizational focus. But the problems of two other occupational groups, farmers and workers, generated cohesive and politically active interest groups. Beginning in 1903 thousands of farmers in both territories joined the Farmers' Educational and Co-operative Union. In some ways reminiscent of earlier agrarian organizations, the

[13]Thompson B. Ferguson to J. W. Shartel, March 4, 1903; Ferguson to J. H. Dillon, December 31, 1907; Ferguson to Dillon, March 21, 1903; Ferguson to J. J. Burke, May 11, 1905, all in Thompson B. Ferguson Collection, Western History Collections, University of Oklahoma, Norman, Oklahoma; *Oklahoma City Daily Oklahoman,* July 3, 1906; *Norman Transcript,* October 11, 1906.

[14]State of Oklahoma, Corporation Commission, *First Annual Report of the Corporation Commission* (Guthrie: Leader Press, 1908), pp. 415-16; *Chandler Tribune,* August 4, 1906; *Norman Transcript,* January 31, 1907, July 26, 1906.

[15]*Norman Transcript,* November 2, 1906. Also see issues of July 19 and August 2, 1906.

Farmers' Union, as it was commonly called, demanded redress of the farmers' grievances against their old adversaries (railroads and grain elevator companies) as well as their newer corporate foes.[16]

The growing political awareness of the farmers was paralleled in the emerging labor unions of the Twin Territories. Although Oklahoma was to enter the Union as a predominantly agricultural state, it already was home to thousands of industrial wage earners. The largest and most important groups were the miners and the railroaders. Indian Territory's coal fields had been significant since the late 1800s. At statehood, in 1907, some 7,000 workers were organized into the United Mine Workers of America. With railway employees leading the way, another 14,000 wage earners had also joined their own unions. In 1903 the separate bodies in both territories combined into the Twin Territorial Federation of Labor, an arm of the growing American Federation of Labor. Like its parent, the local federation endorsed a program of reforms from the moment of its creation.[17]

Working people were also outraged by another of the social changes that accompanied Oklahoma's approach to statehood. The rise of the corporate giants had brought to public prominence an extremely wealthy class of elite status and flamboyant life-style. "Conspicuous consumption" (the indelible characterization by economist Thorstein Veblen) was visible in the garish mansions, yachts, parties, and even the dress of that new class. Their highly publicized spending raised disturbing questions about the direction of American society. A social order long assumed to be remarkably open, fluid, classless, and capable of unlimited opportunity was apparently drifting toward a permanent chasm, a yawning divide that separated the filthy rich from the filthy poor.

One of the clearest local expressions of popular resentment came later from Charles N. Haskell, the state's first governor. To Haskell, the dynamic of history was a struggle between two classes, which he labeled the "producers" and the "parasites." The first were all those whose labor produced wealth, farmers and workers, as well as the honest merchants and local investors who "take part in the development of their country." The "parasites" were those trustlords whose distant manipulations of the marketplace robbed the real producers of the wealth they had themselves created by honest toil.[18]

Haskell's talk of "producers" and "parasites" captured the social fears typical of the times. Others were ready for bold action. The reform spirit was personified in the career of Oklahoma's Kate Barnard. A compassionate, educated, young Catholic, Miss Barnard early chose to devote her life to the underprivileged. But as late as 1904 this meant

[16] Theodore Saloutos, *Farmer Movements in the South, 1865-1933* (Lincoln: University of Nebraska Press, 1964), pp. 184-87.

[17] Keith L. Bryant, "Labor in Politics: The Oklahoma State Federation of Labor During the Age of Reform," *Labor History* 11 (1970):259-63.

[18] Haskell, "Speech at Sulphur," Charles N. Haskell Collection, Oklahoma State Archives, Oklahoma City, Oklahoma.

Kate Barnard, the statehood social reformer known to a generation of the underprivileged as "Our Good Angel, Kate." Courtesy Western History Collections, University of Oklahoma.

no more than work with Oklahoma City's United Provident Association, a typical charity of the day, which collected baskets from the well-to-do for distribution to the "deserving poor."[19]

In that same year, however, her understanding of poverty was transformed by a nationwide tour, financed by the *Daily Oklahoman,* in which she met and talked with some of the most prominent leaders of the "social justice" wing of American progressivism. Soon she came to share with them the new conviction that poverty was not a personal problem (the result of faulty character) but a social problem that had been deliberately imposed—the natural consequence of policies that damned many to helpless want even as it exalted a few to senseless luxury.[20]

The quiet young woman, who had once naively declared that the mission of charity was to "demonstrate what can be done without dollars and to prove that the poor are most effectively benefited by personal effort," returned to Oklahoma. She brought with her the conviction that what the underprivileged needed was not food baskets and discarded clothing, "but justice, and the chance to do an honest day's work for a fair wage. . . . The labor of charity is like pouring water into a sieve. It is the weakest of weapons with which to combat poverty, crime, or disease."[21]

That new perception was soon matched with deeds. Leaving behind the narrow mentality of the United Provident Association, she helped Oklahoma City's underpaid, unskilled workers form their own effective union. She led the expansion of the Women's International Union Label League, an organization that soon enlisted thousands in both territories, to educate consumers to purchase only union-made goods. With statehood imminent, she and like-minded activists wanted to help the victims of predatory wealth. They wanted the new state to be one that would create a new authority as a shield for the underprivileged—a state that would forbid exploitative child labor, that would tax inequitable excess wealth, and that would advance the claims of working men and women.[22]

Each wellspring of the emerging progressivism raised similar issues. Social reformers pressed to bridge the gap between rich and poor; consumers insisted upon strict corporate regulation, tax equity, and a political system freed from corporate domination; and farmers and trade unionists had an entire battery of new remedial legislation. The approach of statehood added urgency to those demands, for a fresh con-

---

[19] Keith L. Bryant, "Kate Barnard, Organized Labor, and Social Justice in Oklahoma During the Progressive Era," *Journal of Southern History* 35 (1969):147. A well written and sympathetic short sketch of Miss Barnard's remarkable career is available in Margaret Truman, *Women of Courage* (New York: William Morrow, 1976), pp. 183-99.

[20] Julia Short, "Kate Barnard: Liberated Woman" (M.A. thesis, University of Oklahoma, 1970), pp. 16-18.

[21] Ibid., p. 12.

[22] Bryant, "Kate Barnard," 148-50.

Charles N. Haskell (above) and William H. Murray (opposite). At the Sequoyah assembly they identified their party with reform and launched their notable careers. Courtesy Oklahoma Historical Society and Western History Collections, University of Oklahoma.

stitution could bring about the instant realization of hopes long deferred. At the same time, impending statehood also compelled the politically ambitious to act. Men isolated from the familiar grooves of patronage in the recent past saw in statehood unmatched opportunities for prominence on a new stage.

The first to act upon that opportunity was a group of Democrats in the Indian Territory. Without significant elections to contest and without federal patronage to disburse, many Democrats in the east had long been politically apathetic. Even such otherwise assertive men as Charles Haskell and William H. ("Alfalfa Bill") Murray had learned to ignore the pointless activities of their political party, leaving Democratic fortunes in the hands of corporate attorneys and old-line partisans. With the certainty of statehood, however, the quick minds of trade, finance, and agriculture learned to act swiftly to establish their political leadership, lest the timeservers from territorial days continue to divide the public offices of the new state.

A much publicized and much misunderstood convention met at Muskogee in 1905. The convention's ostensible purpose was to draft a constitution for a new state, Sequoyah, to be created of the Indian Territory. Haskell, Murray, and other leaders nourished ambition for power. They surely recognized, however, the futility of a statehood separate from Oklahoma Territory. They met without federal authority; both President Theodore Roosevelt and the Congress had already declared that they intended to combine the two territories into a single state. Just as surely, the movers behind the Sequoyah convention recognized that their political prominence in that future state would depend upon the claims they made to future leadership in Muskogee.[23] The Sequoyah convention was the forum for those claims, and the constitution that they wrote there defined their future platforms. The most immediate beneficiaries were Haskell and Murray, one a booster of Muskogee, the other the Tishomingo farmer already known as "Alfalfa Bill." They stamped their personalities on Sequoyah as vice-presidents of the convention and principal authors of its constitution. More than that, they produced one of the earliest and most coherent expressions of the emerging reform agenda.

Borrowing liberally from recent reform measures in a number of states, the Sequoyans provided for strict corporate regulation under a corporation commission and absolutely forbade monopolies and trusts.[24] They mandated tax equity on real property and expanded the tax system to include new forms of corporate and personal wealth that had previously escaped taxation. They also wrote several consumer-oriented measures, including the outlawing of price discrimination. Their con-

---

[23] Paul Nesbitt, ed., "Governor Haskell Tells of Two Conventions," *Chronicles of Oklahoma* 14 (1936):196.

[24] The full text of the proposed constitution is available in W. B. Richards, comp., *Oklahoma Red Book,* 2 vols. (Tulsa: Leader Printing Co., 1912), 1:623-74.

stitution contained an advanced labor code, along with a host of humanitarian measures to enlist the state in the cause of the underprivileged. By the time their wordy document was complete, the Sequoyans had managed to articulate virtually every demand of the growing progressive cause, and its popularity was unquestionable. Submitted for popular approval, the progressive charter of principles won the approval of a phenomenal 86 percent of the electorate.

Although the proposed constitution and separate state were summarily rejected by Congress, the convention had served its purpose. Its leaders had become prominent enough to be remembered in the new, combined state that Congress authorized in the Enabling Act of 1906. The Sequoyah movement had served one other, critical purpose as well. The aborted project began the Democratic party's identification with a cause that previously had borne no partisan label. With the Sequoyah convention, progressivism had begun to merge with the Democratic party.

Two assemblies the following year completed that merger. Final adoption of the long-delayed Enabling Act provided the machinery for a constitutional convention as a prelude to Oklahoma's eventual admission to the Union. The convention's 112 members were to be elected in November, 1906. Spurred to immediate action, Democrats of both territories met at Shawnee in July of that year to "amalgamate" their campaign forces and draft a "suggested platform" for Democratic aspirants. The Sequoyah veterans there fashioned a platform that was little more than a gloss upon the most progressive features of the Sequoyah document.[25] In the fall campaign, virtually every Democratic candidate offered that platform as his own.

In the next month a second assembly convened in Shawnee. The Farmers' Union and the Twin Territorial Federation of Labor met jointly to make their own demands upon convention candidates. Although open partisanship was downplayed, no one could miss noticing that what became the twenty-four "Shawnee Demands" were virtually identical to most of the planks in the previous month's Democratic platform. The principal additions were several specific labor proposals. Circulated among all candidates for convention seats, these demands drew a predictable response. Aware of the voting strength of the two blocs, a total of 124 candidates pledged their support. Just as predictably, 101 of those 124 were also campaigning as Democrats.[26]

As the November, 1906, elections neared for the 112 seats in the Oklahoma Constitutional Convention, the suddenly reinvigorated Dem-

[25]"Some Suggestions for a Platform Which May Be Adopted by Your Club," copy in Peter Hanraty Collection, Indian Archives, Oklahoma Historical Society, Oklahoma City, Oklahoma.

[26]Bryant, "Labor in Politics," 265-67; *Proceedings of the Fourth Annual Convention of the Oklahoma State Federation of Labor,* Oklahoma State Federation of Labor Collection, Western History Collections, University of Oklahoma, Norman, Oklahoma; *Shawnee Oklahoma Union Messenger,* November 1, 1906.

ocratic party pressed its newly seized progressive credentials before the heretofore dominant Republicans. The Democrats had risen above their inferior territorial posture. Their party was now a coalition, born of popular protest and personal ambitions. On the other hand, the Republicans went into the fall canvass virtually unchanged.

Secure in their power, Republicans had been generally deaf to the reform demands that their rivals embraced at the critical transition to statehood. Instead, the Republicans, precisely because of their long-lived power, had developed close ties to business groups, especially the major railroads, that were now the objects of popular criticism. Reform-minded citizens pointed out that Pliny L. Soper, head of the Indian Territory's GOP, also served as corporate counsel to the despised Saint Louis and San Francisco Railroad. Neither could they ignore the habitual influence in western Republican circles of Henry Asp, attorney and principal lobbyist for the tax-dodging Atchison, Topeka and Santa Fe. It was true that some Democrats, including Charles Haskell, had also served corporate interests in the past. But upon reading the lessons of the Sequoyah movement, the ambitious Democrats had severed their connections and denounced the corporations. Soper directed the Republican campaign in the east, and Asp was one of the party's proud nominees for a convention seat from the west. While Democrats vigorously expounded the doctrines of reform, most Republican nominees followed Soper and Asp in timeworn appeals to the Union, the tariff, and Republican prosperity, now endangered by "populistic" legislation.[27]

The Republicans' statehood effort was cursed by an original source of their territorial supremacy—their control over patronage. Antipathy to "carpetbag" rule was so widespread that federal and territorial office-holders, virtually all of whom were Republicans, declined to run for convention seats. Their party, denied the candidacies of its most prominent leaders, was therefore compelled to nominate obscure figures. Moreover, the factional conflict that had grown from continuing patronage jealousies was now an open rupture. In Oklahoma Territory, the McGuire and Frantz factions refused to cooperate with each other in the convention contests; each wanted to concentrate on the congressional contests that would come with statehood. In Indian Territory, the patronage-riddled party proved itself singularly inept in its first election contest. Finally, Republicans in both territories were so mesmerized by the naming of the future state's national committeeman that they stubbornly refused to cooperate. The national committeeman's post would be the key position in the award of poststatehood federal appointments. It was a short-sighted leadership that ignored the Democratic resurgence. Separate, if not openly hostile, groups were responsible for whatever direction the Republican campaign had.[28]

[27] *Norman Transcript,* October 25, 1906.
[28] *Chandler News,* August 2, 1906; *Chandler Tribune,* August 24, 1906; *Chandler Publicist,* July 20, 1906.

Finally, the GOP's campaign for convention delegates was now cursed by another former blessing. Fortified in the past by almost unanimous black support, the GOP made a fatal decision in 1906. Intimidated by a worsening racial atmosphere, the party chose to contest the convention races on a "lily white" basis. The GOP advanced no black candidates, and its district conventions endorsed provisions for racial segregation in the future constitution.[29] Republicans calculated that the loss of black support would be more than matched by gains from racially-conscious whites. They had little chance, however, to compete with the southern-dominated Democrats on that score: segregated schools and transportation facilities were leading planks in the Democratic platform. The only guarantee for the Republicans was that they would alienate 9 percent of the electorate in the combined territories who had proved themselves a vital bloc of Republican loyalists.

The November elections of 1907 made Oklahoma a Democratic state for half a century to come. After nearly two decades of territorial setbacks, the reform coalition that was the state's original Democratic party surprisingly and utterly devastated a divided and misdirected GOP. Not even the most optimistic Democrat had been prepared for the magnitude of their victory. With almost identical strength in each section, the Democrats took ninety-nine of the convention seats, the Republicans, twelve. When the one successful independent candidate announced his allegiance to the majority, the rout was complete.

Stunned Republicans searched for an explanation. It was contained within one statistic. Thousands of Republican voters, at least 12,000 in Oklahoma Territory alone, had chosen to sit out the election.[30] Disaffected blacks, disgruntled victims of factional bloodlettings, and citizens who boycotted a party unresponsive to popular demands—these were the typical Republican stay-at-homes. They had given over power to the party that had suffered for sixteen years as the minority party in Oklahoma Territory and had scarcely existed in Indian Territory.

In taking their victory, the Democrats had gathered more than convention seats. They set the course of the new government. Their crusade for reform already had refashioned their party into a machine activating most farmers, workers, and independent progressives. Now the Oklahoma Constitutional Convention would become a laboratory for progressive democracy.

[29] *Muskogee Cimeter,* September 27, 1906.

[30] The total Democratic vote for delegates from Oklahoma Territory was only about three thousand greater than that received by the party's unsuccessful congressional candidate in 1904. In contrast, the Republican vote fell by 12,000 between the two elections, despite a sizable population increase. Of course, the absence of previous territorial elections in the Indian Territory makes comparison impossible for the east.

CHAPTER 2

A Progressive Constitution

T HE Enabling Act established the basis for the constitutional convention that convened at Guthrie, capital of Oklahoma Territory, on November 20, 1906. Passage of the act had been the work of a Republican Congress. Its implementation was the task of local Democrats. Partisan considerations entered both phases. Before surrendering its jurisdiction, Congress made certain that the constitution would fulfill certain specifications, and it was the duty of the president to proclaim the finished document only if it conformed to the directions of Congress.

Briefly summarized, the congressional restrictions designated Guthrie as the capital until 1913—presumably to ensure stability in a transitional period. Continued prohibition of alcoholic drink was mandated for the Indian Territory and the semiautonomous Osage Nation for a period of twenty-one years after January 1, 1906. Liquor laws for the remainder of the state were left to the convention's deliberations. The act confirmed the tax immunity and inalienability of Indian land allotments and stipulated that all Oklahoma Territory laws in force at the time of admission were to be made applicable to the new state. Congress reserved two sections of each township in Oklahoma Territory for the use of the common schools of the state. It also appropriated $5 million in lieu of the school lands that Indian Territory did not have. Finally, the statute carefully defined five congressional districts and two federal judicial districts for the future state. The final constitution would be submitted to the voters for popular ratification, and the first state officials would be selected at the same election.

Within those guidelines, the creation of a new state government was left to the convention, with its top-heavy Democratic majority. The

The Oklahoma Constitutional Convention in a moment of official decorum. Courtesy Western History Collections, University of Oklahoma.

group was not unlike similar gatherings in other frontier assemblies. It did, however, reflect recent political changes and suggested something of the document that it would produce.[1] Collectively, the delegates were comparatively young—the average age was forty-two—and politically inexperienced. The most experienced territorial Republicans, the appointed officeholders, had been denied election in the popular opposition to their "carpetbag" rule. As a consequence, only seven of the twelve Republican members claimed any previous political experience at all. The transformation of the Democrats that came with the Sequoyah convention and the alliance with organized workers and farmers had brought new men to the command of that party. Only twenty-seven of the hundred members of the Democratic caucus claimed an earlier political post. In contrast, thirty-four of the fifty-five delegates from the Indian Territory had served at the Sequoyah meeting, and another thirty of Oklahoma Territory's fifty-five were members of the Farmers' Union.[2] Nearly all the Democrats had fully endorsed their party's progressive platform, and a total of seventy delegates—sixty-seven Democrats and three Republicans—were pledged to the parallel "Shawnee Demands."

If the convention's membership reflected the diverse sources of Oklahoma's progressivism, its quickly emerging leadership gave them clear expression. William H. Murray and Charles N. Haskell, the principal figures at the Sequoyah convention, were easily the most important

[1] Biographical information on the delegates is available in William H. Murray, *Memoirs of Governor Murray and True History of Oklahoma,* 3 vols. (Boston: Meador Publishing Co., 1945), 2:7-160; Lerona Rosamond Morris, ed., *Oklahoma Yesterday—Today—Tomorrow* (Oklahoma City: Co-operative Publishing Co., 1931); Lewis E. Solomon, "The Personnel of the Oklahoma Constitutional Convention" (M.A. thesis, University of Oklahoma, 1924); and "Autographs, Biographical Sketches, and Comments on the Members of the Oklahoma Constitutional Convention," Western History Collections, University of Oklahoma, Norman, Oklahoma.

[2] Two delegates, apparently neither a member of the Sequoyah convention or of the Farmers' Union, had been elected from the Osage Nation to bring the total to 112.

in this assembly as well. Haskell's earlier connections to railroad interests probably denied him the convention's presidency, but his influence was still enormous. It was he who introduced many of the constitution's provisions on trusts, corporate regulation, the municipal ownership of utilities, and what was euphemistically called "race distinctions." Murray used the reputation that he had won at the Sequoyah meeting and his allegiance to the Farmers' Union to win overwhelming selection as president. As ex-officio member of every committee, Murray made his presence felt on virtually every issue.

Other delegates achieved prominence as specialists. Peter Hanraty, president of the Twin Territorial Federation of Labor, was chairman of the Labor and Arbitration Committee, a post that allowed him to write most of the eventual labor code. Robert L. Williams, formerly the conservative Democratic national committeeman for Indian Territory, had read the election returns. He had learned the lessons of the Sequoyah convention, even if he had not been a member of it. After the convention, Williams had resigned his several posts as corporation counsel and proclaimed his conversion to progressive doctrines. As head of the Committee on Railroads and Public Service Corporations, Williams would sponsor most of the constitution's regulatory provisions. Like Williams, Walter A. Ledbetter, an attorney from Ardmore, had severed his corporate connections and handed in his free railroad passes after the Sequoyah assembly. He became chairman of the Judiciary Committee. The odium of railroad lobbyist was still attached to Henry Asp, one of the Republican "Twelve Apostles," elected from one of the few safely Republican districts. Finally, the able parliamentarian Henry S. Johnston, of Perry, headed the Committee on the Executive Department. It was Johnston who usually directed the Committee of the Whole on the many occasions when President Murray chose to join the floor fight.

Haskell, Williams, Hanraty, Ledbetter, Johnston, and the ever-present Murray led the convention in its long and intricate chore of redeeming its reform pledges. That task was made more difficult as the delegates simultaneously wrestled with a number of unavoidable issues that lay beyond the prevailing reform consensus. One of those was the potentially explosive matter of awarding county seat locations. Many delegates probably shared the sentiments of Holdenville's E. F. Messenger and Sulphur's Cyrus Leeper, both of whom confessed that they brought to Guthrie one unshakeable conviction: that their hometowns must be designated county seats. Under Haskell's firm leadership, the Committee on County Boundaries was able to avoid an open rupture by picking seats for seventy-five[3] irregularly shaped counties that were defined more by complex political compromises than by the logic of geography.

A second unavoidable and divisive issue was the liquor question. Prohibitionists, organized by the Anti-Saloon League, flooded the assembly with petitions demanding that the constitution go beyond the minimum requirements of the Enabling Act to require blanket, statewide prohibition. Aware of the controversy certain to arise, the delegates chose to pass the responsibility to the public. Under Haskell's leadership, an intricate prohibition article was drafted by Ledbetter to be submitted for ratification separately from the constitution. In that way, the passions attached to the issue would be divorced from the main body of the final document.[4]

Like the prohibitionists, suffragettes saw in the Guthrie assembly the opportunity to realize a cherished goal. Before the convention even opened, a majority of at least seventy delegates had yielded to the arguments of the Twin Territorial Woman Suffrage Association and were pledged to support the female vote.[5] Despite that impressive work, the suffragettes' cause ran aground on the shoal of racism. Murray, Williams, Ledbetter, and Haskell repeated the dubious charge that woman suffrage would only increase black political influence because black women were more inclined to use their ballots than were white women. That peculiar argument apparently received dramatic confirmation when the host city held a school board election, the only territorial election open to women's participation. While the anxious delegates watched, a reported 751 black women voted, while only 7 white women went to the polls. The convention cast its own vote on the suffrage provision the following day, and the women's cause failed, 54 to 37, with 21 delegates abstaining. Ironically, women retained only the privilege of voting in school board races. Otherwise, they were inferentially grouped with "felons, paupers, lunatics, and idiots" as unworthy of the vote.[6]

Resolution of the vexing county seat, woman's suffrage, and liquor questions freed the delegates' energies for their new progressive concerns. On those matters, they moved with a speed and a near-unanimity that reflected the reform consensus. The basic document was written in the long session that ran from November 20, 1906, to March 15, 1907. Two shorter sessions, each of six days, would make only minor revisions. Anxious to fulfill their reform pledges in the most tedious detail, the delegates produced a final document that exceeded 50,000 words—easily the world's longest constitution at that time.

The longest substantive section of the charter was Article 9, "Corporations," and it alone exceeded the entire Federal Constitution. The article bristled with anticorporate provisions. Corporations were forbidden to conduct business without an Oklahoma charter. They could

---

[3] The number of counties was increased to its present seventy-seven with the addition of Harmon County in 1909 and Cotton County in 1912.

[4] Jimmie Lewis Franklin, *Born Sober: Prohibition in Oklahoma, 1907-1959* (Norman: University of Oklahoma Press, 1971), pp. 17-19.

[5] One delegate yielded to the extent that he married one of the lobbyists. He was William Tecumseh Sherman Hunt, a Putnam City real estate dealer; the vote-getter was Mamie Shelton of Oklahoma City.

[6] James R. Wright, "The Assiduous Wedge: Woman Suffrage and the Oklahoma Constitutional Convention," *Chronicles of Oklahoma* 51 (1973):421-31.

not contribute to or otherwise "influence" political campaigns. Neither could they own stock in competing firms nor attempt to effect a monopoly. Railroads, the most prominent local examples of big business, were effectively divorced from mining, ending their long control of the Indian Territory coal fields. Long suspected of tax-dodging, the carriers were compelled to pay taxes on all rolling stock and other "movable property" on the same basis as an individual's personal property. A two-cent-a-mile passenger fare was also imposed.

Enforcement of such provisions was generally entrusted to an elected, three-member Corporation Commission that was modeled upon that proposed for Sequoyah. It had enormous investigative and administrative authority; its powers were as great as those of the most ardent statutory commissions in the existing states. The commission was charged with setting rates and establishing standards of service for transportation and utility companies. Although corporations were allowed to appeal the commission's orders, those appeals could go only to the state supreme court, where the company must bear the burden of proof. Moreover, only the commission could present evidence in those judicial appeals. Corporate appeal of any commission order to the federal courts would automatically forfeit the firm's state charter and thereby close its doors.

At other points, the constitution gave even more direct witness to the complaints that had fueled the progressive cause. At two separate places, it declared attempts at monopoly illegal. More specifically still, it directed the legislature to establish a pure food commission to protect consumers from dangerous products. Frustrated consumers also won the prohibition of price discriminations on articles of general consumption. Liberal allowance was made for the municipal ownership of utilities. In fact, the state was expressly granted the right to engage in any business or occupation (agriculture excepted), an open invitation to subject the trusts to the people's own chastening competition.

Along with the redress of consumers' grievances, aroused taxpayers found in the document virtually every demand of the progressive tax crusade. The new state was empowered specifically to levy and collect "license, franchise, gross revenue, excise income, collateral and direct inheritance, legacy, and succession taxes; also *graduated* income taxes, *graduated* collateral and direct inheritance taxes, *graduated* legacy and succession taxes; also stamp, registration, production or other specific taxes." (Article 10, section 12, italics added)

The advocates of social justice were also comforted with the constitutional abolition of the most exploitive forms of child labor and a constitutional Department of Charities and Corrections. That department was to be headed by an elected commissioner. It was anticipated that Kate Barnard would win the post, the only state office open to women, and use it for the further protection of the underprivileged. In addition, the constitution incorporated most of the advanced labor code that was included among the Shawnee Demands. Those provisions were probably as gratifying to the advocates of social justice as to the trade unionists themselves. Certainly, provisions for the eight-hour day in mining and public employment, abrogation of the fellow servant doctrine, compulsory education, and prohibition of contract labor were as appealing to ordinary citizens as to the organized wage earners who had first advanced them.

Finally, the document included most of the instruments of direct democracy that spoke to the delegates' faith in popular government. Carefully worded provisions for the initiative and the referendum fulfilled one of the planks common to both the Shawnee Demands and the Democratic platform. Home rule charters were to be granted cities of greater than 2,000 population, thus freeing local citizens from external legislative influence. Cities were also accorded their own, modified initiative and referendum guarantees. Perhaps the clearest sign of the delegates' passion for direct democracy was their insistence upon making nearly every state office, including assistant mining inspector and clerk of the supreme court, subject to popular election. These were expressions of the naive faith of the progressive era that "the cure for the evils of democracy is more democracy."

Altogether, the convention went far toward fulfilling the dreams of the reformers. To be sure, some specific promises were passed over. The convention failed to provide for an elected commissioner of agriculture or machinery for the recall of public officials, which were two of the Shawnee Demands.[7] The leading plank of the Democratic platform—segregation of schools and transportation facilities—was deleted because of President Theodore Roosevelt's strong opposition. The convention did mandate racially segregated education (a specific allowance of the Enabling Act), but the president's threat to withhold his approval of the document forced the sullen Democrats to leave the rest of their commitment to the First Legislature.[8]

The president's ability to thwart the convention's will in this instance was unusual. The White House had strong objections to the constitution as drafted. In fact, Attorney General Charles Bonaparte detailed fifteen specific complaints. Most dealt with the charter's more "radical" provisions. For example, the attorney general damned the entire article on corporations as "class legislation." Responding to Washington's com plaints, a second session convened on July 10, but it refused to do more than approve minor changes in wording. The only major alteration the delegates would accept was the deletion of Article 9's provision for suspension of corporate charters in the event of appeals to the federal courts. Otherwise, the convention refused to budge from its positions.[9]

---

[7] The constitution did establish an appointed board of agriculture of five members, "all of whom shall be farmers." The elected commissioner was added in 1912.

[8] *Norman Transcript,* January 31, 1907.

[9] *Chickasha Journal,* July 13, 1907; Keith L. Bryant, *Alfalfa Bill Murray* (Norman: University of Oklahoma Press, 1968), p. 67.

Washington's reservations about the constitution may have given the Democratic majority little concern, but it did strengthen the local Republicans' resolve to resist the convention's work. From the opening day, GOP stalwarts heaped scorn upon the Guthrie assembly, constantly reminding voters that the convention and its product were both manifestations of the Democratic party. If that identification was natural enough, it did put the GOP in a hopeless dilemma. Once the convention packed the constitution with the most progressive notions of the day, the Republicans faced the equally disagreeable alternatives of seconding the opposition's program or opposing the finished document and thereby underscoring the equation of popular progressivism with the Democratic party.

Forsaking the opportunity for effective service, the Republicans fell into the trap of automatic partisan opposition at their convention held at Tulsa in August. The convention's dual purposes were to establish a position on the document for the forthcoming ratification campaign and to select party nominees for the simultaneous selection of the original state officers. The Republicans were trapped. While they achieved both goals, they could not erase the contradiction in their positions. On the constitution, the Republicans pledged a fervent opposition, which, if successful, would have meant no statehood at all. In the next order of business, the party nonetheless named candidates for the offices whose very existence they had just chosen to oppose. They exhausted any remaining possibilities for confusion by also endorsing immediate statehood, presumably without a constitution.[10]

The inconsistencies of their resolves apparently were lost on the Republican delegates but could hardly escape other voters. The self-contradictory platform became an impossible burden for the party's nominees in the fall general election. The GOP suffered other disadvantages as well. The August convention had reopened and worsened the factional wounds left over from the previous year. In a bloody intraparty fight, Frank Frantz, governor of Oklahoma Territory, took the gubernatorial nomination and formal party leadership from Bird McGuire, the congressional delegate and Frantz's relentless foe. Frantz won the showdown in a pyrrhic victory. The disgruntled McGuire forces left Tulsa determined to elect their champion to Congress, leaving Frantz and the remainder of the state ticket to their predictable defeat. Unmindful of the recent disaster, both major factions also repeated their earlier error of ignoring the black electorate, choosing to run yet another losing lily-white campaign.

The prevailing Republican disorder was in sharp contrast to the Democrats' vitality in the first state election campaign. Rejecting the discredited convention method of nomination, the Democrats committed themselves to a primary election to select their party nominees in June,

---

[10] *Tulsa World,* August 1, 1907; W. B. Richards, comp., *Oklahoma Red Book,* 2 vols. (Tulsa: Leader Printing Co., 1912), 2:359.

even before the Guthrie convention adjourned. Political tensions and personal rivalries among the ambitious delegates naturally increased. Democratic outsiders hostile to the convention began to exploit the resentments of all those groups dissatisfied with one or another provision of the proposed document. Most of these gathered around the standard of Lee Cruce, a conservative Ardmore banker, in the gubernatorial race, which was the focus of attention.

To head their ticket and parry the Cruce threat, the constitutional leaders turned to Charles Haskell, an extremely shrewd and daring negotiator who probably had been running for the governorship from the very beginning. Haskell had ingratiated himself with the traditional party leaders and heartily cultivated the friendship of farm and labor groups. Even the Republican delegates in the convention had been obliged to concede his ability as a peacemaker. Ministers and other prohibitionists who otherwise surely would have supported Lee Cruce, the long-announced dry, were grateful to Haskell for his part in securing the convention's submission of a statewide constitutional prohibition clause.

Haskell engaged in public debate with Thomas H. Doyle of Perry, a longtime statehood advocate and critic of the constitution, during the primary campaign. It was plain, however, that the nomination lay between Haskell and Cruce. The latter's campaign seemed to be the more heavily financed, but Haskell furnished most of the fireworks. He accused Cruce of a host of unprogressive practices: usurious lending from his bank, opposing bond issues for public schools and other hometown improvements, and using paid workers for electioneering. More serious than any of these was the allegation that Cruce was an insincere friend of the constitution, for he had dared to criticize its provisions and ridicule its authors. Haskell's slashing style was effective. Although his final margin was narrow (51,676 to 48,206, with Doyle an also-ran at 8,820), Haskell bested his rival in every section except Cruce's home area and the extreme western region, where Cruce was much better known.[11]

In contrast with later Democratic primaries, there were few candidates for the lesser state offices, and many Democratic convention leaders won nomination with only token opposition. Peter Hanraty drew no opponent in the race for mining inspector. Kate Barnard, as a woman, had been ineligible to serve in the constitutional assembly, but she had lobbied the convention and played an active role in the 1906 campaign. To no one's surprise, she was the party's unopposed nominee for commissioner of charities and corrections. Robert L. Williams won nomination to the state supreme court. William H. Murray, the convention's dominant figure, chose to campaign for the first state legislature, where he hoped to be named speaker of the house. Unable to cast a ballot in his behalf, voters outside the legislative district indicated the power

---

[11] Richards, *Oklahoma Red Book,* 2:289.

Frank Frantz, doomed but gallant bearer of the Republican banner in the critical statehood contest of 1907. Courtesy Western History Collections, University of Oklahoma.

of the Murray name by nominating his brother, John Shade Murray, a school teacher from the tiny community of Nida, to the post of commissioner of labor. John Shade Murray's victory was all the more remarkable in that he had publicly withdrawn from the race, and his name had not appeared on the ballot in several counties, including his own. The embarrassed Democratic Central Committee, which William H. Murray headed, substituted Charles L. Daugherty, the labor unions' choice, lest they antagonize their labor allies. John Shade's reaction to his astonishing sacrifice is unrecorded.[12] Charles J. West of Enid, who got his start in politics by prosecuting a rate case for the Republican territorial administration under his friend Governor Frantz, capitalized on this record as a railroad foe to win Democratic nomination for attorney general.

Sensitive to Republican charges of a "constitutional cabal," the Democrats wisely left nomination for the two United States Senate seats to men who had not served at the convention. With no delegate in the race, Robert L. Owen of Muskogee, Henry M. Furman of Ada, and Thomas P. Gore of Lawton took the top three positions in a packed primary field. In witness to Democratic harmony, Furman (like Owen, from the old Indian Territory) withdrew in Gore's favor, although the latter had run third. Furman's voluntary action thus made it possible to preserve the informal agreement to allot one Senate seat to each territory.[13]

During the short but bitter statehood campaign, Frantz proceeded to give a good account of himself. Frantz, then only thirty-five, had the advantages of youth, vigor, a handsome presence, and a distinguished military career as one of Theodore Roosevelt's famous "Rough Riders" of the Spanish-American War. Frantz certainly seemed to take his own chances seriously, for he traveled widely, especially in the eastern half of the state, where he was less well known.

Though sorely embarrassed by his own platform, Frantz attempted to take the offensive against Haskell and the Democrats. His speeches repeated the standard partisan ridicule of the convention and attacked the most vulnerable features of its work: gerrymandered legislative and judicial districts, interference with the prerogatives of the courts, and county boundaries. Most of the counties were too small, Frantz maintained, for economical administration. The head of the ticket left it to local Republican workers to argue the corollary: that some county seats were located improperly. This was an important but treacherous argument, and it could not be discussed too openly, lest criticism in Bristow, for instance, reach the voters in the county seat-designate of Sapulpa.

For his part, Haskell may not have been his party's best choice, since

---

[12] Murray, *Memoirs of Governor Murray,* 2:91–92.

[13] Furman's sacrifice would not go altogether unrewarded. With statehood he was appointed presiding judge of the criminal court of appeals (an unfortunate constitutional transposition in nomenclature), where he served with distinction.

his previous record of quick business promotions made him extremely vulnerable in the general election campaign. Republicans tried to capitalize upon Haskell's suspicious connections to railroads and corporations, including the Standard Oil Company, in Ohio, before his removal to Indian Territory.[14] Haskell and his partisans replied in kind. A week before the election, Haskell charged his opponent "with drunkenness, with breaking the laws of God and country, disregarding the ties between husband and wife; [and] with entering into an agreement with oil operators whereby he received stock in a company in return for special privileges."[15]

By the campaign's last stages, the local candidates yielded the spotlight to nationally prominent speakers. William Howard Taft, the Republican secretary of war and Roosevelt's heir-apparent, championed the GOP's position in a legalistic and dispassionate exposition at Oklahoma City on August 24. Contrasting the Guthrie document with the federal Constitution, Taft asserted the superiority of the latter for its simplicity, scope, and diction. The excessively complex and confusing state constitution, Taft declared, erred in its attempt to legislate changing details in an immutable pattern. It was, in that respect, "a code of by-laws" rather than a fundamental instrument of government. In respect to its more radical provisions, the conservative Taft damned it as "flavored with Socialism."[16]

To respond to Taft's charges, the Democrats called upon their beloved William Jennings Bryan, the Great Commoner. Bryan received a hero's welcome as he moved across the territories. At Vinita, Claremore, Tulsa, Sapulpa, Bristow, Chandler, and Oklahoma City, throngs waited to hear the ponderous cadences of the "Silver Tongued Orator from the Platte" as he pronounced the proposed constitution the most progressive ever written. Bryan was too clever to attempt to answer Taft's judicial analysis with a categorical defense; his appeal was to the emotions, flattering Oklahomans for their wisdom in choosing a great constitutional assembly. His benign endorsement of the Democratic slate for state office was all many voters needed. To an audience of 25,000 in Oklahoma City on September 5, Bryan underlined the Republican dilemma: "Secretary Taft suggested that you reject the constitution and postpone statehood, but should you be foolish enough to vote for the constitution, you should put it in the hands of its enemies so they may assassinate it."[17]

In the September, 1907, statehood election, Oklahomans voted overwhelmingly for the constitution and its friends. The popularity of the constitution was universal, and it carried with a statewide margin of five to two. Only in the staunchly Republican counties was the vote

[14] *Shawnee News,* August 28-September 9, 1907; *Oklahoma City Daily Oklahoman,* September 11, 1907.
[15] *Shawnee Daily Herald,* September 3, 1907.
[16] *Oklahoma City Daily Oklahoman,* August 25, 1907.
[17] Ibid., September 6, 1907.

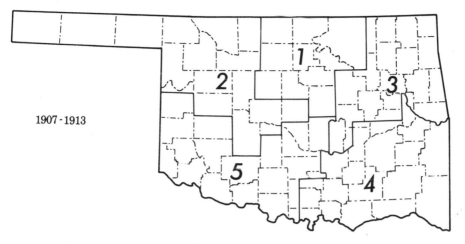

1907-1913

Oklahoma Congressional Districts, 1907-13. From Historical Atlas of Oklahoma, *First Edition, by John W. Morris, Charles R. Goins, and Edwin C. McReynolds.*

even close, and in no county was it rejected. So popular was the constitution that its winning margin was roughly twice that which elected Haskell over Frantz. It was also 76,000 votes greater than that accorded Democratic convention candidates only ten months earlier. The progressive constitution rose above party, attracting Democrats, Republicans, and those who had sat out the campaign of 1906. The separately submitted prohibition clause also carried, but by a narrow margin of 130,361 to 112,258. Seventeen counties appeared in the negative column. Curiously, fifteen of the seventeen were in Indian Territory, which would have been dry in any event.[18]

Earning identification with the constitution paid off handsomely for the Democrats. Their party not only elected Haskell governor but swept every other executive post and all the statewide judicial positions as well. Although the Republican Congress had drawn the congressional district lines in a way that encouraged Republican prospects for at least three of the five seats, the Democratic landslide carried four Democrats to victory. Ironically, the only Republican to escape the deluge was Bird McGuire, whose feud with Governor Frantz had contributed heavily to his party's debility.[19]

It was in the election of the local candidates that the Democrats demonstrated their fundamental strength. In the first statewide test, Democrats gained a clean sweep in many of the counties and at least a plurality of the offices in sixty-two. The Republicans took a majority of the posts in only ten counties, and in three counties the split was

[18] Richards, *Oklahoma Red Book,* 2:292-95.
[19] State of Oklahoma, State Election Board, *Directory of Oklahoma, 1977,* p. 514.

The statehood celebration and beginnings of Democratic political dominance in Oklahoma at Guthrie's Carnegie Library. Courtesy Western History Collections, University of Oklahoma.

even. Although the exact proportions would change with time, Democratic dominance of the courthouses was firmly established in this initial contest. Thereafter, Republicans failed to enter full tickets for the county offices, and ambitious young men just starting their political careers in local races perforce began them as Democrats.

Ninety-two Democrats, representing every corner of the state, took control of the lower house and unanimously chose William H. Murray as their speaker. The seventeen Republican members meekly acquiesced in the Democrats' organizational plans. Unlike their partisan rivals, the Republicans were reduced to a sectional advantage, the northwestern corner of the state, which supplied thirteen of their seventeen representatives.

The Democrats controlled the state senate by a margin of thirty-nine to five. Except for one member from the Okmulgee-Wagoner district, all of the Republican senators came from the northern portion of old Oklahoma Territory. The Democrats of the upper chamber followed their allies in the lower house by choosing another constitutional veteran, Henry Johnston, as their leader in the post of president pro tempore.[20]

Legislative control carried with it control of the new state's first two seats in the United States Senate, since those positions were still filled by state legislatures. Robert L. Owen and Thomas P. Gore, the men who had emerged from the Democratic preferential balloting, thereby were assured election to the Senate. Each of them represented a different version of the ascendant progressive faith.

Robert Latham Owen, the senior senator (his status determined by drawing straws), represented that form of genteel southern progressivism that would soon find its champion in Woodrow Wilson.[21] Like Wilson, Owen was born in Virginia, where his father served as a state senator and a railroad president. From his mother, who was one-eighth Cherokee, Owen received the Indian blood that was a priceless political asset in early Oklahoma. Valedictorian of Washington and Lee University in 1877, Owen migrated to the Indian Territory in the following year. There, while serving as a Democratic stalwart, he built a career as a teacher, editor, lawyer, and banker. Under Grover Cleveland's first administration, he served as superintendent of the Union Agency at Muskogee, which supervised the affairs of the Five Civilized Tribes.

During his long senatorial career, he was a steady follower of what became Wilsonian progressivism—a dignified regulation of economic affairs through expert and efficient administration. As a United States senator, he coauthored (with Virginia's Carter Glass) the Federal Reserve Act and sponsored such measures as the federal income and inheritance tax, the postal savings bank, the direct election of United States senators, public health, and the regulation of corrupt election practices. A generation of Democratic reformers at the national capital found him a steadfast warrior against monopolies and the protective tariff.

Thomas Pryor Gore, the junior senator, was a public man of very different stamp.[22] Born in war-ravaged Mississippi in 1870, he lost his eyesight in two boyhood accidents. A graduate of Cumberland Law School in Tennessee (like a surprising number of early day Oklahoma politicians), Gore lived for five years in Corsicana, Texas, before coming to Oklahoma Territory. In the Lone Star State, Gore had been a member of the Populist party and defended its economically radical program against Democratic party loyalists, among them, ironically, the young William H. Murray, who lived in the same area. After failing to win a congressional seat as a Populist, Gore migrated to Oklahoma Territory, where he forsook his party's label but not its principles. As a Democrat, he was elected to the territorial council in 1902. Thereafter, he was quick to sense a popular issue or to polish a partisan epigram. He was the most resourceful of debaters, demolishing his op-

[20]See John S. Brooks, comp., *First Administration of Oklahoma* (Oklahoma City: Oklahoma Engraving and Printing Co., 1908) for biographical sketches of each state official in every branch of government at statehood.

[21]The only published book-length study is Grant Foreman, *Robert Latham Owen* (Muskogee: First National Bank, 1947).

[22]Gore is the subject of an excellent biography: Monroe Lee Billington, *Thomas P. Gore: The Blind Senator from Oklahoma* (Lawrence: University of Kansas Press, 1967).

Robert L. Owen, senatorial ally of fellow Virginian Woodrow Wilson. Courtesy Oklahoma Historical Society.

ponents with a quip, a sardonic apostrophe, or a dubious "Biblical" quotation. He occasionally enlarged the Holy Scriptures to attribute to them some statement of his own invention. Gore could thus bolster a wavering argument, for he had cultivated the Elizabethan style of the King James Version to perfection.

In Washington, Gore's legislative influence never matched that of his colleague. While the senior senator was always a loyal partisan, particularly during the Wilson years, Gore was too much the maverick

Thomas P. Gore, Democratic maverick and fierce foe of trusts, bankers, and warlords. Courtesy Western History Collections, University of Oklahoma.

to exchange his own cherished principles for any man's leadership. His independence became, in fact, his most consistent quality. If it made him a determined foe of trusts, bankers, and warlords, it also led him to break with his own party's president, once during the First World War and later under the New Deal.

Within the state, the most obvious lesson of the September elections was the massive popular support for the progressive constitution and for the party that authored it. Although he described his personal opinion of the document as "not fit for publication."[23] President Roosevelt could find no grounds on which to deny a proclamation of statehood. After what Democrats considered an unconscionable delay of nearly two months, Roosevelt formally proclaimed Oklahoma's statehood on November 16, 1907.

The voters had chosen to place the constitution in the hands of its friends. Despite its cumbersome length, the document necessarily left much work undone. Many of its provisions were not self-executing. Most of the newly established departments urgently needed statutory authority to enable them to perform their duties. The acts of the First Legislature would vitalize the constitution's general principles and on occasion expand them.

Meeting from December 2, 1907, to May 26, 1908, the legislature turned quickly and enthusiastically to its task. Completion of the state's segregation system was the first order of business. Finally fulfilling the leading plank of their 1906 platform, the First Legislature whooped through Senate Bill 1 with a thirty-seven to two vote in the senate and a ninety-five to ten vote in the house. Transportation companies were given the responsibility of providing separate coaches, waiting rooms, and compartments, "which shall be equal in all points of comfort and convenience." Failure to provide these Jim Crow facilities left the companies liable to fines ranging from a hundred to a thousand dollars for each violation. Black reaction to the predictable measure included small-scale rioting. The Midland Valley station at Taft (an all-black town) was burned, and Lieutenant Governor George W. Bellamy's train was besieged in a brief skirmish.[24]

Political concern over President Roosevelt's disapproval of a Jim Crow constitution had forced the legislature to complete the constitutional convention's segregationist work, and uncertainty over prohibition left the First Legislature to vitalize the separately submitted liquor article. With the governor's full support, Senator Richard A. Billups of Cordell, chairman of the Senate Prohibition Committee, introduced the enforcement statute that forever after would be known as the "Billups Booze Bill." Amended by the house, the final act coupled rigorous enforcement with a state dispensary system. As allowed by the popularly ratified prohibition article, the law authorized the operation of state dispensaries in towns of more than 2,000 people. Counties lacking such populous centers were entitled to one dispensary. The state agencies were authorized to sell liquor only upon the prescription of a licensed physician.

Despite some understandable fears that the system would effectively nullify prohibition, the stiff penalties for abuse (fines of up to $1,000 and imprisonment for as much as a year) apparently deferred fraud.

[23] *Shawnee Herald,* September 6, 1907.
[24] Phillip Mellinger, "Discrimination and Statehood in Oklahoma," *Chronicles of Oklahoma* 49 (1971):373.

Even the most avid prohibitionist must have been pleasantly surprised when the dispensary agent in the capital city reported five weeks' total sales of $3.20. Similarly, Oklahoma City's 50,000 residents consumed only $8.00 worth of Sunnybrook (the agency's brand) between May and August of 1908.[25]

Having attended to convention leftovers, the legislature was free to consider more substantive issues. Close cooperation prevailed, for every branch of the government was headed by a veteran of the Guthrie assembly: Haskell was in the governor's chair; Williams was chief justice; and Murray and Johnston directed the two legislative chambers. A joint legislative committee, working with administrators like Hanraty, Barnard, and Daugherty, drafted the major pieces of legislation. The most important proposals for sweeping social and economic legislation won the approval and the undivided support of the leaders in both the executive and the legislative branches before ever being submitted to the floor.

Predictably, state financing assumed top priority. The Enabling Act had obligated the state to accept the debts of Oklahoma Territory, necessitating the immediate issue of nearly $1.5 million in state warrants. In funding that instant debt and meeting the current expenses of government, the state drew upon the principles of its progressive tax crusade. The First Legislature levied a new, 2 percent gross revenue tax on pipelines, coal mines, and telegraph lines. It added 0.5 percent gross production tax on oil, railroad, and telephone companies, as well as electrical utilities. The first state income tax embraced the progressive feature of graduation. Income under $3,500 annually went untaxed. Between that level and $10,000 the rate was 0.5 percent. Successive increases brought the rate to 3.5 percent for incomes above $100,000.

Despite these new taxes, the property tax would remain the state's prime source of revenue for the foreseeable future. That burden was made more equitable when, as ex-officio chairman of the State Excise Board, Haskell compelled a thoroughgoing upward revaluation of corporate property. Railroad, gas, and electric company assessments increased in some cases as much as 400 percent above the levels listed by Frantz as territorial governor.

The anticorporate drive of early Oklahoma progressivism extended beyond tax reform. The First Legislature enthusiastically continued the constitution's emphasis on regulation by strengthening the already powerful Corporation Commission. Under the fearless and able direction of Jack Love, the commission regained the limits on federal appeals of its orders and required the registration of lobbyists.[26] Elected on the slogan of "Make the Railroads Toe the Mark," Love fought hard to maintain

---

[25] Franklin, *Born Sober*, pp. 25–35.

[26] The two other members of the original commission, James J. McAlester and A. P. ("Potato") Watson, were easily overshadowed by the chairman. For a generally favorable view of the early commission, see Grant Foreman, "Trusts and the People Get Together," *Independent*, December 11, 1916, p. 454.

the constitution's unrealistic mandate of the two-cents-a-mile passenger fares. He did succeed in forcing improved rail service at cheaper rates.

The consumers' counterattack against the "interests" also featured an exceptionally harsh antitrust bill, drafted by Attorney General West. The bill went so far as to earn even Haskell's veto. Haskell asserted that the measure would subject any corporation, however virtuous, to arbitrary administrative action, however inappropriate, upon any accusation of monopoly, however unjust. Despite his veto the governor was careful to make plain his support of antitrust policies. A second bill, more carefully drawn, won his approval at the legislature's end.

The most bizarre consumer bill, credited to Speaker Murray, required hotel proprietors to provide upper bed sheets that were no less than nine feet long.[27] The law further required that the upper sheet must turn back two and one-half feet over the outer covering. Although Republicans generally blasted the measure as yet another example of Murray's contrariness, travelers with experience in the short-sheeting of the frontier could see some sense in the measure.

Much more important but no less imaginative was the new state's pioneer bank guarantee law. Banking in both territories had commonly been lackadaisical for owners and treacherous for depositors. With virtually no regulation of banking, citizens risked what little money they had when they deposited it in ill-managed, ill-capitalized, and ill-protected institutions.[28] The Panic of 1907 and the thirty-day bank holiday that began on October 27, 1907, only underscored the consumers' common plight. The First Legislature quickly turned its attention to the problem.

As part of the new state's comprehensive banking code, the guarantee system was financed by an assessment of 1 percent (to be raised to 2 percent in emergencies) of the average daily deposits of member banks. All state-chartered banks were required to join, and banks holding federal charters were invited to participate.[29] Should a member bank fail, the state banking commissioner would assume the assets of the defunct institution, including the statutory liabilities of its stockholders, and draw upon the fund to pay depositors in full.

The remainder of the banking code sharply limited the discretion of free-wheeling bank officers. Active officers could not secure loans from their own banks. Overdrafts were forbidden. The amount of real estate

[27] The *Saint Louis Times,* reporting the passage of the act on June 26, 1908, felt compelled to assure its readers "We are not jesting."

[28] There had been no regulation at all in the Indian Territory. In Oklahoma Territory, the situation had been hardly better. One year, the territorial banking commissioner, whose office operated on an annual budget of $500, reported that he could not find seven hastily removed banks in order to examine them. See Eugene Gum, "Our Financial Progress Before and After Statehood," in Charles F. Barrett, ed., *Oklahoma After Fifty Years,* 4 vols. (Hopkinsville, Kentucky and Oklahoma City: Historical Record Association, 1941), 1:224.

[29] Forty-seven national banks complied with the provisions of the Oklahoma law, but the comptroller of the currency ordered them to withdraw after the first year.

that a bank could hold was carefully limited. Total deposits were regulated in proportion to capital stock. Finally, the law limited the interest that a member bank could pay on time deposits to 3.5 percent, thus allowing the system to pay for itself.[30]

Despite the alarms of the national bankers, who correctly sensed the threat of competition inherent in guaranteed state banks, the system was an immediate and unqualified success. Deposits in state banks more than tripled in the three years between December, 1907, and January, 1911. Although six member banks failed during that time, the fund lost only $716,670 after their assets had been liquidated. More to the point, not a single depositor lost as much as a dime in any failure.[31] Little wonder, then, that the system served as a model soon to be adopted by seven other states.

In addition to the calls for tax equity and consumer protection, the Guthrie convention had listened closely to the demands of organized labor. Consolidating its strength, the renamed Oklahoma State Federation of Labor appointed a legislative committee to oversee the work of the First Legislature.[32] Housed in the office of Labor Commissioner Daugherty and working closely with Mining Inspector Hanraty and Commissioner of Charities and Corrections Barnard, the committee supplemented the constitution's provisions with an arsenal of weapons that gave Oklahoma's workers a "second Bill of Rights." One typical week saw the adoption of (1) a comprehensive statute outlining the rights of employees and establishing a conciliation service for labor disputes; (2) the creation of the nation's first statewide system of publicly financed employment agencies; (3) the prescription of the eight-hour day on all state projects; (4) the authorization for a college of mining and metallurgy; and (5) the declaration of Labor Day as a state holiday. At other times, the unions also won several safety measures for railroad and mine workers and the prohibition of blacklisting and "yellow-dog" contracts.

Labor's influence was certainly strong but it was not omnipotent. The legislative committee reported at the end of the session that it had introduced a total of eighteen bills, fourteen of which had become law. Three had died in committee, and one, a compulsory education and anti-child labor bill, was vetoed, after barely overcoming strong opposition in the lower house. Defeat on the last bill was especially galling to the unions. It was also ominous for the progressive coalition that

[30]O. P. Sturm, "Liquidation under the Bank Guaranty Law," *Sturm's Oklahoma Magazine,* December 1909, pp. 19-24; Thornton Cooke, "Insurance of Bank Deposits in the West," *Review of Reviews* 41 (1910):625-26.

[31]Oscar Priestley Fowler, *The Haskell Regime: The Intimate Life of Charles Nathaniel Haskell* (Oklahoma City: Boles Printing Co., 1933), pp. 194-213; *Oklahoma City Daily Oklahoman,* January 7, 1911.

[32]Labor's record in the First Legislature is fully covered in Keith L. Bryant, "Labor in Politics: The Oklahoma State Federation of Labor During the Age of Reform," *Labor History* 11 (1970):271-74.

had triumphed with statehood, for the measure had been stoutly opposed by most of the farmers in the house. Equally ominous for that coalition was Speaker Murray's ill-tempered effort to oust the social reformer, Kate Barnard, from the house chamber and slash her department's budget. "Our Good Angel Kate," as she was known to wage earners, had earned the enmity of some of her former allies by attempting to win increased funds for charities and corrections.

Despite such threatening signals, Oklahoma's progressive Democrats could take satisfaction at the end of the First Legislature. They had established their electoral supremacy in two successive and one-sided contests. After drafting what was universally hailed as the nation's most advanced charter of reform principles, they had effectively vitalized and imaginatively expanded them in the First Legislature. When that assembly adjourned, the new state's reformers and the Democratic majority momentarily paused to applaud their achievements before preparing for yet another series of elections. The fall of 1908 would provide them with their third test in as many years. If their confidence was understandable, it was also to be misplaced.

CHAPTER 3

The Reform Spirit Fades

T HE 1908 election season opened propitiously for Oklahoma's Democrats. Triumphant in two successive tests with the Republicans at
home, they were also accorded national recognition for their success
in advancing the progressive cause. Since the ringing approval of their
constitution of 1907, popular-reform journalists—the muckrakers—had
followed their achievements, faithfully reporting the newest experiments
of the brash new state.[1] By the summer of 1908, the ascendant Sooner
Democrats were ready to give their party's national convention the
benefit of their counsel and experience. The Democratic convention
that met in Denver in July found that center stage was all but monopolized by what the conservative *Denver Post* alarmingly referred to as
"that long-haired outfit from Oklahoma."[2]

The prestige of Oklahoma's progressive Democrats was never greater
than during that triumphant July. Not only did the party take the Oklahomans' unanimous first choice, William Jennings Bryan, as its presidential nominee, but it also pledged him to a platform that included
leading provisions of the new state's constitution. The Democratic national platform of 1908 drew directly on the Sooner model for a proposed
federal bank guarantee law that was inspired by the Oklahomans' pioneer
example.

---

[1] Among the better contemporary assessments of Oklahoma's progressivism are: "The
Victory for Popular Government in Oklahoma and its Political Significance," *Arena,* June
1907, pp. 642-43; "A New State's New Ideas," *Nation,* April 4, 1907, pp. 304-305; and
"Oklahoma's Radical Constitution," *Outlook,* October 5, 1907, pp. 229-31.
[2] *Denver Post,* July 5, 1908, quoted in Keith L. Bryant, *Alfalfa Bill Murray* (Norman:
University of Oklahoma Press, 1968), p. 87.

To the Oklahoma delegation, the nomination of Bryan and the notable Sooner accent of his platform was only fitting. After all, as Governor Haskell reminded the party, "Oklahoma was built on Bryanism, and its popular form of government is Bryanism in operation."[3] If that easy equation was greatly oversimplified, it did indicate the influence of the Oklahomans in the councils of their national party. William H. Murray and Robert L. Williams played conspicuous roles in the party's deliberations, and the entire delegation rejoiced as the convention named Governor Haskell to the exalted post of Democratic national treasurer. The personal honors accorded Haskell seemed to affirm the conclusion of the *Denver Post*: The Oklahomans, "fresh from adopting a constitution that is the most radical of any state in the Union, practically controlled the convention."[4]

Although the *Post*'s assessment was probably exaggerated, the prominence of the Oklahoma delegation was both real and understandable. It was the predictable award for their successful articulation of a reform movement that transcended state lines. The irony was that the party's momentary national renown accompanied the imminent collapse of its local strength. Even as Oklahoma Democrats claimed the rewards of making the new state a model of righteous polity, strains were beginning to appear in the original reform coalition—strains that would soon shatter the progressive synthesis and the party that embraced it.

The most apparent source of trouble was the collapse of one of the movement's major pillars: the Farmers' Union. A critical component in the victorious coalition of 1906, the union had brought thousands of farmers to the Democratic fold with its promise of collective organization to influence the marketplace and the government. That promise, however, had not slowed the collapse of farm prices following the nation-wide depression of 1907. Thousands of farmers slid into the ranks of landless tenants and sharecroppers: the number of Oklahoma's landless farmers increased by 120 percent between 1900 and 1910.[5] Farmers' confidence in the union's leadership and its political alliances fell just as rapidly. By the start of 1908, Farmers' Union membership stood at barely 13,000, a decrease of nearly 60 percent from that of 1905.[6] Thinning the ranks of that major source of Democratic strength was certain to have its effect in the coming fall's elections.

Equally ominous was the simultaneous estrangement of a second element in the reform coalition, organized labor. Despite their impressive victories at the Guthrie convention and in the First Legislature, the

[3]"A State Built on Bryanism," Charles N. Haskell Collection, Western History Collections, University of Oklahoma, Norman, Oklahoma, hereafter cited as Haskell Collection.

[4]*Denver Post,* July 10, 1908, quoted in Bryant, *Alfalfa Bill,* p. 87.

[5]The most thorough account of agriculture's "immizeration" is in Ellen I. Rosen, "Peasant Socialism in America? The Socialist Party in Oklahoma Before the First World War" (Ph.D. diss., City University of New York, 1976), pp. 77-91, 102-103.

[6]Robert L. Tontz, "Membership of General Farmers' Organizations in the United States, 1874-1960," *Agricultural History* 38 (1964):155.

political ambitions of trade unionists had been repeatedly frustrated by the rural bloc in the house of representatives. For example, a stringent anti-child labor bill, heartily endorsed by both the State Federation of Labor and Charities and Corrections Commissioner Kate Barnard, was stoutly resisted by agrarian house members who remembered their own youthful work on the farm. That particular bill barely passed the legislature, only to meet the governor's veto. The disappointed labor leaders reacted to such reversals by preparing a list of "enemies" to defeat in the 1908 campaign. Virtually every name on the list was that of a rural Democrat, and House Speaker "Alfalfa Bill" Murray's was conspicuously at the top. All were slated to become victims of labor's ballots and efforts in the 1908 elections. Moreover, the federation's ire was directed at more than individuals; it extended to "any official or party that [continued] to boost them,"[7] a label that could apply only to Democrats.

The disaffection of organized agriculture and labor with the Democrats accompanied yet another handicap for the party and its efforts. Governor Charles Haskell, whose work at the Sequoyah and Guthrie assemblies had given birth to the statehood coalition, had no sooner scored his Denver triumph than he fell victim to personal scandal. Upon Haskell's admittance to the inner circle of the Bryan campaign, William Randolph Hearst's newspaper chain directed a series of journalistic broadsides at the new Democratic national treasurer. Details of Haskell's earlier sharp promotions, inflamed charges of past dishonesty, and pointed suggestions of previous collusion with the Standard Oil Company were paraded daily in the Hearst papers, giving Republican nominee William Howard Taft ammunition to attack a sorely embarrassed Bryan. There was too much hard evidence in print to dismiss the charges as a mere partisan smear; hence, the Bryan forces compelled Haskell's humiliating resignation from the post on the obviously hollow grounds of "onerous and engrossing" gubernatorial duties in Oklahoma.[8]

Although Bryan was able to divorce himself from the scandals surrounding Haskell, Oklahoma's Democrats could hardly deny their incumbent governor and the man who had helped them mold their party. Compounded with the estrangement of organized farmers and workers, the Democratic prospects, which had looked so bright only a few months before, dimmed considerably as the November election neared. The third test of party strength in as many years made 1908 a major test for officials who had been installed less than twelve months earlier.

On the other side, the twice-beaten Republicans had cause to antici-

---

[7] *Proceedings of the Fifth Annual Convention of the Oklahoma State Federation of Labor* (Oklahoma City, 1908), Oklahoma State Federation of Labor Collection, Western History Collections, University of Oklahoma, Norman, Oklahoma; Keith L. Bryant, "Labor in Politics: The Oklahoma State Federation of Labor During the Age of Reform," *Labor History* 11 (1970):271-76.

[8] Josephus Daniels, *Editor in Politics* (Chapel Hill: University of North Carolina Press, 1941), pp. 539-47, quotation from p. 546. The Haskell Collection contains scattered material relating to the affair.

pate a vastly improved showing. Not only did they expect to profit from
the Democrats' troubles, but they also could predict electoral gains from
a critical but easily forseeable source. In the two previous elections, the
Republicans' prestatehood strength had dissolved in no small part because many of the party's traditional supporters, especially most of the
30,000 black voters, had not bothered to go to the polls. The successive
defeats in 1906 and 1907 had failed to show the GOP the folly of its
lily-white policy, but their rivals' militant and successful racism was
worse. Blacks were convinced that they had nothing to gain by staying
home on election day after the adoption of the Democrats' Jim Crow
transportation bill. It was a prospect that the Democrats richly deserved,
and, in a campaign critical for the new state, it was a prospect for electoral disaster.

For all these reasons, the results of the November 3, 1908, balloting
were more explicable than the swollen Democratic victories of the previous two years might have foretold. The party was barely able to put
Oklahoma's seven electoral votes in the Bryan column. Despite an increase of 5,000 in the vote total since the statehood contest, Bryan took
nearly 12,000 fewer votes than Haskell had claimed in 1907. In fact, his
was a minority victory, for the Great Commoner's 122,363 ballots were
only 48 percent of the total. In contrast, Haskell, as head of the Democratic ticket, had won 54 percent fifteen months earlier. Most of the
difference was accounted for in the surprising surge of protest from the
Socialists. Their party had more than doubled its showing to take 9
percent of the vote in the presidential race, enough to empty the Democrats' presidential victory of much of its meaning.

Returns in the congressional contests were even less favorable to their
party. The GOP scored a major reversal of the 1907 results to take a
majority of the congressional seats. Bird McGuire held his First District
seat for the party, and Dick T. Morgan and C. E. Creager ousted Democratic incumbents to give the GOP the Second and Third districts for
a three to two advantage in the delegation. Since United States senators
were not yet chosen by popular vote and the Democrats still controlled
the legislature, Thomas P. Gore's return to Washington was assured.
The share of Republican seats in the statehouse gave the party an even
third of the legislative seats.[9]

The state legislative races most clearly demonstrated the source of the
Republican resurrection. The largest Republican gains came in places
like Holdenville, Okmulgee, and Guthrie—each one of which counted
a sizable black electorate. For that reason, the election of Guthrie's
A. C. Hamlin to the state house of representatives was especially significant. The first (and for two generations, the only) black to serve in the
Oklahoma legislature, Hamlin stood as a visible reminder of the reacti-

---

[9] State of Oklahoma, State Election Board, *Directory of Oklahoma, 1977,* pp. 516-17;
Oliver L. Benson et al., *Oklahoma Votes, 1907-1962* (Norman: University of Oklahoma,
Bureau of Government Research, 1964), p. 49.

vated black role in the reinvigorated Republican party.

Altogether, the November, 1908, election results represented a major setback for the party that had swept the field in 1906 and 1907 and, thereby, had received such national acclaim only a few months earlier. The degree of the reversal was measured partly in the minority presidential and congressional results and the relative drop in its legislative power; it was measured more completely in the visible loss of Democratic cohesion that followed the constitutional and statehood victories. The growing enmity between the agrarian and labor blocs and the embarrassment of the scandal surrounding Haskell had taken their toll. Only 86 of the original 110 house members were returned to the Second Legislature; the remainder of the reforming veterans had fallen to the opposite party or to rivals within their own. Only a handful of the legislators who met in Guthrie in 1909 owed anything at all to Governor Haskell or to Commissioners Charles Daugherty, Peter Hanraty, and Kate Barnard. Thus the legislative-executive harmony that had generated so many progressive measures in the first assembly would be lacking in the second.

For that reason, the 1908 election served to break the momentum of Oklahoma's progressive drive. So closely had reform been identified with the Democratic coalition of 1906–1907 that the defeat of party meant the defeat of program. The Republicans, happy enough to count on their rivals' misfortunes, still refused to grasp reform issues. Because of the suddenness of their opportunity, reform forces had failed to establish independent bases of strength. Sooner progressivism had been rushed into an early marriage with the Democratic party. In sickness and in health, the fate of one would largely determine the fate of the other. After 1908 the one was sick indeed, and the Democrats' debility soon spread to the reform impulse. It, too, grew infirm, and politics succumbed to cynical manipulations for partisan and personal advantages.

The very different tone of public affairs was quickly registered in the legislative session that met from January 20 to March 10, 1909. Only four days into the session, the Second Legislature took up a politically inspired investigation of the governor. Jim Harris, whose hatred of everything Democratic served him well as Republican state chairman, orchestrated the attack upon Haskell. Charges that the governor had misappropriated nearly $6,000 in outlays for legal services made banner headlines in the GOP newspapers. Republicans and the minority of anti-administration Democrats attempted to turn the legislative process into a forum for scandal, if not impeachment. This, the earliest of many attempts to use the legislature as a rampart from which to assault the executive, came to little; the faithful Democratic majority was able to prevent any serious investigation.[10]

Still, the sound and fury signified something: the displacement of reform efforts by partisan machinations. The short-circuited legislative

[10] An excellent account is available in Frederick S. Barde, "The Oklahoma Legislature," *Sturm's Oklahoma Magazine,* March 1910, pp. 28–30.

investigation was the first example of partisan self-preservation. The reduced Democratic majority had its own interests to protect—interests just as partisan as those of the frustrated Republican scandalmongers. Determined to fortify their party for future contests, the Democrats rallied to strike back at the most vulnerable point of the resurgent Republican strength—the black vote. Poring over census and voting returns, eager Democratic mathematicians were convinced that all three Republican congressmen elected in 1908 would have been defeated except for the solid black voter support they had received. The 1907 statehood census had recorded 4,507 adult black males in McGuire's First District; 3,329 in Morgan's Second; and 11,825 in Creager's Third.[11] In each case, the number of eligible black voters easily exceeded the Republican's winning margin.

The solution to the Democrats' problem was a proposed constitutional amendment to require a literacy test for voting. The purpose of the change was transparent in the heart of the proposal—an infamous "grandfather clause": those eligible to vote on or before January 1, 1866, their descendants, and foreign immigrants were specifically exempted from the literacy test. In effect, only blacks would be subject to the test, and even fairly literate blacks could be barred by rigid application of the amendment by intolerant (and normally Democratic) election officials.

The Republicans, still willing to sacrifice their black constituency in the hope of recovering their strength with white voters, presented only half-hearted opposition to the blatantly unjust measure. Nonetheless, the determined Democratic majority took no chances with the amendment's ratification. Dredging up the evils of "black rule" and other imaginary horrors, a shrill and thoroughly racist Democratic campaign drowned out the feeble protests offered by blacks and some Socialists.[12]

The form they prescribed for the state question revealed the craftiest Democratic preparation of all. They offered a ballot of confusion. There was no simple choice between an affirmative and negative vote. Rather, printed at the bottom of the proposal were words, "for the amendment." In order to vote in opposition, the voter had to cross out the words with a lead pencil. An affirmative vote was easier; any ballot returned unmarked was routinely recorded in favor of black disfranchisement.[13] In that way, ignorant or careless voters as well as those without a discernible

---

[11]U.S. Department of Commerce and Labor, Bureau of the Census, *Population of Oklahoma and Indian Territory, 1907* (Washington: Government Printing Office, 1907), p. 36.

[12]The campaign is thoroughly treated in Phillip Mellinger, "Discrimination and Statehood in Oklahoma," *Chronicles of Oklahoma* 49 (1971):373-77. The Socialists' divided stance is analyzed in Garin Burbank, *When Farmers Voted Red: The Gospel of Socialism in the Oklahoma Countryside, 1910-1924,* Contributions in American History, no. 53 (Westport, Conn.: Greenwood Press, 1976), pp. 69-89.

[13]"The Grandfather Clause in Oklahoma," *Outlook,* August 20, 1910, p. 853.

preference were put automatically in the affirmative column. No sequel
to this tactic is recorded in Oklahoma politics.

Placed on the August 2, 1910, primary election ballot (so that its
effects could be felt in that year's general election), the proposition
carried by an official count of 135,443 to 106,222. What made the results
notable was that the number of ballots counted on the measure was
20,364 greater than the total vote cast in the four simultaneous gubernatorial primaries.[14] More than 20,000 votes for black disfranchisement
were, in fact, utterly blank ballots. How many were cast by voters oblivious to every other matter and how many managed more dubiously to
find their way to ballot boxes involves an intriguing but unanswerable
question. In either case, the deed was done; and the Democrats' stalwart
defender, the *Daily Oklahoman,* crowed over the removal "finally and
forever [of] the Negro race from Oklahoma politics."[15]

Whatever its ethical worth, the artful disfranchisement of black voters
was one of the Second Legislature's few "reforms." It was also a rare
example of Democratic party unity. Once that issue was resolved, the
party began to splinter into intense rivalries. The legislators turned their
energies to the most narrow matters, of which the location of state institutions consumed nearly all the remaining time. Institutions were prizes
born of endless logrolling. Legislators worked fitfully to win state bounty
for their home folks.

Since the former Oklahoma Territory already boasted a number of
continuing institutions (including the capitol, state university, agriculture
and mechanical college, and three normal schools), representatives of
the old Indian Territory combined to establish new institutions and
locate them in the east. Chickasha, in the old Chickasaw Nation, took
the Oklahoma Industrial Institute and College for Girls (later renamed
the Oklahoma College for Women and, eventually, the University of
Sciences and Arts of Oklahoma). A school of mines, authorized by
the 1908 legislature, was located in Wilburton. New normal schools at
Tahlequah, Ada, and Durant gave the east the same number of teacher
training schools as the west. A new state preparatory institute at Claremore was similar balance for the one already operating at Tonkawa.

The sudden creation of so many institutions of higher education spoke
less to public need than to political opportunism. More necessary but
no less opportunistic was the assignment of other institutions, which also
seemed biased toward the east. Since 1890, territorial and state convicts had been incarcerated under contract at the Kansas state prison
at Lansing. McAlester's boosters won that city the lucrative site for a new
penitentiary. Criminals, brought under heavy guard from Kansas, did
much of the actual construction of "Big Mac" in 1910. Pauls Valley

---

[14] *Directory of Oklahoma, 1977,* p. 629. The Democrats, Republicans, Populists, and
Socialists fielded primary candidates at the same election.

[15] *Oklahoma City Daily Oklahoman,* August 7, 1910.

was named the site of a training school for delinquent boys, and nearby Wynnewood provided one for delinquent girls.

The Second Legislature also dealt the east a series of eleemosynary institutions. Eastern Oklahoma Hospital for the mentally afflicted went to Vinita. The all-black town of Taft won the predictably segregated institution for black patients. State homes for the orphaned at Pryor, the blind at Fort Gibson, and the deaf at Sulphur completed the distribution of future centers for appropriations and patronage.

Western representatives were far from inactive during the intensive dealings. They claimed new district "A. and M." colleges for Lawton and Goodwell, a reformatory for Granite, and a mental hospital for Enid.[16] Moreover, they kept the grandest prize of all—the state capital. Since the First Territorial Legislature of 1890, Guthrie and Oklahoma City had wrestled for the seat of government. The Enabling Act of 1906 had apparently decided the issue by designating Guthrie as the state capital until 1913. That unique provision of the Republican Congress rankled the Democratic leaders of the new state government. Despite its two decades of capital status, Guthrie had not yet provided a suitable capitol. Even worse, the Logan County center was a nest of republicanism, where the GOP's opposition and ridicule was brilliantly articulated by Frank Greer's *Oklahoma State Capital.*[17]

Democratic discontent with Republican Guthrie led the legislature to adopt a bill allowing any town to seek the capital by petition and agreement to meet general requirements. Several made intriguing bids, perhaps none more so than Granite's offer of an ideal forty-acre tract, "all of it granite mountain."[18] In the end, however, only three cities—Guthrie, Oklahoma City, and Shawnee—managed to fulfill all of the requirements. Governor Haskell then called a special election for June 11, 1910, to give voters an unusually complicated state question. State Question 15 actually involved two issues: "Shall the Capital be located?" and "Where?" No one offered a hint of "when," but it is likely that most voters assumed their preference was for a permanent site after 1913.

Led by an energetic group of twenty-five business and professional men, Oklahoma City launched a massive campaign of publicity. Civic leaders of what was already the state's most populous city stressed its central location, superior rail facilities, absence of black local officials (an effective argument in the southern counties), and bountiful enthusiasm. "One-half million dollar free capitol guaranteed" was their promise. Haskell made his own choice apparent with his active campaigning on behalf of an Oklahoma City site. The governor spent the final two

[16] Edward Everett Dale and Gene Aldrich, *History of Oklahoma* (Edmond: Thompson Book and Supply Co., 1972), p. 323.

[17] The fullest account of the removal and the source for the following paragraphs is Gerald Forbes, *Guthrie: Oklahoma's First Capital* (Norman: University of Oklahoma Press, 1938).

[18] Oscar Priestly Fowler, *The Haskell Regime: The Intimate Life of Charles Nathaniel Haskell* (Oklahoma City: Boles Printing Co., 1933), p. 305.

*Governor Haskell ready for business at his new office, June 12, 1910. Courtesy
Western History Collections, University of Oklahoma.*

weeks energetically boosting his own choice, returning to Guthrie only
to gather up his papers.

By the evening of the June 11 balloting, the results were certain. A
strong majority (96,448 to 64,522) favored "locating" the capital, and
Oklahoma City was their choice by a three-to-one margin over Guthrie,
with Shawnee a very distant third.[19] His own preference confirmed,
Haskell astounded everyone—public officials no less than private citizens—by instructing his secretary, W. B. Anthony, to take the state seal
immediately to the winning city. On the morning of June 12, 1910,
Oklahomans awoke to learn that the capital was now at Oklahoma
City—specifically, at the Huckins Hotel, where Haskell's hand-lettered
sign, "Governor's Office," hung over the clerk's desk. Haskell was blandly
confident in his course. "Under the law," he announced, "Oklahoma City
is the state capital, and I have simply done my duty."[20]

Others were not so sure. John H. Burford, head of Guthrie's legal com-

[19] *Directory of Oklahoma, 1977,* p. 629.
[20] *Oklahoma City Daily Oklahoman,* June 13, 1910.

mittee, secured a rain of writs that so intimidated some state officials that a majority stayed in Guthrie. The state supreme court remained for several months. Some of the more timid officials thought it wise to sign their documents in both "capitals."

Amid the uproar over Oklahoma City's sudden coup, the state supreme court added to the confusion by invalidating the special election for a technicality of wording. But Haskell was not to be deterred. A special legislative session convened after his proclamation of November 19, 1910, to regularize the removal. Meeting in Oklahoma City, the legislators wasted little time before designating that city as the "permanent and immediate" capital. Before adjourning, the session also approved acquisition of the "Culbertson site," a 650-acre area in the northeastern part of the city. The capitol, to be built at Northeast Twenty-third Street and Lincoln Boulevard, would sit on a 15-acre tract, and an adjoining half-acre would allow construction of an executive mansion. The remainder would be platted and sold by a capital commission, with the state guaranteed $1 million from the lot sales.[21]

Guthrie made one last stand. Ignoring the local Anti-horse Thief Association's intriguing offer to prevent forcibly the removal of state records, the city staked its legal position on the Enabling Act's designation of Guthrie as the state capital until 1913. In a quick and split decision (three to two), the state supreme court upheld the legislature's action.[22] With unaccustomed speed, an appeal was laid before the United States Supreme Court. By a seven-to-two vote, the High Court ended the controversy by affirming a state's right to determine its own capital, unbound by prior congressional restrictions.[23]

The dramatic capital relocation fight stood with black disfranchisement as the Second Legislature's most memorable acts. Each in its own way testified to the remarkable determination of the governor. Nonetheless, Haskell's success at the expense of the blacks and Guthrie did not obscure his declining fortunes. In his final month in office, the governor was indicted by a federal grand jury on charges arising from his earlier territorial dealings in Creek town sites. Three civil suits—one stemming from the Hearst charges and two from unsavory business practices in his native midwest—kept him before the courts as his term ended and further damaged the first governor's reputation.[24]

Haskell's fall from grace only paralleled the fate of the progressive coalition that he had overseen. Its momentum broken in 1908, the coalition shattered two years later in the divisive campaign to select Haskell's

---

[21]Unknown to the participants, the site sat atop a major oil pool to be developed in the 1920s. By the end of World War II, the oil derricks surrounding the capitol had become an emblem for the state and earned for it nearly $5 million in royalties. Edgar S. Vaught, "A New Chapter in an Old Story" (Unpublished ms., 1946), Oklahoma Historical Society, Oklahoma City, Oklahoma.

[22]*Coyle* v. *Smith,* 28 Okla. 121 (1911).

[23]*Coyle* v. *Smith,* 221 U.S. 559 (1911).

[24]The criminal charge was later dropped for technical errors in procedure.

Cautious and dignified (even in trying circumstances), Lee Cruce campaigns for the Democratic nomination for governor in 1910. Courtesy Western History Collections, University of Oklahoma.

successor. Although four hopefuls filed for the Democratic gubernatorial nomination, the battle revolved around two dissimilar candidates who personified the tensions buried within state progressivism.

One of those was Lee Cruce. A humorless, self-made banker from Ardmore, Cruce had been Haskell's primary foe in 1907. His campaign that year had been based on his thinly disguised hostility to the more notable features of the proposed constitution, especially its pervasive anticorporate tone. His defeat had changed neither his position nor his ambition. Over the next three years, Cruce cautiously put together a coalition of various dissident elements in anticipation of the 1910 race.

Cruce's major opponent for the Democratic nomination was William H. Murray. With Haskell, Alfalfa Bill had been instrumental in aligning the Democratic party with the reform demands of aggrieved farmers, workers, and consumers, and he had ridden their support from the Sequoyah convention through the speakership of the first house of representatives. His 1910 campaign was eloquent testimony to the fate of the reform platform that had so vigorously triumphed in 1906 and 1907. Murray's well-known opposition to what he took to be labor's more extreme demands—particularly, safety and anti-child labor bills— had been a major cause of labor's estrangement from the Democratic party. He no longer carried the influence with farmers he had enjoyed before the dissolution of the Farmers' Union. Finally, his abrasive and crude personality had alienated him from the most notable representatives of the state's progressive social justice forces. His ill-tempered feuds with Kate Barnard and any others who crossed him were already legendary.[25]

Singularly unsuited to the effort of reassembling the earlier progressive coalition, Murray suffered a serious defeat at the hands of Cruce. His 40,166 votes gave him only 32 percent of the total, well distant of Cruce's comfortable plurality of 44 percent. Murray was not the only constitutional convention leader to fail in the 1910 primary, however. Milas Lasater, E. D. Cameron, and Peter Hanraty all lost renomination to the executive posts that they had helped fashion after their stunning victories of 1906.[26]

Behind the descent of Haskell and the defeats of Murray, Lasater, Cameron, and Hanraty was the collapse of the original reform coalition. Oklahoma progressivism was entering a metamorphosis. Increasingly, leadership was falling, if only by default, to aspiring businessmen and professionals who had balked at the shrill antibusiness tones of the constitution's drafters. The historian George Brown Tindall, who has traced their rise across the South, appropriately calls such people "business progressives"; and their agenda, whether in Oklahoma or elsewhere, had a common pattern.[27]

Believing in the fundamental justice of the social order, they looked to economic growth to correct gently any temporary maladjustments that might exist. Since development perforce required investment, they eschewed the more extreme demands of their radical rivals. Rather, they insisted that government could cooperate with enlightened capital by making itself more efficient, that is, more businesslike. They rejected crude political appeals to class grievances in favor of the calm promotion of public morality and economic growth directed by men like themselves: dignified, respectable, and — by definition — progressive.

In many ways, Lee Cruce was the perfect representative of those values. A self-made man, he had climbed the ladder of respectability with deliberate calculation. As he emphasized, he was no politician, and his only previous public service had been briefly as a regent for the state university. His profession was banking, and he had been president of the Ardmore National Bank since 1903. His was the personality of the successful banker. Reserved, cautious, deliberate to a fault, Cruce was uncommonly suspicious of others' disorder and extravagance. His primary campaign stressed a predictable blend of the negative and the positive — against free textbooks, for black disfranchisement, and above

---

[25] The Murray campaign is treated in Bryant, *Alfalfa Bill,* pp. 91-97.

[26] *Directory of Oklahoma, 1977,* p. 517.

[27] George B. Tindall, *The Emergence of the New South, 1913-1945,* History of the South, vol. 10 (Baton Rouge: Louisiana State University Press, 1967), pp. 219-53.

all else, against frightening away investment capital and for efficient and economical government.

Cruce led the Democratic ticket into the November general election against a Republican slate headed by J. W. McNeal, who, like Cruce, was a national banker. In contrast to the three previous contests, the 1910 party battle was calm, dignified, and boring. Democratic party lines held well enough to give Cruce a near majority—49 percent in the four-party field. His total was nearly 14,000 fewer than Haskell's in 1907.[28]

One probable cause for the Democratic decline was the party's eroding popular appeal. Another was the marked drop in voter turnout. Despite an increase in population of 243,000 between 1907 and 1910, nearly 3,000 fewer ballots were cast in the latter year. The difference was largely attributed to lessened voter interest, but the effect of black disfranchisement could not be ignored. The systematic disfranchisement of blacks allowed the Democrats to reverse the results of the preceding congressional elections. Bird McGuire and Dick Morgan held on to their First and Second District seats, but the Democrats took a majority of the delegation by replacing the Third District's C. E. Creager with former congressman James Davenport. Davenport's successful comeback was undeniably aided by the disfranchisement of a fifth of his district's voters. For the same reason, the GOP's existing share of state legislative seats was reduced by just under 25 percent.[29]

Following his oath of office (which Cruce, with typical caution, had taken at both Guthrie and Oklahoma City), the second governor presented the legislature with a comprehensive program that belied Murray's later remark that his conqueror's notion of government was that it existed "merely to pass criminal laws and to pay the salaries of public officials."[30] True, the Cruce program was played in a different key from the aggressive Murray's, but it was no lullaby for political slumber. Actually, it was a model of southern business progressivism with its watchwords of moral decency and government efficiency.

A believer in the virtues of buttermilk, Cruce was particularly concerned with the state's uncertain battle with Demon Rum. He proposed direct assault on the foe under a new enforcement officer responsible only to the governor, who would end the notoriously lax enforcement efforts of many county officials. He also hoped to discourage habitual liquor law offenders by a new statute raising a third violation to felony status. Finally, he directed the dismantling of the state's experimental dispensary system, an agency that offended both his moral sentiments and his views on economy in government.[31]

---

[28] *Directory of Oklahoma, 1977,* pp. 515, 519.

[29] The GOP picked up three senate seats but lost fifteen in the house for a net loss of twelve of their earlier total of fifty-one. Benson et al., *Oklahoma Votes,* p. 49.

[30] William H. Murray, *Memoirs of Governor Murray and True History of Oklahoma,* 3 vols. (Boston: Meador Publishing Co., 1945), 3:221.

[31] Jimmie Lewis Franklin, *Born Sober: Prohibition in Oklahoma, 1907-1959* (Norman:

The governor's conscientious concern for his fellow citizens' moral behavior also compelled him to lay before the legislature a brace of sumptuary proposals for Sunday "blue laws," as well as gambling control and outlawing prostitution. Although the less troubled legislators managed to ignore each recommendation, Cruce was able to assert his own executive authority in his crusade for public morality. In a courageous move, he deferred enforcement of the state's death penalty during his term, acting on the conviction that the punishment was applied in a discriminatory manner and repugnant to civilized behavior.

Less farsighted was his administration's assertion of martial powers to prevent sporting contests. On July 4, 1911, the governor prevented a scheduled boxing match at Sapulpa with the threat of martial law. During the next two years, similar events at McAlester, Dewey, Oklahoma City, and again at Sapulpa were stopped by state militiamen acting under the governor's orders but without formal proclamations of martial law. In April, 1914, Cruce did issue the state's first martial law proclamation, preventing horse racing at the Tulsa fairgrounds. Ignoring a 1913 Cruce-sponsored statute, that city's Jockey Club attempted to hold the race anyway, but the militiamen fired shots in the air, unnerving the animals and convincing the would-be bettors that the governor meant business.[32]

Cruce's sincere concern for civil morality was typical of his own style and the respectability of his contemporaries in surrounding states: prudent businessmen of the progressive persuasion. Typical, too, was Cruce's determination to turn his office into an efficient promoter of industrial development. Presiding over like-minded executives of the Southern Commercial Club, he worked to promote regional development through long-range and coordinated state planning. For his own state, the governor sought and won federal assistance for surveying oil and gas fields, developing water power sites, and planning highway construction. Similarly, Cruce persuaded the legislature in 1911 to establish a state highway department, financed by a one-dollar license fee on Oklahoma's few motor vehicles, to coordinate the state's eventual placement of the roads.

The embryonic highway department became, however, a rare example of executive-legislative accord. Mesmerized by the vision of efficiency, Cruce ran headlong into a wall of legislators whose purposes ran to the more narrowly political. This was most evident in his struggles with what Cruce derisively and accurately labeled the "institutional spending bloc." The reorganization of administration, the abolition of superfluous institutions, and the curtailment of nonessential services—all urged by the governor to redeem his campaign pledge to reduce state expenditures—

University of Oklahoma Press, 1971), pp. 51-56.

[32]Orben J. Casey, "Governor Lee Cruce," *Chronicles of Oklahoma* 52 (1974):456-75; Casey, "Governor Lee Cruce and Law Enforcement, 1911-1915," ibid. 54 (1976):435-60; *Oklahoma City Daily Oklahoman,* April 15, 1914; *Tulsa Daily World,* April 10-16, 1914.

were blocked by legislators more concerned with patronage for themselves and appropriations for their districts. After six weeks' debate on the governor's economy program, only one bill had passed—a minor one relating to sheriffs' fees. By adjournment time, the legislators had defeated or emasculated most of the major recommendations. Moreover, they had sorely embarrassed the governor's economy drive by appropriating nearly $9 million—more than twice the figure that he had criticized during Haskell's second biennium.

While the governor fumed at the legislators' contempt for a banker's efforts at good management, they went about the process of preparing the state for congressional redistricting. Population growth since statehood rewarded the state with three new congressional seats after 1910, and several weeks were consumed as legislators surveyed the lush prospects for gerrymander. Eventually, Cruce fought the legislature to a standstill. Congressional redistricting was deferred until 1913, and the three seats would be filled at large in 1912. On the even more hazardous issue of state redistricting, Cruce's rational proposals met total defeat. His request that the legislature equitably reapportion itself on the basis of the new census was stonily rebuffed. Only minor changes were allowed in the distribution of house seats and district judgeships, and nothing at all was done to equalize the senate divisions.

Altogether, Cruce's well-intentioned program had borne little fruit at mid-term. If the disintegration of the original reform coalition had been accomplished, it was not replaced by a new cohesion. The governor's proposals for businesslike reforms were repelled by a legislature intent upon its parochial interests. In the 1912 elections, the governor tried to meet the politicians in their own arena. The result was more than a setback. It allowed his opponents to take the offensive.

Presidential politics provided the first skirmish. The nomination battle between New Jersey Governor Woodrow Wilson and Speaker of the House Champ Clark emphasized and deepened the division between Oklahoma Democrats. A faction of antiadministration Democrats aggressively backed Wilson's candidacy against Clark, the choice of the governor's faction. Anti-Cruce forces won the fight at the county conventions by electing 295 delegates pledged to Wilson against 251 committed to Clark. Though the state convention divided the Oklahoma delegation to the Baltimore national convention equally, ten for each contender,[33] even Wilson's eventual victory failed to heal the gaping division between the governor and his foes.

Despite that division, the Democrats were able to claim the state's Electoral College vote over their hapless foes. The GOP was unable to choose between the incumbent president, William Howard Taft, and Theodore Roosevelt, his bolting predecessor. The Bull Moose faction and the regular Republicans ran campaigns notable for confusion and

[33] *Oklahoma City Daily Oklahoman,* February 24, 1912.

lack of vigor, campaigns so inept that they virtually handed victory to the Democrats. More important than Wilson's victory, however, was the fact that for the third successive election the Democratic ticket received a lower percentage and vote total than in the preceding race. The 1907 Haskell victory with 54 percent (134,162 votes) had declined over five years to leave Wilson a minority victor—47 percent (119,156 votes). Most of the difference went to the Socialists, who increased their showing more than fourfold in the same interval. In contrast, the Republicans benefited not at all from the Democratic decline. Although they returned their two incumbent congressmen, their share of the total delegation declined with the election of the Democrats' three at-large candidates. In the statehouse, the GOP did even worse by losing five senate seats and eight house seats.[34]

The minority victory of Wilson and the success of the remainder of the ticket hardly amounted to absolute Democratic supremacy. Even less did it testify to Democratic unity. Into the wounds of existing discord, Governor Cruce poured rock salt. In the Democratic primaries of 1912, he had repeatedly intervened in legislative contests to urge the defeat of incumbent "spenders" by candidates pledged to his economy program. Posing always, and sincerely, as the watchdog of the treasury against legislative waste, the governor fiercely denounced the Democratic legislators who had opposed his economy efforts. In the end, Cruce failed to purge his foes, a failure that destroyed whatever chances he might have had to face a friendly legislature in the latter biennium of his term.

The governor's blunder was exacerbated when he daringly published his next legislative recommendations thirty days before the legislature convened.[35] The able document declared a new war with the legislative spenders, while it also gave them time to mobilize their arguments and bring up reinforcements. Reinforcements were in ample supply because Cruce had named a number of institutions for elimination. Citing the fact that 30 percent of the state's expenditures were for higher education, the governor reasoned that the educational burden was altogether disproportionate to the state's needs or resources. He asked for elimination of five of the six district agricultural schools, indicating that only the institution at Goodwell need survive. Even less promising was Cruce's call to abolish half of the state's six teacher training schools. Because he failed to designate which institutions were to be eliminated, the governor put all the potential victims on notice and allowed legislators to rally in defense of their constituents' hard-won institutional plums.

More threatening still to the political interests of the lawmakers was

[34] *Directory of Oklahoma, 1977,* pp. 522-23; Benson et al., *Oklahoma Votes,* p. 49.
[35] *Regular Biennial Message of Governor Lee Cruce to the Legislature of 1913 Oklahoma* (Vinita: Leader Printing Co., 1913), copy in Oklahoma Governors Collection, Oklahoma State Archives, Oklahoma City, Oklahoma.

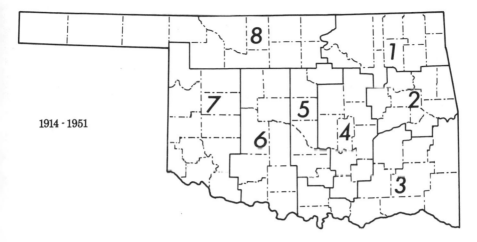

Oklahoma Congressional Districts, 1914-51. A ninth congressman was elected at-large from 1932 through 1940. From Historical Atlas of Oklahoma, *First Edition, by John W. Morris, Charles R. Goins, and Edwin C. McReynolds.*

Cruce's recommendation to abolish several government offices, including those of state printer, all superior judgeships, and several district judgeships. He also advocated the outright abolition of township government and the consolidation of five county posts into two. The governor's legislative foes could be expected to rush to the defense of their allies; even more would they oppose Cruce's proposals to reduce their own numbers. Measuring his distance from political realities, he called for the reduction of forty-four senate seats to twenty and ninety-nine house seats to fifty. Abolition of their own jobs was not high on the list of legislators' priorities.

Their own preferences soon became clear, and they showed that the Fourth Legislature was in no mood to cooperate with a governor whose political vision was, at best, farsighted. Quickly scuttling the governor's program (much of which would see adoption over the next several decades), the legislature retaliated with a series of investigations of state officers and institutions. House Speaker J. H. Maxey, then thirty-four years old, spearheaded a special investigation committee that brought the State Board of Affairs, the Department of Charities and Corrections, the State Health Department, and the School Land Commission under extremely critical scrutiny. Before their fury was spent, the legislators had impeached three officers, two of whom—Insurance Commissioner Perry A. Ballard and State Auditor Leo Meyer—resigned before their scheduled senate trials. State Printer Giles W. Farris was removed by the senate on house-drawn charges of neglect, corruption, incompetence, and fraud connected with publication of the *Oklahoma Red*

Book. Meanwhile, the embattled governor escaped impeachment by only a one-vote margin in the investigation committee. The Fourth Legislature did approve an official resolution of censure, no less contemptuous for its lack of effect.[36]

So intent was the assembly upon ferreting out its foes and felons— there was notable legislative confusion of the two—it failed to pass essential appropriation bills during the regular session. In the resulting special session, the governor took one substantive defeat after another, his influence reduced to stubborn defenses of his integrity and a series of bitter veto messages. In the stalemate, Cruce retained his office (despite the taint of the censure resolution), but the legislature maintained the institutional spending so pleasing to constituencies. The most significant act of the special session was the completion of congressional redistricting—a redistricting calculated to maximize Democratic chances against the Republicans.

By that time, though, the Democrats faced challenges other than those offered by their traditional rivals. True, even black disfranchisement had not yet broken the GOP. But it was also true that the party that was most effective in cutting into Democratic strength (leaving the Democrats with minority victories in every campaign since 1908) was the Socialists. In addition to their rivalry with the tenacious Republicans and the rising Socialists, the Democrats also had to worry about their internal problems. The business progressives' agenda had floundered before the narrow interests of the shortsighted, and the now-defunct reform consensus of statehood was still unmatched by any cohesion beyond the most immediately partisan.

The best evidence of the Democrats' subsequent predicament was the common assessment of their party's strongest gubernatorial aspirant for 1914. A veteran neither of the Sequoyah and constitutional conventions nor of the ranks of enlightened capitalists, Al Jennings, the evident man-to-beat, was a graduate of a different school—the federal prison at Columbus, Ohio, where he had served time for bank robbery. The likely gubernatorial succession of a dignified bank president by a convicted bank robber measured the breadth of the Democratic crisis.

[36] State of Oklahoma, Legislature, House of Representatives, *Journal,* 4th Leg., extra. sess., pp. 1078, 1086, 1136, 1181-99; Walter Ferguson, "How the Investigation Looks to a Republican," *Harlow's Weekly,* January 25, 1913, pp. 24-25.

CHAPTER 4

Williams Democracy and
the Challenge of Socialism

.

I N THE two years following the Cruce administration, Oklahoma's
dominant political party faced critical tests. A gubernatorial election, followed by an especially intense presidential campaign, took the
measure of the Democratic party's electoral appeal as well as its evolving
ideology, particularly when it confronted its most vigorous challenge.

In the first of those tests, the 1914 gubernatorial race, all signs pointed
to a party turnover in state government. For once, the Republicans were
ready to present a united opposition with a ticket of John Fields for
governor and John H. Burford for the United States Senate.[1] Moreover,
their campaign was a refreshing change from the GOP's standard appeals
to established partisan loyalties. Fields was especially attractive for that
reason. An acknowledged follower of the Theodore Roosevelt brand of
progressivism, he seemed likely to appeal to farmers of whatever political
party. He had formerly served ably as director of the Oklahoma Agricultural Experiment Station and as a professor at the agricultural college.
Since 1902 he had also edited the popular *Oklahoma Farmer*. Under his
aggressive leadership, the GOP, for the first time since statehood, was
set for a well-coordinated and issue-oriented campaign, calculated to
transcend their own minority partisan following.

Republican harmony contrasted sharply with the Democratic disarray.
Governor Cruce's unyielding struggles with the legislature had won the
admiration only of Republicans. Within his own party, factional strife

---

[1]Finally breaking with their record of divisive factionalism, the Republicans named
their slate in a preprimary convention, sparing their candidates a public nomination fight.

had left many soreheads and no ready leadership. One consequence was a record field filing for nomination in the Democratic primary, where ten aspirants sought the lieutenant governorship alone. Six candidates filed for the nomination for governor, and their primary campaigns testified to the general Democratic disorder.

For the first time, prominent state party leaders waged open war upon one another in campaigns noteworthy for personal vilification. Only Robert N. Dunlap of Muskogee, a glad-hander who was incumbent state treasurer, appeared to have no enemies, but neither did he have a program or much of a chance. Dunlap was an early victim of more forceful campaigners. One of them was Attorney General Charles West, who had been grooming himself for the governorship since the territorial days. Joining these two statehouse veterans in the race were two others. Robert L. Williams, elected as the first chief justice of the state supreme court, resigned from the bench to make the race; James B. A. Robertson, another contender, did not resign his place as supreme court commissioner.

Because the harsh campaigns of these four statehouse Democrats divided the loyalties of the party wheelhorses, it seemed altogether possible that the nomination might fall to one of the two outsiders in the field. F. E. Herring, though a member of the constitutional convention, had little to offer beyond anonymity. The other, Al Jennings, was already painfully famous.

For all of his notoriety in 1914, Jennings was the product of a quite respectable family.[2] His father, J. D. F. Jennings, had served in several states as a physician, a Methodist minister, and as an attorney before coming to Oklahoma in the 1889 land run. In his new home, the elder Jennings was later elected probate judge of Pottawatomie County. Like several of his brothers, Al Jennings was educated to follow his father's path as a jurist and, in 1892, young Al was elected county attorney of Canadian County. After the defeat of his reelection bid in 1894, he moved to Woodward, where he entered a legal partnership with his brothers Ed and John.

But in 1895 Al's life took an ill-fated turn. A wild gunfight involving Temple Houston, the flamboyant son of the great Texan, left Ed Jennings dead and John badly wounded. Along with a third brother, Frank, Al Jennings left the law for a life of crime, ostensibly to revenge their brother's death. The Jennings gang briefly became the terror of the Southwest, robbing saloons, banks, post offices, and trains, with the practiced assistance of "Little Dick" West and "Dynamite Dick" Clifton.[3]

---

[2] An excellent biographical sketch of Jennings, from which this is taken, is available in Glenn Shirley, *West of Hell's Fringe: Crime, Criminals, and the Federal Peace Officer in Oklahoma Territory, 1889-1907* (Norman: University of Oklahoma Press, 1978), pp. 387-425. The 1914 gubernatorial campaign, particularly Jennings's role, can be followed in Duane Gage, "Al Jennings, the People's Choice," *Chronicles of Oklahoma* 46 (1968): 242-48.

[3] Clifton's nickname was something of a misnomer. In one of the gang's more spectacular raids, Dynamite Dick attempted to blast open a safe carried on a train. The inept

Jennings was finally apprehended by United States marshals in December, 1897, and sentenced to a life term at the federal prison at Columbus, Ohio. In 1900 that sentence was commuted by President McKinley to five years, less good behavior. Released in 1902, Jennings received a full pardon from President Roosevelt and returned to Oklahoma, where he practiced law in Lawton before moving to Oklahoma City in 1911. Emboldened by a strong showing in a 1912 race for county attorney—he won the Democratic nomination but lost in the general election—Jennings prepared a highly romanticized autobiography for the *Saturday Evening Post,* starred in a motion picture of his life, and announced for the governorship in 1914. The reformed desperado, describing himself as a "very much misunderstood man," ran a predictably aggressive and colorful campaign, stressing little beyond his new-found commitment to honesty. He did, however, mention his "special qualifications" on the subject of prison reform.

Whatever its prospects for levity, the Jennings candidacy was no joke. Democratic party managers rightly feared that the bloodlettings of the four statehouse rivals would hand "that outlaw" the nomination. In fact, only that fearsome prospect kept the party from an open rupture. The more respectable contenders closed ranks and calmed their differences to choke off the threat. The final balloting was the closest in the young state's history, and the results remained in doubt for two days. When the final returns trickled in from rural precincts, Jennings had carried Oklahoma, Logan, and Stephens counties, and had a total vote of 21,732. That was enough to beat both the state treasurer and the attorney general, but not the two leaders. Williams took the nomination by a 2,101-vote margin over Robertson, who placed second.[4] So close was the balloting that an official protest or, at the least, continued post-primary feuding was a very real possibility, but one that was averted when Robertson graciously extended Williams his support and made his own plans for 1918. Jennings left for California and a career, appropriately enough, in the movies.

Williams's narrow victory ended the ludicrous prospect of a convicted criminal at the head of the state ticket, but it hardly augured favorably for Democratic prospects in the general election. Fields offered the strongest challenge yet from an always hungry and suddenly unified Republican party. Williams, on the other hand, had won little more than a fourth of his party's primary vote, and the rest of the ticket (with the exception of United States Senate nominee Thomas Gore) had suffered equally close contests. Dramatically reversing the situation of the eve of the constitutional convention balloting, the GOP was running a

Clifton used too much dynamite and blew the train up, leaving the safe intact. Shirley, *West of Hell's Fringe,* p. 396.

[4]State of Oklahoma, State Election Board, *Directory of Oklahoma, 1977,* pp. 523-24; Oliver L. Benson et al., *Oklahoma Votes, 1907-1962* (Norman: University of Oklahoma, Bureau of Government Research, 1964), p. 74.

well-coordinated campaign based upon a cross-party appeal embracing progressive principles. This time it was the Democrats who took the more conservative ground. They were also becoming the victims of their own intense factionalism.

One further development darkened Democratic prospects. By 1914, the Socialist party had become a formidable challenge to both established parties, but especially to the Democrats, from whose ranks the Socialists recruited the disillusioned reformers. The sudden appearance of a strong Socialist opposition illuminated the transformation of the dominant party and its departure from the idealism of 1907.[5] Already far along, the metamorphosis of progressivism would be completed in the intense heat of militant socialism.

Sooner socialism dated from the early days of the hectic land runs. As early as 1895, Mont Howard and G. G. Halbrooks had established a Socialist "local" at Medford, in the Cherokee Strip. During those formative years, it drew its inspiration chiefly from native sources, largely oblivious to European versions of orthodox Marxism. Edward Bellamy's utopian novel of 1888, *Looking Backward,* had stirred considerable interest in Oklahoma, as it did elsewhere. Perhaps even more important to the emerging radical cause was Laurence Gronlund's *The Co-operative Commonwealth,* a brilliant attempt to translate Karl Marx's "scientific socialism" into an American language. Gronlund's title became for many Socialists a common (and perhaps euphemistic) synonym for the cause itself.[6]

[5]Oklahoma's experience with socialism has drawn a good deal of recent scholarly attention. The earliest systematic treatment of the question, Howard Meredith's "A History of the Socialist Party in Oklahoma" (Ph.D. diss., University of Oklahoma, 1970) is now supplemented by three newer and considerably more analytical works. Ellen I. Rosen's "Peasant Socialism in America? The Socialist Party in Oklahoma Before the First World War" (Ph.D. diss., City University of New York, 1976) puts the phenomenon in the widest possible context by using the party's success as a test for several sociological models that attempt to account for a broader rural radicalism. If difficult reading, the result is a most suggestive treatment of the social sources of the party's growth. Garin Burbank's *When Farmers Voted Red: The Gospel of Socialism in the Oklahoma Countryside, 1910-1924,* Contributions in American History, no. 53 (Westport, Conn.: Greenwood Press, 1976) is a topical treatment, especially strong on the movement's cultural significance and its political struggles at the local level. The single best treatment of Sooner socialism is James R. Green's *Grass-Roots Socialism: Radical Movements in the Southwest, 1895-1943* (Baton Rouge: Louisiana State University Press, 1978). Putting the movement within a broad context of region and native radicalism, Green's book provides an unusually sensitive treatment of the Oklahoma experience.

As will soon be evident, this treatment of socialism relies heavily upon the evidence and arguments of Rosen, Burbank, and Green. Less directly it is also indebted to Lawrence Goodwyn's *Democratic Promise: The Populist Moment in America* (New York: Oxford University Press, 1976). Although Goodwyn writes of another agrarian movement in another time, he does so with an acute sensitivity to the social and cultural issues involved, as well as to issues that are truly political in the broadest sense of the term. Our understanding of socialism's sources and significance consciously draws upon that form of analysis. Into it we have read much of the evidence that we gratefully borrow from Rosen, Burbank, and Green.

[6]Green, *Grass-Roots Socialism,* pp. 13-14, 18.

Of course, neither of those books had been specifically directed at Oklahoma's frontier audience, and the eventual state Socialist movement drew upon sources richer than any literary visions. Local traditions were much more important to the party's early history. In the old Indian Territory, the Knights of Labor had left a legacy of opposition to the wage system that outlasted the union itself, which had vanished from the territory's coal fields in the late 1890s. In both territories the Farmers' Alliance left memories of a strong and active cooperative resistance to the agricultural market system. But the most important contribution to territorial socialism was the short-lived Populist party, especially in its most radical version: the collectivist strain of "middle-of-the-road" populism that had steadfastly refused absorption with the reformist Democrats.[7]

Although such indigenous sources provided early socialism with an initial base of support, its early growth was, nonetheless, quite slow. It was 1900 before the Socialists formally organized their political party to present a ticket for that year's elections in Oklahoma Territory. The party's nominee for congressional delegate received only 796 votes, a mere 1.1 percent of the total. Even with better organization and preparation, the party's congressional candidate was unable to win as many as 5 percent of the ballots in 1904, the last territorial contest.[8]

One probable reason for the party's slow growth was that the Democrats' emerging progressive wing was systematically and effectively raiding the Socialists' platform. By the time of the constitutional convention campaign, the Democratic program embraced nearly all the substantive issues that Socialists had raised in the territorial era, including the explicit constitutional permission for state-owned enterprises. The Socialists stoutly maintained their independence, however, and ran their own candidates for convention seats. None made much of a showing in the Democratic sweep. Again, in 1907, the Socialists opposed both the progressive Democrats and the standpat Republicans, criticizing the proposed reform constitution for its shortcomings on woman's suffrage and the restrictions placed upon the initiative and referendum. The significance of those caveats was lost on the electorate. The new document won roaring approval, and the Socialists' gubernatorial nominee mustered a scant 9,740 votes, 3.8 percent of the total.[9]

While organized socialism gathered few votes in its early opposition to the reform Democrats, the movement did benefit from the progressive atmosphere of early statehood. The battle with the progressives forced the Socialists to sharpen their own analysis and organization. Progressive denunciation of corporate evil and social inequity raised the very issues that socialism was most likely to thrive upon—issues that were

[7] Ibid., pp. 12-43.

[8] W. B. Richards, comp., *The Oklahoma Red Book*, 2 vols. (Tulsa: Leader Printing Co., 1912), 2:305-306.

[9] *Directory of Oklahoma, 1977*, p. 515.

often beyond the accepted limits for debate in more conservative regions. Finally, the early climate of political change encouraged by the reformers allowed their radical critics a tolerant hearing, a forbearance proved to be all the more precious by its brevity.[10]

Still, the worth of any political party is measured by electoral success. Against that standard, the Socialists' initial encounters with the progressive Democrats had done little to establish them as a significant political force. In the three campaigns after statehood, however, their party began a period of notable and consistent growth. From a base of fewer than 10,000 votes in 1907, the Socialists' following grew to more than 21,000 in 1908, nearly 25,000 in 1910, and more than 41,000 in 1912.[11] Admittedly, none of those swelling totals was enough to elect a Socialist governor or presidential electors, but along the way, the party had elected a number of local officials. In a number of counties, it replaced the Republicans as the leading opposition party. In addition, its dues-paying membership had come to exceed that of every other state in the Union, not merely as a percentage of the electorate but in absolute numbers as well.[12] By 1914, the Socialists had not driven the Democrats from the statehouse, but they had driven them to an attitude of near panic.

The rapid increase of Socialist strength was indebted to several causes. The most obvious was the estrangement between the Democratic party and organized workers and farmers, a split that left for the Socialists thousands of potential recruits, many of whom made the transition. As early as 1908, the United Mine Workers had rejected the leadership of progressive Democrats and replaced them with active Socialists as union leaders. By 1911, even the traditionally conservative skilled urban workers of Oklahoma City responded favorably to a Socialist's mayoral candidacy. In that same year, J. Luther Langston, secretary-treasurer of the Oklahoma State Federation of Labor, announced his conversion to socialism. Meanwhile, the collapse of the Farmers' Union after the Panic of 1907 sent thousands of disgruntled farmers into the Socialist camp.[13]

The Democrats' split with their labor and agrarian constituency had been accompanied by their movement toward a more businesslike brand of progressivism. The declining influence of workers and farmers had left middle-class professionals and merchants more firmly in charge of Democratic fortunes. Never comfortable with the more extreme demands of the statehood leaders, these elements were now ready to call a truce in the war against corporate interests. Symptomatic of the transition was the new tone adopted by the *Daily Oklahoman,* the traditional bellwether of Democratic doctrines. Under the direction of E. K. Gaylord, who prided himself as the leader of respectable opinion, the

---

[10] Green, *Grass-Roots Socialism,* pp. 62-63.

[11] *Directory of Oklahoma, 1977,* pp. 515, 519, 522.

[12] In 1910 the party's official membership was 5,482, exactly 800 more than were enrolled in New York's state party, even though New York had nearly six times Oklahoma's population.

[13] Green, *Grass-Roots Socialism,* pp. 66-68, 193-204.

Oklahoman was preaching that Oklahoma's immature fling with "punitive" anticorporate legislation must end if the state were ever to attract the outside investment capital necessary to develop its resources.[14] Equally suggestive were Lee Cruce's efforts at business progressivism, a program that, despite its dismal legislative performance, foretold his party's future and much calmer course. Especially after black disfranchisement emasculated the GOP, the Democrats became more comfortable with conservative positions, unmindful of threats to their political supremacy.

The Republicans' repeated ineptitude left them incompetent to exploit the majority party's neglect of reforms that had been shining promises only a few years earlier. Those changes were being translated into consistent declines in the Democratic electoral strength, losses that redounded not to the Republicans but to the Socialists. For example, between 1907 and 1910, the Democrats' gubernatorial vote dropped by 14,000. The Republicans made no improvement at all; in fact, they suffered a decline as well. It was the Socialists who made the only gain; their gubernatorial vote climbed by 15,000 between the two elections.[15]

Socialists profited from those political changes mainly because of the impoverishment of the rural countryside. Historians familiar with early voting patterns have long recognized what sophisticated statistical analysis has only recently made more precise. The Socialists consistently won their largest followings from those areas that were predominantly rural, where farm values were low, tenancy and indebtedness commonplace, economic growth minimal, and cotton and wheat preeminent.[16] Oscar Ameringer's droll observation that "Socialism grows when every other crop fails"[17] sounded crudely deterministic, but it did not miss the point: Oklahoma's socialism was fundamentally a movement of the rural poor.

But it was not their poverty alone that turned men to socialism. Rather it was the social circumstances of their poverty. Like their forefathers who had settled successive American frontiers, Oklahoma's settlers had come to this, the final frontier, hoping to claim their birthright of independence. For many, the promise had been fully redeemed. For others, though, that dream was turning into a nightmare of unrewarded toil. In the old Indian Territory, dissolution of tribal land tenures had rewarded only the large-scale land speculators, not the small-scale farmers. Locally known as "grafters" (a term less of defamation than simple description), these men operated behind a complex façade of legal formalities to take virtual control of the allotments of ignorant Indians and all but monopo-

[14] Burbank, *When Farmers Voted Red,* p. 102.

[15] *Directory of Oklahoma, 1977,* pp. 515, 519. Of course, there is no way to demonstrate that the difference was a direct consequence of fourteen thousand Democrats and another thousand Republicans switching their individual votes.

[16] The statistical analysis is most fully developed in Rosen, "Peasant Socialism in America?" pp. 109, 137, 140, 141, 143, and 144.

[17] *Oklahoma City Oklahoma Pioneer,* January 26, 1910, quoted in Green, *Grass-Roots Socialism,* p. 252.

lize the best farmlands of eastern Oklahoma.[18] Quickly, they had turned their holdings to the commercial production of cotton, acting as land-lords supervising landless tenants. The latter were in ample supply, for no free land was available to them: the federal Homestead Act did not apply to the Indian Territory. What did prevail was the supremacy of a relatively small number of landlords, a supremacy which, coupled with the stimulation of land prices attendant to rapid settlement, doomed thousands of farmers to the status of landless tenants and sharecroppers. By 1910 in no fewer than twenty-five eastern Oklahoma counties, at least 70 percent of all farm units were operated by landless tenants. Already more prevalent than in any state of the Deep South, tenancy was also on the increase, both in its number of victims and in its demands upon them.[19]

The different method of settling the former Oklahoma Territory had left land speculators fewer opportunities. There, the Homestead Act was in force; consequently, most of the land had originally been granted as quarter-sections to independent farmers. As a result, a considerably higher proportion of western farmers owned their land after statehood. That ownership tended, however, to be burdened by exacting mortgages. Mortgage loans as a source of vitally needed credit may have been inevitable in a quickly developing economy, but just as inevitable were the onerous interest rates on the credit-starved frontier. Although no data are available on mortgage interest rates of the time, the published local rates for short-term loans probably ran parallel to them; at nearly 20 percent, Oklahomans paid higher interest than any farmers in the nation.[20] In the best of times, the mortgage-burdened wheat farmers of western Oklahoma fared poorly. In the worst of times, their problems approached the ill-fortunes of the eastern tenants.

The bitter statement of W. L. Thurman both captured the conviction of his fellow Socialists and came remarkably close to squaring with official statistics. According to Thurman, by 1915 three of every four Oklahoma farmers had already been reduced to tenancy or were approaching that fate under the threat of mortgage foreclosure. The actual figure was 71 percent, but Socialists were not likely to quibble over the difference.[21]

Statistics began to capture the dimensions of Oklahoma's rural crisis. For its human texture, consider Oscar Ameringer's description of the state's rural poor. A veteran Socialist organizer, Ameringer was no stranger to squalor. He would never forget his first contact with the Oklahoma countryside. He wrote of

---

[18] A masterful account of tribal dissolution and its effect upon land ownership is Angie Debo's *And Still the Waters Run: The Betrayal of the Five Civilized Tribes* (Princeton: Princeton University Press, 1940), pp. 3-125.

[19] Computed from Rosen, "Peasant Socialism in America?" p. 125.

[20] Ibid., pp. 91-104, 160.

[21] Ibid., pp. 166-68.

toothless old women with sucking infants on their withered breasts. I found a hospitable old hostess, around thirty or less, her hands covered with rags and eczema, offering me a biscuit with those hands, apologizing that her biscuits were not as good as she used to make because with her sore hands she could no longer knead the dough as it ought to be. I saw youngsters emaciated by hookworm, malnutrition, and pellagra, who had lost their second teeth before they were twenty years old. . . . The Oklahoma farmers' standard of living was so far below that of the sweatshop workers of the New York east side . . . that comparison could not be thought of.[22]

Between the statistics of farm ownership and Ameringer's grim descriptions of their victims lay the central social truth: the so-called "agricultural ladder" had broken down.[23] The farmer's presumed ability to move from the ranks of landless laborer to independent yeoman was cruelly, systematically, and increasingly denied. The power of the landlords, the unavailability of affordable land, and the exactions of creditors all conspired to keep growing numbers of farmers at the brink of ruin.

What made the rural crisis so explosive—and took it into socialism—was its victims' belief that their plight owed little to the distant manipulations of an otherwise just social order and even less to themselves. What brought men to socialism was the conviction that their misery was the price forced upon them by a wicked economic system. To them, the wrongs of commercial capitalism were not born of its temporary impediments; that was the progressive position. To Socialists, wrong was inherent to its very nature. In becoming Socialists, they split even with the local reformers who decried the machinations of Wall Street. As radicals, they believed that the enemy's lair was also to be found on Main Street.

Ultimately, it was that radical, class analysis, with its focus on local manifestations of power, that set the Socialists apart from even the most progressive Democrats. Patrick Nagle, perhaps the state's foremost native radical, gave that analysis indelible phrasing in a famous tract that argued that the miseries of Oklahoma's rural folk should be charged to the "interlocked parasites in the electric light towns."[24] Nagle's colleague, L. D. Gillespie, made that indictment specific by naming the "interlocked parasites": "the gentry constituting the eminently respectable citizens of the cities and county seat towns; the directors and officers of the chambers of commerce; the deacons and pillars of the aristocratic churches . . . , the bankers, the credit store managers, the landlords, and the corporation lawyers."[25]

[22] Ameringer, *If You Don't Weaken: The Autobiography of Oscar Ameringer* (1940; reprint ed., Westport, Conn.: Greenwood Press, 1969), p. 232.

[23] Green, *Grass-Roots Socialism,* pp. 68-69.

[24] Nagle, *The Interlocked Parasites,* Bulletin no. 1 (Oklahoma City: Oklahoma Socialist party, 1914). Published as a campaign pamphlet for the 1914 gubernatorial race, *The Interlocked Parasites* was circulated in 250,000 copies.

[25] "Hunger in the Land of Plenty," *International Socialist Review* 17 (1916):283.

In some ways, that was an assault upon respectability itself, but it was also an attack upon the very groups who were coming to dominate the Democratic party, especially in the southern counties. One study of seven counties in that region and their 166 most prominent Democratic leaders showed that 96 followed careers in law, business, or medicine. Even in that predominantly rural area, only thirty earned their livings as farmers—a category that, one suspects, likely included more landlords than tenants.[26]

Especially in the state's cotton belt, there was some evidence to support the Socialists' charge that this interlocking commercial and political elite used its power in its own selfish interest. Of necessity, these were the small capitalists who supervised a labor-intensive agriculture. As landlords, they also controlled access to the soil. As creditors, they determined the cost and conditions of credit. And as politicians, it was they who regulated public affairs. Responsible for local taxation, they tended to underassess their own business property. But as directors of local spending, they favored the needs of their "electric light towns" at the expense of the rural community. For example, in Marshall County (where 81 percent of the farmers were landless tenants), the county seat, Madill, had but one-fourth of the county's total population, but sixty-one of the county's seventy-one teachers were assigned to that city's schools. Even in the understaffed and miserably financed rural schools, the curriculum tended to reflect the academic desires of the town middle class that produced the teachers and their supervisors but rarely the students. The school system reinforced the divisions between "two well-defined groups of people—the banker-merchant-landlord class and the tenant-small landowner class."[27]

Oklahoma's rural poor, isolated from the gentry's political power (but not from its effects), were also isolated from the town gentry's culture. The town of Madill boasted of itself as a "Progressive Church Town"; and its civic leaders proudly pointed to the impressive new high school, country club, and active commercial club. But the 1,200 tenant families in Marshall County's countryside had few churches, inadequate schools, and no clubs at all—country, commercial, fraternal, or otherwise.[28]

Most important, the rural poor, in their very poverty, were alien to the values of the rising town gentry. The latter were inveterate boosters of their new state's limitless opportunities, convinced that a fair field lay open for exploitation by the industrious, the frugal, and the upright. Taught in their schools and preached in their churches, those doctrines rang of truth, and they were pleasantly confirmed in the townsmen's own rise to success and prominence. If others had failed, their

---

[26]Burbank, *When Farmers Voted Red,* pp. 91-92.
[27]Rosen, "Peasant Socialism in America?" pp. 208-10, 220-22; Green, *Grass-Roots Socialism,* pp. 258-60; Charles E. Gibson, "Farm Children in Oklahoma," *Child Labor Bulletin* 7 (1918):50-51.
[28]Green, *Grass-Roots Socialism,* p. 258.

failure was the unfortunate consequence of their own indolence, waste, and folly. Therefore, the usual attitude was that the rural poor could be ignored. At best, they might be pitied—not for their poverty but for their moral faults that made their poverty inescapable, even just.[29]

The recruits to socialism saw the matter differently. To them, tenancy, land speculation, absentee ownership, and credit terms (if available at all) had shattered the prospects for individual mobility. In its place was an unbridgeable chasm of class, not a temporary divide to be spanned by diligent individual effort. To the smug advocates of middle-class values, Socialists could respond with bitter satire. Take, for instance, Oscar Ameringer's parody of the advice of respectable editors: "The trouble with you tenant farmers . . . is that you spend your money foolishly. Take your table for instance. What's the use to squander good money on [food, when] there are all kinds of mussels in the nearby creek. . . . Grasshoppers are plentiful too. . . . John the Baptist became a great man on a grasshopper diet." By the time Ameringer reached his inevitable conclusion—"Everybody can have a farm . . . if they only save hard enough"[30]—his faithful readers were not as inclined to meditate upon their own moral shortcomings as upon the moral shortsightedness of what commonly passed for respectability.

The social and cultural alienation of the rural poor was the keenest expression of the crisis in commercial agriculture. That very isolation provided a void for socialism to fill. In doing that, socialism became more than a deviant political party; it was nothing less than a massive social movement to reconstruct the shattered social order of the countryside.

For the constituency often denied formal schooling, Socialists brought education to match their commitment to agitation. Beyond the reach of the gentry's town schools, they established their own, to meet on Sundays and couple the explication of Marxism with more elementary instruction. Together with their allies in neighboring states, they even established a short-lived "People's College" at Fort Scott, Kansas. Wagonloads of books provided party members their own traveling libraries closer to home. At one time, the party also maintained its own bookstore in Oklahoma City.[31]

More important to the Socialists' educational effort in the countryside was a vibrant radical press. Easily the most significant of the radical newspapers was Julius Augustus Wayland's *Appeal to Reason*. Published at Girard, Kansas, and claiming a weekly circulation of three million (larger than that of the *Saturday Evening Post*), the *Appeal's* special Sooner edition was reaching more than 20,000 homes after 1910. Even

[29] This interpretation is most emphatically advanced in Burbank, *When Farmers Voted Red,* pp. 97-105.

[30] *Sentinel Sword of Truth,* January 1, 1913, quoted in Green, *Grass-Roots Socialism,* pp. 146-47.

[31] Ibid., pp. 127-28, 134.

Patrick Nagle, consummate Socialist spokesman and critic of Oklahoma's "para-sites in the electric light towns." Courtesy Oklahoma Historical Society.

if outraged conservatives damned the sheet as the *Squeal to Treason,* it was the most popular radical publication ever offered in America, certainly in Oklahoma. In addition, its large staff of agents, nearly 6,000 of whom peddled subscriptions in Oklahoma and Texas, became the celebrated "Appeal Army" that founded party locals on the side as they spread Socialist doctrines to the countryside.[32]

Wayland's newspaper was not the only one to challenge the commercial elite and its town press. Dozens of small weeklies sprang up across Oklahoma to give immediacy to the local effort. Foremost of these was the *Oklahoma Tenant Farmer,* which Patrick Nagle published in Kingfisher after 1912. A former Democrat and United States marshal, Nagle broke with his original party as his legal practice took him increasingly to the defense of tenants and debtors. As a Socialist editor, he smoothly combined radical zeal with an intimate knowledge of tenancy. Even Democrats begrudgingly admitted that the *Oklahoma Tenant Farmer* was the Southwest's most authoritative journal on what they liked to call "the land question." To radicals, Nagle's 1914 pamphlet, "The Interlocked Parasites," was the clearest exposition of the social struggle between town and country.[33]

The radical education of the Socialist press was supplemented by the dramatic excitement of the movement's summer encampments. Modeled on the brush arbor revivals of the fundamentalist churches, the encampments provided a forum for both education and agitation, as well as a welcome break in pervasive social monotony. They also attracted followers by the thousands. For example, in 1912, some 20,000 Socialists descended upon Snyder (population: 250) for a week of festivity and inspiration. At that particular assembly, Kate Richards O'Hare, one of the most prominent southwestern organizers; "Mother" Jones, the grand old lady of radical labor; and Eugene V. Debs, founder and presidential candidate of the Socialist Party of America, labored to give an appreciative audience hope for a future as magnificent as its present was miserable.[34]

With all of this—the Sunday schools, the libraries, the Socialist press, and the encampments—socialism was providing its followers more than a party, more than a platform, more than an outlet for their frustrations. Those who took up socialism were, in essence, outcasts. Before their conversion, they were subservient in a society that worshiped independence, poor in an age of material progress, and excluded from the society of the towns' middle class citizens. When they embraced this alien political cause, they became still more estranged from the culture that had nurtured them. Especially in the southern counties, where the bulk

[32]Ibid., pp. 128-35; Rosen, "Peasant Socialism in America?," pp. 257-58.

[33]Green, *Grass-Roots Socialism,* pp. 135-43; H. L. Meredith, "The Agrarian Reform Press in Oklahoma," *Chronicles of Oklahoma* 50 (1972):82-94.

[34]Green, *Grass-Roots Socialism,* pp. 151-62; Ameringer, *If You Don't Weaken,* pp. 263-67.

of residents had migrated from the rural South, their affiliation with the Socialists necessarily implied the repudiation of the party of their fathers. Even worse, was not socialism understood to be the declared foe of family, morality, even Christianity?[35]

It was no trivial thing for a man to become a Socialist in rural Oklahoma. In order to win followers, socialism had to offer more than a political program. It had to offer its own culture, its own values, its own institutions, all to prepare its converts for the inevitable cultural assault of their foes. Because it was able to do these, socialism became a real threat in the Oklahoma countryside. But also because it did these things, the threat was more than political. To the faithful followers of both established political parties, socialism was the stark repudiation of everything they valued. As a social movement, it threatened more than their offices, for socialism defied their own sense of order and propriety. Ultimately socialism and its ragtag constituency denied them the sense of justice implied in their own success.[36]

For all these reasons, the general election campaign of 1914 became a critical test for the new state's politics. Leading the Socialists into combat were Fred W. Holt and Patrick Nagle. Holt, the gubernatorial candidate, was a veteran of the United Mine Workers, and his union affiliation personified the shift that had taken much of organized labor out of the Democrats' statehood coalition. Nagle, a former Democrat and now the Socialist nominee for the United States Senate, symbolized the dissatisfaction with the Democrats of tenant farmers and hard-pressed debtors. Able campaigns from Holt and Nagle and an organizational network that extended into virtually all the state's precincts challenged and frightened the dominant Democratic party.

The Socialist platform emphasized that threat and indirectly testified to the changes that had befallen the Democrats. Eschewing obscurant Marxist rhetoric, the third party's platform of 1914 echoed many of the Democratic principles of eight years past.[37] Like the group that had swept the constitutional convention elections, the Socialists endorsed a battery of proposals regulating wages, hours, and working conditions in nonfarm

---

[35] Socialism's foes were eager to emphasize its inherent antagonism with Christianity, especially in its Protestant fundamentalist form. That argument was a powerfully negative one in rural Oklahoma and one that the movement's followers were forced to counter. To the more secular of them, particularly the party organizers who were not native to the region, the rebuttal was a simple denial that political radicalism necessarily conflicted with traditional religion. At the same time, many radicals, especially those native to the area, asserted that socialism was, in fact, the clearest expression of the moral imperative of Christianity. In that way, their political radicalism often drew sustenance from a radicalized version of pervasive religious beliefs, becoming—like their press and their schools—another example of the Socialists' cultural "counterinstitutions." This view is fully developed in Burbank, *When Farmers Voted Red*, pp. 14-43; but also see Green, *Grass-Roots Socialism*, pp. 162-75, and Rosen, "Peasant Socialism in America?" pp. 239-41.

[36] Burbank, *When Farmers Voted Red*, pp. 97-105; Rosen, "Peasant Socialism in America?" pp. 259-61.

[37] The platform is discussed in Burbank, *When Farmers Voted Red*, pp. 9-10.

employment. The old direct legislation proposals were updated, as the Socialists advocated liberalized initiative and referendum procedures and woman's suffrage. In addition, the party reaffirmed its earlier opposition to the Democratically-sponsored disfranchisement of black citizens.

The heart of the platform was its "Renter's and Farmer's Program." For its impoverished rural constituency, the party offered proposals that went well beyond what the Democrats had pledged, even at the height of their progressive stance. They did not advocate the confiscation of existing private landholdings, but they did offer several schemes to enlarge the public domain and open it to the use of landless farmers, who would gain permanent rights of occupancy; formal title would remain vested in the state. Further, the State Board of Agriculture was to encourage "cooperative societies" among farmers, freeing them from the power of creditors and dealers who were so prominent among the "interlocked parasites." Finally, Socialists advocated state-owned banks, insurance companies, grain elevators, and warehouse facilities to provide farmers essential services at cost.

Only in its agrarian planks did the platform endorse an agenda that even approached collective ownership of the means of production. Even on that subject, the specific proposals could be read as logical, if extreme, extensions of the constitution's existing provisions for public enterprise. In a sense, therefore, Sooner socialism was less Marxist than progressive, closer to the principles of the statehood reformers than to those of foreign revolutionaries. Its radicalism lay less in its specific program than in its vigorous efforts to marshal the rural poor for conflict with the local establishment—the merchants, creditors, and landlords who held sway in the "electric light towns." These were, after all, the men into whose hands the Democratic party had been delivered. As a group, they were perfectly represented by the party's current standard-bearer, Robert L. Williams.

Born and educated in Alabama, Williams was a splendid example of the men who had prospered after coming to the Oklahoma frontier.[38] After several abortive forays in the West, the young and ambitious Williams finally settled in Durant, where he opened a successful legal practice. In time, he became one of the most successful corporation lawyers working in the Indian Territory, and his practice specialized in representing the railroad interests who opened the territory to a commercial promise.

His political ascension had kept pace with his growing prosperity. After the usual ventures into school district and city council elections (the only offices available to whites under the Indian regimes), he became a major figure within the councils of the territory's Democratic party. In 1904 he was chosen Democratic national committeeman for the Indian Territory, giving him titular leadership over the local Demo-

[38] Williams's biography is available in Edward Everett Dale and James D. Morrison, *Pioneer Judge: The Life of Robert L. Williams* (Cedar Rapids, Iowa: Torch Press, 1958).

crats. That leadership evaporated, however, when Charles Haskell, William Murray, and other ambitious men seized control of the Sequoyah constitutional convention and made it the launching pad for their own political careers in the new state. In the process, they had managed to link their party with the emerging demands for progressive reform.

Williams had read the shifting political winds, turned in his free railroad passes, and announced his conversion to the anticorporate cause. If enough to win him a seat at the Guthrie constitutional convention, his new reform posture was, nevertheless, visibly stooped. At the convention, he was notably involved in calming some of the more extreme notions of his fellow Democrats, and it was commonly understood that he was the most conservative of the constitution's chief architects. Still, his unquestioned legal ability won him nomination to the state supreme court in 1907. He won election in his party's statehood sweep and designation as chief justice from his colleagues.

Williams was a dedicated jurist whose opinions often ran beyond the profuse.[39] Still, he found time to oversee his continuing personal affairs—affairs that made for success in southeastern Oklahoma. Well before his close primary victory, Williams had helped organize several banks in which he continued to hold substantial interests, in addition to a cottonseed-oil company and an insurance firm that he controlled. Land remained the key basis of his prominence, however, and his holdings included nearly 3,000 acres of prime farmland in Bryan County, land operated as a modern cotton plantation, land on which teams of tenants toiled. For Robert L. Williams, the early promise of Oklahoma as a "magnificent country for a young man with integrity, determination, and unconquerable will" had been fully redeemed.[40]

His successful primary campaign of 1914 was chiefly indebted to its model organization. His way opened by local "Good Government Clubs" composed of likeminded businessmen, Williams undertook an exacting schedule of speaking engagements, which usually began with the candidate's reception at a local hotel, where he met with "the boys" to size up the local "situation." Next came a dinner sponsored by the local ladies' aid group at the church. Finally and inevitably, the candidate came to the public square for a "speaking" that not infrequently would run for two hours. In that campaign, Williams had joined every other candidate in belaboring the friendless Cruce, but his own thoughts on government came quite close to those of the frustrated business progressive. They certainly were closer to the incumbent's than to Fred Holt's or Patrick Nagle's.

In the general election struggle, the Democrats hoped to end the Socialist threat largely by belaboring it with silence. They closed ranks

[39] On one notable occasion, Williams took seventy pages to trace the history of statemaking since the birth of the nation in order to establish the simple point that crimes committed before statehood were fully punishable. See *Higgins* v. *Brown,* 20 Okla. 355 (1907).

[40] Quoted in Burbank, *When Farmers Voted Red,* p. 93.

Robert L. Williams: governor, banker, lawyer, landlord, and Democratic champion against the Socialist heresy. Courtesy Western History Collections, University of Oklahoma.

around their candidate and bravely announced the alliterative slogan, "We Will Win With Williams." Downplaying the Socialist threat, they emphasized their struggle with the yet unbowed GOP in appeals to ingrained partisan loyalties. The result was success inasmuch as party lines held well enough to give them victory. It was, however, their narrowest victory to date. Williams's 100,597 ballots represented a fall-off of nearly 19,000 Democratic votes since the 1910 election, and his winning percentage (39.7 percent) was less than two points above Fields's 37.8 percent for the GOP. The shocking news was that the Socialist vote had climbed by more than 113 percent since 1910. More than one-fifth of Oklahoma's voters had returned Socialist ballots in the governor's race, and the party had actually carried three counties and displaced the GOP as the leading opposition party in twenty-five others, including most of the state south of the Canadian River. Their strength was even apparent in the usually sluggish races for the lesser state offices, where the Democrats had come to expect routine majorities. Not so in 1914: rarely did Democratic candidates draw more than 45 percent of the vote; Socialists regularly pulled about 22 percent and Republicans around 33 percent.

In the congressional races, the Socialists also proved themselves to be a force to be reckoned with. Thomas P. Gore became the state's first popularly elected senator, but Nagle had received 21 percent of the ballots to leave Gore a minority choice of 48 percent of the voters. Similarly, the Democrats won seven of the eight races in the new congressional districts (losing only to Dick T. Morgan in the Eighth District); but, for the first time, Democratic candidates received a minority (46 percent) of the total congressional vote. Again, the Socialists made the difference. By polling 53,000 votes, their congressional candidates had taken 21.6 percent of the total—not enough to elect a congressman, but enough to place second in both the Third and Seventh districts and trail the GOP by only 217 votes in the Fourth. The pattern was even more ominous in the state legislative contests. For the third time since their strong 1908 showing, the Republicans suffered a net loss of seats. But, this time, the Democrats did too, as five Socialists were elected to the state house and one to the state senate. At least 100 Socialists were also elected to local, township, and county offices.[41]

Shaken by their close call, the Democrats swiftly closed ranks behind their new governor. The 1915 legislature was one of the briefest of early statehood. Meeting only seventy-eight days, it consciously worked to exorcise the Socialist menace. One tactic was the quick approval of a series of measures frankly designed as counterweights to socialism. A maximum hours law for women workers was adopted, partly in the hope of inducing labor's return to the Democratic fold. The state's first welfare laws were also approved by this legislature, in its attempt to head off socialism's appeal to the downtrodden. Widows and orphans were made eligible to receive state assistance, but very little of it. A widowed mother could draw no more than ten dollars per month for herself and children from a fund administered by the county commissioners. Moreover, no county could disburse more than $8,000 annually.

The 1915 assembly approved the provision of benefits to Confederate

[41] Directory of Oklahoma, 1977, pp. 526-28; Benson et al., Oklahoma Votes, pp. 49, 78; Green, Grass-Roots Socialism, pp. 286-93.

veterans, but the ten dollars a month pension hardly matched the existing federal grant to Union veterans. Finally, the legislature appealed directly to Oklahoma's disaffected farmers with new laws regulating warehouses and cotton gins and extending school land leases to five years.[42] More radical proposals, such as a graduated land tax to encourage the breakup of commercial estates, were ignored, as were the Socialists' demands for state-owned agricultural facilities to replace the commercial middlemen. On balance, therefore, the Fifth Legislature's reputation as the state's most conservative yet was well earned. Even the *Daily Oklahoman* was pleased to conclude that the assembly had done nothing to alarm anxious business interests.[43]

On the contrary: the legislators were notably more cooperative with Williams than with Cruce. Whether Williams's greater sagacity or the need to present some coherent alternative to radicalism prompted their record, the legislature joined the governor to slash the state budget and modernize governmental operations. The first was achieved primarily by deferring capital expenditures for building projects and pruning institutional appropriations. Except for the completion of the capitol, few improvements were authorized, and nearly every state institution suffered budget cuts. Meanwhile, Williams continued to press Cruce's fight against wasteful duplication, especially in higher education. Connell Agricultural and Mechanical College at Helena was transformed into a reformatory, and Haskell A. and M. at Broken Arrow was abolished outright. The same fate was scheduled for Murray A. and M. at Tishomingo. The school was saved, however, when Congressman Murray managed to win it timely federal appropriations for the new dormitories that kept his monument open.[44]

Changes in governmental machinery also included an overhaul of the inefficient judicial department, under which Williams had suffered at first hand. Many of the reforms that Cruce had vainly sought now won approval. Most were procedural in nature, designed to increase the efficiency of the court system, although the enlargement of the state supreme court (from six to nine members) was of major interest. A corresponding increase was made in the size of the supreme court commission. Meanwhile, the governor continued Cruce's battle for public morality, pushing grand jury investigations of gambling and prohibition law violations in a dozen counties and speaking out for decency at every opportunity.

Notoriously parsimonious with his own money, Williams was impatient with a tax system that remained inadequate, even for reduced needs. Hoping to bring the budget into a businesslike balance, the gov-

[42] State of Oklahoma, Secretary of State, *Message of Governor Robert L. Williams to the Sixth Legislature (1917)*, Oklahoma Governors Collection, Oklahoma State Archives, Oklahoma City, Oklahoma.

[43] *Harlow's Weekly,* April 3, 1915.

[44] William H. Murray, *Memoirs of Governor Murray and True History of Oklahoma,* 3 vols. (Boston: Meador Publishing Co., 1945), 2:126.

ernor won approval of increased ad valorem and gross production taxes, a nominal inheritance tax, and (in 1917) the reinstitution of the state income tax. None was burdensome to taxpayers of great wealth. The income tax, for example, carried a maximum levy of only seven and one-half mills on $10,000.[45]

The administration's most significant accomplishment was the adoption of the nation's first oil and gas conservation statutes. The recent opening of the rich Cushing and Healdton fields had ended any hint of balance between supply and demand in the Oklahoma oil fields. The Cushing Field alone produced five times as much oil as the available pipelines could transmit. Independent producers were helpless victims of the resulting collapse of crude prices, and tens of thousands of barrels were daily lost to irretrievable waste. Responding to desperate cries for state regulation, the legislature empowered the Corporation Commission to supervise the oil industry and hold production to reasonable market demand. As embodied in subsequent commission orders and, later, copied by several states, those statutes became the Bible of the oil and gas industry until the greater crisis of the Great Depression forced even more drastic action.[46]

At one level, the first biennium of the Williams term was a notably placid period of state government. For the first time, no major scandals erupted to test the harmony between the governor and the legislature.[47] Surprisingly, given the slimness of his election, Williams was able to dominate public affairs without enduring the internal dissension that plagued other strong chief executives. His firm control propelled the state far toward realizing the goals of the new breed of business progressives. Although government expanded slightly, most notably in its supervision of the self-destructive oil industry, more efficient operation allowed welcome reductions in overall spending. The result seemed to confirm the wisdom of Williams's typical belief that government could best function as "one great business enterprise to be administered according to business sense and business judgment."[48]

At the same time, the Williams administration testified to the decline in Oklahoma's progressivism. Labor's victories were minimal; an impending agricultural crisis went unarrested; and the crusade for social justice was feeble. Absent was the fierce anticorporate tone of the statehood reformers. Unlike theirs, the Williams version of reform was more dis-

---

[45] *Message of Governor Williams to the Sixth Legislature.*

[46] Blue Clark, "Beginning of Oil and Gas Conservation in Oklahoma," *Chronicles of Oklahoma* 55 (1977):383-86.

[47] Corporation Commissioner A. P. ("Potato") Watson was impeached and removed from office in March, 1915, for having accepted bribes from commission-regulated utilities. At the same time, Insurance Commissioner A. L. Welch was also impeached, but he was acquitted in his senate trial. Neither of those affairs damaged the governor's reputation or his accord with the legislature. State of Oklahoma, Legislature, Senate, *Journal,* 5th leg., reg. sess., March 16, 1915, pp. 1308-37.

[48] Quoted in Dale and Morrison, *Pioneer Judge,* p. 246.

tinctly middle class, more devoted to efficiency, economy, and moral uplift. It was also much less willing to challenge existing forms of power. The old talk about "producers" and "parasites" had been left to the Socialists, who had radically redefined the terms to include as parasites the new breed of reformers themselves—even Robert L. Williams, governor, banker, corporation lawyer, and landlord.

What made the Socialist movement disturbing was not its surprisingly strong performance in the 1914 elections, troubling as that was. Other events submerged worry about the uncertainties of rural life, all beyond the mastery of state Democrats, but all likely to test their authority. Chief of these was the great war raging in Europe. Already it had closed off markets for American exports, the most important of which was cotton. Across the South, some $500 million of sorely needed income was lost in one year alone. In the context of Oklahoma's economically moribund and socially explosive cotton economy, the ruin could turn despair into desperation, even without America's participation in the war. If that involvement came, even the most sagacious dared not predict the consequences.

CHAPTER 5

War at Home and Abroad:
World War I and its Aftermath

JUST before the primary nomination of Governor Williams, the Great
World War had begun. During the early part of his administration,
public attention shifted from the state capitol to the European battle-
fields and Washington, where President Wilson labored to keep the
nation free from the Old World's latest and most destructive folly. The
new state administration benefited from the initial diversion. A breathing
spell after the divisive passions of the Cruce years was welcome. Nonetheless, the war could not be ignored; for many citizens, the effects of
that distant struggle, when mixed with developments closer to home,
proved to be disastrous.

The outbreak of European war brought the collapse of much of the
American cotton market, a collapse that caused a first-year loss estimated at half the crop's value.[1] In Oklahoma, that ruin was played
against an agonizing series of changes within the state's cotton economy.
Even before the price decline, cotton farmers had helplessly watched
the accustomed pattern of merchant-supplied credit—the familiar "fur-
nishing" system—give way to a credit mechanism dominated by local
bankers. Farm credit, an absolute necessity for all but the most prosperous growers, came to be the monopoly of Oklahoma's town bankers,
a change that had the effect of increasing agricultural interest rates,
even as it heightened the existing tension between towns and rural

[1] George B. Tindall, *The Emergence of the New South, 1913-1945,* History of the South,
vol. 10 (Baton Rouge: Louisiana State University Press, 1967), pp. 33-34. The price collapse
came at a time when the existing local level, according to the *Oklahoma Farmer-Stockman,*
February 26, 1914, was already but half of the estimated cost of production.

areas. Despite the constitution's toothless limitation of 10 percent maximum interest, cotton farmers were soon paying twice that rate on seasonal loans. By 1915, the federal comptroller of the currency, J. S. Williams, could calmly announce that no fewer than 300 banks in Oklahoma were routinely saddling farmers with interest rates that were legally defined as usurious.[2]

In Oklahoma, virtually every cotton grower required credit, and the great bulk of them, being tenants, also required land. Bankers charged their price, and landlords did too—a share of the crop. And while bankers were raising their fees, landlords generally were raising their demands as well. By the 1915 season, the customary rental of one-fourth of the cotton and one-third of the corn had increased to improve the landowner's share and reduce the grower's proportion, a reduction that meant that the actual producer received much less when the crop was sold, especially after the drop in prices was included in the calculations.[3]

Not surprisingly, then, the Oklahoma cotton belt soon became a battleground of class antagonism. Across the green hills of southeastern Oklahoma, farmers were organizing. In Choctaw County, a Growers' Protective Association enlisted 9,000 members, all determined to fight usury in the courts. The Pittsburg County Farmers' Emancipation League took up the same fight. In Sequoyah County, L. C. McNabb, the popular county attorney, resigned his office to lead angry farmers pressing antiusury lawsuits. Farther west, in McClain County, the Oklahoma Renters' Union was marshaling sharecroppers to resist the increased exactions of landlords.[4]

Perhaps the largest of these spontaneous associations and the one fated to become the best known was the Working Class Union (WCU). Founded in 1914 near Van Buren, Arkansas, the WCU spread across Oklahoma's cotton belt over the next three years, ultimately enlisting thousands of recruits. At its peak, its estimated membership ranged between 18,000 and 35,000. The WCU was an odd amalgam of class-conscious radicalism, chiliastic religion, and mystic ritual—all heavily laced with an anarchic commitment to political violence. The last was its most distinguishing feature, for the desperate legions of the Working Class Union eschewed even the peaceful methods of the ballot-box Socialists in favor of their own "direct action," the barn burnings, floggings, shootings, and bank robberies that violently underscored their discontent.[5] In that respect, they called up local visions of the dreaded Industrial

---

[2] Cited in Garin Burbank, *When Farmers Voted Red: The Gospel of Socialism in the Oklahoma Countryside, 1910-1924,* Contributions in American History, no. 53 (Westport, Conn.: Greenwood Press, 1976), p. 18. The Oklahoma total compared to 317 in Texas. Together, Oklahoma and Texas banks comprised nearly three-fifths of all national banks receiving an average interest greater than 10 percent on their loans.

[3] James R. Green, *Grass-Roots Socialism: Radical Movements in the Southwest, 1895-1943* (Baton Rouge: Louisiana State University Press, 1978), pp. 299, 301.

[4] Ibid., pp. 301-303.

[5] Sherry Warwick, "The Working Class Union," *Chronicles of Oklahoma* 52 (1974): 180-90.

Workers of the World (IWW), the nationwide radical labor union with whom the WCU was said to be allied.[6] Indeed, their acceptance of violence as a political instrument probably surpassed that of the IWW; the feared "Wobblies" were, after all, most noted for their violent rhetoric, the WCU for its violent deeds. Reports of WCU outrages—the burning of a landlord's barn here, the flogging of a foe there—soon filled the columns of the county seat newspapers, and the anxiety of one side soon equaled the desperation of the other.

WCU-inspired or not, a rash of bank robberies soon afflicted the state. Special targets were those institutions accused of usurious lending. By 1916, when Oklahoma banks were being robbed at four times the national rate, insurance companies were forced to cancel their coverage of state banks on the ground that, as the state's most astute political journal put it, "public sentiment against the banks was so severe as to encourage robberies."[7] For some of the "public," it truly was. When Henry Starr, no amateur at robbing banks, was finally captured in eastern Oklahoma, the *Appeal to Reason* was pleased to publish his defense: Bankers were "in the robbery business too."[8]

In the face of these spasms of mass rage, political leaders were sure to respond. Linking the Socialist party to the worst episodes of violence, Democrats ended their earlier forbearance of radical dissent. The *Tishomingo Remonstrator,* which, as late as 1912, could bill itself as "the only anti-Socialist magazine in the southwest,"[9] was soon joined by G. E. Guthrie's *The Kumrid,* published at Okemah and also singularly devoted to combating the rising tide of radicalism.[10] The existing commercial press also began to exploit conservative fears of violent upheaval. Not only did they attempt to tar the Socialist party with every outrage; they also began to question even the mildly reformist ideas that had earlier been granted a respectful hearing. In the same way, disruption in the countryside helped push the state's dominant party rightward. Incidents

[6] The best account of the IWW is Melvin Dubofsky's *We Shall Be All: A History of the Industrial Workers of the World* (Chicago: Quadrangle Books, 1969). The union's forthright acceptance of "sabotage" as an industrial weapon caused its followers' expulsion from the Socialist Party of America in 1912. As Dubofsky makes clear, however, the Wobblies were far more often the victims of violence than its perpetrators. In fact, one of their martyrs was Frank Little, a part-Cherokee Indian from Oklahoma, who headed the Union's Agricultural Workers Organization before being lynched in Butte, Montana. The AWO's emphasis fell upon the organization of migrant farm workers, not tenant farmers. Any connection between the AWO and the WCU was probably one of common style and ideology rather than formal affiliation.

[7] *Harlow's Weekly,* December 13, 1916, quoted in Green, *Grass-Roots Socialism,* p. 342.

[8] *Appeal to Reason,* April 17, 1915, quoted ibid., p. 340. See also Green's discussion of "social banditry," particularly his imaginative use of a straw presidential poll taken in 1912 among the inmates of the state penitentiary at McAlester, pp. 335-44.

[9] Andrew Allen Veatch to Robert L. Williams, Robert L. Williams Papers, Oklahoma Historical Society, Oklahoma City, Oklahoma.

[10] Guthrie's son, whom the editor proudly named Woodrow Wilson Guthrie, later became famous under the name of "Woody." He also would have considerably greater sympathy for the rural poor and political radicalism than his fiercely anti-Socialist father.

of trouble, gaudily reported, gave fearful critics a handy weapon against their Socialist rivals.

That instrument was all the more valuable because the governing party was simultaneously confronted with a vital and unwelcome change in the state's election laws. In 1915 the United States Supreme Court invalidated Oklahoma's "grandfather clause" as a transparent violation of the equal suffrage guarantees of the Fifteenth Amendment.[11] That decision triggered a chain of events that added fuel to the flames of party strife. Before they were played out, those events threatened to create an open anti-Democratic alliance involving blacks, Republicans, and Socialists, more than enough to break the party's stranglehold on state government.

In the immediate aftermath of the High Court's decision, Democratic leaders, unwilling to accept black political participation, wrestled with the dilemma of continuing black exclusion while also satisfying the objections of the federal courts. Taking advantage of the prevailing uncertainty, the Socialists seized the opportunity to attack the Democrats at a vulnerable point: their control of the state's election machinery. The so-called "Nagle Election Law," heartily endorsed by the Republicans as well, proposed to break the dominant party's control over the state, county, and precinct election boards by requiring equal tripartite representation on each one of those critical boards. Circulated as an initiative petition, the measure earned a place on the ballot by drawing 64,037 signatures in less than two months.[12]

Confronted with the dual challenge of renewed black voting and a Republican-Socialist coalition's control of the election machinery, Governor Williams called a special legislative session to meet in January, 1916. Few legislative meetings have been subject to such delicate deliberations, for the governor and legislators foresaw a vital test of party fortunes later in that same year. Carefully, the Democratic majority prepared its two-part solution. The first was a proposed constitutional amendment to replace the voided grandfather clause. The amendment required a literacy test for voting, and it exempted only certain former servicemen and their descendants from the literacy requirement.[13] Like the earlier grandfather clause, the exemption would still leave all but a handful of blacks subject to the exacting literacy requirement. Unlike the grandfather clause, however, this proposal might also ensnare a number of illiterate whites, presumably Socialists. As a constitutional amendment, the measure would first have to win approval in a popular referendum.

A second legislative measure amended the state's election law immediately, without the delay and uncertainty of popular approval. In all subsequent elections (including the referendum of the new literacy test),

[11] *Guinn* v. *United States,* 238 U.S. 347 (1915).
[12] William S. Harmon, "Oklahoma's Constitutional Amendments: A Study of the Use of the Initiative and Referendum" (Ph.D. diss., University of Oklahoma, 1951), pp. 12-13.
[13] Ibid., pp. 13-16.

voters would have to register under Democratic precinct officials. All those eligible to vote in 1914 (while the grandfather clause was still in effect) were to be automatically registered. Those ineligible to vote in 1914—virtually all of the blacks—had to register between April 30 and May 11 or be forever barred from political participation. In either form, registration, for the first time, required voters to declare their place of residence and partisan identification. That information was defined as a public record, subject to publication.[14]

Vainly, the Socialists and the Republicans circulated petitions to repeal the new election law by referendum vote. The Republican motive was clear: the exceedingly brief registration period would still leave most blacks unenfranchised. If anything, the Socialists' purpose was even more urgent: they knew how vulnerable their tenant constituency could be to the intimidation of landlords and creditors once their partisan identification became known. Apparently, the same point was not lost upon the most desperate and least scrupulous Democrats. In Johnston County, which the Socialists had nearly carried in 1914, the editor of the *Capital-Democrat* immediately began publishing lists of Socialist registrants, with the pledge to identify "every varmint in the county who registered that way." In neighboring Marshall County, the Socialists' banner county, the even more diligent editor of Madill's *Marshall County News-Democrat* carefully noted that 113 Socialists left the county after the registration files were opened, implicitly supporting the Socialists' charge that their followers were being systematically "rented out." If true, it would be little wonder. Marshall County's *Kingston Messenger* all but confessed that "it is to head off this class of voters that the law is framed."[15]

When the Republicans and Socialists failed to overturn the registration law within the allotted time, they concentrated their combined efforts on defeating the proposed literacy test, which Governor Williams ordered placed on a special election ballot on August 1, 1916. United in the charge that the proposal amounted to a devious Democratic trick to disfranchise all opposition, the two parties helped send the amendment down to a resounding defeat, 133,140 to 90,605.[16]

While rejecting the literacy test, voters on the same day selected party nominees for the 1916 general election. Unlike the fight over the suffrage proposal, the primaries were unusually quiet. It was the first time that

[14]The statutory change remained in effect until it, too, was struck down by the United States Supreme Court in 1939 (*Lane* v. *Wilson,* 307 U.S. 268 [1939]), Justice Felix Frankfurter arguing for the Court that the Fifteenth Amendment "nullified sophisticated as well as simple-minded modes of discrimination." The Oklahoma case presumably fell in the latter category. A good brief discussion is available in June Tompkins Benson, "Election Practices in Oklahoma" (M.A. thesis, University of Oklahoma, 1954), pp. 22-23.

[15]*Tishomingo Capital-Democrat,* May 11, 25, June 1, 1915; *Marshall County News-Democrat,* October 19, 1916; *Kingston Messenger,* April 14, 1916; all cited in Garin Burbank, "Agrarian Radicals and their Opponents: Political Conflict in Southern Oklahoma, 1910-1924," *Journal of American History* 58 (1971):11.

[16]State of Oklahoma, State Election Board, *Directory of Oklahoma, 1977,* p. 634.

no gubernatorial or senatorial nominees were chosen. In the absence of the glamour races, most statewide attention centered on the nominations for two Corporation Commission seats. A. P. ("Potato") Watson, impeached and removed the previous year, ran for the long term, seeking vindication. He did not find it; Watson placed last in a field of five led by Campbell Russell, the unreconstructed and irrepressible Alabamian who remained a stormy petrel in Oklahoma politics for twenty years. W. D. Humphrey was the easy winner for the Democratic nomination to Watson's unexpired term.[17]

The Democratic primary was otherwise uneventful except for the defeat of Congressman William H. Murray for renomination from the Fourth District. Despite a record of independence in his two congressional terms, Murray was able to campaign on a record of support for many of the key features of President Wilson's New Freedom—tariff reduction, rural credits, and antitrust law revision. But all those issues lost their impact with the rise of another that, to his constituents, overshadowed all others: preparedness. Murray had given his support for the president's call for increased military preparations, and his two major primary opponents, H. H. Smith and Tom McKeown, had made the most of it. Both campaigned strenuously against swollen military spending and the prospect of American involvement in the war.[18]

Even before the primary, Murray could foresee the emotional effect of the war issue. At his own party's state convention of 1916, he had received a thunderous ovation worthy of his long record of popular leadership. When he spoke in favor of military preparation as a cruel but unavoidable necessity, however, the cheers suddenly turned to boos and hisses.[19] Evidently, his constituents felt preparedness to be both cruel and avoidable, for in the August primary balloting, Murray lost to McKeown by 279 votes, while Smith ran a close third. The two critics of war preparation received between them 63 percent of the district's Democratic vote.[20]

In the subsequent general election campaign, the Democrats wisely played down the dangers of war to emphasize the president's record as a reformer. Wilson was popular with every faction of Oklahoma Democrats. The Williams administration, able to join the acclaim that "He Kept Us Out of War," worked tirelessly to see that Wilson improved greatly over his 1912 performance. The president added nearly 30,000 votes to take an outright majority, 51 percent, over the Republican candidate, Charles Evans Hughes, who finished with 36 percent. Allan L. Benson, the Socialist nominee in Eugene Debs's familiar place, won only 15 percent of the presidential vote, despite his efforts to keep the menace of war alive. Benson is best remembered for his proposal to

[17] Ibid., p. 528.
[18] Keith L. Bryant, *Alfalfa Bill Murray* (Norman: University of Oklahoma Press, 1968), pp. 130–42.
[19] Ibid., p. 134–35.
[20] *Directory of Oklahoma, 1977*, p. 528.

require a national referendum before a declaration of war, affirmative
voters being the first to go. The Socialist vote was 3,516 above Debs's
showing in 1912, making Oklahoma the one state in which the party
improved its strength between the two elections.[21]

The day belonged, however, to Woodrow Wilson, who proved even
stronger than the local ticket in the state. In the congressional races,
James S. Davenport lost his place in the seesaw First District to Republican challenger T. A. ("Bert") Chandler by 269 votes. The GOP also
retained its hold on the Eighth District by reelecting Dick T. Morgan
to a fifth consecutive term. Otherwise, it was a Democratic sweep. Many
of the legislative seats went to the Democrats uncontested, and their
advantage reached eighty-five to twenty-six in the house (where each of
the Socialist incumbents was defeated) and thirty-eight to five in the
senate, with one Socialist holdover.[22]

Two state questions, both pushed by the Socialists and the Republicans, were decided at the same election. State Question 80 accompanied
the proposed Nagle Election Law; it would have amended the constitution to forbid the legislature's adoption of any registration law (implicitly
overturning the recently enacted statute) and left future suffrage changes
to popular approval. As governor, Williams used his prerogative to place
the two on the general election ballot, where adoption would demand
approval by a majority of all votes cast, not just a majority of votes
recorded on the particular questions. The governor's strategy of using
the so-called "silent vote" proved to be wise because both measures
won overwhelmingly favorable responses only to fall short of the total
affirmative vote necessary for adoption, the Nagle proposal by fewer
than 5,000 ballots. The distribution of the vote in the official returns
lent some credence to the charge lodged by Socialists and Republicans
that election officials had deliberately created a ballot shortage of 20,000
to ensure the amendment's defeat (presumably by the silent vote).[23] More
suspect was the singular method that the State Election Board used to
calculate the total vote cast and, thus, the affirmative vote necessary for
adoption. Rather than figure on the basis of total presidential vote—the
method employed in every preceding and subsequent instance—the election officials subtracted the total number of ballots issued, minus the
number returned mutilated or unused. The difference was critical. By
the usual method, the Nagle measure (though not the other) would have
been approved, with more than 800 votes to spare. Only by the unprecedented decision did it fail.[24] The Socialists and Republicans immediately
cried foul and implicated the governor, perhaps unfairly, in the alleged

[21] Ibid., p. 530. On Benson and his imaginative antiwar proposal, see David A. Shannon,
The Socialist Party of America: A History (Chicago: Quadrangle Books, Quadrangle
Paperbacks, 1967), pp. 90–92.

[22] *Directory of Oklahoma, 1977*, p. 531; Benson et al., *Oklahoma Votes*, p. 49.

[23] H. M. Sinclair, *Making Oklahoma Safe for the Democratic Party, or How the Williams
Machine Stole the Election of 1916* (Oklahoma City: The Author, 1917). Sinclair was
secretary of the state Socialist party.

conspiracy to defeat the Nagle measure. The two parties also made common cause in jointly filed lawsuits to overturn the board's way of reckoning.

Within his own party, however, Governor Williams remained the unchallenged leader, and he comfortably presided over the Democratic-controlled legislature of 1917, the least productive in the state's history. No serious opposition developed as the legislators routinely disposed of local bills and appropriations. Nothing of much significance was accomplished in the boring session. The state did appropriate $688,215 to match federal grants made under the new Federal Highway Act of 1916; but aside from a few bridges, there was little highway construction. The assembly's principal diversion was watching the completion of the new capitol, a structure still unfinished when the governor and legislature occupied it in early 1917—to save rent. No one seemed to mind, even after the state accepted formal delivery on July 1, 1917, that the edifice was without a dome; there were plans to add one later. Those plans were eventually deferred because of the unanticipated American declaration of war and the consequent inflation of structural steel prices. Still domeless in 1982, the uncompleted capitol is only one result of the effects of the First World War upon the state.

The legislature had already adjourned by the time of the American declaration of war on April 6, 1917, and the governor did not choose to call a special session thereafter. The conduct of state affairs was, therefore, exclusively in the executive's hands during the war. The state administration, under Williams's watchful eye, ably devoted itself to the new demands of modern war: organizing draft boards to secure manpower for the army, promoting the sale of war bonds to raise revenue, and propagandizing the home front to save food and fuel—and to think rightly. The Williams administration emerged with nothing except unstinting praise in all but the last of those enterprises.

Just after the American declaration of war, the Williams administration created a state council of defense without authority of formal statute. The council's mission was to educate the civilian population to its responsibilities. County branches of the council were staffed by prominent clergymen, editors, bankers, and county farm agents.[25] These were nonpartisan agencies or, more accurately, bipartisan, for the Socialists refused their assent to what they proclaimed to be a "rich man's war and

[24] Harmon, "Oklahoma's Constitutional Amendments," pp. 24-25, argues that logic was on the side of the election board, since the method that it adopted theoretically allowed for a more exact calculation of true voter turnout. However, that method did not allow for the possibility of misnumbered stubs and, if accurate, implied the implausible situation in which some twelve thousand voters had left the voting booths without having bothered to cast a presidential ballot. At a minimum, this peculiar method, employed without precedent and without pretense of statutory authority, emphasized the problem of the Democratic monopoly of the election machinery that the measure was determined to correct.

[25] O. A. Hilton, "The Oklahoma Council of Defense and the First World War," *Chronicles of Oklahoma* 20 (1942):18-42.

a poor man's fight." As early as 1914, the Socialists' state platform had pledged their opposition to the war and threatened to "refuse to enlist; but if forced to enter military service to murder fellow workers, we shall choose to die fighting the enemies of humanity in our own ranks rather than perish fighting our fellow workers."[26]

If those hard words were never acted upon, the Socialists' opposition to the conflict could not be denied. Neither was it to be countenanced. Persuasion gave way to coercion as patriots added the suppression of socialism to the worthy objects of their war work.

This was especially the case after August, 1917, when the accumulated frustrations of southeastern Oklahoma briefly exploded into the tragicomic affair locally known as the "Green Corn Rebellion."[27] To their existing grievances against bankers and landlords, the region's tenants now added hatred of the war and of the powerful men who they felt had caused it and stood to profit from it. The result was that the isolated spasms of violence over the previous months gradually came together into one mighty upheaval, sponsored by the Working Class Union and identified with the Socialist movement.

There had been scattered refusals to register for the draft and a series of dynamitings and shootings, as well, before the main rebellion began on August 2, when a sheriff's posse was ambushed near Lone Dove, in Seminole County. By the next morning, an estimated 1,000 rebels had collected at several points in the Canadian River valley, armed with guns, dynamite, and a vision. That vision was as heroic to them as it would have been hopeless to anyone else, for they planned to march east, collecting recruits along the way, until they could merge with the great rebel army of the Industrial Workers of the World. They would live off the countryside by eating the ripening corn in the fields, hence the rebellion's name. They would march triumphantly into the nation's capital, where they would subject the "Big Slick" (President Wilson) to citizens' arrest, end the war, and, as they liked to say, "restore to the working class the full product of its labor."

Within three days, it was all over, the bravado silenced, the vision shattered. The Green Corn rebels were victims of posses, militiamen, and, not least, their own ignorance. Few conscripts had rushed to their cause, the mighty rebel host of the IWW never materialized, and the nation was still at war. The only important consequence was that, within Oklahoma, the Socialists were now associated with the ultimate defiance, and their suppression became systematic. The disavowals of stout-hearted Socialist leaders were drowned by the vigilante chorus. Even their erst-

---

[26] Quoted in Burbank, *When Farmers Voted Red,* p. 111.

[27] The Green Corn Rebellion is the subject of a modest secondary literature. The fullest account is in Charles C. Bush, "The Green Corn Rebellion" (M.A. thesis, University of Oklahoma, 1932). More analytical treatments are available in Warwick, "The Working Class Union," pp. 190-95; Burbank, *When Farmers Voted Red,* pp. 133-56; Green, *Grass-Roots Socialism,* pp. 357-68; and John Womack, Jr., "The Green Corn Rebellion" (unpublished paper in authors' possession).

while Republican allies dropped out of the pending suits over the defeat of the Nagle law and joined in the persecution. Few voices of protest were heard when the Socialists' newspapers were denied mailing privileges, their agitators were silenced, and many of their followers were escorted from the state by self-appointed vigilantes, who enjoyed the tacit approval of county defense councils.

Of course, attempts to suppress dissent were nationwide. The Oklahoma phase was significant only in the part played by the state administration to encourage or, at least, countenance the hysteria. That it did so was testimony to its fears, reasonable or misguided, of disloyalty, sedition, and espionage. The fears were also fed by the fact that only in Oklahoma did the Socialist party represent anything like a real threat to the governing party. The war provided the occasion—however eagerly or reluctantly seized—to wreck the Socialist movement, once and for all. By the war's end, the party's two most recent gubernatorial candidates—J. Tad Cumbie and Fred Holt—had been jailed. Its dues-paying membership had dropped by 65 percent, and the number of party locals had fallen from 1,100 to 470. For all practical purposes, the Socialist party of Oklahoma was dead.[28]

Although the wartime repression had its most telling effect upon the Socialists, it was hardly confined to them. Oklahoma had its own chapters of the American Protective League, an organization that boasted 250,000 "silent watchers for disloyalty," who were not so silent, as it turned out. In partnership with the county defense councils, these patriotic citizens determined who should donate how much to Liberty Loan drives, Red Cross campaigns, and war savings stamps crusades. Compulsion was especially likely for those of suspected disloyal tendencies. In addition to the Socialists, these included the state's small number of German-born citizens, who, despite their thorough acculturation, were always watched and, not infrequently, harassed.[29]

In Tulsa County an especially zealous defense council was able to call upon citizens eager to strike a blow for liberty and against a dissident minority at the same time. In that regard, they had the full support of the city's most respectable elements, who feared the prospect of IWW or Socialist influence in the oil fields. When the home of J. Edgar Pew, a prominent oilman, was bombed, eleven presumed Wobblies were immediately charged with the offense, along with six men who offered to testify in their defense.[30] As they awaited trial, the *Tulsa Daily World*

[28] The best accounts are in Green, *Grass-Roots Socialism,* pp. 368-82; and Burbank, *When Farmers Voted Red,* pp. 108-32. The nationwide antiradical repression is well treated in H. C. Peterson and Gilbert Fite, *Opponents of War, 1917-1918* (Madison: University of Wisconsin Press, 1957).

[29] For a good example of the official diligence paid the suspect, see "Report of the Oklahoma State Council of Defense, January 26, 1918," copy in Clayton H. Hyde Collection, Western History Collections, University of Oklahoma.

[30] Angie Debo, *Tulsa: From Creek Town to Oil Capital* (Norman: University of Oklahoma Press, 1943), p. 101.

provided compelling evidence of the prevailing hysteria with an editorial entitled "Get Out the Rope": "A knowledge of how to tie a knot that will stick may come in handy in a few days. It is no time to dally with enemies of the country. . . . The first step in the whipping of Germany is to strangle the IWW's. Kill 'em. . . . Don't scotch 'em: kill 'em. It is no time to waste money on trials."[31]

Indeed it was not. Inspired by that piece of advice, a mob calling itself the "Knights of Liberty" donned white robes and removed the prisoners from the jail. On the edge of town, the Knights whipped their captives, poured hot tar in their wounds, and ordered them to leave the community. Even the *World* addressed itself to the outrage—except that it detected no outrage at all. On the contrary: it applauded the "patriotic" action that involved "the sterling element of citizenship, that class of taxpaying and orderly people who are most of all committed to the observance of the law."[32]

In a surprisingly short time the war ended, its termination coinciding with the close of Williams's term as governor. The suspicions and hatreds that surrounded the defense councils would embitter Oklahoma politics for a troubled decade. After a brief period of quiet—the benumbing effect of the war—political passions would erupt once more. Before the storm, however, there would be a deceptively calm interlude.

For all the political fury that the war aroused, state elections in 1918 were so placid as to approach boredom. In the August Democratic primary, everything went according to the plans of the professionals. James B. A. Robertson, the dependable party man whose loyal acceptance of Williams's narrow victory in 1914 had spared the embattled Democrats an unseemly fight, was conceded from the beginning to be the front-runner. He enjoyed the support of most party workers, Governor Williams, and the oil industry. His superior organization decided the campaign. Showing strength across the state, Robertson took a near-majority (45 percent) in the seven-man primary field, besting his nearest rival, former Congressman William H. Murray, by two-to-one. In other races, the prevailing Democratic lethargy left several incumbents uncontested in the wartime balloting. In two of the rare close races, Secretary of State Joe S. Morris barely eliminated the perennial contender, William C. Murray (no kin to William H.); and J. A. Whitehurst, candidate for the presidency of the State Board of Agriculture, finished only seventy votes ahead of T. F. Wilson (not to be confused with Superintendent of Public Instruction R. H. Wilson; George Wilson, a rival for the educator's post; or Woodrow Wilson, whose election inspired a number of Wilsons to seek office.)[33]

[31] *Tulsa Daily World,* November 9, 1917, quoted in Green, *Grass-Roots Socialism,* p. 371.

[32] Ibid., November 12, 1917.

[33] *Directory of Oklahoma, 1977,* pp. 531-32.

The listlessness of the Democrats' preparations contrasted with the frenzied activity within the Republican camp. In a strongly contested race, Horace G. McKeever, an Enid attorney, bested several respected leaders to take the GOP's gubernatorial nomination. Though a newcomer to politics, McKeever was a true believer. His general election campaign was a furious crusade against the president—so furious that it often seemed that McKeever's race was against Woodrow Wilson himself. Ignoring the possibilities of a coalition effort with dissident Democrats or Socialists, he led a strictly partisan effort on behalf of the party that was "never 'too proud to fight' and never advocated a 'peace without victory.'"[34] His straight-out partisanship was a fatal error, for it only consolidated the opposition.

In the general election, held six days before the Armistice, Robertson handily defeated McKeever, 104,132 to 82,865. The dismal decline of the Socialists was evident in the vote received by Patrick Nagle, their gubernatorial nominee—7,438, hardly one-sixth of their strength two years previously. The Socialists thus routed and the Republicans once again the victims of their own ineptness, the remainder of the Democratic ticket prevailed with monotonous regularity. Running for reelection as a staunch supporter of the president, Senator Robert L. Owen led the ticket with 105,009 votes, and each of the party's nominees for the lesser state offices won with majorities ranging from 54 to 56 percent. In the congressional races, the Democrats improved on their 1916 performance by taking seven of the eight seats; Dick Morgan's faithful northwest district was the only one to elude them. In none of the congressional races did the Socialists draw as many as 800 votes. Nor did any of their candidates win a state legislative seat. Although the Democrats suffered a net loss of four seats in the house and five in the senate, their control was still more than adequate.[35]

Legislative Referendum 33, submitted by the Sixth Legislature, attracted more interest in the election than did the competition for governor or senator. It was the woman's suffrage amendment to the state constitution. Though known to be opposed by the outgoing governor, it carried 106,909 to 81,481, with the cities supporting it overwhelmingly, and the southern rural counties leading the opposition.[36]

The 1918 election produced a record low turnout. Not even two-thirds of the 1916 voters found their way to the polls in 1918, and the gubernatorial vote total was 59,252 fewer than in 1914. Robertson received only 3,535 votes above the Williams total. Although Williams had won with the slimmest of margins, Robertson was able to lead his party to a smashing victory. The obvious difference was the large number of Socialists from 1914 who sat out the election in 1918, unwilling to join

[34] *Tulsa Daily World,* August 4, 1918.
[35] *Directory of Oklahoma, 1977,* pp. 533-34; Benson et al., *Oklahoma Votes,* p. 49.
[36] *Directory of Oklahoma, 1977,* p. 636. Out of grudging admiration for the women's war work, the bachelor Williams agreed not to stump against the amendment.

either major party and fully aware of the dismal prospects of their own.

James Brooks Ayers Robertson, the state's fourth governor and the first to be chosen from the Oklahoma Territory side, was a fitting victor. A native of Iowa, he had settled in Chandler in 1893, where he became an avid joiner and faithful Democratic worker. Both Haskell (who appointed him to a district judgeship) and Cruce had favored him as their successor, but neither had been an asset at the end of a bruising term of office. Williams was, and with the support of the incumbent governor and most party professionals, Robertson drafted a program calculated to give something to every group: for farmers, state-sponsored marketing cooperatives; for business, lower property taxes; for educators, support for school consolidation; and for everybody, a reprieve from the specter of radicalism. In temperament and philosophy, he was prepared to continue the cautious reforms of the business progressives, determined to set the state on a course of economic growth that had been regrettably "retarded . . . by 'freak legislation,' by the exploitation of spectacular and unnecessary 'fads' and 'isms,' and by the unseemly and undignified wrangles of public officials."[37]

With his allies in firm control of both branches of the state legislature, Robertson presented a comprehensive program to overcome the state's legacy of political immaturity and clothe it in "the habiliments of full grown manhood."[38] For a time, it appeared that the governor's program would encounter no serious opposition. But as the specifics of his general course became clear, he met a major rebuke from the people themselves. Citizens who applauded the governor's commitment to economic growth were not yet prepared for the state spending that far exceeded prewar levels of appropriations.

In his first legislative message, Robertson sought a $50 million bond issue, to be matched by liberal federal grants for a statewide network of hard-surfaced roads along routes to be determined by a new five-member highway commission.[39] Dutifully submitted to popular vote by the legislature, the bond issue was strenuously debated in a full-scale campaign. In the end, the bonds lost, not to some "spectacular 'ism'" but to the wrangles of public officials and to the voters' suspicions of a breathtakingly costly expansion in state government. Several prominent officials led the opposition (including the state auditor, Frank C. Carter, who disallowed the salary claims of state employees working for the measure's adoption).[40] The voters turned out in greater numbers for the May, 1919, special election than they had for the recent gen-

---

[37] State of Oklahoma, Secretary of State, *Governor J. B. A. Robertson's First Message to the Seventh State Legislature,* pp. 2-3.

[38] Ibid.

[39] Ibid., pp. 3-7.

[40] Robertson committed a grievous error in naming his potential appointees to the proposed highway commission; the excluded naturally found flaws in the referendum and led the opposition to it.

An avid joiner and party wheelhorse, Governor J. B. A. Robertson directed Democratic fortunes in the tense post-World War War I era. Courtesy Western History Collections, University of Oklahoma.

eral election. They defiantly buried the bonds, 171,327 to 69,917.[41] The cornerstone of the governor's program was smashed, although a more modest road-building program did eventually build or authorize 1,300 miles of paved roads during Robertson's term.

Other proposals, less expensive and not subject to popular approval, were effected, wholly or partially, in a busy legislative session of 1919. True to the governor's promises, cooperative marketing agencies, sponsored and regulated by the state, soon flourished, especially in the west. Low interest rates on school land loans to tenant farmers were likewise approved as a limited gesture toward encouraging land ownership as "the antidote for anarchy and . . . Socialism."[42]

Meawhile, the support of the institutional bloc was assured by increased appropriations to strengthen and expand state facilities. The six normal schools were advanced to the status of teachers' colleges; the preparatory school at Tonkawa advanced to that of a junior college; and the school at Claremore was converted to Oklahoma Military Academy. Education laws were amended to encourage the efficient consolidation of rural schools and the creation of "union graded" districts. In addition, two tuberculosis sanitaria and two hospitals for war veterans were established.

To conciliate the state's newly enfranchised women voters, the governor urged ratification of the woman's suffrage amendment to the federal Constitution. He won it only in a special session, called after the regular assembly had withheld its consent. On the other hand, he secured speedy ratification of the Eighteenth Amendment, preserving the unbroken record of Oklahoma governors' aggressive support of prohibition.

Two adjustments were made to the tax system. The legislators applied the minimal state income tax to corporations. At the same time, they approved the governor's demand to lower ad valorem taxes. The consequent reductions in revenues and postwar inflation eventually required emergency appropriations from a special session of 1920. To coordinate state spending and introduce a measure of efficiency, the legislature also approved the state's first, and widely heralded, budget law, which would be quietly scrapped in 1921.

One probable cause for the governor's remarkable success with the Seventh Legislature was their shared fear of the radical menace. Easier school land loans encouraged acquisition by tenants. That concern did not, however, extend to more radical steps, e.g., tough antiusury laws and graduated land taxes. The meager school land measure was the single positive gesture to heal discontent. On the repressive side, and with scarcely a murmur of debate or a vote in opposition, the legislators eagerly joined the governor in erecting a wall of antiradical statutes. Among other forbidden things was the desecration of the American flag, the display of any red flag, and the teaching of foreign languages in

[41] *Directory of Oklahoma, 1977*, p. 636.
[42] *Governor Robertson's First Message*, p. 9.

the first eight grades of the public schools. The capstone of the system was a criminal syndicalist act, endorsed by Robertson and adopted with only four dissenting votes in the legislature. Setting a maximum penalty of ten years' imprisonment and a $5,000 fine, the law forbade the advocacy in any form of doctrines endorsing crime, violence, "or other unlawful acts or methods as a means of accomplishing or effecting industrial or political revolution."[43] Scarcely a ripple of protest against these repressive measures was to be found in the newspapers, all of which acknowledged and feared the radical threat.

The governor truly earned his reputation as radicalism's determined foe. Convinced that industrial conflicts were evidence of an unholy design to upset the political system, Robertson drew upon his military powers to curb strikes, calling upon the militia more often for that one purpose than any of his predecessors had used it for all purposes. By the end of his first year in office, he had exceeded the appropriation allotted the adjutant general's office by $100,000 in order to beat back the first signs of trouble.

Amid the general postwar wave of strikes, the governor's unbending stance repeatedly sent guardsmen to confront angry picket lines. When the Drumright telephone operators went on strike in September, 1919, the governor detected the hand of the detested Industrial Workers of the World. His response was to dispatch six companies of militiamen, more than enough to allay the tensions of the community, but just enough (or so the union leaders charged) to embolden the telephone company to reject the recommendations of an independent arbitration board. In the more serious nationwide coal strike of November and December, 1919, Robertson declared the walkout to be an "insurrection," placed two regiments of national guardsmen in the Oklahoma coal fields, and frantically proclaimed martial law in six coal-producing counties.[44] Only the national coal settlement in early 1920 resolved the issue.

By the heavy-handed use of repressive legislation and his own military powers, as well as by the more subtle enactment of a comprehensive program for the efficient promotion of economic growth, Robertson, by mid term, had steered the Democratic party safely away from the shoals of radicalism. But the party was hardly free from threat. Already, in

[43] James Arthur Robinson, "Anti-Sedition Legislation and Loyalty Investigations in Oklahoma" (M.A. thesis, University of Oklahoma, 1955), pp. 19-24. The first attempt to enforce the criminal syndicalist act came in late December 1923, when Arthur Berg, an unreconstructed Wobbly, was charged with circulating seditious literature and organizing a society teaching violence. Acquitted on the second charge, Berg appealed his conviction on the first. In early 1925, the state criminal court of appeals, while upholding the act's constitutionality, reversed Berg's conviction on a technicality of trial procedure. No further proceedings were brought against him, and the act remained dormant until 1940. Ibid., pp. 24-28.

[44] *Oklahoma City Daily Oklahoman,* October 30, 1919; Guy Harold Parker, "Uses and Legal Questions of Martial Law in Oklahoma" (M.A. thesis, University of Oklahoma, 1935), pp. 138-39.

the special election of November, 1919, the Democrats had sustained a shock when the previously impregnable Fifth District congressional seat, vacated by the death of Joe B. Thompson, had gone to John W. Harreld, a conservative Republican and attorney from Oklahoma City who defeated former Congressman Claude Weaver.[45] The Democrats blamed their defeat on a light vote. The truth was that this special election was an omen of disaster. Within a year, that disaster would strike in full force and overwhelm the Democrats' partisan vessel. At the same time, it would usher in the wildest political era in the state's history.

[45] *Directory of Oklahoma, 1977,* p. 535.

CHAPTER 6

Republican Resurrection and Radical Resurgence

NATIONALLY, 1920 proved to be very much a Republican year. Accumulated frustrations against Woodrow Wilson and his administration allowed the Republican party to return to the White House in the person of its affable Ohio senator, Warren G. Harding, and his promise of a "return to normalcy." Harding's election and the GOP's comfortable victory in the congressional elections launched a full decade of Republican ascendancy. Politically and philosophically, the 1920s did approach the familiar "normalcy" of the pre-Wilson era. In Oklahoma, 1920 was also a banner year for the Republicans. It was hardly normal, though, that the state Republican party, all but dormant since statehood, swept the Oklahoma ballot boxes. Moreover, the 1920 elections ushered in an unprecedented period of impassioned political strife, rather than a calm return to "normalcy."

Like their counterparts in Washington, the Oklahoma Democrats had good cause to approach the 1920 canvass with caution. The unequaled turmoil that had accompanied the war and the economically troubled first years of peace had wounded the state's ruling party. Despite their record of political domination, the Democrats were the victims of attacks from without and within. The first internal tensions to surface focused on the Senate seat held since statehood by the fiercely independent Thomas P. Gore, who had stoutly resisted preparation for war and participation in the League of Nations.

Rather than a relaxed confidence, anger was the dominant mood of the state party convention, and it was directed at Oklahoma's junior senator. A furious resolution deplored Gore's steadfast opposition to the president's war and peace proposals. "With the blush of shame and the lament of sorrow," the dominant faction, headed by Governor

J. B. A. Robertson and Senator Robert L. Owen, officially censured Gore's maverick course.[1]

It was plain that the party would throw its support to any strong contender against the embattled senator in the August preferential primary. When Representative Scott Ferris, a loyal Democratic partisan through seven sessions, announced his candidacy for Gore's Senate seat, every other likely contender removed himself from the race. For the first time since statehood, the chief contest in the Democratic primary was a two-man affair. It was also an out-and-out test of the national administration's prestige. No other contest in the state's history has been decided on one issue so clear-cut as Gore's apostasy, and in few elections have the rank and file so grimly taken sides.

For their part, the Republicans spent most of their factionalism in a tough convention battle to select their national committeeman. Jake L. Hamon of Ardmore, a colorful oilman in the free-spending, high-living, rugged individualist tradition, won the post over John Embry of Chandler and James J. McGraw of Oklahoma City. Jim Harris and Bird McGuire led the successful forces of Hamon, whose great wealth was no handicap. The Republicans thereupon sat back to enjoy their Chicago convention, where the Oklahoma delegation first supported Illinois Governor Frank O. Lowden, only to switch to Harding at the strategic moment, under Hamon's adroit leadership. Oklahoma was thus represented in the celebrated "smoke-filled room." At home, the GOP's nominating primary occasioned little interest, for John W. Harreld, the upset victor in the recent special congressional election, was by far their strongest senatorial possibility. All factional differences forgot, the Republicans approached the fall campaign splendidly united behind Harreld and against Wilson and the League of Nations.

By contrast, the Democrats' confidence steadily deteriorated through a series of quarrels from their state convention in February to the national convention in July and the senatorial primary in August. Only the short-lived presidential candidacy of Robert L. Owen stirred the faction-ridden party to anything like its old ardor. After Owen's hopes evaporated in San Francisco, [2] the party was thrust into the maelstrom of the Senate race.

Although both Ferris and Gore were known for their jocular speech-

---

[1] *Muskogee Daily Phoenix,* February 6, 1920. Gore's independent course in foreign affairs can be followed in Monroe Lee Billington, *Thomas P. Gore: The Blind Senator from Oklahoma* (Lawrence: University of Kansas Press, 1967), pp. 82-120. This was not the first time that Gore had been snubbed by the party leadership. Although he had attended the 1918 state convention, his presence was officially and pointedly ignored. *Oklahoma City Daily Oklahoman,* September 24, 1918.

[2] Owen might have made a strong presidential nominee, for his platform was easily the most progressive of any leading contender. Hoping to downplay the foreign affairs issues, Owen urged a profit-sharing system with labor and use of the Federal Reserve Board to "fix and stabilize the per capita wealth of the country." In any event, his candidacy could hardly have served the Democrats worse than did that of their eventual nominee, James M. Cox.

Senator Gore's irreconcilable opposition to President Wilson's diplomacy did lead to divorce—one from which both he and his party suffered. Courtesy Western History Collections, University of Oklahoma.

making, the contest was devoid of pleasantry or personality. Loyalty to Wilson, especially his war and League policy, was the issue, and it was decided in Ferris's favor, 106,454 to 80,243. Ferris built his winning margin on the basis of large majorities in the state's major cities. Oklahoma City, probably influenced by the *Daily Oklahoman*'s stinging indictments of Gore, gave Ferris a three-to-one majority, and he also carried Tulsa, Shawnee, Enid, and Muskogee. The rural areas were noticeably kinder to the incumbent. Gore carried twenty-five predominantly rural counties in all, including such former Socialist strongholds as Dewey, Ellis, Johnston, Marshall, and Sequoyah counties.[3]

[3]State of Oklahoma, State Election Board, *Directory of Oklahoma, 1977* (Oklahoma City, 1977), p. 537; Oliver L. Benson et al., *Oklahoma Votes, 1907-1962* (Norman: University of Oklahoma, Bureau of Government Research, 1964), p. 113.

"Miss Alice." Congresswoman Alice Mary Robertson. Courtesy Western History Collections. University of Oklahoma.

The Ferris victory proved to be costly for the Democrats, perhaps as costly as Gore's renomination might have been. The primary struggle had kept fresh the gaping ideological wounds opened by the war. Many of Gore's long-standing agrarian following remained inconsolable, and there was little in the Ferris nomination to pull the old Socialists back into the Democratic fold. On the contrary, the unrepentant Socialists would not forgive the party that had rejected one of the irreconcilables against Wilson's fateful intervention in the war. Neither were they likely to forget that Harreld, the Democrats' fall opponent, had cast one of his few congressional votes in favor of seating the Milwaukee Socialist, Victor Berger.[4]

At the presidential level, the Democratic campaign never had much of a chance in Oklahoma. Although the major daily newspapers tried to play up the contest as a battle over the League of Nations, the election was anything but the "solemn referendum" that the ailing president had asked for. James M. Cox, the presidential nominee and titular head of the Democratic ticket, was an uninspiring campaigner, despite his gallant defense of the League charter in a major October address in Oklahoma City. Moreover, his party was racked by frustrations and tensions that were directed as much toward Oklahoma City as toward Versailles.

The 1920 election saw a record turnout, expanded by the first participation of women voters. Oklahoma for the first time cast its electoral vote for a Republican candidate: Harding easily defeated Cox, 243,831 to 217,753. Eugene Debs, the familiar Socialist nominee and current inmate of the Atlanta federal prison—he was confined for his antiwar speeches under the draconian sedition law—received but 25,726 votes. It was nothing more than a respectable protest. The total for Debs did not deny Harding a majority victory, and the Socialists' 5 percent showing was their smallest share since 1907, barely equal to one-third of their strength in the last prewar campaign.[5]

Harding led most of his ticket to victory in an election marked by unusual straight-ticket voting. Every Republican nominee for statewide office won, as the GOP took one Corporation Commission post, a seat on the criminal court of appeals, and all four vacant slots on the state supreme court.[6]

In the United States Senate race, Harreld defeated Ferris by a margin that surpassed even that of Harding to become the state's first Republican senator. The Democrats also lost three incumbent congressmen, and the

<hr/>

[4]Berger, long a leader in Socialist party circles and a duly elected congressman from Wisconsin, was refused his seat by the House of Representatives in April, 1919. At the time, Berger was appealing his conviction under the federal Espionage Act. After that denial, a special election was held in Berger's Milwaukee district to fill the vacancy. Again, Berger was elected; again, the House majority refused to seat him. David A. Shannon: *The Socialist Party of America* (Chicago: Quadrangle Books, Quadrangle Paperbacks, 1967), p. 124.

[5]*Directory of Oklahoma, 1977,* p. 537.

[6]Ibid., pp. 537–38.

GOP took a majority of the state's delegation for the second time since statehood, winning five seats to three. Only the Third, Fifth, and Seventh districts remained Democratic, and narrowly so. The surprising Republican winners were J. C. Pringey, Alice Robertson, and Manuel Herrick. Pringey, a Lincoln County farmer, was perhaps as dumbfounded as his rival to find himself the Fourth District's congressional representative. Alice Robertson of Muskogee—"Miss Alice"—had the distinctions of being only the second woman elected to Congress and also the one Republican winner in the entire history of the Second District.[7] The granddaughter of famed Indian missionary Samuel Austin Worcester, she was born at an Indian mission outside Muskogee and was more than sixty-five years old when sent to Congress. After her many years of service to the Indian Territory (and although she was an inveterate foe of extending suffrage to her sex), she ran a simple campaign from behind the cash register of her cafeteria in Muskogee. Her advertisements, virtually her only contact with the district's voters, combined the daily menu with biblical quotations and her forthright platform: "I am a Christian, I am an American, I am a Republican." That was enough to assure election in 1920. In whatever measure Miss Alice's triumph was part of President Wilson's presumed referendum on American participation in the League of Nations, the result must have disappointed him badly. The new congresswoman had already made plain that she was "against any league which includes nations that worship idols."[8]

Manuel Herrick's election from the Eighth District provided the most compelling evidence possible of the extent of the Republican triumph. True, the district had been a faithful Republican bastion through Dick Morgan's six terms in Congress, but Herrick was no Morgan. The popular incumbent had died shortly before the August primary, too late for any Republican of standing to join Herrick in filing for the position. Herrick, who had received just fifty-six votes when he had sought the office as an independent in 1918, was thereupon certified as the unopposed Republican nominee, and his candidacy had to be accepted by the outraged Republican leaders. So massive was the Harding landslide that it pushed Herrick into the national Capitol.

It would be charitable to describe the new congressman as eccentric. Herrick was born in Ohio on September 20, 1876, to John Herrick and his simpleminded wife, Balinda. Balinda evidently took as her own the angelic injunction given Mary, for she named her child Manuel and raised him to believe that he was the Christ. The family homesteaded in the Cherokee Strip in 1893, and Manuel became a preacher, though unwelcome in every church. He also became a perennial seeker of public office, though he won none, and his aspiring political career was punctuated by trips to the territorial insane asylum. In 1920 he reached his

[7]A good short sketch is available: Louise B. James, "Alice Mary Robertson—Anti-Feminist Congresswoman from Oklahoma," *Chronicles of Oklahoma* 55 (1977):454-61.
[8]Ruth Moore Stanley, "Alice M. Robertson: Oklahoma's First Congresswoman," *Chronicles of Oklahoma* 45 (1967):226.

goal, and he left behind a notice that he ordered published—"just like I wrote it, capital letters and all"—by the local press:

BEWARE!

February The 22, 1921
Manuel Herrick Left Today on the 9 O'clock Train To Assume his Duties In washington D. C. Before Leaving he Stated That all news paper Reporters who are wise and value Their good health while They have got It will Stay awa from him ESpecially those Representing The Daily Oklahomian and Daily news—Manuel Herrick.[9]

Herrick's stunning victory provoked little mirth.[10] Among the Democratic partisan newspapers, there was much sadness at the repudiation of President Wilson, so apparent in the election returns. The *Daily Ardmoreite* was particularly incensed that the Democrats should have deserted their invalid leader to follow the sirens of materialism, comparing the Democratic renegades to a "hop fiend" who had tasted "insidious hasheesh."[11] All agreed that the party's internal civil war was chiefly responsible for the debacle in Oklahoma. The *Daily Oklahoman* comforted partisans with the thought that the party would somehow survive; it always had.[12] Few other papers ventured the uneasy prophecy that a resurgent Democracy would soon recover from the holocaust.

Though not a candidate himself (Oklahoma's governors, always elected in nonpresidential years, have been able to stay clear of the massive voter shifts like that of 1920), Governor Robertson's part in the campaign was creditable. Mounting dissatisfaction with his own administration neutralized his efforts in behalf of the Democratic cause. His use of the militia during the previous winter, for example, had irritated many voters, and they noted that every county subjected to martial law had gone Republican in the fall voting.[13] The governor was also criticized for giving too much attention to politics. State business had undoubtedly suffered in July, when the governor attended the Democratic National Convention and the lieutenant governor also left the state—to be followed, in turn, by the senate president pro tempore and the speaker of the house. It was an unprecedented situation; the state, for a time, had no acting governor at all. The situation was hardly brightened when each succes-

[9]Herrick left Congress in 1923, eventually to die after his commitment to a California mental hospital. His biography is available in Gene Aldrich, *The Okie Jesus Congressman (The Life of Manuel Herrick)* (Oklahoma City: Times-Journal Publishing Co., 1974), quotation from p. 153.

[10]One exception was Thomas Gore, who could barely conceal his satisfaction that "Harding, Harreld, . . . [Jim] Harris, Herrick, and hell [had] formed a combination that simply could not be beaten. . . . The country did not go Republican. It simply stayed American." Gore quoted in *Tulsa Daily World*, November 6, 1920.

[11]*Ardmore Daily Ardmoreite*, November 4, 1920.

[12]*Oklahoma City Daily Oklahoman*, November 4, 1920.

[13]*Ada News*, November 5, 1920.

sively exercised his temporary pardoning power before leaving the state.[14]

Under the circumstances, the Democrats were fortunate that half of the state senators were holdovers, including several elected from doubtful districts in 1918. While the Republican delegation was the strongest in history, Democratic control of the upper house remained decisive. Across the capitol's rotunda, the GOP was able to organize the lower house for the first and only time since statehood by capturing fifty-five of the ninety-two seats. Two women were chosen, Mrs. Bessie McColgin, Republican, and Mrs. Lamar Looney, Democrat. Both gratified the proponents of woman's suffrage in their first national test. Like the two women, most of the members of the Tenth Legislature were inexperienced. Fewer than a quarter of the house members, for example, had served in the preceding session, so great was the turnover.[15]

The latter biennium of Governor Robertson's term likely would have been troubled, even without the unprecedented wreckage visited upon his party in the 1920 elections. Commodity prices began falling in 1920, and by 1921, the wheat, cotton, and livestock markets were in full retreat. Land values, inflated during the war when thousands of farmers had further extended themselves to secure credit, declined through the decade. In the nationwide postwar depression, banks failed, factories closed, and industrial workers were either laid off or subjected to drastic wage reductions. Meanwhile, employers attempted, with considerable success, to resist the labor union movement that had been nurtured by the war. In consequence, the state was rarely free from strikes. In addition, the worst race riot in the state's history—and one of the nation's bloodiest—erupted in Tulsa in 1921. Reeling from all these tribulations, the state administration was also forced to fend off vicious attacks from a bloodthirsty legislature.

From the beginning, Republicans had campaigned against the Democrats' inefficiency and feuding and the party's habit of "politics as usual" to the detriment of sound public administration. Now, with the opportunity to rectify the alleged mismanagement of affairs, the Republican legislative majority was unable to accomplish much in the way of constructive lawmaking. Under the direction of Republican House Speaker George B. Schwabe of Nowata, an implacable partisan, the lower house proved to be little more than an agency of obstruction and embarrassment to the Robertson administration. Many secret investigations were undertaken with the intent of bringing impeachment charges against the chief officers of administration. The Republican majority soon dissipated its opportunities for constructive work in a series of ill-organized attempts to discredit its partisan foes.

Martin Trapp was the first prominent victim of the house headhunters.

[14] *Oklahoma City Oklahoma News,* July 3–8, 1920.

[15] The lack of continuity in the lower chamber was quite exaggerated, but the general condition is typical. Rarely have as many as half of the members served previously. Mayes County alone changed its representative at every election for the first twenty-one sessions.

The lieutenant governor was formally impeached for "fraudulent conspiracy to defraud Seminole County" of $43,434.80, advanced by him for road-building bonds, voted in anticipation of federal aid. On another charge, the house accused Trapp of taking an excessive profit of $38,943.23 in a million dollar bond issue voted by Creek County. In his private life, the lieutenant governor was an investment counselor who specialized in municipal securities—an avocation that provided a basis for the house accusations. However unseemly his transactions looked to his critics, Trapp apparently had done nothing illegal. At his senate trial, the charges were swiftly quashed by a strict party vote, twenty-seven to sixteen.[16] Despite their failure before the Democratic senate, the house managers also attempted to impeach State Treasurer A. N. LeeCraft and Governor Robertson, himself. Both attempts failed.

Because of the interparty bickering in the legislature, no appropriation bills—and little else—had been approved by the end of the regular sixty-day session, when legislative pay would drop to two dollars per day. Valuing their services more than that, the representatives abruptly adjourned on April 2, 1921. The senate stayed in session. The governor was forced to convene a special session to reconvene the recalcitrant house. The necessary appropriations were finally passed to set a new record of more than $20 million for the biennium. But the sum was artificially inflated by the war's reduction in purchasing power and, despite its size, was less than the governor had requested and less than state institutions required to maintain minimum services. Two acts of modest consequence were the creation of a soldier's relief commission for the state's war veterans and the first grant of state aid to local school districts. The amount was modest ($100,000), but it was a precedent for greatly expanded freedom in the 1930s from the poverty of local district financing. By the close of the special session, little else had been achieved, and the GOP had wasted its rare chance for statesmanship.

Even after the legislature's adjournment, the governor was not free from partisan harassment. The most sensational charges levied against Robertson were the climax of his difficulties with the Republican officials of Okmulgee County.[17] In March, 1922, a grand jury was called by District Judge Mark L. Bozarth to investigate the failure of Okmulgee's Bank of Commerce in the previous November. The panel returned twenty-three indictments against more than thirty persons, including the governor and his former bank commissioner, Fred G. Dennis. The state officials were accused of accepting bribes to permit the Guaranty State Bank to remain operating after they knew it to be insolvent. Guaranty State was shortly thereafter absorbed by the Bank of Commerce. The

---

[16] State of Oklahoma, Legislature, Senate, *Journal of Proceedings of the State Senate Sitting as a Court of Impeachment, March 14-26, 1921,* 8th leg., reg. sess., March 26, 1921, pp. 107-108.

[17] The protracted affair can be traced in the *Okmulgee Daily Times,* March, September, and October, 1922.

merger with the diseased institution had killed the larger bank, and feeling ran high, for no court could restrain the passionate hatred of depositors toward any men who allowed a bank to fail. The Republican-controlled courts of Okmulgee County proceeded to fan that resentment into a political issue. Both the district judge and the county attorney were bitterly criticized for their partisan handling of the case, especially their refusal to allow the governor to appear in his own defense before the grand jury. Only after the state supreme court assumed jurisdiction, in a mandamus suit brought by Robertson against Judge Bozarth, was the governor finally exonerated.[18] Most citizens not already biased against the governor saw the whole sorry affair as one more incident of politically inspired harassment.[19]

It was not the last test. Contemporaneously with his difficulties at Okmulgee, Robertson was forced to defend his integrity in a quarrel with a hometown editor. I. B. Nichols, editor of Chandler's *Lincoln County Republican,* accused the governor of securing a block of flats valued at $100,000 in Oklahoma City. When an editorial suggested that such real estate success was indeed amazing for a man on a salary of $4,500 per year, Robertson sued for libel—$100,000 worth.[20] By that time, the 1922 gubernatorial campaign was in progress, and public attention, long weary of such wrangles, shifted to the more colorful spectacles of the hustings. Robertson, whatever the propriety of his personal deeds, was already a ruined man.

The administration's bruising political struggles were repeatedly interrupted by episodes of social upheaval. On May 31, 1921, the most serious mass violence in the state's history erupted in Tulsa.[21] Following the arrest of Dick Rowland, a young black accused of assaulting a white girl, rumors began to circulate that Rowland would be taken from the jail and lynched. The *Tulsa Tribune* openly speculated that a lynching was not at all unlikely; at least 141 had already occurred in the state. When armed blacks gathered around the courthouse to prevent Rowland's removal (a tactic that had succeeded in a similar incident at Muskogee), rioting broke out full-scale. Within hours, the governor declared martial law throughout the county and dispatched 6,000 guardsmen to the city. The guardsmen herded Tulsa's blacks into a mass detention center at McNulty Park, but the rioting continued, and as many as 25,000 whites systematically looted the black community for three days. By the time

---

[18] *Oklahoma City Daily Oklahoman,* September 4-11, 1922; *Robertson v. Bozarth,* 87 Okla. 716 (1922).

[19] Such is the theme apparent in the governor's correspondence of September and October, 1922, preserved in the J. B. A. Robertson Collection, Western History Collections, University of Oklahoma, Norman, Oklahoma.

[20] *Chandler Lincoln County Republican,* August-September, 1922.

[21] A good brief account of the riot is available in Carter Blue Clark, "A History of the Ku Klux Klan in Oklahoma" (Ph.D. diss., University of Oklahoma, 1976), pp. 16-21. Transcriptions of important contemporary newspaper accounts are available in Kaye M. Teall, ed., *Black History in Oklahoma: A Resource Book* (Oklahoma City: Oklahoma City Public Schools, 1971), pp. 204-208.

their fury was spent, the mob had gutted two square miles of black-owned property. The fatalities included at least nine whites and seventy blacks.

Although the guardsmen left Tulsa on June 4, the continuing wave of postwar strikes sent them to one place or another almost every month. The miners walked out in 1919; the bricklayers struck in Oklahoma City and Norman in 1920; the state's packinghouse workers struck in 1921; and the railway shopmen struck in 1922. The last two strikes were national in scope.

The ugliness of the Tulsa race riot and the bitterness of the repeated labor confrontations were symptoms of the social disorder that accompanied Oklahoma's entry into the postwar world.[22] Population statistics measure and partially explain the disorder. Between 1900 and 1920, the state's population climbed by a dizzying 123 percent, and within the state the proportion of urban dwellers increased from 8 percent to 30. Two economic forces helped account for this massive relocation. The first was the continuing misery in the countryside, especially the Oklahoma cotton belt. The exactions of King Cotton annually sent thousands of tenants and their children to seek refuge in the state's growing urban centers, especially Oklahoma City and Tulsa. The unplanned and unsettling growth of those two cities in particular was caused by the second economic change: the rapid expansion of the oil industry. A national leader of oil production since its entry into the Union, Oklahoma partook of the intoxicating discovery of new pools opened during and just after World War I. By the time the boom reached its peak, half the state's land surface was either under production or under lease.

With the riches pouring from the oil fields came a host of problems. Oil towns sprang up as if by magic; producers and workers descended on formerly dusty villages or rural crossroads. While the black gold rushed forth, whole communities yielded to the lure of instant wealth, and money quickly gained was as quickly spent—spent on the prostitutes, the gamblers, and the bootleggers who were attracted like insects to the lights of the drilling rigs. By 1921, Tulsa alone counted fourteen bordellos and fifty gambling halls to service the lusty drillers, roustabouts, and drifters who had been drawn to the state's center of oil production. Some communities worked mightily to restrain the vice: Tulsa's bordellos were all confined to the one district tacitly reserved for them. But no town could control the wave of disorder that spread forth nightly from the roadhouses that lined the paths to the wicked oil towns.

The resulting fear of crime was not entirely exaggerated. Oklahomans also sampled other modern changes like the automobile, the movies, and the more sophisticated sexual attitudes that were revolutionizing American life. Coming, as they did, alongside demographic shifts and a rowdy

[22]The following general analysis is indebted to Clark, "A History of the Ku Klux Klan in Oklahoma," pp. 1-35.

oil industry, these changes made Oklahomans especially sensitive to disorder. In the oil-boom years, the people were concerned, apprehensive, and afraid.

Those fears were enlarged by the prevailing malaise in public affairs. The exploding economy brought not only new wealth but also new tensions over the distribution of money. Old grievances remained between workers and employers, tenants and landlords, town and country, "producers" and "parasites." The Socialist party may have been destroyed, but the bitterness that had helped create it lingered.

All these elements came together to bedevil Robertson's last years in office. They also came together to create a movement that fastened itself on Oklahoma for most of the next decade—the Ku Klux Klan. In the process, party barriers were demolished, along with the reputations of dozens of men in two administrations. Before its force was spent, the Klan's influence had reached into every courthouse, every state office, and the campaign headquarters of both major parties. However mawkish and ridiculous it might appear to a later generation, the Klan was a powerful force for a full decade.

Oklahoma's latter-day Ku Klux Klan was not a sudden growth. Its spirit, at least, was present in the wartime acts of prejudice and repression. Tulsa's Knights of Liberty had used both Klan methods and Klan garb in its savage attack upon dissidents in 1917. A fear of minorities—blacks, Jews, Catholics, foreigners, and radicals—had been latent since early statehood and, with the end of the war, these were the familiar scapegoats of the discontented majority. The insane savagery of the Tulsa race riot could be partly explained by the competition between blacks and whites for the few jobs that were available. Emotionally, people were not yet ready for peace. The Klan had only to take the psychic condition of an overwrought people and, through its silly rituals and ludicrous parades, mold a powerful pseudopatriotic cult of flag-worship and "Americanism." By late 1923, only three years after its resurrection, the Klan enrolled an estimated 100,000 Sooners in its "Invisible Empire."

The Klan, with its klaverns, klaliffs, klokards, kligripps, kludds, and klokans,[23] was more than a motley collection of simple-minded men on the lunatic fringe. Some simple men did help satisfy their urge to power in the secret hocus-pocus and the animalistic violence of the hooded order, but it was far from simple men who furnished the direction to the KKK. At the state level, its foremost proponents included administrative officers and faculty members of leading colleges, prominent ministers, lawyers, doctors, and businessmen—all of whom shared the protective anonymity of pillowcases and mystic robes and rationalized their unholy connection with lawlessness as a bulwark against sedition

---

[23] The ritualistic order provided its own names for various offices. A klavern was a local Klan unit, a klaliff a klavern vice-president, a klokard an official lecturer, a kligripp a secretary, a kludd a chaplain, and a klogan an official investigator. Clark, "A History of the Ku Klux Klan in Oklahoma," p. 72.

Apostles of fear and foes of modern thinking, Oklahoma's Klansmen employ its technology: Bartlesville Klansmen initiate members beneath an electric cross. Courtesy Western History Collections, University of Oklahoma.

and immorality. Convinced that they were preventing a breakdown of law and order, politicians of both major parties also hastened to take the Klan obligation and memorize its absurd creed.

The secret terror became an instrument of political intimidation. It was always—and, perhaps, primarily—an agency that sought to regulate public morality.[24] Despite its fierce antiblack, anti-Jew, anti-Catholic, and anti-immigrant rhetoric, the Klan's fury fell only infrequently on those minorities, who, after all, were relatively rare in Oklahoma. Most of its attention and most of its violence were directed at the offenders of what the general public regarded as respectable morality. Among the sinners who earned the censure of a vigilant and hypercritical order were bootleggers, wife-beaters, gamblers, impure women, and the like. By 1922, it was estimated that the Klan was responsible for a flogging a night in Tulsa County and one a week in Oklahoma County. More determined champions of decency were not above beating, castrating, or burning the sign of the fiery cross into the flesh of alleged evildoers.[25] Citizens who tolerantly suggested that law enforcement might better be left to duly constituted authorities got the same treatment. Such incidents of violence, which reached their peak in 1923, furnished an outlet for human cruelty, while they also satisfied righteous desires to guard community rectitude.

It was not surprising that the Klan's mysteries and ceremonious titles

[24] The moralistic basis of the Klan's appeal is well presented in Charles C. Alexander, *The Ku Klux Klan in the Southwest* (Lexington: University of Kentucky Press, Kentucky Paperbacks, 1966), pp. 20-35.

[25] The most comprehensive treatment of Klan violence is in Clark, "The Ku Klux Klan in Oklahoma," pp. 139-68. A less disinterested contemporary resume of the outrages commonly attributed to the order is available in Howard A. Tucker's *History of Governor Walton's War on the Ku Klux Klan, The Invisible Empire* (Oklahoma City: Southwest Publishing Co., 1923).

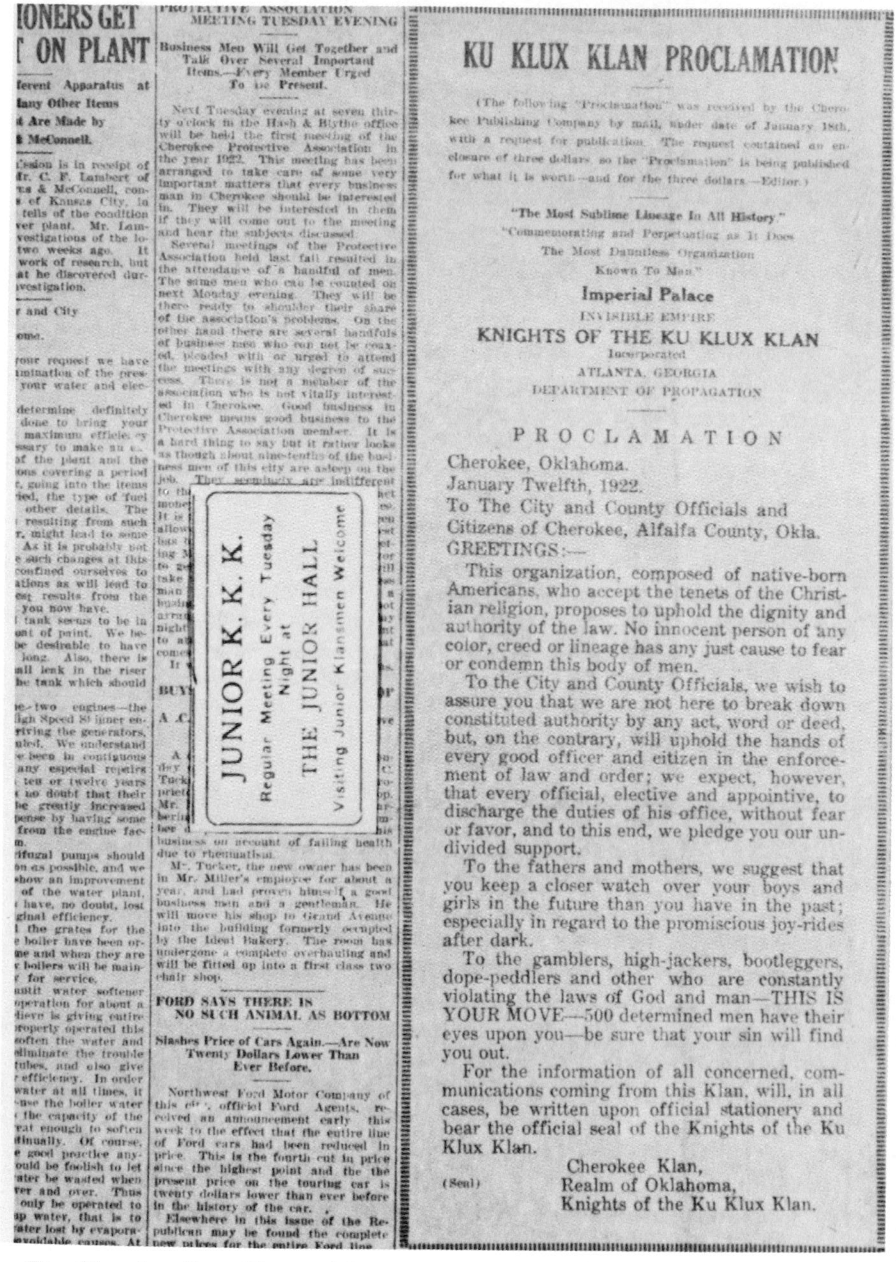

ferent Apparatus at
Many Other Items
t Are Made by
McConnell.

cssion is in receipt of
Mr. C. F. Lambert of
rs & McConnell, con-
s of Kansas City, in
tells of the condition
ver plant. Mr. Lam-
vestigations of the lo-
two weeks ago, but
work of research, but
at he discovered dur-
ivestigation.

r and City
ome.

rour request we have
timation of the pres-
your water and elec-

determine definitely
done to bring your
maximum efficiency
ssary to make an e-
of the plant and the
ions covering a period
r, going into the items
ied, the type of fuel
other details. The
resulting from such
r, might lead to some
As it is probably not
e such changes at this
confined ourselves to
ations as will lead to
est results from the
you now have.
I tank seems to be in
ent of paint. We be-
be desirable to have
long. Also, there is
all leak in the riser
he tank which should

ie-two engines—the
igh Speed 80 liner en-
riving the generators,
ufed. We understand
e been in contiguous
any especial repairs
tien or twelve years
n no doubt that they
be greatly increased
pense by having some
from the engine fac-
m.

ifugal pumps should
on as possible, and we
show an improvement
of the water plant.
have, no doubt, lost
ginal efficiency.
the grates for the
e boiler have been or-
ne and when they are
r boilers will be main-
r for service.
until water softener
operation for about a
dieve is giving entire-
roperly operated this
soften the water and
eliminate the trouble
fubes, and also give
r efficiency. In order
water at all times, it
use the boiler water
the capacity of the
rat enough to soften
dinually. Of course,
e good practice any-
ould be foolish to let
ater be wasted when
rer and over. Thus
only be operated to
up water, that is to
ater lost by evapora-
voidable causes. At

Business Men Will Get Together and
Talk Over Several Important
Items—Every Member Urged
To se Present.

Next Tuesday evening at seven thirty o'clock in the Hoch & Blythe office
will be held the first meeting of the
Cherokee Protective Association in
the year 1922. This meeting has been
arranged to take care of some very
important matters that every business
man in Cherokee should be interested
in. They will be interested in them
if they will come out to the meeting
and hear the subjects discussed.
Several meetings of the Protective
Association held last fall resulted in
the attendance of a handful of men.
The same men who can be counted on
next Monday evening. They will be
there ready to shoulder their share
of the association's problems. On the
other hand there are several handfuls
of business men who can not be coax-
ed, pleaded with or urged to attend
the meetings with any degree of success. There is not a member of the
association who is not vitally interested in Cherokee. Good business in
Cherokee means good business to the
Protective Association member. It is
a hard thing to say but it rather looks
as though about nine-tenths of the business men of this city are asleep on the
job. They seemingly are indifferent
to th...

[advertisement, boxed text rotated]

JUNIOR K. K. K.

Regular Meeting Every Tuesday
Night at

THE JUNIOR HALL

Visiting Junior Klansmen Welcome

BUY...

A C...

A
day ...
Tuck...
priett...
Mr.
berin...
her d...
business on account of failing health
due to rheumatism.
Mr. Tucker, the new owner has been
in Mr. Miller's employe for about a
year, and had proven himself a good
business man and a gentleman. He
will move his shop to Grand Avenue
into the building formerly occupied
by the Ideal Bakery. The room has
undergone a complete overhauling and
will be fitted up into a first class two
chair shop.

FORD SAYS THERE IS
NO SUCH ANIMAL AS BOTTOM

Slashes Price of Cars Again.—Are Now
Twenty Dollars Lower Than
Ever Before.

Northwest Ford Motor Company of
this city, official Ford Agents, received an announcement early this
week to the effect that the entire line
of Ford cars had been reduced in
price. This is the fourth cut in price
since the highest point and the the
present price on the touring car is
twenty dollars lower than ever before
in the history of the car.
Elsewhere in this issue of the Republican may be found the complete
new prices for the entire Ford line

KU KLUX KLAN PROCLAMATION

(The following "Proclamation" was received by the Cherokee Publishing Company by mail, under date of January 18th,
with a request for publication. The request contained an en-
closure of three dollars so the "Proclamation" is being published
for what it is worth—and for the three dollars.—Editor.)

"The Most Sublime Lineage In All History."
"Commemorating and Perpetuating as It Does
The Most Dauntless Organization
Known To Man."

Imperial Palace
INVISIBLE EMPIRE
KNIGHTS OF THE KU KLUX KLAN
Incorporated
ATLANTA, GEORGIA
DEPARTMENT OF PROPAGATION

PROCLAMATION

Cherokee, Oklahoma.
January Twelfth, 1922.
To The City and County Officials and
Citizens of Cherokee, Alfalfa County, Okla.
GREETINGS:—

This organization, composed of native-born
Americans, who accept the tenets of the Christian religion, proposes to uphold the dignity and
authority of the law. No innocent person of any
color, creed or lineage has any just cause to fear
or condemn this body of men.

To the City and County Officials, we wish to
assure you that we are not here to break down
constituted authority by any act, word or deed,
but, on the contrary, will uphold the hands of
every good officer and citizen in the enforcement of law and order; we expect, however,
that every official, elective and appointive, to
discharge the duties of his office, without fear
or favor, and to this end, we pledge you our undivided support.

To the fathers and mothers, we suggest that
you keep a closer watch over your boys and
girls in the future than you have in the past;
especially in regard to the promiscious joy-rides
after dark.

To the gamblers, high-jackers, bootleggers,
dope-peddlers and other who are constantly
violating the laws of God and man—THIS IS
YOUR MOVE—500 determined men have their
eyes upon you—be sure that your sin will find
you out.

For the information of all concerned, com-
munications coming from this Klan, will, in all
cases, be written upon official stationery and
bear the official seal of the Knights of the Ku
Klux Klan.

Cherokee Klan,
(Seal)   Realm of Oklahoma,
Knights of the Ku Klux Klan.

The Cherokee Republican of January 20, 1922, offers a warning to "gamblers,
high-jackers, bootleggers, [and] dope-peddlers," as well as those merely given to
"promiscuous joy rides after dark." Courtesy Western History Collections, University of Oklahoma.

had much the same appeal as those of a lodge. Nor was it unusual that many pious men found their church duties all but indistinguishable from their membership in the Klan. The Masonic lodges and the Protestant churches were never reduced to adjuncts of the Klan, but their memberships did overlap, and many insecure men were confused by their allegiances.

In the Red River counties, the Klan's leadership also conspicuously overlapped with another group. The state's cotton belt, long scarred by wounds of class and status, added the Klan issue as another source of division. The Klan drew most of its membership from the town residents, particularly those an admiring editor liked to call "the best people."[26] Businessmen and professionals, as well as prominent clerics, showed a disproportionate enthusiasm for the Klan's presumed moral crusade. According to one Klan spokesman, the Atoka County Klan included virtually every chamber of commerce member in the entire county; and, in Marshall County, the Madill Chamber of Commerce was said to include the entire leadership of the local Klan "klavern."[27] Neighboring Johnston County boasted of a Klan "of highest standing, composed of preachers, doctors, lawyers, merchants, in fact men from every walk of life."[28] Conspicuous by its absence was the "walk of life" that would have included most of the county's residents: tenant farmers.

The Klan's claim on the finest clientele was not disputed by the area's lesser residents. Especially among the veteran agrarian radicals, the Klan was but one more manifestation of the "interlocked parasites" of their well-remembered battles. Because of that belief, the old followers of socialism remained steadfast in their opposition to the Klan and its pretensions, and that opposition was repaid in kind. When not venting their hatred of distant "wops," "dagos," and "Krist killers," the region's Klansmen were quick to turn on "inferior types" closer to home: "the sorriest, dirtiest, most lowdown white trash . . . ever to steal the breath of life," mere "cattle," whose evident moral failure and political radicalism made them enemies of their community's decency and respectability.[29]

While the Klan was rising to poison Oklahoma's political waters, a second movement of a different character also appeared and proceeded to elect the state's fifth governor and set the stage for an explosive confrontation. The postwar agricultural depression, abetted by the deflationary policies of the Federal Reserve Board, slashed farm prices by half and reduced many farmers to ruin. Together with their old allies in organized labor, then targeted for destruction by antiunion campaigns, Oklahoma farmers were ripe for any well-organized move-

[26] Tishomingo *Johnston County Capital-Democrat,* December 13, 1923, quoted in Garin Burbank, *When Farmers Voted Red: The Gospel of Socialism in the Oklahoma Countryside, 1910-1924,* Contributions in American History, no. 53 (Westport, Conn.: Greenwood Press, 1976), p. 163.

[27] Burbank, *When Farmers Voted Red,* p. 163.

[28] *Madill Record,* February 23, 1922, quoted ibid.

[29] *Madill Record,* May 1, 1924, quoted ibid.

ment that promised relief from their distress. The contemporary example of North Dakota's Non-Partisan League was an example of boldly aggressive state action to redress similar grievances. Inspired by that model, farm and labor leaders retraced their steps to the scene of their triumphant 1906 convention in Shawnee. Assembling there on September 17, 1921, they formed the Farmer-Labor Reconstruction League. The parent groups were the Oklahoma State Federation of Labor, the Farmers' Union, and the railroad brotherhoods. Conspicuously serving as midwives for the new coalition were the unrepentant Socialist leaders, Oscar Ameringer, Patrick Nagle, and J. Luther Langston. Before leaving Shawnee, the league settled upon its immediate strategy: the formation of a platform and the selection of candidates to be entered in the 1922 Democratic primary.[30] That decision, urged by Farmers' Union president John A. Simpson of Weatherford, was dispassionate, dictated by electoral mathematics, not by any preference for Democratic principles. Their candidates' principles would be determined by their own independent program.

That program and those candidates were selected at a second convention, also held at Shawnee, in February, 1922. As in North Dakota, the Socialists left their imprint on the platform, for it represented a polished new version of the 1906 demands. The league endorsed outright government ownership of railroads and public utilities and urged the creation of state-owned banks and warehouses, as well as a system of state insurance. In addition, it called for a guaranteed minimum price for farm commodities and new job security for workmen. Finally, the coalition emphasized its opposition to all forms of militarism, particularly to high military spending.[31]

Emboldened by their own enthusiasm and aware that every political observer was anxiously watching their deliberations, the delegates picked their slate, multipartisan in origin, but all to be listed on the Democrats' preferential primary ballot. John Calloway ("Jack") Walton, Oklahoma City's mercurial one-term mayor and the favorite of that city's well-organized trade union council, was picked for governor. The convention also endorsed William Darnell, a former Socialist from Custer County, for lieutenant governor; E. P. Hill, a former Democratic state senator from McAlester, for attorney general; and Joe H. Strain of Claremore for state treasurer. For the strategic place on the Corporation Commission, the league endorsed Frank C. Carter to replace the intractable Campbell Russell.[32]

The reaction of orthodox Democrats to the league's slate was fierce but fatally unorganized. Unable to agree on candidates of their own, the old-line partisans lapsed into division and uncertainty. Most of the stand-

---

[30] E. T. Bynum, *Personal Recollections of Ex-Governor Walton: A Record of Inside Observations* (Oklahoma City: The Author, 1924), p. 11.

[31] Gilbert C. Fite, "Oklahoma's Reconstruction League: An Experiment in Farmer-Labor Politics," *Journal of Southern History* 12 (1947):535-44; *Shawnee Morning News,* February 24, 1922.

[32] *Harlow's Weekly,* March 3, 1922.

patters ensconced in the "courthouse rings" favored former Oklahoma Supreme Court Justice Thomas H. Owen of Muskogee for the governorship, but a large number chose to back State Superintendent of Public Instruction R. H. Wilson, the candidate who was also endorsed by the Klan. Moreover, Wilson enjoyed the support of the state's oil industry. E. W. Marland, Ponca City's princely oilman, held the purse strings for Wilson's campaign, while Marland's confidential attorney, former Chief Justice Samuel W. Hayes, served as the campaign manager. Possibly either Owen or Wilson could have defeated Walton, but it was much less likely that both could, since their rival candidacies could only divide the considerable anti Walton sentiment. Knowing that, leaders of both campaigns tried desperately to join forces as the election approached, but neither candidate would withdraw without liberal and unacceptable concessions from the other.[33]

While his opponents worked in vain to find a common ground for coalition, Walton was proving the effectiveness of a new style of campaigning, one so successful that countless later candidates would inflict it upon Oklahoma audiences. String bands, intemperate raillery at the opposition, and political buffoonery—all calculated to dramatize the candidate's personality—made Walton the star of the best show in Oklahoma. Surpassingly handsome, Walton charmed people of all classes. To many reformers, his disjointed but strangely eloquent presentation of the latest Shawnee platform made him truly the people's advocate. Farmers waited in the fence corners to see him pass, and workers recalled with pleasure his jailing of the director of the Oklahoma City Chamber of Commerce during that city's tense packinghouse strike. Even the hostile listened, spellbound, and were converted. When Jack Walton opened up on his opponents, the blackest of infamies unfolded. When he foretold the people's coming victory, vistas of prosperity obliterated the parched landscape. If he was content to leave specifics to the league's founders (who formulated his strategies and paid his expenses), Walton nonetheless revealed himself a master of rough-and-tumble politics matched by few—if any— in the state's history.

In the August primary, Democratic voters ignored the gaps in Walton's logic and syntax to give the league's choice a comfortable plurality— 44 percent of the vote and a lead of nearly 35,000 ballots over Wilson, his closest rival. So much activity had been concentrated on Walton that the Reconstruction League failed to do nearly so well for its other selections. Darnell lost his bid for the lieutenant governorship by 2,490 votes to the two-term incumbent, Martin E. Trapp. Strain also lost, by a larger margin, to an incumbent, State Treasurer A. S. J. Shaw; and Hill, the league's choice for attorney general, finished last in his race. On the other hand, Carter took the nomination in a badly divided field for the Corporation Commission seat; and other league candidates were victorious in races for four other lesser state offices, three supreme court

---

[33] Ibid., June 16, June 30, July 7, July 14, 1922.

Jack Walton, champion of the Reconstruction League and star of the best show in Oklahoma. Courtesy Western History Collections, University of Oklahoma.

judgeships, one seat on the criminal court of appeals, and thirty posts in the state legislature.[34]

The outcome could not have been happier for the Republican leaders, who gleefully counted on the unorthodox turn of events in the Democratic primary. The momentum from the 1920 sweep, moreover, appeared to help the Republicans in their long-frustrated design to win control of state government. Their gubernatorial candidate, John Fields, had come within a handful of votes of beating Robert L. Williams in 1914, and he anticipated little difficulty against the imposter who headed the Democratic ticket. Nearly every respectable political observer agreed.

Although he was conceded the advantage at the beginning of the fall canvass, Fields was in a peculiar position. Eight years earlier, he had been the reformer, campaigning against the conservative Democrat, Williams. But in the intervening years, he had developed close ties with business and banking interests. Confronted by Walton and his radical constituency, Fields muted his earlier commitment to reform. In 1922 he was the conservative who aimed to bring "good" Democrats into a coalition dedicated to a "safe and sound, businesslike administration." Toward his Democratic rival, the Fields campaign consisted of little more than undisguised red-baiting. That tactic was resoundingly trumpeted by the candidate's faithful Republican press, who eagerly took up the fight against the Socialists and other assorted radicals, whom they saw behind Walton's smiling face.[35]

One effect of that tactic was to scare a number of prominent Democrats into the Fields camp. A hastily formed "constitutional Democratic Club," organized by Campbell Russell, enlisted a host of earlier party notables: Ben F. Wilson (former house speaker), Bob Dunlop (past state treasurer), F. F. Herring (veteran of the constitutional convention), Charles F. Colcord (territorial marshal, then an Oklahoma oilman), Alger Melton (former state chairman and manager of Williams's 1914 race), along with the current attorney general, Prince Freeling, and the head of the Taxpayers' League, L. E. Paterson. The conservative bolters clanged the alarm against the radicals who had supposedly taken over the Democratic party and committed it to the Shawnee Demands. It was, however, the Constitutional Democrats, Russell, in particular, who produced evidence of what might have become the most damaging issue in the contest: Walton's financial vagaries. It seemed, according to several affidavits, that the poor boys' champion had recently found the wherewithal to make several large stock purchases, including some suspiciously made just after his primary victory.[36] The potential damage of those allegations was neutralized by their source: a bunch of well-heeled renegades whose extravagant prophecies of doom had already destroyed most of their

[34] *Directory of Oklahoma, 1977,* pp. 538-39; Fite, "Oklahoma's Reconstruction League," pp. 547-49.

[35] Fite, "Oklahoma's Reconstruction League," pp. 549-51.

[36] Bynum, *Personal Recollections of Ex-Governor Walton,* pp. 35-36; *Tulsa Daily World,* October 7, 1922.

credibility. Walton, equal to any challenge to invective, casually dismissed his critics as a band of "intellectual prostitutes," "just common, ordinary liars."[37]

While the Constitutional Democrats grew more impassioned, other party regulars were accepting Walton, apparently in the belief that they could pry him from his radical advisers once he was safely elected under their tutelage. Governor Robertson, who originally preferred Owen for his successor, came out unreservedly for the ticket, as did former governors Haskell and Cruce. In addition, Senator Robert L. Owen and both Thomas Gore and Scott Ferris threw their support to the cause, along with countless lesser figures.

For their part, the radicals never wavered in their adherence to Walton. J. Luther Langston, Oscar Ameringer, and Patrick Nagle, all former Socialists and prime movers behind the Farmer-Labor Reconstruction League, allowed nothing to jeopardize Walton's chances. They sacrificed George Wilson, the league's president, by forcing him to resign his position after he had made an impolitic attack on the American Legion in a speech at Atoka. Their own respect for the militantly patriotic organization must have been limited, at best.[38] Through the fall campaign, they tirelessly worked to finance Walton's bid with new $3.50 membership dues collected from thousands of farmers and laborers who joined the Reconstruction League. They probably did not know that less simple folk were also buying their own tickets for the Walton bandwagon, including oilmen like E. W. Marland, Charles Page, and Harry Sinclair.[39] While those contributions placed Walton on the prongs of a forked allegiance, he remained, to the trusting radicals, "Our Jack."

By election day, Walton's magnetism had overcome Fields's supposed advantage. He took the governorship by a count of 280,206 to 230,469, the state's greatest margin since Wilson's victory of 1916. Fields won most of the urban centers. He carried Oklahoma City, Tulsa, Enid, Okmulgee, Bristow, Stillwater, Ponca City, and Pawhuska, but Walton's overwhelming advantage in the rural areas drowned out the GOP's best opportunity since statehood. The tally sheets indicated an uncommon number of split tickets, as Walton carried some counties that otherwise went all Republican, while Fields was taking majorities in some places without a single Republican face in the courthouse. The unprecedented ticket-splitting benefited Walton: for every outraged Democrat who crossed the line, two Republicans scratched for Walton. Such was the force of the Reconstruction League in knocking askew the customary party alignment. For the Socialists, their movement into the Democratic party by way of the league left their own party a virtual nonentity, as reflected in the trifling vote (3,941) accorded its formal nominee, O. E. Enfield.[40]

[37] *Tulsa Daily World,* October 1, 1922.
[38] Bynum, *Personal Recollections of Ex-Governor Walton,* pp. 20-22.
[39] Ibid., pp. 37-47.
[40] *Directory of Oklahoma, 1977,* p. 541; Benson et al., *Oklahoma Votes,* p. 83.

Because Walton had sustained most of the opposition blows, the Democratic candidates for the lesser state offices all prevailed by majorities of 100,000 or more. The landslide also returned Democrats to control of the house of representatives and strengthened their existing advantage in the senate; Democrats picked up five senate seats and a whopping fifty-six in the house to climax the most abrupt party turnover in the legislature's history. Included in the Democratic victors were virtually all of the thirty league-endorsed nominees. Also included were an even larger number, perhaps an outright majority, who had enjoyed the backing of the Ku Klux Klan. Finally, Oklahoma's congressional delegation returned to a more familiar division, as four of the five Republican seats won two years earlier were restored to Democrats. Only Milton Garber, the Enid publisher who had defeated Manuel Herrick in the primary, held on to take the reliable northwest (Eighth District) for the GOP.[41]

In sum, the Democrats had miraculously recovered from the debacle of two years earlier; all things considered, they had won their strongest victory since statehood. It was a remarkable achievement. It was also a disturbing one because, this Democratic party bore only a slight resemblance to the party of the past. To traditional Democrats, the Walton candidacy had added a series of alien groups—veteran Socialists, Republican farmers, Wilson-haters, and most of the politically active blacks, all of whom had done unremitting battle against every Democratic enterprise of the previous fifteen years. For the moment, they forgot their differences in their romance with "Our Jack." It would not be long before that romance soured, and this obscure man would fall just as fast as he had risen. While falling, he would also threaten to bring everybody else down with him.

[41] *Directory of Oklahoma, 1977*, pp. 541–42; Benson et al., *Oklahoma Votes*, p 49; Clark, "A History of the Ku Klux Klan in Oklahoma," p. 196.

CHAPTER 7

Governor Walton and the Ku Klux Klan

THE INAUGURATION OF Jack Walton as the state's fifth governor in January, 1923, was a folk spectacle the like of which Oklahoma had never seen. The governor-elect had previewed it in his campaign speeches, repeating his mass invitation four hundred times: "When I am elected governor, there will not be any inaugural ball, and there will not be a tea dansant. I am going to give an old-fashioned barbecue. It will be a party for all the people, and I want you all to come."[1] Come they did, by the tens of thousands, and reporters had a field day embroidering the human interest story of frontier democracy acclaiming its hero in the Andrew Jackson tradition. Miles of trenches were cut through the state fairgrounds to accommodate the chefs who prepared tons of beef, most of it proudly donated; and thousands of gallons of coffee were eagerly consumed by the surging mob. Twelve jazz bands added to the revelry.[2] The nervous adjutant general, Charles F. Barrett, was still awed sixteen years later when he wrote of the "barbecue that suppressed [sic] all records for size and the outflow of public spirit."[3]

Who was this man around whom such expectations radiated? His past was so obscure that, even now, the details are often lost to contradiction and uncertainty, so that only the principal facts are known.[4] He was born March 6, 1881, on a farm near Indianapolis, Indiana. When he was

[1] *Oklahoma City Daily Oklahoman,* January 10, 1923.
[2] "Homeric America," *Nation,* January 24, 1923, p. 86.
[3] Barrett, ed., *Oklahoma After Fifty Years,* 4 vols. (Hopkinsville, Kentucky and Oklahoma City: Historical Record Association, 1941), 2:431.
[4] The conflicting accounts of Walton's biography are taken from *Harlow's Weekly,* August 11, 1922; *Tulsa Tribune,* November 17, 1922; *Oklahoma City Daily Oklahoman,* October 2, 1948; E. T. Bynum, *Personal Recollections of Ex-Governor Walton: A Record*

six, the family moved to Lincoln, Nebraska, where he stayed until he joined the field artillery in 1897. His service continued through the Spanish-American War, although his duties took him no farther than Little Rock, Arkansas. For the next few years, the trail is overgrown with conflicting testimony. Walton was variously identified as a salesman, railroader, hotel clerk, and some sort of engineer. After working on Mexican railroads, he came to Oklahoma City (even the date is uncertain, ranging from 1903 to 1909), where he worked as a salesman for an engineering firm and, in 1917, as a civil engineer. In the same year, he entered public life as a commissioner of public works. After brief war service, he returned to the city which, after a spirited campaign, elected him its mayor in March, 1919.

His years in the capital mayoralty drew him the publicity that later made him a gubernatorial candidate. The pugnacious executive plunged into battles with his commissioners for control of the police department. Prosaic business was deferred in favor of sensational investigations into the city's moral conditions. Citizens were generally impressed by the results of his "purity squad" raids, although some voiced concern about the arbitrary methods used in the mass arrests and imprisonments that attended the mayor's much-publicized forays into the demimonde. Whether by conviction or by calculation, Walton always sided with organized labor in the community's labor disputes that grew out of the unsettled postwar economy. Himself a union member (appropriately enough, of the Stage Hands and Theatrical Workers Union), the mayor gave his open sympathy to the packinghouse workers during their long strike. His jailing of the president of the chamber of commerce provided a touch of comic opera.

As the gubernatorial election approached, Walton also moved to curry the favor of the Socialists by inducing the police to use part of their benefit fund to purchase stock in the faltering *Oklahoma Leader,* long the movement's most effective journal. For a police department to be the partial owner of a radical newspaper was incongruous with traditional views of law and order. Nevertheless, the move paid off handsomely for Walton. Socialists and trade unionists gave him the support that resulted in the Reconstruction League's endorsement in 1922.

The diverse coalition that had put Walton in the governor's chair began to come apart almost as soon as the last celebratory barbecue had vanished. Despite their decisive legislative majority, the Democrats were fractured by rival cliques, with league followers, Klan sympathizers, and old-line partisans going their separate and thoroughly antagonistic ways. Walton was caught in the middle. Some of his advisers, like Patrick Nagle, urged the speedy vitalization of the Shawnee platform, while others, like C. H. Ruth, cautioned restraint in the interest of overcoming the

of Inside Observations (Oklahoma City: The Author, 1924), pp. 3-7; and Howard A. Tucker, *History of Governor Walton's War on the Ku Klux Klan, The Invisible Empire* (Oklahoma City: Southwest Publishing Co., 1923), pp. 3-6.

wariness of party conservatives and businessmen. Contenders for the governor's favor hardly knew from one day to the next which faction had the upper hand. Indeed, Walton himself did not know: he vacillated from one opinion to the opposite. Only his policy on pardons was consistent. Like Cruce, he refused to permit the death penalty. Unlike any previous governor, he was unusually responsive to the blandishments of attorneys and families of convicted criminals, some of whom received clemency before they arrived at the state prison.[5]

Most of the credit for the Ninth Legislature's record for advanced legislation must be given to the "Committee of Twenty-one," which the Reconstruction League had selected to manage its legislative program. Neither the committee's leadership nor the impact of Walton's astonishing victory at the polls, yielded a substantial legislative dividend. A minor improvement was the expansion of marketing cooperatives begun under the previous administration. Other laws strengthened the existing warehouse and inspection acts to conform to the minimum demands of cotton and wheat farmers.

Aside from these, ameliorative statutes, the league experienced a series of frustrations. Radical proposals for state-owned grain elevators and a state insurance system died at the hands of conservative Democratic legislators. The proposal for state-owned banks was also defeated.[6] In fact, the pioneering bank guaranty system, dating back to Haskell's administration, was dismantled, over the angry protests of the league's representatives. However, repeal was inevitable. Too many state banks had withdrawn from the system and applied for federal charters. Many of the remainder had failed in the postwar depression, leaving the survivors incapable of paying the outstanding obligations of a system that was long since bankrupt. It could have survived only with a massive transfusion of state dollars because even the least healthy of institutions would have required protection. Under the circumstances, the league could win no more than a feeble gesture to indignant debtors in a reorganization of the Banking Commission and the stipulation of harsh penalties for bank officers who violated the state banking code.[7]

The legislature nonetheless earned a reputation for reform, not for its embrace of the radical labor and agrarian demands but for its expansion of state services administered by a score of new welfare, educational, and regulatory agencies. For example, more than a million dollars (ten times the previous allotment) of "weak school aid" was freely granted; the first free textbook law was adopted (amended by the Klan members to forbid the purchase of any volumes teaching evolution); and $3 million more in highway revenues accrued from an additional one-cent gasoline levy.

   [5]Charles C. Alexander, *The Ku Klux Klan in the Southwest* (Lexington: University of Kentucky Press, Kentucky Paperbacks, 1966), pp. 138-39.
   [6]Ibid., p. 138.
   [7]Thornton Cooke, "Collapse of Bank Deposit Guaranty in Oklahoma and Its Position in Other States," *Quarterly Journal of Economics* 68 (1923):108-39.

Despite that record, Walton's support from the league cooled appreciably in the face of his demonstrated inadequacy and vacillation. As his original constituency withered, the governor moved in two directions to bolster his declining fortunes. The first was to patronage, long used to strengthen a governor's hand. None, however, had used it with Walton's abandon in creating more jobs for the jostling rivals, alternating his favors with scant regard for the consistency of public administration. The capitol and the governor's home were besieged by job-hunters; and Walton, ever ready to please, kept their hopes alive by impulsively announcing the appointment of nonentities to high posts. In addition, he forced state departments to employ his friends in offices that were already overstaffed and to create sinecures for deserving, if obscure, campaign supporters.[8]

When the traditional departments had absorbed their limit of political favorites, the governor looked to the state's educational institutions as a new source of patronage jobs. His scheme of including college presidents, professors, and janitors among his appointees was the beginning of his ruin. While previous executives had not been above interference with the state's schools, Walton's crude assaults on the university and the agricultural college aroused educators, alumni, and students to the menace of his rule. Walton heartily distrusted higher learning and its practitioners, few of whom, he rightly believed, had supported his candidacy. Believing that all state agencies should bend to the chief executive's will, he pursued his fatal course with a determination that bordered on madness.

Walton's first frontal assault was directed at the administration and governing board of the university. When President Stratton D. Brooks and two members of the board of regents resigned under pressure, Walton accepted the advice of his more temperate counselors to name to the board two incorruptible men—Frank Buttram of Oklahoma City and C. J. Wrightsman of Tulsa, both oil millionaires. The governor apparently wanted to name Dr. Forney Hutchison, a highly respected Methodist minister from Oklahoma City, to the university's presidency, but Hutchison refused the appointment. Walton then turned to a cracker-barrel philosopher, R. L. ("Battleaxe") Glover, a radical agitator from the Rush Springs area. Unfortunately for Walton's designs, his own appointees to the board of regents indignantly blocked that move.[9] After many months of public wrangling, Dr. William Bennett Bizzell, then president of Texas A. and M., was selected.

Amid the furor, a majority of the senate Democrats, alarmed at the reaction to Walton's disregard for the integrity of the university, publicly remonstrated with the governor to leave the institutions of higher learn-

<hr>

[8] Bynum, *Personal Recollections of Ex-Governor Walton,* pp. 85ff.; State of Oklahoma, Legislature, Senate, *Transcript of Proceedings of the Senate Sitting as a Court of Impeachment,* 9th leg., extra. sess., November 8-9, 1923, pp. 261-353.

[9] Bynum, *Personal Recollections of Ex-Governor Walton,* p. 84.

ing undisturbed.[10] Walton's answer was to name a new Board of Agriculture to do his bidding in reorganizing Oklahoma A. and M., which was constitutionally governed by that board. More successful this time, the governor got George Wilson, the erstwhile president of the Reconstruction League and a former Socialist, appointed by the new board as the college president, over the anguished protests of John A. Whitehurst, the popularly elected president of the Board of Agriculture, and A. E. Whitworth, the lone survivor of the initial purge. Seven hundred Stillwater residents protested the rash appointment and defiantly cornered the governor in a capitol corridor. At the school, students broke out signs: "We Want Educators, Not Agitators," and, less imaginative but more pointed, "To Hell with George Wilson." Wilson's inadequacy was plain to every eye except Walton's, and the determined governor went ahead to have Wilson installed under military guard.[11] Beset on every side by contempt and derision, Wilson was a pathetic prisoner. Luckily, his stay was short, for Walton soon tired of his inept puppet and peremptorily ordered the Board of Agriculture to fire Wilson. Their collective backbone stiffened by the example of the university regents, his appointees refused, whereupon the governor ousted them to name yet a third board, which eventually replaced Wilson with Bradford Knapp, whose economic views tended more toward the orthodox than did Wilson's.[12]

At the beginning of Walton's ill-fated and heavy-handed interference with the state colleges, he had also reached out for one other source of strength to augment his diminishing league following. At a time when the largest single group opposing him was the Ku Klux Klan, Walton had secretly turned to the Klan's emissaries, meeting behind closed doors with Klan potentates, hoping to make new friends without losing the old. At one of those closed-door meetings in late January, Walton paid Dr. W. T. Tilley, a Muskogee Kleagle (head of a local unit), a twenty-dollar Klectoken (initiation fee) to become a "Klansman at Large." So impressed was the hooded order with Tilley's proselyting that it conferred lifetime membership on the Muskogean.[13]

After the public uproar over his meddling with the university and the agricultural college, Walton turned to the Klan once more—not to join it but to make war upon it. Already threatened by impeachment talk, in the summer of 1923, Walton launched a grand diversionary maneuver to recapture the imagination of the people and regain his lost following. His strategy was to paint all foes with the brush of the Klan, elevating himself as the people's continuing champion against

---

[10] *Oklahoma City Daily Oklahoman,* April 30, 1923.
[11] *Tulsa Daily World,* May 15-June 4, 1923; *Oklahoma City Times,* May 21-23, 1923.
[12] Alexander, *The Ku Klux Klan in the Southwest,* pp. 138-39.
[13] Ibid., pp. 136-37; Bynum, *Personal Recollections of Ex-Governor Walton,* pp. 71-72. After their break with the governor, his former Socialist and Reconstruction League advisers, especially Patrick Nagle, acquired and published copies of correspondence relating to Walton's dalliance with the Klan. See *Oklahoma City Oklahoma Leader,* December 14, 1923.

intolerance and terror. To be sure, the Klan richly deserved punishment, but not subversion of civil liberties with unparalleled ruthlessness. Walton's methods, moreover, were crudely ineffective, so ineffective that the Klan emerged stronger than before.

Already, following outbreaks of Klan violence in the Henryetta area in June and July, Walton had declared martial law over Okmulgee County.[14] Suddenly seizing the opportunity afforded him by more alleged Klan outrages, he declared martial law on specified parts of Tulsa County on August 13 and, on September 1, extended military rule across the entire county. In accordance with the governor's orders, military officers imposed a sundown curfew on the city, suspended the powers of the police department and the county sheriff's office, and forbade any criticism of state or military authority. The governor's proclamation of martial law, one of the most intemperate documents in state history, darkly described a "general state of lawlessness" existing for more than a year and charged the Tulsa authorities as being in "secret sympathy" with "scores" of Klan assaults. By the proclamation, the privilege of the writ of habeas corpus was suspended, a direct violation of the state constitution.[15]

Grand Dragon N. Clay Jewett, the state Klan leader, met Walton's challenge, vowing that "Jack Walton and all his cohorts will never be able to break the power of the Ku Klux Klan."[16] The *Tulsa Tribune,* one of the few remaining pro-Walton newspapers, angrily broke with the governor. In retaliation, Walton imposed military censorship on the *Tribune*'s editorial page, although he relented a day later when threatened with a federal lawsuit. On September 11 the governor met with Tulsa's civic leaders and laid down his terms for the removal of the military occupation: the ouster of the county sheriff, police chief, police commission, and jury commission. The Tulsans voted to resist, and the troops remained.[17]

Four days after delivering the Tulsa ultimatum, Walton extended martial law to cover the entire state and imposed "absolute martial law" on Oklahoma County, where a grand jury was scheduled to convene to investigate the governor. His garrulous proclamation labeled Klansmen and all their sympathizers "enemies of the Sovereign State of Oklahoma," to be "dealt with accordingly" by the 6,000 guardsmen he called up.[18] That ominous language was no worse than his earlier counsel that citizens should shoot any Klansmen who bothered them, with the guarantee of an executive pardon "in advance." The Oklahoma

---

[14] *Okmulgee Daily Times,* June 24–July 13, 1923.

[15] Executive Proclamation No. 1154, September 4, 1923, Secretary of State's Files, Oklahoma State Archives, Oklahoma City, Oklahoma.

[16] *Oklahoma City Times,* September 7, 1923.

[17] Alexander, *The Ku Klux Klan in the Southwest,* pp. 145–46. A full account of Tulsa's experience with military rule is available in Carter Blue Clark, "A History of the Ku Klux Klan in Oklahoma" (Ph.D. diss., University of Oklahoma, 1976), pp. 181–87.

[18] *Tulsa Tribune,* September 16, 1923; *Oklahoma City Daily Oklahoman,* September 16, 1923.

County action, however, was raw official power: guardsmen trained machine guns on the doors of the county courthouse to prevent the grand jury from assembling.[19]

On September 26, as legislators hurried into Oklahoma City, they were turned away from the capitol by military forces acting under Walton's orders. In a hurried meeting at the Skirvin Hotel, the displaced lawmakers planned their next move. Attempting to win the support of veterans, Walton had already called for a special election on October 2 to consider a soldiers' bonus measure. Acting in furious haste, the governor's enemies, led by the intrepid Campbell Russell, prepared an initiative petition to add a second question to the ballot: a constitutional amendment authorizing the legislature to call itself into special session, without the governor's invitation. Quickly gaining the necessary number of signatures, the issue was placed on the October 2 ballot on the basis of a formal opinion by Attorney General George F. Short.[20]

Now desperate, Walton secured a court order enjoining the State Election Board from placing the question on the special election ballot, but the injunction was immediately lifted by the state supreme court. When the election board approved submission of the measure, Walton fired its members and named a new board, which ordered county officials to prevent the election. On October 1, the day before the scheduled vote, the new board's order was overturned by the courts, leaving Walton with but one last card. He played it, ordering the national guard and local police forces to stop the balloting, by force if necessary. "There may be bloodshed, but there will be no election," he promised.[21]

He was wrong on both counts. The election proceeded without incident in most of the state. Only in Cimarron, Delaware, Harper, and Johnston counties was the governor's desperate order obeyed. In the remainder of the state, the voting went ahead; most sheriffs and constables, along with not a few guardsmen, deserted to the enemy. The Russell measure passed by a crushing majority, 209,452 to 70,638.[22]

Within hours after the returns were conclusive, William D. McBee of Duncan, chosen as legislative leader after the September 26 confrontation at the capitol, issued a call for a special legislative session to meet—its purpose obvious—on October 10. On the eighth, Walton made one last feeble assertion of his prerogative by issuing his own call for a special session to convene on October 11 for the purpose of enacting a curb on the Ku Klux Klan. Two days later, he dramatically offered

[19] Alexander, *The Ku Klux Klan in the Southwest,* pp. 144, 147.
[20] Clark, "The Ku Klux Klan in Oklahoma," pp. 193-95.
[21] Ibid., p. 194; *Oklahoma City Daily Oklahoman,* September 16-October 4, 1923.
[22] State of Oklahoma, State Election Board, *Directory of Oklahoma, 1977,* pp. 637-38. Unnoticed in the excitement were the results of voting on three other measures placed on the same ballot. The soldiers' bonus bill was defeated (120,219 to 142,082), as were measures to amend the state's workmen's compensation system and to pay off all claims pending against the bank guaranty fund. Voters approved measures to open executive offices to women and to guarantee a minimum fifteen dollars per child school appropriation. Both were later invalidated by the state supreme court as improperly submitted.

to resign in exchange for the adoption of a stringent "antimask" law, but the gathering legislators were in no mood to countenance any more of Walton's histrionics. McBee gave their reply: "Nobody has asked Governor Walton to resign. Nobody wants him to establish himself as a martyr on a side issue and close the books on his official acts and the doings of his subordinates."[23]

The legislature thereupon met in its self-called special session, summarily ignored the governor's agenda, and gathered evidence for his impeachment. Walton's former sponsors in the Farmer-Labor Reconstruction League joined the legislative majority as the house quickly shaped twenty-two charges of impeachment. Rumors that Walton was prepared to empty the state prison by a blanket pardon spurred immediate action, and two articles were hastily adopted and sent to the senate on October 23. Upon their receipt, Walton was officially suspended from office, pending his senate trial on all twenty-two counts, and Lieutenant Governor Trapp, himself only recently the object of an impeachment trial, assumed the governor's duties.[24]

The impeachment articles comprehensively summarized Walton's official misdeeds and were abundantly verified by the testimony taken by the house managers, who were commanded by the young, non-Klansman representative from Tulsa County, Wesley E. Disney. The trial opened on November 6. Walton's defense was the assertion that his deeds were necessary responses to the Klan's reign of terror. This was especially argued against the six articles that grew out of the martial law proclamations. For his defense on those counts, Walton planned to call as many as a thousand witnesses in an attempt to prolong the trial and reduce all issues to a Klan-versus-governor question. On November 16, Disney effectively ended that possibility when he moved to drop those particular six counts to devote the prosecution to the remaining sixteen, any one of which, if upheld, was grounds for the governor's removal. His prospects for legal defense and political martyrdom thereby cancelled, Walton dramatically walked out of the proceedings on the following day, announcing that, "I do not care to stand this humiliation any longer. . . . You may proceed as you wish."[25]

After two more days of testimony, the senate voted on the remaining sixteen counts of impeachable offenses, charitably acquitting the governor on the most dubious five. Eleven were sustained. They involved Walton's illegal collection of campaign funds, padding state payrolls, preventing the assembly of a lawful grand jury, issuing improper deficiency certificates, paying a private chauffeur with state funds, suspend-

[23] *Oklahoma City Daily Oklahoman,* October 10, 1923.

[24] Alexander, *The Ku Klux Klan in the Southwest,* pp. 152-53. Although assuming the duties of governor, Trapp did not take the formal oath of office—an omission that he later used to justify his claim never to have been the actual governor and, thus, his eligibility in 1926.

[25] Clark, "The Ku Klux Klan in Oklahoma," pp. 200-201; Walton quoted in Alexander, *The Ku Klux Klan in the Southwest,* p. 154.

ing the writ of habeas corpus, making excessive use of his pardoning authority, and being generally incompetent.[26] Walton was firmly retired in disgrace—though neither quietly nor permanently, as it turned out.

Destroyed also was the radical political accord of farmers, workers, and Socialists. The Farmer-Labor Reconstruction League had won its last election and fought its last fight. Because of their identification with the discredited regime, the high-minded reformers who had sought to give the state government a fresh infusion of progressive leadership were ruined, their political influence permanently broken.[27] Patrick Nagle, the old Socialist who had overcome the stigma of war resistance to become an adviser to "Our Jack," died, a sad and crushed man, a few months later, and much was buried with him. In the countryside, the old indignation that had fueled the nation's strongest grass-roots radical movement began to give way to resignation and fatalism. Only the truly gullible mind could fully believe that Walton was the innocent victim of a ruthless conspiracy. No longer would throngs gather to hear "Our Jack's" latest assault on the predatory interests. Only a pitiable and powerless minority could close their minds to all evidence and grant him the status of martyrdom—"the only way," George Bernard Shaw once commented, "a man can become famous without ability."[28]

Walton's speedy disgrace forever ended the Reconstruction League that had put him in office. It also gave new life to his avowed enemy, the Ku Klux Klan. The Klan was probably in decline by the summer of 1923, when Walton had fatally chosen to make war upon it. At the year's end, the Klan, fortified by its resistance to Walton's petty despotism, was stronger than ever. By 1924, the state Klan counted 100,000 members and swept its candidates to victory in a series of city elections, especially in the eastern part of the state.[29] Although the pace of its violence slowed, the Klan remained for several years the key organization—or, at least, the central issue—in state politics.

Only the able stewardship of Walton's successor was able to minimize the Klan's immediate capacity for mischief. Martin Edward Trapp was no stranger to politics, yet his administration was surprisingly free of it, and Trapp fully earned his self-description of "all business." If his ideas were of the commonplace stock of the state's business progressives and his speeches typically tiresome, he was an effective administrator who succeeded in untangling the badly knotted threads of public business.

[26] Alexander, *The Ku Klux Klan in the Southwest,* p. 154.

[27] One common story told of the radicals' disappointment with Walton is probably apocryphal, but it illustrates their contempt for his intellectual capacity. It concerns a Reconstruction League orator's recounting how the governor, once in office, had betrayed his friends for personal gain. "As Browning said," the unnamed orator recited, "'Just for a handful of silver he left us.'" Walton, informed of the charge, is supposed to have said, "Who is this fellow, Browning? Get him in here to say that to my face."

[28] Hesketh Pearson, *G.B.S.: A Full Length Portrait* (Garden City, N.Y.: Garden City Publishing Co., 1942), p. 67.

[29] Clark, "The Ku Klux Klan in Oklahoma," p. 205; Alexander, *The Ku Klux Klan in the Southwest,* pp. 199–200.

Martin E. Trapp, Walton's lieutenant governor and successor. Courtesy Western History Collections, University of Oklahoma.

Born on a Kansas farm on April 18, 1877, Trapp had come to Logan County as a boy and, after attendance at the Edmond normal school, served briefly as a teacher. He gained an insight into territorial politics as an advertising solicitor and reporter for Frank Greer's *Oklahoma State Capital.* As a traveling salesman, he acquainted himself with thousands of voters. In 1904 he won his first political race, to become clerk of the predominantly Republican county, his rare success as a Democrat largely credited to his drawing a black opponent on the GOP side. With statehood, he was chosen as the first state auditor, but attempting to shift to the state treasurer's office in 1910, he suffered his first defeat. Out of office for four years, Trapp worked as an investment broker, buying and selling municipal securities and profitably stimulating the interest of local officials in public works projects. In 1914 he returned to the campaign trail to win a close race for the lieutenant governorship and was reelected in 1918. Even his rough handling by the Republican legislature of 1921 did not seriously damage his political reputation, and he won a third term (after beating the Reconstruction League's choice in the Democratic primary) in 1922. Two years after his own acquittal on impeachment charges, Walton's folly propelled him to the governor's chair.[30]

No friend of the Klan—but no fool, either—the new governor recalled the Ninth Legislature into special session, and the legislators took up the matter ignored after Walton's final summons: some controls on the Klan. With Walton safely out of the way, even moderate Klansmen agreed on the propriety of legislation restricting the order's right to visit mayhem on its foes. On November 20, Senator Tom Anglin of Holdenville presented the new administration's remedy: a law requiring the registration of membership in all secret organizations and prohibiting the wearing of masks in public places. The firm opposition of the more extreme Klansmen in the legislature forced the deletion of the registration feature. Wesley Disney accurately prophesied that the adoption of a toothless anti-Klan law would leave Walton free to charge in the impending 1924 United States Senate race that the government was Klan-dominated. The bill passed in its amended form. Despite its weakness, the statute was the first adopted by any state to regulate the wearing of masks by the Klansmen. In approving it, Trapp helped remove the immediate threat of further disruption by the hooded terrorists.[31]

With the Klan issue temporarily compromised, the Ninth Legislature, in early 1924, meekly complied with Trapp's demands that they undo much of their earlier work. So chastened were its members that even the erstwhile radicals acceded to the governor's request that they reduce the commitments they had made to the free-spending Walton a year earlier. The same, more conservative approach prevailed as Trapp directed the Tenth Legislature in 1925. Trapp took credit for the busi-

[30] Barrett, ed., *Oklahoma After Fifty Years,* 2:437-38.
[31] Alexander, *The Ku Klux Klan in the Southwest,* pp. 154-57.

nesslike restoration of the state's credit, chiefly by forcing the repeal of nearly ten million dollars' worth of Walton-era appropriations. Institutional building suffered most from the new spirit of legislative economy, although the 1925 assembly also cut common school aid to little more than a third of the 1923 appropriation.

The most significant achievement of the Trapp administration was a highway construction program that in three years made more road improvements than had been done in the preceding twelve. Supervising the modern building program was a new and powerful highway commission, consisting of Cyrus S. Avery of Tulsa and Frank J. Gentry of Enid, Democrats, and Roy M. Johnson of Ardmore, the minority member. The creation of an efficient highway commission had been Trapp's first priority, the provision of revenues his second. Recalling Robertson's ill-fated road bond issue, Trapp elected to put the road building program on a pay-as-you-go basis, financed by increases in gasoline taxes. Two separate increases, one in 1924 and a second, smaller one in 1925 brought the total state levy to three cents a gallon. Motor vehicle license fees were also increased by 2.5 percent. Thanks to the 3 percent gross production tax on the healthy oil industry, general state revenues steadily climbed. The ad valorem tax was largely turned to local needs, for by 1926, receipts from the gross production levy reached $10 million to provide, by far, the most lucrative source of state income.[32]

Solicitude for business was apparent in the governor's dealings with the powerful oil companies and utilities. All but obsequious to the oil company executives, Trapp withheld aggressive enforcement of the state's existing conservation statutes to let the companies have their way in the oil fields, and the prevailing high oil prices seemingly confirmed the wisdom of the governor's laissez faire policy. Meanwhile, the utility companies effectively voided the constitutional mandate of a public referendum on franchise renewals by an act of the Tenth Legislature that turned renewal authority over to the Corporation Commission. Although there was some argument within the legislature, it was a routine debate between rival corporate interests, and the state's consumers were all but voiceless. The fact that the utilities could even raise such an issue indicated to what extent the administration of 1925 differed in spirit from that of 1907, when every branch of state government insisted on subjecting corporate power to popular democracy.

Under Trapp's businesslike rule, the few expansions of state authority came not at the expense of corporate privilege but in the direction of more efficient state management. One example was the new attempt to manage Oklahoma's wildlife population. At the governor's urging, the Tenth Legislature limited hunting seasons and strengthened conservation services by adding three new enforcement agencies: a forestry commission, a fish and game commission, and a conservation commission.

[32] S. T. Bisbee, "Relation of the Oil Industry to the Revenues of the State of Oklahoma," *Harlow's Weekly,* October 18, 1924, p. 8.

Only the temptations of patronage limited the executive and legislative commitment to the professional management of resources.

Equally typical of Trapp's approach to government was his insistence that the state penitentiary become self-supporting, especially after the required retrenchment of 1925. Convinced that prisons should pay their own way, the governor placed a national guard officer, Colonel William S. Key, over the McAlester facility and ordered the creation of prison industries within the walls of "Big Mac." The use of convict labor on state projects far removed from the institution was ended because the cost of providing adequate security was excessive. The governor pointed to the experience of using convict labor to build the state capitol, where twenty-seven guards had been required for sixty-three prisoners. Thirteen convicts had escaped anyway.[33] There could have been no better argument.

The governor's ingrained caution did not prevent his use of troops, but the guard was never used as indiscriminately as under Walton. Renewed disturbances in the southeastern coal fields in 1924 led him to send the militia to Wilburton from July through September of that year. With some justice, the fading United Mine Workers Union charged that the governor's military intervention cost them its hopes for a closed shop and allowed the operators to maintain a 30 percent wage reduction.[34] A year later, during the nationwide coal strike, the operators hysterically demanded protection in the McAlester field. The governor delayed, arguing from his recent experience that the presence of troops would only aggravate the ill-feeling. His predecessor in Oklahoma City, Robert L. Williams, then a federal district judge, on October 23, 1925, removed the pressures on the administration with a crippling injunction that eventually broke the strike.[35]

The most dramatic disruption of state affairs came not from the coal fields but from the United States senatorial campaign of 1924. The retirement of Senator Owen and the continuing presence of the Ku Klux Klan—most recently demonstrated in its disruption of the Democrats' 1924 national convention in New York—opened the door for Jack Walton's bid to return to power.[36] Within the state, the dominant party had hoped to compromise the Klan question by sending to New York a delegation of Klansmen pledged to William G. McAdoo, while naming Scott Ferris, an anti-Klansman, as national committeeman. Walton's flamboyant return to the hustings guaranteed that the Klan matter could not be so easily resolved.

Predictably, Walton's campaign was a vitriolic attack on the continuing menace of the Invisible Empire, which he self-righteously blamed for

[33] *Oklahoma City Daily Oklahoman,* November 3, 1923.

[34] *Henryetta Free-Lance,* July 22, 1924.

[35] *Oklahoma City Daily Oklahoman,* September 2, 1925.

[36] The Democratic National Convention had been sorely rent by the issue of officially censuring the Ku Klux Klan. The intensity of the struggle was reflected in its outcome— defeat of the specific Klan censure by the count of 543 3/20 to 542 7/20. George B.

his martyrdom and for crushing the hopes of the downtrodden. Walton's unexcelled talent for demogoguery guaranteed that every other legislative, economic, and social issue immediately receded into the background. The primaries of both parties became battlegrounds for the Klan.

Among the Democrats, Walton's rivals virtually handed him the anti-Klan issue, since he was the only avowed foe to enter the primary. The others either professed neutrality—a hopeless no man's land in the war of extremes—or, sympathetic toward the Klan, fought among themselves for its endorsement. Perhaps only Prince Freeling, a former attorney general and Walton foe from the beginning, appreciated the magnitude of the crisis. Freeling sagaciously proposed that each Democrat entered against Walton in the primary withdraw, except for one to be chosen by the party's central committee.[37] The plan failed because none of the leaders (a group that did not include Freeling) was willing to make the sacrifice.

Forgotten in the turmoil was the organization that only two years earlier had exerted such wrenching force on state politics. The survivors of the Farmer-Labor Reconstruction League, gathering at El Reno, endorsed C. J. Wrightsman. That endorsement, itself, was a sad commentary on the league's demise, for the oil millionaire was admired only for his defiance of Walton during the university controversy.

If little regard was paid to the Reconstruction League's endorsement, all eyes watched anxiously for the Ku Klux Klan to bestow its favors. Thomas Gore, bidding for a comeback, would certainly not win it, for his well-remembered opposition to the war ruled him out with the patriotic order. One possibility was Congressman E. B. Howard of Tulsa, a Klansman himself and inveterate foe of Walton. On July 29 a group of Klan leaders endorsed Howard. Three days before the primary, however, the *Fiery Cross,* the official state Klan newspaper, came out officially for Wrightsman. Any remaining possibilities for confusion were exhausted when N. Clay Jewett, the state Grand Dragon of the Klan, immediately followed the official editorial with telegrams to every Klan local that endorsed Howard as the Klan's true choice.[38]

The result was a lesson in the hazards of a divided field in a plurality primary. The split Klan endorsements for both Howard and Wrightsman assured Walton his victory with 91,510 votes, 31 percent of the total. The two Klan-endorsed candidates split between them 45 percent of the ballots, but Howard, the more popular of the two, was still nearly 7,600 votes short of Walton's total. Howard had commanding majorities in the northeast, and Gore (who placed third) ran very well in the northwest. But Walton proved unbeatable in the big-voting Democratic counties

Tindall, *The Emergence of the New South, 1913-1945,* History of the South, vol. 10 (Baton Rouge: Louisiana State University Press, 1967), pp. 243-44.

[37] *Tulsa Daily World,* August 3, 1924.

[38] Alexander, *The Ku Klux Klan in the Southwest,* pp. 201-202.

of the south, where the countryside's distrust of the Klan pretensions brought the tenant class to Walton's side once more.[39]

The Klan's bewildering flip-flop, which gave the deposed governor the Democratic nomination, virtually guaranteed a Republican victory in November. Indeed, it was with that development in mind that Jewett had deliberately split the Klan's Democratic vote. A devout Republican, Jewett had calculated that the most vulnerable opponent for his own party was the disgraced former governor, and he used the powers of his exalted office deliberately to befuddle the pliant Democratic Klansmen into giving their party's nomination to their most despised enemy.[40] Meanwhile the Republicans had their own battle to fight over the nefarious order.

In a field of six contenders for the GOP senatorial nomination, the two chief rivals were William B. Pine and Eugene Lorton. Lorton, the publisher of the *Tulsa World,* had a ready campaign organ and impressive testimonials from a host of party stalwarts whose credentials dated to the territorial years.[41] Lorton was a fervent anti-Klansman, and he pitched his campaign to that issue against Pine, a wealthy oilman and Klan member. Lorton's anti-Klan crusade was not enough, however, for the party's rank and file, many of whom saw an unpleasant parallel between Lorton's and Walton's methods of campaigning. With the stout assistance of Grant McCullough, the Tulsa banker who was Lorton's bitter personal enemy, Pine easily won a clear majority with 60,129 votes to Lorton's 24,374.[42] The *World* petulantly refused to support Pine in the general election, the embittered Lorton justifying his position with the curious argument that Pine was not a Republican and Walton was not a Democrat.[43]

Despite Lorton's apostasy, the GOP came out of its primary contest much less divided than the Democrats. The depth of that party's division over the Klan issue was apparent in the returns from the other primary races. While Walton, the Klan's foremost foe, emerged to head the ticket, four of the six supreme court nominations went to avowed Klansmen, and a Klan-endorsed candidate received the nomination to the Corporation Commission. Small wonder that Democratic State Chairman R. L. Davidson, attempting shortly after the primary to mediate the savage factional dispute, remarked, with masterful understatement, "The sore spot has not healed."[44]

A majority of the county committeemen had opposed Walton in the primary and were frankly dismayed at the result. As the general election approached, the state vice chairman, Mrs. O. H. Cafky of Forgan,

---

[39] *Directory of Oklahoma, 1977,* p. 544; Oliver L. Benson et al., *Oklahoma Votes, 1907-1962* (Norman: University of Oklahoma, Bureau of Government Research, 1964), p. 115.
[40] Alexander, *The Ku Klux Klan in the Southwest,* p. 202.
[41] *Tulsa Daily World,* August 3, 1924.
[42] *Directory of Oklahoma, 1977,* p. 543.
[43] *Tulsa Daily World,* August 8, November 4, 1924.
[44] *Oklahoma City Daily Oklahoman,* August 10, 1924.

together with Kirby Fitzpatrick of Ardmore, began organizing the anti-Walton Democrats in support of Pine. The most celebrated bolter was the incumbent United States Senator, Robert L. Owen, who announced his support of a Republican for the first time in his life. In a withering attack on the deposed governor, Owen warned that, "Walton's election would discredit, demoralize, and injure the Democratic party and impair the high standards of Oklahoma in the United States Senate. He has already done the state enough harm."[45] Joining Owen was Campbell Russell, who advertised himself as "an unreconstructed Democrat, with all rights reserved." Russell briefly considered making the race himself as an independent write-in candidate but decided it would be dangerous to divide the anti-Walton vote. In early October, he went to work for Pine.[46] Though not an active Pine supporter, E. B. Howard set the pattern for most Democratic leaders by concentrating on the presidential and state supreme court races, leaving Walton to his fate. In an election eve blast, Howard accurately charged that Walton had been nominated by "parties interested in Republican success" in an attempt to "get the entire Democratic ticket."[47] To forestall that possibility, Howard and Governor Trapp worked tirelessly on behalf of the Democratic ticket, Walton not included.

The former governor was not, however, without some party support. In one of the strange aberrations of politics, the badly defeated Prince Freeling, who had bolted the ticket in 1922, when Walton was elected governor, now announced that he would support Walton for the Senate, despite his own preprimary judgment that "if the Walton platform is Democracy, then I have lived a lie."[48] In addition to Freeling, a small contingent of "Anti-Ku Klux Democrats," quickly organized by Frank Carter and Porter Newman, campaigned actively for Walton. Of course, the star of the show was the candidate himself. In a campaign schedule of ten speeches a day, Walton excoriated the Ku Klux Klan and promised to "skin the Klan" and to "run the Kluckers into the Gulf."[49] His talent for invective never failed him, as he slashed out at all of his political foes, both Democrats and Republicans. "The political preachers," as he called them, were special targets of his cannonades. One, the Reverend F. D. Gregory of Sulphur, filed a $50,000 libel suit against Walton after the former governor allegedly told a Sulphur town meeting that Gregory "would steal the pennies from St. Peter's eyelids and ravish the Virgin Mary."[50] For their part, the "political preachers" were not slow in responding. Reverend M. O. Harper, leader of a determined speakers' bureau of 130 Protestant clergymen, called the deposed governor "a worse traitor to the country than Benedict Arnold" and enjoined his

[45] *Shawnee Morning News,* October 10, 1924.
[46] *Oklahoma City Daily Oklahoman,* August 27, October 3, 1924.
[47] *Tulsa Daily World,* October 31, 1924.
[48] *Shawnee Morning News,* August 9, 1924.
[49] *Tulsa Daily World,* October 26, 1924.
[50] *Oklahoma City Times,* October 6, 1924.

rallies: "A Democrat who is guilty of voting for Jack Walton should go to jail for 30 days, and a Republican who votes for him should go to the penitentiary for 99 years."[51]

Despite the typical vigor of his rabble-rousing, Walton's defeat was certain because of the ready opposition of all Klansmen, virtually all Republicans, and probably most Democrats. Fearful that the entire Democratic ticket would be jeopardized as it had been in the Harding landslide four years earlier, the Democratic leaders redoubled their efforts in behalf of John W. Davis, their party's presidential nominee. The result was a welcome split in the Oklahoma ballot. Davis, who nationally suffered the worst defeat yet administered a Democratic candidate, nonetheless saved Oklahoma's electoral vote by a margin of 30,000 votes over President Coolidge. Remaining aloof from the state and national Klan controversy, Davis recovered a third of the counties that had gone to Harding in 1920; he carried 49, and Coolidge, 28. Although his was a minority victory—Senator Robert M. LaFollette, campaigning as the independent Progressive candidate, drew 41,141 votes—the Democrat's success was welcome news to his partisans within the state. Equally welcome was the tally in the senatorial contest, where Pine buried Walton by a count of 339,646 to 196,417. Pine thereby became the state's second Republican senator, and the chilling prospects of Walton's return to power had been avoided.[52]

Although Walton, in his humiliation, blamed his loss on the vengeance of the Ku Klux Klan, the fact was that the Klan came out of the contest scarcely better than did Walton. Jewett's machinations in behalf of the minority party may have won Pine a Senate seat for the GOP, but they also became the stake that soon penetrated the monster's heart. After the 1924 race, the power of the Oklahoma Klan was in swift decline. Thereafter, it remained a talking issue, as politicians of both parties made their rivals' past memberships strong campaign weapons. Never again would its endorsement become the maker of a political career. Ironically, Pine's victory, while putting the Klan that supported him on the path to extinction, strengthened the Democratic party that lost the second of its Senate seats. In rejecting Walton, the Democrats had purged themselves of a poisonous minority; and their loyalty to the national ticket at a time when the party was at its lowest ebb elsewhere affirmed their continuing vitality.

[51] *Shawnee Morning News,* October 14, 1924.
[52] *Directory of Oklahoma, 1977,* pp. 544-45.

CHAPTER 8

Henry S. Johnston and the Four Horsemen

OKLAHOMA had removed one governor in an impeachment notable for its drama. The governor chosen at the next successive
election would be impeached and removed, too, but in a way marked by
pathos. Henry S. Johnston was that man, and his regime must be remembered as one of the most bizarre in state history. His own personality
was at once exceedingly complex and disarmingly simple. Clustered
around him was an egregious collection of people: a legendary "woman
governor," a needlessly harsh legislature that had tasted blood in impeaching one governor and thirsted for more; and an executive office
filled with misfits and mystics. Meanwhile, the Ku Klux Klan acted out
its last performance in a long public spectacle, and rival groups eager to
exploit the riches of a maturing state did battle for domination. Finally,
the volatile political movements of the war and its aftermath left the
state's ruling party less a party than an umbrella for jealous factions.
Through it all, the man who would become the victim of a blind and
consuming hatred was an inoffensive and high-minded gentleman whom
fate had picked from obscurity in 1926 and damned to disgrace in 1929.

Martin Trapp, who had succeeded to the governorship after the 1923
removal of Walton, had never acknowledged that he was the governor
of Oklahoma. Because he never had been elected to the office and
never had taken the governor's prescribed oath, he asserted that he
was eligible to enter the governor's race in 1926 and filed therefor. He
might have succeeded because many citizens, grateful for the period of
relative quiescence that had followed the stormy Walton, were rightly
impressed by Trapp's unruffled demeanor and his success as a legislative
leader. In the friendly suit of *Fitzpatrick* v. *McAlister,* however, the
state supreme court construed literally the constitutional prohibition of

successive gubernatorial terms and voided Trapp's candidacy.[1] By the court's reasoning, Walton himself was not disqualified, but the deposed governor had already announced for John W. Harreld's Senate seat, leaving the governor's race open to more respectable candidates.

Disillusioned by their lone attempt at slate-making, the farmer-labor group did not make an organized attempt to regain political power. Some labor leaders did endorse O. A. Cargill, Oklahoma City's mayor and an avowed anti-Klansman, but Cargill lacked Walton's flair for campaigning and never developed a statewide following. His primary opponents were old-timers, thoroughly familiar to every voter. J. B. A. Robertson sought a political comeback, as did William M. Franklin, a former senator and clerk of the supreme court, and William M. Darnell, the sometime Socialist who had sought to be Walton's running mate as the league's choice for lieutenant governor in 1922. Henry S. Johnston of Perry had the oldest credentials. Though he had served in the constitutional convention and the First Legislature, Johnston had not held an elective office since 1910. He was, however, a faithful party worker, and his management of the delegates pledged to prohibition and William G. McAdoo at the 1924 Democratic National Convention had interested most of the drys and church leaders in his gubernatorial candidacy. He was also the clearly expressed favorite of the Ku Klux Klan.[2]

The support of Klansmen, prohibitionists, and churchmen gave Johnston an irreducible minimum of support, perhaps enough for a plurality nomination. Of the remaining candidates, Darnell seemed to have the best chance. Several prominent Democrats were active in his behalf, and he was endorsed by both the conservative *Daily Oklahoman* and the left-wing *Oklahoma Leader*. Had the Trapp administration added its support, Darnell likely would have overtaken Johnston. Since Darnell was an anti-Klansman, Trapp's endorsement of the one man able to beat the Klan candidate could have been expected. Trapp, however, stewed in resentment at the supreme court's decision in the *Fitzpatrick* case, which Darnell had publicly defended. The executive's spite probably cost Darnell the governorship.[3]

The Democratic party was in a serious dilemma. Twice, in 1922 and 1924, Walton had been the choice of only a minority; and his nomination had split the party, fatally so in 1924. Party leaders blamed their tribulations on the plurality system that permitted the leading candidate, however small his margin, to go into the general election against a Republican opposition that was almost always united. Nearly every executive since Haskell had advocated a runoff contest between the primary's

[1] 121 Okla. 83 (1926). Trapp had given ample notice of his intentions. During the 1924 filing period, the governor had sought to file for the office, but the election board refused to accept his application on the ground that there was no imminent vacancy.

[2] The Johnston campaign, emphasizing the role of the Klan, is treated in David C. Boles, "Effect of the Ku Klux Klan on the Oklahoma Gubernatorial Election of 1926," *Chronicles of Oklahoma* 55 (1977):424-32.

[3] *Harlow's Weekly*, July 24-August 7, 1926.

front-runners, and Trapp had sponsored such a law by the initiative route. The supreme court, by curious reasoning, had declared it unconstitutional.[4] In 1926, Trapp's elimination had left no strong contender in the race, and whoever won in the closely packed field would lead a divided party into the general elections.

The hazards of the plurality system were much less for the minority party. The Republicans had never claimed fickle blocs of farmers and workers, hence there were no standard expectations, or calculations, to be upset. Moreover, Republicans were generally less susceptible to divisions over the Klan question. Thus their own primary was a comparative model of decorum, in which Omer K. Benedict, Tulsa postmaster and former editor of the *Oklahoma City Times,* won over W. J. Otjen of Enid. Neither side was troubled that Benedict had successfully used the Klan issue against Otjen, who admitted to being a former member and pled contrition. After all, Benedict was just as "former" and equally contrite about his own past affiliation with the hooded order.[5] In the senatorial balloting, Harreld easily took his party's nomination for a second term.

On the Democratic side, Johnston, as expected, led the divided field with 36 percent of the vote, thus winning the nomination and inviting a new schism over the Klan. More promising for party fortunes were the results in the senatorial race. The party finally threw off its enslavement to Jack Walton when Sixth District Congressman Elmer Thomas defeated him by 18,794 votes. Walton's old ally, a divided opposition, failed him in a relatively small field of five candidates, three of whom never had much of a chance. After the field narrowed to Thomas and Walton, it was finally possible to corner the deposed governor, especially since Thomas drew his chief support from the southwestern corner of the state, heretofore a hotbed of Waltonism. Consolidating the existing anti-Walton sentiment in the rest of the state, Thomas was the ideal candidate, not for any views he entertained but because his Washington service had kept him clear of the upheavals of the previous four years.[6]

Somewhat surprisingly, Johnston also proved to be a much better candidate than might have been expected. Though the Klan's announced favorite, he was hardly its creature, and his support proved to be broader than a single organization could provide. His ardent prohibitionism won him the allegiance of drys and churchmen, both within and without the Klan's ranks, and his 1907 progressive credentials were attractive to the legions of voters weary of the state's more recent reputation for political buffoonery. Even his Klan connections were much less a handicap than they might have been. For all the fears of politicians, the Klan's moment

[4] *Dove* v. *Oglesby,* 114 Okla. 114 (1925).
[5] *Tulsa Daily World,* July 29, 1926.
[6] State of Oklahoma, State Election Board, *Directory of Oklahoma, 1977,* pp. 545-48; Oliver L. Benson et al., *Oklahoma Votes, 1907-1962* (Norman: University of Oklahoma, Bureau of Government Research, 1964), p. 116.

had passed. In the person of the moderate, circumspect Perry attorney, the old KKK no longer seemed frightening.

Johnston's general election campaign had to overcome the organized opposition of disgruntled fellow Democrats. For the fourth consecutive time since 1920, a number of party leaders deserted their own party's ticket. Governor Trapp, angry at Supreme Court Justices E. F. Lester and J. W. Clark, who had ruled him ineligible for self-succession, refused to endorse a ticket that included the hostile judges. Judge Thomas H. Doyle of the criminal court of appeals refused to support Johnston's gubernatorial candidacy. Though both men were from the same town, Doyle was a Catholic, and he could not excuse the religious prejudices that Johnston took no pains to conceal. Walton openly worked for Benedict, as did Paul Nesbitt, his speaker and chief lieutenant in the Ninth Legislature. O. A. Cargill's following, including J. Luther Langston, the Socialist veteran of the Reconstruction League, and other labor leaders, deserted to the Republicans. The addition of Senator J. H. McCurley, a Waltonite from Bokchito, gave the "soreheads' revolt" a legislative complexion.[7]

Benedict, an implacable partisan whose editorials had punctuated the Oklahoma party battle for two decades, ran on a platform of tax reduction, business encouragement, and tolerance. Although he tried to pin the Klan tag to Johnston, his own former membership effectively negated that issue, and his campaign subsequently extended little further than his partisan base. For his part, Johnston proudly stressed his own record of unbroken party regularity, his patriotism, and his knowledge of the state constitution. He never discussed the Klan issue.

Since both candidates emphasized their own partisanship, the election returns were not surprising. Oklahoma voters, casting a large proportion of straight ticket ballots, returned to their customary voting patterns, i.e., Democratic. The impact of the two gubernatorial candidates was only to modify those patterns with slight sectional variations. Benedict did better than GOP gubernatorial nominees usually fared in the eastern half of the state, while Johnston, a west-sider from the Eighth Congressional District, did better than average in the old Oklahoma Territory and held Benedict to a draw in the normally rock-ribbed Republican Eighth.[8]

The rest of the ticket won handily, with every Democratic nominee elected to the statewide offices, including the incumbent supreme court justices (who overcame Governor Trapp's spiteful endorsement of their rivals) and their new colleague on the high court, Robert A. Hefner. The mayor of Oklahoma City (and, earlier, of Ardmore), Hefner retired the last of the justices elected in the year of the great Harding landslide, to restore the Democratic monopoly of statewide offices. The First District changed its representative and its party allegiance for the sixth consecutive time when E. B. Howard of Tulsa regained his old seat from S. J.

---

[7] *Tulsa Tribune,* November 4, 1926.
[8] Benson et al., *Oklahoma Votes,* p. 83.

Montgomery, the 27-year-old war veteran from Bartlesville. Howard was one of the seven Democratic congressional victors; the GOP held on only in Milton Garber's northwest. Democratic candidates were also sent to the state legislature in good number. Though the Democrats lost three seats in the state senate, they picked up seven in the lower house.[9]

The Democrats reserved their greatest joy for the recovery of one of the lost United States Senate seats, as Elmer Thomas ousted Senator Harreld by 36,025 votes. Thomas was helped by the indifference of many Republicans to Harreld. Senator Pine and his special friends were noticeably cool to the senior Republican because Harreld had refused to share his control of federal patronage after Pine's election in 1924.

In winning a Senate seat, Elmer Thomas reached the goal of a political career that had begun with statehood and eventually stretched past mid-century. For nearly thirty years, he would represent the state in Washington, and yet he has remained one of the least known of Oklahoma's political figures.[10] Even after his elevation to the Senate, to which he was destined to be reelected three times, he never became a popular idol nor a particularly forceful official. His amazing electoral vitality would owe little to public adulation and less to an identification with important issues. Rather, his political strength was compounded of his consummate mastery of political organization. Drawing upon his handsome presence, the franking privilege, the seniority system, and the calculated distribution of patronage, he built and maintained a political network that soon reached into every village. Luck would favor him: his senatorial campaigns would always come in Democratic years, and his primary rivals would include some of the most bitterly despised political figures in the state's history. Above all else, it was his native intelligence, attention to detail, and acute sensitivity to public moods that eventually made him one of the state's most successful, if least remembered, public men.

Seven state questions added to the ballot's length in 1926. Each failed, perhaps from a mood of pervasive naysaying, perhaps reflecting the voters' slide rightward. The first explanation accounts for the defeat of measures to increase legislative pay and to call a second constitutional convention. The second more reasonably explained the failure to override the recent legislative repeal of the pioneering anti-convict labor law as well as the more recent statute for state-supplied school textbooks. The frenzied campaign of the oil interests and their lobbies also helped bury Campbell Russell's initiative petition to increase the gross production tax to the level of the ad valorem tax rate.[11]

The state's seventh governor was of typical frontier background.[12]

[9]*Directory of Oklahoma, 1977,* pp. 549-50; Benson et al., *Oklahoma Votes,* p. 49.

[10]The only full-length study of Thomas is Eric Manheimer's "The Public Career of Elmer Thomas" (Ph.D. diss., University of Oklahoma, 1953).

[11]*Directory of Oklahoma, 1977,* pp. 639-40.

[12]This sketch of Johnston's biography is taken from the *Tulsa Daily World,* August 22, 1926.

Ill-fated Governor Henry S. Johnston, the second of Oklahoma's two successively impeached chief executives. Courtesy Western History Collections, University of Oklahoma.

Born in Indiana, Johnston had stopped over in Kansas before coming to the Cherokee Strip in 1893. There he built a law practice and settled into politics, losing more frequently than he won, for his area was Republican. His personal appearance was that of a frail, bookish county seat lawyer. His considerable knowledge of constitutions, laws, folkways, diseases, crops, and religions was exceeded only by the strength of his opinions on each subject. In principle, he was a Democrat of the Grover Cleveland era, suspicious of tariffs, monopolies, railroads, and liquor. In style, he was like the pioneer preachers whose techniques he had adopted and perfected. His bony, loose-jointed frame, his reedy voice, his threshing gestures, and his interminable invocations to the Almighty long remained his quaint but characteristic political assets.

Johnston's old-fashioned virtues were occasionally outweighed by old-fashioned faults. While he frequently displayed a narrowly intolerant attitude toward his enemies, he was often fatally blind to the weaknesses of his friends. As an administrator, he was prone to indecision; and although his state papers were subject to a perfectionist's craftsmanship, his public speeches and conferences revealed an uncontrollable tendency to digress along tangents of maddening irrelevancy. Johnston's disorganized philosophical excursions may have been a mystic source of strength for the man himself, but more than one visitor left the governor's office bewildered by the strange talk that bore little apparent connection to the public business under consideration. At bottom, his greatest fault was one with his greatest virtue: absolute loyalty to the Democratic party and to the people that gathered around him.

By any measure, the Eleventh Legislature would not win high marks. Perfunctory at best were most of its deeds: technical modifications of election laws, minor changes in county and municipal government, and the routine approval of appropriations. Desultory debate ended in a reorganization of the Highway Department to establish a new five-member board in place of the three-member agency of the Trapp years. More to their credit, the legislators modestly expanded the state's role in social welfare by building a new hospital for crippled children and making generous grants for their care. The largest appropriation yet made for school aid, $1.5 million, helped the least prosperous local school districts. Despite such measures, there was nowhere evident a zeal for thoroughgoing reform. Weak executive leadership, a more complacent public mood, and a more conservative legislature left no room for extensive reorganization or an expansion of regulatory measures. Even a modest bill to reapply the state income tax to corporations died a quick and generally unmourned death, its warrant signed, according to the bill's author, by the governor's indifference.

It was generally true that Johnston's legislative relations were characterized more by indifference than by overt hostility. The governor drew around himself a strange circle of sycophantic advisers whom he trusted to make executive decisions that, in past administrations, had awaited consultation with interested senators and representatives. None of these persons was more significant than Mrs. Mayme O. Hammonds, whom Johnston appointed as his confidential secretary. The post itself had been in disrepute since the Walton regime, and Mrs. Hammonds did little to restore public confidence in it. Although a fairly recent acquaintance of the governor, she was married to his state health officer and was a niece of Judge James R. Armstrong, formerly of the criminal court of appeals and a prominent figure within the governor's inner circle. Mrs. Hammonds enjoyed Johnston's unquestioning confidence, and most state business actually pivoted around this slight woman who made it her business to insulate the governor from unseemly pressures, including the historic prerogative of legislators to see the governor on questions of state policy, patronage, and district affairs.

It was that quality that most excited the legislature's enmity. Unable to win the governor's ear or, often, even to approach it, Johnston's critics soon portrayed him as a bizarre mystic who allowed a woman to rule the administration while he retreated to his office for long periods of solitary meditation, studying Rosicrucianism, or enraptured by the imparted wisdom of L. Howell Lewis, his personal astrologer. Admittedly, Johnston was a dreamer who possessed great faith in the signs of the zodiac—so much faith that he once soberly announced that he had delayed signing a bill until Lewis had advised him that the heavenly portents were favorable. Nonetheless, Johnston was, at worst, a dilettante mystic, at least compared to Judge Armstrong. That gubernatorial adviser, whose influence was believed to be second only to Mrs. Hammonds's, claimed definite psychic powers. In his office, Armstrong kept cages of canary birds, through which he purported to communicate with spirits of superior intelligence about the conduct of public business.[13]

Though peculiar enough, Johnston's eccentricities were, on the whole, inoffensive and easily tolerated. What legislators found insufferable was the governor's indecision and insensitivity to their political interests. They were particularly incensed at the administration's Highway Department, which controlled a growing part of the state's patronage and spending. Unable to press their personal demands upon the governor, they fumed as the department distributed jobs and awarded contracts with scant regard for their desires. That resentment was channeled into the first organized effort to unseat Johnston by four legislators never friendly to him—H. Tom Kight of Claremore, E. P. Hill of McAlester, Tom Johnson of Antlers, and Robert L. Graham of Oklahoma City, the so-called "Four Horsemen." Though each was a Democrat, the four set out to effect Johnston's ruin. Knowing that an unseemly patronage squabble would appear too petty as grounds for criticism, they chose to lift their assault to higher ground: the Highway Commission's preference for asphalt over concrete surfacing in road construction. Though hardly

[13] *Blackwell Morning Tribune,* September 16, 1927; Aldrich Blake, "Oklahoma Goes Rosicrucian," *Nation,* September 14, 1927, pp. 247-48; *Oklahoma City Daily Oklahoman,* January 10, 1929.

a monumental test of statesmanship, the issue did promise scathing revelations from disgruntled contractors. But the real nature of the fight—control over state hiring and spending—did not escape the Four Horsemen and other legislative realists.

The "Ewe Lamb Rebellion," an affair of both low politics and low comedy, was the result.[14] Well after their formal adjournment, the legislators drew upon the initiated measure that had been passed in 1923 to depose Walton and called themselves into a special session in late November, 1927. Meeting at the Huckins Hotel, the special session chose E. P. Hill as their speaker. The supreme court, which had also been a target of legislative criticism, ruled on December 3, 1927, that the earlier initiative had been improperly submitted and, therefore, that the legislature could not meet on its own motion.[15] Although the court had upheld Johnston's contention that a new session could not convene without his express call, the determined legislative sharpshooters chose to ignore both the state's high court and the old constitutionalist to organize an investigating committee, which hastily brought impeachment charges against Johnston on December 10. Two days later, they added charges against Harry B. Cordell, president of the State Board of Agriculture. The governor maintained his refusal to recognize the rebel body, and he was sustained by State Auditor A. S. J. Shaw and State Treasurer R. A. Sneed, who announced that they would not honor any legislative salary claims.[16]

In a proclamation of December 12, Johnston boldly protested the invasion of his prerogative, charging the Four Horsemen with sinister motives and "illegal, unlawful, and treasonable actions." At the mercy of scheming legislators, "the State of Oklahoma and its constitutional government is [sic] in grave danger of being thrust into the throes of civil war," the document warned. In addition, the governor ordered Adjutant-General Charles F. Barrett to prevent any rebel attempt to occupy the capitol and declared martial law on the fourth floor of that building.[17] Several rounds of fisticuffs ensued when Senate President Pro Tempore Mac Q. Williamson led a taxicab brigade of senators through the rotunda; but the senators, unequal to General Barrett's tactics, were outmaneuvered, and the executive-judicial coalition had won the first round.

After the skirmish at the capitol, the senators retreated to the Huckins,

[14] The revolt took its name from a Biblical phrase (II *Samuel* 12:3) injected by Johnston into a tense conference with legislative leaders, who implored him to dismiss Mrs. Hammonds. "Must I give up this one little ewe lamb?" Johnston asked plaintively.

[15] *Oklahoma City Daily Oklahoman*, December 4, 1927; *Simpson* v. *Hill*, 129 Okla. 90 (1927).

[16] *Oklahoma City Daily Oklahoman*, November 22–December 13, 1927.

[17] Ibid., December 13, 1927. An unexpected observer of the capitol confrontation was Jack Walton, who happened by when the guard surrounded the building. His only comment to the *Oklahoman*'s reporter was "it doesn't look as though he had quite as many as I had out."

where they organized as a court of impeachment. Tempers cooled during the Christmas holidays, however, and when a district judge enjoined the convening of an impeachment court, the senators voted, twenty-two to sixteen, to drop the impeachment charges that had been prepared by the house. On December 29, they quietly obeyed General Barrett's order to disperse.[18] Unlike Walton, Johnston had relied upon the courts to sustain his authority, and his danger had momentarily passed.

The revolt continued to simmer throughout the campaign year of 1928, as both sides took their cases to the people. The Democratic primaries were critical to Johnston's tenure because the Four Horsemen and the other victims of his military power during the previous winter would be certain to demand his head when the next legislature convened in January, 1929. Although Johnston reaped no great outpouring of public sympathy in the elections, neither did his foes. In fact, E. P. Hill, one of the original Horsemen and the speaker of the irregular house, lost his seat to a challenger in the Democratic primary. Otherwise, the primaries were a poor gauge of public opinion; neither side could claim a clear-cut victory. Neither Johnston nor his enemies could have foreseen that a swift reversal in the political tides, governed by forces more powerful than any in state politics, was about to produce a tidal wave that overwhelmed the governor's prospect for a complete term. Johnston had survived the Ewe Lamb Revolt in December, 1927, and the August primaries of 1928, but the November elections would seal his doom.

Though the campaign of 1928 deeply affected Oklahoma, the fortunes of a governor were decidedly secondary to the voters' absorption in the presidential contest. Through the first half of the year, entrenched Democratic officials in the statehouse and county courthouses had every reason for optimism. Not since the Williams regime had their party been so firmly in control of the state and county governments. The Harding aberration of 1920 was largely forgotten, especially after the success of the otherwise dismal Davis candidacy in 1924. The presidential nomination of Alfred E. Smith changed all that. One needed neither an astrologer nor a cageful of canaries to foretell the results of his candidacy in Oklahoma, for he was of the wrong political background (New York's Tammany Hall), the wrong religion (Roman Catholic), and the wrong moral views (a dripping wet critic of national prohibition). The one thing right about Al Smith was that he was a Democrat.

That was enough for Governor Johnston, the faithful party man who had often known defeat as a steadfast Democratic loyalist in enemy territory. Although he personally disliked Smith and could hardly have been blind to the prospects, Johnston, as titular head of the state party, felt compelled to support him. Admittedly, as a militant dry, a Protestant, and a Klansman, he had no little trouble explaining himself to the people.

[18] Ibid., December 27–31, 1927. See also "Head-Hunting in Oklahoma," *Independent* 109 (1927):642–43; "Oklahoma's Punctured Impeachment," *Literary Digest,* January 14, 1928, p. 11.

Within months, he had severed his connections with several party and Klan leaders, as well as the organized drys, "out of respect for the party," as he told his Perry neighbors.[19] By October, he had rationalized his position sufficiently to undertake four speeches a day in behalf of the national ticket. In lengthy, defensive addresses, the embattled governor also pleaded for a friendly legislature to help him secure a new tax system, a budget law, a textbook commission, and a criminal code, sounding at times as if he were a candidate himself. The prosaic and time-worn issues he belabored in defense of the Democracy were no match for the fury of rostrum and pulpit and the insistent whispering campaign against Tammany Hall, the Roman Catholics, and the wets.[20]

Among the Democratic renegades, former Senator Robert L. Owen (who four years earlier had first bolted his party upon Walton's nomination for his Senate seat) was the recognized leader. He was joined by dozens of previously unsullied Democratic wheelhorses who publicly or privately bolted the ticket. One of the relatively few to join Johnston in the aggressive advocacy of the Smith campaign was Jack Walton, who had endorsed the New Yorker even before the nominating convention. Walton's support may have been as damaging as Owen's opposition, but endorsements of party leaders probably made little difference. The Democratic rank and file had already found the man from the sidewalks of New York culturally unacceptable to their rural and small town Protestant values. Even Smith's daring Oklahoma City address in September assailing the Anti-Saloon League, the Ku Klux Klan, and religious bigotry had no chance of turning the indignant tide.[21]

Among the state's major newspapers, the Smith candidacy commonly was greeted either by silence or by open hostility. Its one important effect was an historic reversal for the Tulsa papers. The *World,* heretofore a reliable foe of any Democratic enterprise, surprisingly endorsed Smith. Eugene Lorton, the *World's* publisher, had begun to sour on standpat Republicanism after his poor showing in the senatorial primary of 1924. Lorton was ambitious for a diplomatic appointment, and because the Republicans failed him, he switched to support Democratic candidates until the second administration of Franklin Roosevelt. (He was rewarded only with a modest assignment to a Canadian arbitration commission and returned to the Republican fold in 1940.) The *Tulsa Tribune,* on the other hand, staunchly Democratic until the Walton administra-

---

[19] *Blackwell Morning Tribune,* April 20, 1928.

[20] The anti-Smith cause not infrequently rose well above a whisper. Mordecai F. Ham, visiting revivalist at Oklahoma City's First Baptist Church, expressed the ultimate implications of the Smith candidacy in his advice to his congregation: "If you vote for Al Smith you're voting against Christ, and you'll be damned." Ham quoted in George B. Tindall, *The Emergence of the New South, 1913-1945,* History of the South, vol. 10 (Baton Rouge: Louisiana State University Press, 1967), p. 247.

[21] The speech, as well as the social issues involved, are fully treated in Elton Harvey Wallace, "Alfred E. Smith, The Religious Issue: Oklahoma City, September 20, 1928" (Ph.D. diss., Michigan State University, 1965).

The Sooner delegation to the Seventy-first House of Representatives: Charles O'Conner (First District), Wilburn Cartwright (Third District), W. W. Hastings (Second District), Jed Johnson (Sixth District), Milton Garber (Eighth District), James V. McClintic (Seventh District), U. S. Stone (Fifth District), and Tom McKeown (Fourth District). Also pictured are the Tulsa World's *Eugene Lorton and Senator Elmer Thomas. Courtesy Western History Collections, University of Oklahoma.*

tion, switched to the GOP and long remained undeviatingly Republican.

The anti-Al Smith earthquake rocked the state to its political foundations. Ignoring the dissension in state government, an unprecedented number of Oklahoma Democrats went to the polls to vote against Al Smith. Frank A. Parkinson, Republican state chairman, appeared optimistic when he had offered an election eve prediction of a 50,000-vote majority for the GOP,[22] but even he underestimated the influence of the prohibition and religious issues. Parkinson's optimism was short by nearly 125,000 votes, as Hoover trounced Smith by a margin of 394,046 to 219,174, to win the greatest majority recorded in Oklahoma to that time. Smith carried only eight counties, all in Little Dixie, and all nar-

[22] *Oklahoma City Daily Oklahoman,* November 5, 1928.

rowly. Everywhere else, his unpopularity was pronounced. In some rural precincts that had never voted Republican, Hoover won majorities of three and four to one. Riding his long coattails was every other Republican nominee for statewide office, all of whom awakened to joyful news on Wednesday morning. E. R. Harding, the earlier beneficiary of the Harding landslide, returned to a six-year term on the Corporation Commission by beating his erstwhile colleague, Frank Carter, by 18,000 votes. The available seat on the court of criminal appeals and the three openings on the state supreme court were all taken by Republicans. The GOP also won the congressional seats in the Fifth District and in the First, which continued its habit of biennial party reversals. Of course, the Eighth District merely reaffirmed its Republican ways. Veteran Democrats in the five remaining districts plowed through the landslide to survive, running far ahead of Smith.[23]

"Rum and Romanism," assiduously battled by some of the sons of the Rebellion, spelled defeat for many Democratic legislators, friends and foes of Johnston falling indiscriminately. Tom Johnson, himself one of the original Four Horsemen, was beaten in Pushmataha County, where acknowledged Republicans were probably less numerous than practicing vegetarians. Generally, however, Johnston Democrats fared worse than antiadministration nominees. Regardless of the Democrats' factional affiliations, the Republicans sent solid delegations from three counties (Tulsa, Payne, and Creek) and displaced Democratic incumbents in a number of traditional Jeffersonian strongholds. Altogether, the GOP gained three senate seats and twenty-six in the lower chamber, six short of the number necessary to organize the house, but more than enough to produce an unbeatable anti-Johnston coalition with the remnant of dissident Democrats.[24] It was the handwriting on the wall for the governor, whose impeachment promptly became the first order of business for 1929.

The storm signal went up in the attempted organization of the state house of representatives. Under the traditional rules, Allen Street was chosen speaker, but Street, who hoped to keep peace with the embattled administration, was forced out after only six hours. James C. Nance, then of Cotton County and a frankly anti-Johnston man,[25] took his place, as nine Democrats joined the solid Republican phalanx to amend the house rules and place antiadministration members at the head of every important committee. Quickly, the determined anti-Johnston majority voted thirteen articles of impeachment against the governor, eleven of which became the basis for his senate trial. Most were petty or, at

---

[23] *Directory of Oklahoma, 1977,* pp. 551–52.

[24] Benson et al., *Oklahoma Votes,* p. 49.

[25] Nance was the author of the corporate income tax bill that had been defeated after Johnston had done nothing to advance it. Nance had previously served in the Ninth Legislature from Stephens County and later represented McClain County, as well. With Holdenville's Tom Anglin, he was one of the two men elected to leadership of both legislative houses.

best, technical charges, and none of them alleged dishonesty or malfeasance. But the inclusion of the final count—general incompetence—was the means for subjecting the entire administration to the review of an impeachment court.

The revelations of 141 witnesses filled a 5,433-page transcript,[26] one of the most remarkable documents in state history. Johnston's impeachment was a lesson in the pitfalls of public administration. It was the story of the intrigues of palace politics, of shameful advantage taken by unworthy advisers in the name of a governor whose greatest crime was his misplaced trust. Colorful names were daily paraded before the public and the senate—Hawkshaw Cooper, Jose Alvarado, Eugene Gum, and Buck Ethridge. The central character of the drama, Mrs. Mayme Hammonds, was never called. However, her influence over the administrative departments, her arbitrary manner toward legislators, her feud with another woman in the executive offices, even her use of a state plumber's wrench to fix her gas stove—these and many other details, some of them significant and some of them petty, were introduced as evidence against her employer.

The governor, when he was finally called and sworn, could not undo the damage of the preceding testimony. Yet during his week-long ordeal, he aroused some admiration and considerable sympathy for his candid affirmation of the principles of a man who believed himself wronged. Most of all, his testimony revealed Johnston to be an executive oblivious to the deeds committed in his name. That heads of departments had been unable to pass Mrs. Hammond's secretarial barrier seemed a surprise to him. Confronted with allegations of Armstrong's unworthy influence over the decisions of the Highway Department, the governor replied, "I never heard of that before."[27] Through it all, the gentlemanly governor was remorselessly pressed by the house prosecutors, especially Tom Kight of Claremore and John C. Head of Idabel.[28]

The trial's result was a foregone conclusion, for Johnston had been beaten before it began—beaten perhaps as early as Al Smith's presidential nomination. Though no charges had yet been investigated and no witnesses heard, he had been suspended from office on January 21, 1929,

---

[26] State of Oklahoma, Legislature, Senate, *Transcript of Proceedings of the Senate Sitting as a Court of Impeachment,* 12th leg., reg. sess., January 21–March 25, 1929, 2 vols.

[27] Ibid., 2:4433.

[28] The prosecution was especially effective in challenging the qualifications of Johnston's appointees, Johnston at times provoking unintended merriment with his unsophisticated view of proper credentials. Of Mrs. George Waters, appointed warden of the Granite reformatory, Johnston confidently cited these qualifications: "First of all, she is a graduate of Stillwater College, Oklahoma A. and M. Next, she is a school teacher; next, she is a mother of several children, and she helped Dr. Waters, who was a widower and who had a family, and she reared two children in peace and quietude." Concerning a physician appointed in consultation with Dr. Hammonds to serve in the tuberculosis sanitarium at Talihina: "This young man had specialized along the lines of mental and nervous diseases, specialized on the line of—oh, germs, and things of that type." Johnston's testimony is available ibid., 2:3536–4440, quotations from 2:3799 and 2:3814.

his duties assumed by Lieutenant Governor William J. Holloway. After two months of trial, Johnston's ordeal ended. Verdicts of guilty were not brought on any of the specific charges by anything approaching the necessary two-thirds vote of the impeachment court. Such was evidently the senators' design, for the members carefully distributed their ayes and nays to make certain of his acquittal on all but the general charge of incompetency. Acquittal on the remainder was quite meaningless, however. The incompetency article had been taken up first and overwhelmingly approved, thirty-five to nine, seven of the governor's staunchest Democratic friends joining two Republicans to resist, if vainly, all pressures of the impeachment-bent majority.

Though technically sufficient (and freely predicted by the state's political writers), Johnston's removal on the single charge of incompetency was of debatable wisdom. Perhaps there was some truth in William H. Murray's later observation that "the people have a right to elect a fool; and the best way to cure them of that habit is to let him stay in office."[29] Most would agree with Murray's verdict on the real sources of Johnston's failure: "He ought not to have been elected governor, because he lacked executive ability and because he arrived slowly at sound conclusions and judgment; and he was too careful of others' feelings."[30] In any event, Johnston and his family left the capitol to receive a civic reception upon their return to Perry. After the next election, he had the consolation of being sent to the state senate, where he served with many of the same men who had removed him. Like Walton, he thereafter continued to seek vindication in various candidacies but with even less success.

The senate's removal of Johnston affirmed that body's power in state government. Although the Ku Klux Klan, aroused by its former member's endorsement of a Catholic's presidential bid, tried to claim the credit for another governor's scalp, the truth was that Johnston likely would have been impeached and removed even without the Klan's opposition, fervent though it was. By surrounding himself with undependable advisers who insulated him from the legislators' pressures, Johnston had threatened their access to patronage and state contracts, especially lucrative in the expanding Highway Department. His defiance of 1927's "Ewe Lamb" rebels was truly pyrrhic, for it made future compromise all but impossible. After the Republican sweep of 1928, Johnston's competency had as little to do with it as his mysticism. The senate had learned that the prizes of government were worth having. Now, the governor had learned just how much they were worth.

Lest any miss the point, the two houses forgot their customary legislative duties and remained in session to the end of May with the avowed purpose of humbling unbowed members of the state supreme court. The

---

[29] Quoted in *Harlow's Weekly*, February 12, 1938.

[30] Murray, *Memoirs of Governor Murray and True History of Oklahoma*, 3 vols. (Boston: Meador Publishing Co., 1945), 2:114. Murray, elected governor himself in 1930, could never be accused of those faults.

targets were Chief Justice Charles W. Mason and Associate Justices Fletcher Riley and J. W. Clark. The legislature's attack on the three was urged on by the powerful *Tulsa World.* After taking up the cudgels for a Republican legislator, O. O. Owens, who had been fined $5,000 for contempt of the high court in 1928, the *World* had been threatened with libel action.[31] Libelous or not, the *World's* intemperate editorials merely foretold the eleven articles of impeachment that were brought against Clark, the first to be tried. The eleven included the convenient charge of incompetency. After a trial nearly as long as the governor's, Clark was acquitted on all counts. Their passions spent, the senators then sustained demurrers to similar charges against Justice Riley and to all but one of those against the chief justice. Mason won full acquittal in the subsequent and speedy senate trial.[32]

Whatever the injustice done Johnston's career and the reputations of the three judges, most citizens were glad to get the entire mess finally resolved. Having impeached two elected governors, the state was acquiring a reputation of embarrassing notoriety.[33] William Judson Holloway, the genial lieutenant governor who assumed Johnston's office on March 20, 1929, was generally given good marks for the respite from controversy. The Arkansas-born son of a Baptist minister, Holloway was an alumnus of Ouachita College in 1910 and later a graduate student at the University of Chicago, making him the first college graduate to become an Oklahoma governor. In the time-honored tradition, he had studied law while teaching school—he was the principal of the high school at Hugo—and earned his law degree from the well-patronized southern legal factory at Cumberland, Tennessee. Admitted to the bar in 1915, he became county attorney of Choctaw County the following year. His political career was interrupted by war service. Remaining in the national guard after the Armistice, he saw active duty in the coal fields under Governor Robertson in 1919. In 1920 he was elected to the state senate, where he became the recognized leader of the fledgling school bloc at a time when few members understood the importance of heavy state financial aid. He was chairman of the committee that recommended the Ninth Legislature's unprecedented educational appropriation of 1923. Rising rapidly, young Holloway became the senate's president pro tempore in 1925; and, in 1926, with the grateful support of the schoolteachers, he far outdistanced twelve other candidates in the lieutenant governor's race. During Johnston's impeachment ordeal, rumors abounded that Holloway, hardly a disinterested party, was a partner with his former senate colleagues in the removal effort. Whether he was an active member of the legislative cabal, he was certainly the beneficiary.

[31] *Tulsa Daily World,* August 17, 1928.

[32] Riley managed to outlive the opprobrium of impeachment, but Mason lost his place in the primary of 1930 and Clark in 1932.

[33] Cortez A. M. Ewing, "Impeachment of Oklahoma Governors," *American Political Science Review* 24 (1930):648-52.

William J. Holloway brought tanquility to public life after the turmoil of successive gubernatorial impeachments. Courtesy Oklahoma Historical Society.

In his twenty-two months at the helm of state government, Governor
Holloway succeeded in restoring the equilibrium of public business and
earned considerable respect as a competent administrator. As the regular
session of the Twelfth Legislature had been devoted almost entirely to its
more exciting judicial duties, he was compelled to call a special session
to consider his reorganization and economy proposals. Of the latter, he
was able to realize his declared goal of keeping biennial appropriations
under $30 million without seriously impairing existing functions. Despite
another promise, however, the existing $2 million deficit grew steadily
larger in the Great Depression, which began a few months after Holloway
took office. The revenue system, substantially unaltered since statehood,
was on the verge of total inadequacy; and the governor properly stressed
the need for budgetary reform to avoid the chaos of hit-and-miss appropriations. The legislature refused to act, however, and his proposed state
tax commission failed to win approval.

Holloway's reorganization proposals likewise made little headway. The
governor, understandably willing to sacrifice a great deal to keep peace
with headstrong legislators, yielded on most of his ideas for departmental
reform. Like previous executives, he put forward a sensible plan to consolidate state colleges, but the legislators had no intention of destroying
their institutional fiefdoms. He was, however, able to raise the standards
of teacher certification, and he tolerated no interference with the heads
of state institutions.

Predictably, reorganization of the Highway Department, the object of
unremitting criticism under Johnston and no small element in his removal, received top priority for a new administration. The five-member
board established under Johnston was ousted and its duties assigned to
a new, three-man commission. Although there had been rumors that the
Republicans would be granted control of the department to repay their
work in Johnston's removal,[34] the Democrats allotted themselves a majority of the seats. The chairman of the new agency was Lew Wentz,
a prominent Republican spokesman and oil millionaire from Ponca City.
Though never a candidate for elective office in his own right, Wentz
consistently played the role of financial angel to assorted Republican
causes. Archly partisan Democrats gagged at his appointment, but Wentz
and his two Democratic colleagues—S. C. Boswell of Durant and L. C.
Hutson of Chickasha—cooperated to give the department a record for
construction up to that time: 607 miles of paving, 1,205 miles of graveled
road, 1,458 miles of additional improvements, and 200 bridges. In addition, several toll bridges that burdened the state's growing traffic were
purchased outright. The governor, like Robertson and Trapp before him,
had visions of even greater highway construction; but the legislature,
recalling the fate of Robertson's proposal, refused to submit a road bond
issue. The improvements, therefore, were financed by an increase in the
gasoline tax from three to four cents per gallon.

[34]Murray, *Memoirs of Governor Murray,* 3:233.

Looking to the future, Holloway also appointed a number of executive commissions, staffed by leading citizens of both parties, to survey the needs of the common schools and recommend revisions in the archaic tax system. Few of their recommendations could be acted upon during his brief administration, but their appointment provided welcome relief from the bitterly partisan bloodlettings, impeachments, and other scandals that had stained much of the politics of the 1920s.[35]

Thus, by the end of the 1920s, most of the passions that had inflamed Oklahoma's recent political history had been quieted. Although the Klan tried to claim credit for the defeat of Al Smith and the removal of Henry Johnston, its power was clearly broken, and the organization that had been such a source of discord became little more than a distasteful memory. Even its former members, like Governor Holloway, tended to regard it as the most recent manifestation of recurring human folly. Earlier, the radical passions that had flowed into the Farmer-Labor Reconstruction League had been cooled by the betrayal of their loyalty. Apathy, not agitation, would become the central quality of the state's heartland, and political diversion, not radical expectation, its reward.

As the 1930s opened, therefore, the causes and the men who had brought about the recent political upheavals had disappeared. But new forces—economic depression, unprecedented federal demands, and eventually a second world war— would work unpredictable effects upon state government.

[35] *Oklahoma City Daily Oklahoman,* January 12, 1931. Although Holloway had entertained hopes for a United States Senate seat, he was never a candidate for public office after his brief gubernatorial term. Settling at Oklahoma City, he became a successful corporation attorney and a prominent spokesman for the state's oil interests.

CHAPTER 9

Murray: Fighting a Depression with Martial Law

THE GREAT DEPRESSION in Oklahoma connoted many things. It meant a young novelist named John Steinbeck locating a place named Sallisaw on the map and creating a fictional family named Joad. It meant a young man from Okemah, Woody Guthrie—Woodrow Wilson Guthrie, his fiercely anti-Socialist father had named him—blown with the dust, first to California, then to New York, losing his father's political preferences along the way. It meant oil prices plummeting to twenty cents a barrel, the closing of coal mines in the southeast and lead and zinc mines along the Kansas-Missouri border. It meant food riots in Oklahoma City and anxious national guardsmen patrolling the state. It meant a disaster so devastating that hundreds of thousands left the state, the least favored to be nicknamed Okies, giving the nation an enduring symbol of human misery and the migrants from the state an indelible badge of shame.[1]

Politically, the depression brought an era of unprecedented activity, but not to the Republicans, whose stunning victories of the previous ten years were erased as they became identified with the misery. To the Democrats fell the electoral advantage of the depression, and the advantage stretched into the next half century. The immediate challenge of addressing the crisis also fell to them. With the GOP reduced to a negligible factor in the events to follow, all attention was riveted on the Democratic primaries of 1930, where the choice of public officials would cer-

[1] An excellent study is W. Richard Fassey, "'Talkin' Dust Bowl Blues': A Study of Oklahoma's Cultural Identity During the Great Depression," *Chronicles of Oklahoma* 55 (1977):12-33. Also see H. Wayne Morgan and Anne Hodges Morgan, *Oklahoma: A Bicentennial History,* States and the Nation Series (New York: W. W. Norton for the American Association for State and Local History, 1977), pp. 161-70.

154

tainly be made. One hundred three Democratic candidates contested the fifteen elective state offices in that year, along with record fields for Congress and state legislative and judicial posts. Amid the clamor of rival personal ambitions, the formal machinery of political parties became irrelevant. In 1930—and in the years to follow—Oklahoma voters aligned themselves for or against powerful personalities with little respect for the public resolves or private machinations of their party officials.

The voter who relied on his newspapers to interpret the trend in the Democratic gubernatorial race would have been badly misinformed. According to the pundits, the leading contender would surely come from a field that included former Governor Martin Trapp, former First District Congressman E. B. Howard, incumbent State Auditor A. S. J. Shaw, and one very attractive newcomer, Frank Buttram, the wealthy Oklahoma City oilman who had defied Walton during the memorable controversy over the university. Buttram's genial conservatism and his promise to end the state's emerging reputation for political buffoonery made him the leading candidate of the state's businessmen. It also won him the early and unflinching endorsement of E. K. Gaylord's powerful *Daily Oklahoman,* which never tired of reciting Buttram's rags-to-riches biography and record of civic leadership.[2] Among the others, Howard provided most of the early fireworks. The first statewide candidate seriously to advocate old-age pensions, Howard was also noted for his proposal to fight the spread of chain stores with a steeply graduated tax that was calculated to drive the multiple-unit retail stores out of business. To his newly won following among the elderly and small businessmen, Howard added his existing support from the prohibitionists, the Farmers' Union, the *Tulsa World,* and labor leaders to give him an irreducible minimum of support that seemed certain to assure him of one of the runoff spots in the new double primary system.

Before the first primary, one other candidate was mentioned casually by the metropolitan press, as though his efforts were not to be taken seriously. But many country weeklies, more observant than their urban cousins, knew better than to ignore William H. Murray. Alfalfa Bill had grown a bit seedy in appearance since his last political success, in 1914. His untrimmed walrus mustache became his trademark. On the rural hustings his wrinkled cotton suit—its legs forever rising above the ankles to reveal six inches of long underwear was a political if not a sartorial asset. With the support of his old allies from the constitutional convention of nearly a quarter-century earlier, the intrepid Murray had borrowed forty-two dollars from the First National Bank of Tishomingo and had launched a campaign unmitigated in its gall and unmatched for its success.[3]

More than a decade before, Murray had been written off as a political

[2] Francis W. Schruben, "The Return of Alfalfa Bill Murray," *Chronicles of Oklahoma* 41 (1963):42-43.

[3] William H. Murray, *Memoirs of Governor Murray and True History of Oklahoma,* 3 vols. (Boston: Meador Publishing Co., 1945), 2:364-66.

has-been. His defeat in the intense congressional campaign of 1916, followed by a dismal performance in the governor's race two years later,
had apparently forever removed him from serious political consideration. So poor were his future prospects that he left his ingrate neighbors
in 1919 to wander nomadically through Latin America for four years.
He was back in Oklahoma briefly, in 1923-24, to recruit a collection
of frontier-seekers for an ill-conceived agricultural colony in the Gran
Chaco of Bolivia. Murray's Bolivian venture lasted five years and ultimately cost him $84,000. Virtually penniless, he returned to Tishomingo
in August, 1929, just in time to sense the possibilities of another revolt
directed at the scheming "interests."[4] He took the popular side in a
utilities franchise controversy precipitated by the 1929 legislature's passage of a law that seemingly vitiated the plain constitutional injunction
against perpetuities. Announcing for the governorship and crossing the
backroads of the state, he subsisted on a diet of cheese and crackers,
professing all the while to be certain of victory.[5] "The country folk is
aroused," he confidently noted.[6]

For a time, the metropolitan press continued to slight the old-timer's
chances to concentrate on their own favorites. In fact, even in late May,
the *Tulsa Tribune* dismissed Murray as a "Texas Ranger, Type B."[7] By
July, however, the *Daily Oklahoman* was forced to recognize the threat
from the unrepentant old agrarian. A front page editorial informed the
Oklahoman's readers that "AN UNCONSCIONABLE LIAR SEEKS THE GOVER-
NORSHIP."[8]

Murray was right. The country folk were aroused, and quite possibly
the scorn of the more respectable elements added to the resentment of
the dispossessed. In any case, Alfalfa Bill exploited that smouldering
constituency deliberately and brilliantly. Early in the race, his allies had
scraped together the money to buy the *Blue Valley Farmer,* an old
Socialist weekly published at Roff. It was a poor economic investment
because the paper had only 430 recorded subscribers. Placing the paper
under the direction of his distant cousin, Cicero I. Murray, Alfalfa Bill
turned it into a legendary campaign organ. With press runs of up to
450,000 copies, the *Blue Valley Farmer* blanketed the countryside with
Murray's views on the greedy men of wealth and the iniquities of the
city. In its pages, the candidate fought the depression and its arrogant
creators, while extolling his own program: rigid economy, road construction to give jobs to the unemployed, and most of all, the constant
theme of tax reduction, never neglecting to remind the farmer and the
small homeowner of the unfair burden of taxation that they bore.[9] His
way prepared by the *Blue Valley Farmer,* Murray dramatized himself

[4] On the Bolivian "exile," see Keith L. Bryant, *Alfalfa Bill Murray* (Norman: University
of Oklahoma Press, 1968), pp. 151-72.
[5] Murray, *Memoirs of Governor Murray,* 2:365-67.
[6] Quoted in Bryant, *Alfalfa Bill Murray,* p. 177.
[7] On the metropolitan press, see Schruben, "Return of Alfalfa Bill," 41-44.
[8] *Oklahoma City Daily Oklahoman,* July 1, 1930.

"Alfalfa Bill" Murray, unrepentant old agrarian, takes his candidacy to Okla-homa's rural and small-town folk. Courtesy Western History Collections, University of Oklahoma.

wherever he went. More forceful than all the metropolitan editorials reviling him was his image of the courthouse lawn Socrates, discoursing on every topic, battling the depression, and munching his cheese and crackers. In manner more than issue, the poor had found their champion.

Paralleling the class division in the gubernatorial fireworks was a senatorial contest for the seat held by Republican William B. Pine. A number of prominent Democrats, united on belaboring Herbert Hoover and all Republicans, crowded into the race. The recently deposed governor, Henry S. Johnston, like Jack Walton before him, sought vindication with a Senate bid that won some support from citizens who believed that the harmless old gentleman had not really deserved the fate that had befallen him. Along with Johnston, two other former governors—Lee Cruce and J. B. A. Robertson—entered contention, Cruce campaigning for total prohibition, Robertson for repeal of the Eighteenth Amendment. Most of the "best people" looked to C. J. Wrightsman of Tulsa, an oil millionaire whose activity reached back into territorial days. Like Buttram,

---

[9]Bryant, *Alfalfa Bill Murray*, pp. 178-79. Murray's views on the moral wickedness of the cities are well expressed in his "Campaign Speech Delivered at Altus," copy in William H. Murray Collection, Oklahoma State Archives, Oklahoma City, hereafter cited as Murray Collection.

A veteran Oklahoma politician, former Senator Thomas P. Gore effectively renewed his battles with the trusts, bankers, and warlords. Courtesy Western History Collections, University of Oklahoma.

his wealth was something of an early advantage in the race, amply underscored by his extensive newspaper advertising. Another figure, however,
rose from the political grave. Former Senator Thomas P. Gore, apparently retired in the bitter primary of 1920, returned from Washington as
eloquent as ever and eager to use his oratorical powers on issues he had
discussed with such marked success three decades before: the iniquities
of the trusts, bankers, warlords, and diplomats.[10] For all of its practiced
campaigners, however, the senatorial struggle attracted scant attention.
Like other political news, the Senate race was overshadowed by the
intense interest in the question of who would be governor.

Murray's triumph was the startling news of the first primary. He ran far
ahead of the field, gathering 134,243 votes to Buttram's distant second-
place showing of 69,501. The legislature's Democratic majority, sorely
embarrassed by Walton's minority nomination in 1924, had already provided for a runoff primary in the event that no candidate received a
majority, and Buttram was assured a second chance. It would be a slim
one, however, for Murray had carried fifty-four counties in rolling up
a massive rural vote. Outpolling his combined rivals by as much as three
to one in some rural areas, Murray had performed an amazing achievement for a man who had not won an election in sixteen years. Nearly
as surprising were the Senate returns. Gore took a strong rural vote to
bury the three former governors and lead Wrightsman into the runoff by
179 votes.[11]

The brief runoff campaign lent itself to a natural pairing. Gore tied
his campaign to Murray's, intensified his attacks on the "monied interests," and managed to deliver a good many quips, all to the effect that
a rich man could not enter the sacred precincts of the Senate. The pairing was inevitable: Murray and Gore, the impoverished but unbowed
advocates of the people, pitted against Buttram and Wrightsman, the
shining symbols of special privilege. As local political leaders climbed
aboard the Murray-Gore bandwagon, a searing drought in the interval
between the two primaries further stirred the resentments of the afflicted
against the comfortable rich. Nonetheless, Buttram doggedly continued
his fight with dignity (*for* dignity, some said), perhaps expecting that the
eliminated candidates would consolidate their strength in a determined
crusade to save the state from the menace of Murray and his wild-eyed
following.[12]

The daily newspapers, now thoroughly alarmed, were mischievous
beyond the limits of fairness in reporting Murray's side of the campaign. The *Daily Oklahoman* was especially malicious in its attacks

[10] The Gore campaign is covered in Monroe Lee Billington, *Thomas P. Gore: The Blind
Senator from Oklahoma* (Lawrence: University of Kansas Press, 1967), pp. 141-46.
[11] State of Oklahoma, State Election Board, *Directory of Oklahoma, 1977*, pp. 552, 554.
[12] J. S. Russell, "Is Oklahoma About to Become Radical?," *Harlow's Weekly*, July 12,
1930, pp. 4-5; A. L. Beckett, "Murray Not an Accident," ibid., August 2, 1930, pp. 6-8.

on Murray's dress, manners, and language.[13] The enmity of the metropolitan press probably boomeranged to Murray's favor, as it seemed to verify everything that Murray had said of his enemies—especially with rural citizens whose own dress, manners, and language were not much different from the candidate's. Meanwhile, Buttram's efforts suffered greatly after Wrightsman, his ally, confirmed the worst suspicions of the distressed with avowals that wealth was necessary for public service—a "gentleman" could not live on a politician's salary. Wrightsman's grossly misplaced homilies about his butler's dispensing handouts from his mansion's back door doomed whatever hope remained for the two.[14] In the August runoff, Murray trounced the hapless Buttram by a two-to-one margin. Gore's victory over Wrightsman was smaller but comfortable.[15]

Worsening economic conditions made a Democratic sweep all but inevitable in November. Murray, considerably subdued as political meetings moved indoors, recaptured much of his old-time eloquence and passion in his formal speeches. For example: "The flames ignited by economic errors, now consuming the huts and cabins of the poor, will eventually destroy the mansions and palaces of the rich, and the rich seem not to comprehend."[16] Meanwhile, Gore struck the party's keynote in all his speeches: "If the people are satisfied with things as they are, they should vote the Republican ticket."[17]

To the Democrats, that was a certain bet. The Hoover sweep of 1928 was completely reversed in the general elections, as Murray carried sixty-four counties to roll up an unprecedented 301,921 votes to 208,575 for Ira Hill, the Republicans' gubernatorial sacrifice. Though he trailed in Oklahoma City, Tulsa, Enid, Stillwater, and Bartlesville, not even the continued opposition of the Tulsa and Oklahoma City dailies could damage his standing in the rural areas. The Murray landslide was strong enough to return Gore to his familiar seat in the Senate. Gore, who still had many Democratic enemies (who were reminded of the former senator's war record by an intensive Republican radio campaign), had a much closer race, but he retired the Republican incumbent with a 23,249-vote majority.[18]

The remaining Democratic statewide nominees, less objectionable to the city voters, had majorities that exceeded even Murray's. Included with the winners were a number of second-level politicians who, though relative newcomers to the statehouse in 1930, would later survive the

[13]The *Oklahoman* reluctantly endorsed Gore in the runoff and concentrated its fire on Murray. The paper charged that Murray scorned soap and water, lived without a bathtub in a dirt floor shack, and ate pancakes and syrup with his bare hands. For a sample of the hysteria, see the *Daily Oklahoman,* August 11, 1930. Murray's reception, a classic in political ribaldry, is recounted in his *Memoirs,* 2:380.

[14]Billington, *Thomas P. Gore,* pp. 143-44.

[15]The vote totals were: Murray, 220,255; Gore, 179,366; Buttram, 125,838; and Wrightsman, 128,573. Source: *Directory of Oklahoma, 1977,* pp. 552, 554.

[16]Murray, *Memoirs,* 3:484.

[17]*Tulsa Daily World,* November 4, 1930.

[18]*Directory of Oklahoma, 1977,* pp. 555-56.

vicissitudes of party turmoil and reappear on the ballot with monotonous regularity: Mabel Bassett, John Rogers, Jess G. Read, Harry B.
Cordell, Frank Carter, James E. Berry, and W. A. Pat Murphy. The
careers of each of them would extend into the 1940s, and Berry would
be elected lieutenant governor as late as 1950. Rogers, no kin to the
famed humorist, would eventually capture the record. First elected state
examiner and inspector in 1930, he would serve in that capacity until
the office itself was abolished in 1979. Whether the group's longevity
was to be attributed to the voters' admiration or to simple inertia could
not be determined.

In the congressional campaigns, the Democrats regained their seven-
to-one advantage when Wesley E. Disney, the young Tulsan who had
prosecuted Walton, took the First District seat from its Republican
incumbent, Charles O'Conner, by 260 votes. Disney's triumph, the first
of what became seven victories, put an end to the district's record of
changing its party affiliation in every election since its boundaries were
drawn in 1914. Only Milton Garber's reelection from the faithfully Republican Eighth District gave the party a place in the congressional
delegation. Not much brighter was the GOP's performance in the state
legislative races, where the reinvigorated Democrats cut their rivals'
house representation to nine seats, thirty-eight fewer than after the
aberrant results of 1928.[19]

The Democrats' 1930 sweep all but obliterated the hapless Republican
party within the state and struck a mighty blow at the earlier signs of
an emerging two-party system. It also rendered meaningless the factional
divisions within their own party during the 1920s. The stunning triumphs
of Murray and Gore were especially important for that reason. Virtually
alone of the candidates for the major offices, neither of them had been
touched by the furor over the Ku Klux Klan or the brief partisan realignment sponsored by the Farmer-Labor Reconstruction League. While the
state party had divided into two hostile factions, Gore had remained in
Washington, D.C. where he practiced law; and Murray had led a pathetic
colony to failure in the wilds of Bolivia. Discredited and useless to their
party in the turbulent twenties, they re-emerged to prove, among other
things, how irrelevant recent battles had become. The question remained
open, however, whether those aging captains could adapt the party to
the challenges of depression politics.

The new governor would be a critical part of the answer. His election
to the governorship had been an immense personal victory for which
the party organization could claim no credit. In January, 1931, Murray
reaped his personal reward. Twelve thousand spectators, including forty
survivors of the constitutional convention, looked on as the patriarchal
Uriah Dow Murray, 91-year-old frontier preacher, administered the oath
of office to his 61-year-old son. Alfalfa Bill asserted his ability to meet

[19] Ibid.; Oliver L. Benson et al., *Oklahoma Votes, 1907-1962* (Norman: University of
Oklahoma, Bureau of Government Research, 1964), p. 49.

the crisis, firm in the conviction that "running a government is very much like running a farm." Perhaps in vindictiveness toward his still vocal critics, Murray pledged that, "I shall honestly and honorably represent those who choose to call themselves the 'better element,' but this is one time when Oklahoma Indians, niggers, and po' white folks are going to have a fair-minded governor too."[20] From the moment of Murray's swearing-in ceremony, Oklahomans knew that for all his crudities they had a governor of immense personal appeal, a powerful advocate and a dangerous foe.

Whatever the measure of his political success, it is unlikely that Murray will ever be matched by any Oklahoma governor for the entertainment he gave.[21] Born during Reconstruction in the little community of Toadsuck, Texas, he suffered the usual privations of frontier farm families before escaping at eleven from a domineering stepmother to work at chopping wood, picking cotton, punching cows, selling books, and teaching school. In the meantime, he perfected the high-flown oratory that passed for political debating in a state torn by Populist strife and, the better to prepare himself, read law, reported courthouse doings for two country newspapers, and worked in the Democratic ranks for Governor Jim Hogg. Failing in his first race for the Texas state senate, he emigrated to Tishomingo, capital of the Chickasaw Nation, in 1898. There he became involved in tribal politics, married Mary Alice Hearell, the niece of the tribe's chief executive, and became one of the foremost attorneys working in the tangled mass of Indian land claims.

Settling on a fine Washita Valley farm, Murray also experimented with several crops, claiming to grow the first alfalfa in the Chickasaw Nation. By the time of the Sequoyah and Oklahoma constitutional conventions, his progressive principles had energized his drive for prominence. He became a prime mover in both causes, as the vice-president of the first convention and the president of the second. After a single term in the state house of representatives, which he served as speaker, he briefly returned to private business to satisfy his debts and, in 1912, was elected to Congress from the state at large. Two years later he won a second term from the newly defined Fourth District but lost his reelection bid of 1916 in the uproar surrounding the coming American participation in the world war. A second defeat, this time in the gubernatorial primary of 1918, sent him on his long self-exile to Bolivia, an exile ended by his brilliant campaign of 1930.

His long absence from the state had done little to tone down his most notorious eccentricities.[22] Irascible, obscene, and indifferent to the feelings of others, Murray was brutally contradictory when opinions con-

[20]Quoted in Bryant, *Alfalfa Bill Murray,* p. 190.

[21]Details of Murray's biography are available in his *Memoirs;* Bryant, *Alfalfa Bill Murray,* and Gordon Hines, *Alfalfa Bill: An Intimate Biography* (Oklahoma City: Oklahoma Press, 1932).

[22]Murray's legendary peculiarities attracted considerable attention from the national press. For examples, see Wayne Gard, "Alfalfa Bill," *New Republic,* February 17, 1932,

troverted his own, for he could not tolerate criticism. He was boastful to the point of braggadocio, and he never let anyone forget his supposedly superior knowledge of political science and constitutional principles. His stubborn attitude could goad a man to fury or silence him to irreconcilable hatred. His fellow officeholders found the governor particularly insufferable when his towering will crossed their own. In time, nearly all became the object of Murray's scorn. Attorney General J. Berry King was a mere "law clerk," whose opinions were "notorious." Commissioner of Charities and Corrections Mabel Bassett was "contemptible." Secretary of State Frank C. Carter was an outright criminal. And State Treasurer A. S. J. Shaw was dismissed with the gubernatorial sobriquet of "Jackass Shaw."[23]

To Murray's credit, he usually proved to be more circumspect with duly elected senators and representatives, whose prerogatives he respected. But even the legislators would have to contend with Alfalfa Bill's often bizarre notions of statesmanship, notions that seemed to touch every human activity. His first official message to the legislature, for example, included such dubious schemes as the construction of a dormitory for legislators, designed as protection from the wiles of lobbyists, particularly those "brazen ladies who get the unsophisticated member from the small town or country into their graces until he ceases to resist temptation."[24] He coupled that with a demand for drastic revision of the state's higher education system that made, in his telling, "high-toned bums" of its students. By eliminating all duplication of departments at the various state colleges, requiring college professors to remain in their offices eight hours a day, and abolishing the "deplorable educational error" of intercollegiate athletics, he hoped to trim 30 percent from the state's higher education budget.[25] The college people, deriding him as a meddling fool, were alarmed. The legislators, however, soon learned to separate the governor's personal prejudices from the more urgent public business and, for the most part, ignored Murray's pet ideas on

pp. 11-12; Louis Cochran, "Imperial Alfalfa Bill," *Outlook,* December 30, 1939, pp. 555-56; and William Gunn Shepherd, "King of the Prairies: Alfalfa Bill," *Collier's,* November 28, 1931, pp 12-13.
[23] The secondary officials, who usually fought each of his proposals, were fully capable of responding in kind. To Secretary of State Carter, Murray was "the most monumental liar in Oklahoma." Attorney General King, his most determined statehouse foe, once responded to a gubernatorial request by labeling it "idiotic" and reminded the governor that he could not frighten him "physically, mentally, politically, or officially." Walter L. Gray, "The Long Ballot in Oklahoma" (M.A. thesis, University of Oklahoma, 1952), pp. 64, 57-58.
[24] *First Message of Governor William H. Murray,* Oklahoma Governors Collection, Oklahoma State Archives, Oklahoma City. The governor's concern for the legislature's morality was a continuing one. In 1933 he complimented legislators after his "scouts" reported considerably less philandering by the members and the removal of whisky stores from the capitol's basement. *Second Message of Governor Murray,* ibid.
[25] *First Message of Governor Murray.* During his first six months in office, Murray replaced more educators than any governor except Jack Walton. Bryant, *Alfalfa Bill Murray,* p. 204.

morals, agriculture, education, and penology. For example, his plan to
restore stocks and lashes for convicts was quickly brushed aside. Less
successful at ignoring the governor's peculiar penal notions were the
magistrates of surrounding states, who would have to contend with
Murray's standing offer to parole any criminal who agreed to leave Oklahoma—an offer that exported 2,214 felons to Oklahoma's neighbors.[26]

The nation's journalists found it easy to belittle Murray but impossible
to ignore him. His quaint, unkempt appearance, his pretentious speeches,
and his unorthodox ideas of statesmanship made him many things, but he
was never dull. Moreover, he was often a shrewd interpreter of popular
moods. When he ordered that the state save the $3,000 appropriated for
the governor's inaugural ball in favor of a square dance with himself as
caller, he struck a popular mood. When he ordered the mansion's lawn
plowed so that unemployed men could plant potatoes, he attracted publicity for his kind-heartedness. Even when he ordered that the chairs in
the governor's office be chained to the radiators—"to keep folks from
putting their faces plumb into mine"—he was accepted as an amiable
crank.[27]

Although some detected in Murray the dread signs of demagoguery,[28]
his worst critics were mistaken. He could not be dismissed as a senile
buffoon or semiliterate barbarian. Murray's long experience in politics
had taught him the need for a bit of showmanship, and that need he
unabashedly fulfilled. Experience had also taught him the necessity of
personal power in a state in which impeachment had become an occupational hazard of the governorship. Deliberately tailoring his public
poses to popular moods and adroitly dispensing patronage, a gubernatorial weapon in a time of spectacular unemployment, Murray was able
to take firm control of state government and make the party machinery
totally subject to his personal command. His most trusted allies soon
filled virtually every party post, from which they distributed state jobs
to Murray's legions. His critics raged in impotence as Murray added
relatives, supporters, and grateful, needy men to an ever-expanding state
payroll. Soon, even the lordly senators came to understand the meaning
of the governor's power and his challenge. "If you've got any impeachment ideas in your heads," he roared, "hop to it. It'll be like a bunch
of jackrabbits tryin' to get a wildcat out of a hole."[29] The language was
vintage Murray, but he swiftly and permanently ended the legislature's
nasty habit of impeachment.

For all the attention focused on the governor's personal habits, his
administration was not without substance. Tax reform, the major theme
of his campaign, was detailed in his first message to the legislature.
Altogether, Murray proposed twenty-four bills, the collective effect of

[26] Bryant, *Alfalfa Bill Murray,* p. 246.
[27] Gard, "Alfalfa Bill," p. 11.
[28] That view is most vigorously advanced in Reinhard H. Luthin, *American Demagogues:
Twentieth Century* (Boston: Beacon Press, 1954), pp. 102-26.
[29] Quoted in Hines, *Alfalfa Bill,* p. 285.

which would have been a thorough overhaul of the state's tax system. The major elements included increased and broadened corporate taxes, a personal and corporate income tax at one-half the federal rate, and abolition of the state property tax. The capstone of his proposed reforms was to be a tax commission, designed to bring order to the state's tax collections.[30]

The lower house, elected in the Murray landslide and led by his old ally, Carleton Weaver, warmly received his proposals. There, the tax commission bill was adopted, with only three dissenting votes, three hours after its introduction. The state senate, however, was less acquiescent. Half its members had been elected while Murray was still in Bolivia, and the body was experienced at ignoring a governor's wishes. Indeed, the veteran members had helped remove at least one chief executive. In the upper chamber, twelve Republicans joined a maverick Democratic minority to weaken or defeat virtually every executive recommendation.[31]

By the end of the legislative session, the governor's program had been reduced to one major success. The Oklahoma Tax Commission became his only enduring achievement. The commission, empowered to make valuations of public service property and report its findings to the State Board of Equalization, managed to bring some uniformity to the complex problem of industrial assessments. It devised orderly procedures for the collection of all taxes except those on real estate, personal property, and intangibles, which were still to be collected by the counties. County excise equalization boards were also established with the object of bringing local property under a uniform assessment system and apportioning the revenues among local spending units. Upon its creation, the Tax Commission increased assessments on corporate property by $65 million, while cutting personal assessments 20 to 25 percent.

The work of the commission did bring some relief to most taxpayers but at a fearful price. Because the legislature had failed to approve the remainder of Murray's program, especially the increased corporate and personal income taxes, the state slid deeper into debt. Ad valorem collections declined sharply. Moreover, the governor's cautious budget recommendations of $26,475,000 had been shelved in favor of appropriations that totaled nearly $35 million. Although Murray forced department heads to return some $3 million to the treasury, state fiscal reform was more distant than ever.

Upon presenting his legislative program, a determined Murray had forewarned the Thirteenth Legislature that "the roll will be called and the firebells will be rung before this is over."[32] Following the adjournment, the governor wasted little time before taking the initiative route for his celebrated "Firebells Campaign" of 1931. The governor's sup-

---

[30] *First Message of Governor Murray.*
[31] Bryant, *Alfalfa Bill Murray,* pp. 193–94.
[32] *Harlow's Weekly,* February 7, 1931.

porters organized Murray Tax Reform Clubs in every county to speed circulation of seven initiative petitions that captured the essence of Murray's program. If unable to browbeat the legislators, he proved that he still retained a considerable popular following. In an action without precedent or sequel, he secured more than 119,000 signatures on each of the seven proposals within three days. The number far exceeded Murray's own expectation of 71,000 signatures and might have been greater still had not petition forms been exhausted in many rural areas.[33]

While opponents challenged the petitions' validity in protracted legal maneuverings, the governor abruptly called a special election for December 18 on the four leading proposals. Alarmed at the governor's audacity, his foes united, as they had never been able to do before, to check his designs. Their primary target was a proposal for a steeply graduated income tax that reached a maximum levy of 10 percent on corporate income above $100,000. That threat to wealth, especially in its corporate form, paled before a second measure that called for escheat to the state of all corporate-owned land not sold within ten years. A proposed budgeting law was intended to strengthen the governor's power over appropriations at the expense of the legislature. It would have established a state budget officer responsible only to him and forbade the legislators to exceed the executive's budget requests without a three-fourths vote. Finally, the governor coupled a proposal for appropriating $2 million for free textbooks with the demand to limit the powers of the state superintendent of public instruction by excluding him from a new state board of education and state textbook commission.

A heavily financed "Citizens' Committee" was formed to defeat the Murray proposals. Generously supported by business interests and heartily endorsed by the metropolitan press, the committee was spearheaded by Attorney General J. Berry King, who blistered the governor in a series of radio speeches. Murray himself was in rare form, and his speeches were free from the demagoguery that might have been expected in view of the radical nature of his proposals. He insisted that the proposed income tax was not confiscatory, as the Citizens' Committee charged, but a necessary and equitable measure to restore the state's solvency. Budgetary reform was, as he maintained, long overdue; and his penetrating analysis of the ill-coordinated educational system was unanswerable. Even the apparently wild-eyed measure for the escheat of corporate landholdings would do no more than enforce a provision of the state constitution. For nearly a quarter century, corporations had been forbidden to own land not essential for the conduct of their business. The Murray proposal merely activated that prohibition. Through it all, Murray remained unruffled, refused to debate the eccentricities of his personality, and counted on his personal popularity to put the measures over.[34]

Murray was beaten. Whatever the emergency demanded, many people

[33] Ibid., October 31, 1931.

were aroused by the dark suspicions of the Citizens' Committee that the firebells measures were designed only to tighten the hold of a Murray dictatorship. In the countryside, where Murray had always drawn his greatest support, two days of rain before election day kept the rural voters at home, and all four measures were defeated. The income tax measure was the most popular, yet it lost, 235,918 to 208,144; and the budget proposal lost by 51,000. Some of the measures carried in more than fifty counties, but in each case, the cities delivered crushing negative majorities. For example, nearly a third of the 240,028 negative votes on the escheat measure came from the two metropolitan centers, Tulsa and Oklahoma counties.[35]

Silencing the firebells signaled the end of Murray's opportunity to battle the depression with massive structural changes. Hostile lawmakers, jealous executive officers, and a powerful metropolitan press had played on voters' fears of a comprehensive scheme to shift the tax burden, no matter how unsatisfactory the familiar system might prove to be. In the process, they also had reduced the issue of reform to one of personality, a mutation made easy by the governor's many peculiarities. Politicians hated his arrogance; conservatives feared his radicalism; and the respectable detested his crudeness. Distrust of Murray had grown to the point that he no longer had a dependable constituency, a loss confirmed when his remaining three initiatives succumbed to even worse defeat in the July, 1932, elections.[36]

Unable to arrest the spreading disaster with legislation, the governor fought back with the one weapon suited to his office and his instincts: martial law. From May, 1931, to April, 1933, there were few days when some part of Oklahoma was not subjected to the presence of national guardsmen. Altogether, Murray issued an astonishing thirty-four proclamations of martial law, the first time the military power had been used to such an extent. His contention was that power had always belonged to the office, but it had not been exercised by a governor who understood it.[37] He made his first full-scale use of the guard on May Day, 1931, when fear of supposed Communist activity in the Henryetta area provoked his order to the adjutant-general. Antiradical hysteria, no stranger to Oklahoma, was intensified by the hard times and the report that some nitroglycerine had disappeared from an oil company's stores.[38]

It was not long afterward that the governor became involved in the "Bridge War," the most dramatic and best-remembered incident in the prolonged campaign to close all toll bridges in the state. The Highway

[34] Ibid., October 24, October 31, 1931. A good secondary account is available in William S. Harmon, "Oklahoma's Constitutional Amendments: A Study in the Use of the Initiative and Referendum" (Ph.D. diss., University of Oklahoma, 1951), pp. 124–30.

[35] Harmon, "Oklahoma's Constitutional Amendments," pp. 129–30; *Directory of Oklahoma, 1977*, pp. 641–42.

[36] *Directory of Oklahoma, 1977*, p. 642.

[37] *Oklahoma City Daily Oklahoman*, January 6, 1935.

[38] Ibid., May 1, 1931.

Governor Murray inspects his troops on the Red River, guaranteeing that no Texan shall cross. Courtesy Western History Collections, University of Oklahoma.

Department had completed three free bridges over the Red River, paralleling privately owned toll bridges at Durant, Marietta, and Ringling. When the Durant-Denison Bridge Company, a Texas corporation that operated toll bridges at two of the crossings, obtained a federal court injunction to prevent the opening of the free bridge at Durant,[39] the governor ordered the Highway Commission to barricade the approaches to the toll bridges. By a proclamation of July 23, the national guard was ordered to oppose "all interference whatsoever," except that of the "superior executive power of the President of the United States."[40] In response, Governor Ross Sterling of Texas sent his rangers to obstruct traffic on the Texas side of Oklahoma's newly built free bridges.

On July 25, United States District Judge Collin Nesbitt, sitting at Muskogee, enjoined the Highway Commission and the national guard from preventing traffic on the toll span at Durant. Murray promptly defied the court and hurried to Durant to take personal command of his troops. The publicity was gratifying: photographs of the governor

[39]Ibid., July 17, 1931.
[40]Executive Proclamation No. 1456, July 23, 1931, Secretary of State Files, Oklahoma State Archives, Oklahoma City, hereafter cited as State Files.

slouched in the uniform of the guardsmen appeared on the front pages of newspapers throughout the country. The inevitable caption was "Horatio at the Bridge." On July 27, Murray extended his martial law declaration on the free bridge to reach the Texas state line, about seventy-five feet south of the southern end of the bridge.[41] Already, he had ordered the Highway Department to plow up the Oklahoma approaches to the toll bridges. Outmaneuvered, the courts dissolved their injunctions against the opening of the free bridges.[42] The legal battle continued for nearly a year before the federal appellate courts finally upheld the governor's authority on the grounds that Oklahoma controlled both banks of the Red River. Troops remained at the scene most of that time. The bridges remained free forever.

Murray's boldest invocation of martial law followed the first skirmish of the Bridge War by little more than a week. Hastened by ruinous overproduction in the Seminole, Oklahoma City, and East Texas fields, the price of oil dropped below twenty cents a barrel in the summer of 1931. Responding to the desperate pleas of helpless independent oil producers, the governor warned, on July 28, that if the price did not rise to one dollar a barrel by August 1, he would shut down the state's production.[43] On August 4 he carried out his threat, declaring 3,106 martial law zones, each defined as a circle with a radius of fifty feet from the center of every producing oil well in the state. Asserting that, "as reported to me by my secret scouts," violence was imminent in the oil fields "unless all these wells are at once closed down," Murray named cousin Cicero "proration umpire."[44] Under Cicero's command, troops shut off the flow of oil and, later, strictly limited it to 5 percent of the daily allowable. Still firing off executive orders, the governor kept the guardsmen in the oil fields, over the mounting protests of the integrated companies. Finally, the temporarily cowed Fourteenth Legislature passed an acceptable conservation law and the Corporation Commission could regain control. By that time, oil production had been under military control for a total of 618 days, with the guard's expenses paid by a special tax imposed on the offending oil companies.[45]

Amid the battles with private bridge companies and the haughty petroleum "majors," Murray continued to file executive orders without letup. The governor did not hesitate to call out the militia to secure what he believed to be justice for the oppressed. Colonel Zack Miller, sometime proprietor of the 101 Ranch near Ponca City, was jailed for failure to pay alimony. Murray believed that he detected the foul hand

[41] Executive Proclamation No. 1450, July 27, 1931, State Files.

[42] *Oklahoma City Daily Oklahoman,* August 6, 1931.

[43] For background on the Corporation Commission's conservation efforts and Murray's role, see Blue Clark, "Beginning of Oil and Gas Conservation in Oklahoma, 1907-1933," *Chronicles of Oklahoma* 55 (1977):375-91.

[44] Executive Proclamation No. 1460, August 4, 1931, State Files.

[45] Executive Proclamation No. 1519, September 21, 1932, State Files; Bryant, *Alfalfa Bill Murray,* pp. 198-200.

of his arch foe Lew Wentz behind the deed and ordered the adjutant-general to secure Miller's release. He then issued an executive pardon that expressly prohibited Miller's re-arrest, melodramatically describing him as the unfortunate victim of a vicious conspiracy "to despoil him of his property and patrimony and home."[46]

In March, 1933, Governor Murray ordered a state bank moratorium,[47] and when Enid's First National Bank refused to comply, troops closed the offending institution and enforced martial law on the surrounding sidewalk. Meanwhile, tax sales of farms and homes were halted by declarations of martial law in eleven counties and the threat of it in others.[48] Poor men arrested as vagrants were turned out of jail on his orders. After Oklahoma City health officials forbade the practice of feeding hundreds of unemployed men from the surplus of Saint Anthony's Hospital kitchens, the governor retaliated with a threat to declare a military zone around the hospital, ending the city's authority. The same health authorities condemned as unsanitary the distribution of substandard skimmed milk sold to the poor by the O.K. Milk Association, a cooperative of two thousand farmers in the Oklahoma City area. Murray's own relief organization continued to purchase two thousand gallons daily at the prevailing rate of two cents a gallon. When M. C. Graham, the association's agent, was arrested on complaint of the city health officer, Murray responded in an unusual executive proclamation that granted Graham a full pardon and prevented future arrest by declaring a military zone of Graham's home, office, and automobile.[49]

After such incidents, no one was disposed to disbelieve the governor when he rang for the adjutant-general, and the threat of martial law was usually sufficient to gain his desired objective. For example, the Phillips Petroleum Company, which had been involuntarily supplying commercially worthless free gas from its open pipelines for a year, decided on a very cold day to shut off the supply of its uninvited consumers. Murray gave the company thirty minutes to turn the gas back on. It did.[50]

His eccentricities and imaginative use of military power made Murray a national figure by 1932. In fact, by that time, he was probably the nation's best known state executive, except for New York Governor Franklin D. Roosevelt. Emboldened by the reams of publicity that attended his every deed, and never doubtful of his own abilities, Alfalfa Bill set out on his grandest quest yet. He would be president.

[46] Executive Proclamation No. 1537, November 28, 1932, State Files. Wentz, a Ponca City oil millionaire, was chief spokesman of Oklahoma City's Republican party and William Holloway's appointee as chairman of the State Highway Department, holding the post during Murray's first biennium. In the latter half of his term, Murray was able to force Wentz's removal by a reorganization of the department.
[47] Executive Proclamation No. 1570, March 2, 1933, State Files.
[48] Executive Proclamation No. 1709–1714, April 14, 1934, State Files.
[49] Executive Proclamation No. 1729, July 30, 1934, State Files.
[50] *Oklahoma City Daily Oklahoman,* March 12, 1932.

Murray campaigning for president, promising "Bread, Butter, Bacon, and Beans." Courtesy Western History Collections, University of Oklahoma.

The inspired editorials of the *Blue Valley Farmer* began the Murray boom as early as April 9, 1931, when an anonymous contributor (perhaps himself) wrote: "Bill Murray is presidential timber and must answer the call of the people."[51] Already he had appeared on Lincoln's Birthday, in the unaccustomed habiliments of striped trousers and frock coat, at the Great Emancipator's tomb in Springfield, Illinois, to deliver an eloquent tribute and to intone the prayer, "O Father of all Mercies, send us another Lincoln."[52] He seemed ready to answer his own prayer. In 1932 he traveled more than ten thousand miles in seventeen states, preaching an alliterative program of "bread, butter, bacon, and beans."[53]

His strategy was apparently to win second- and third-choice commitments that would become effective once the leading candidates deadlocked, but although the Oklahoman attracted crowds wherever he spoke, more came from curiosity than from conviction. He entered five presidential preference primaries, making a decent showing only in North Dakota. Even there, he could not come within 20,000 of Franklin Roosevelt's 52,634 votes. As the months passed, the campaign became ever more futile and Murray ever more desperate, lashing out at Roosevelt with venomous, personal attacks.[54]

Henry S. Johnston nonetheless went through the motions of nominating Murray at the Democratic National Convention in Chicago. In an address notable for the multitude of historical giants invoked, the deposed governor favorably compared Murray with Washington, Jefferson, Jackson, Lincoln, Franklin, Demosthenes, Lord Coke, Luther Burbank, Daniel Webster, and Patrick Henry—with Saint Paul thrown in for good measure.[55] The delegates, however, remained notably unimpressed. On the first ballot, Murray received just twenty-three votes. His own delegation was unanimous, for it was handpicked. The only other Murray vote came from his own brother, George Murray, a North Dakota delegate whom he had not seen in thirty-four years. Although Murray allowed the Oklahoma delegation to join the Roosevelt bandwagon on the final ballot, his support for the patrician New Yorker remained cool at best.[56]

Back home, the voters' dissatisfaction with the current order was foretold in the Democratic primary, which produced many extremely close races. Veteran congressmen W. W. Hastings, Tom McKeown,

---

[51] *Blue Valley Farmer,* April 9, 1931.
[52] *Oklahoma City Daily Oklahoman,* February 13, 1931.
[53] A campaign song of the same name featured such inspired verses as:
   Give us the good old days, give us the good old days.
   Give us back the old familiar scenes.
   Then we'll have money to pay the rent.
   Murray for President.
   Bread, Butter, Bacon, and Beans.
New York Times, March 3, 1932, quoted in Bryant, *Alfalfa Bill Murray,* p. 224.
[54] The entire campaign is treated in Bryant, *Alfalfa Bill Murray,* pp. 214-36.
[55] Murray, *Memoirs,* 3:546-55.
[56] Bryant, *Alfalfa Bill Murray,* pp. 235-36.

F. B. Swank, and J. V. McClintic were all forced into runoffs; of the group, only McClintic won the second primary with any comfort. The first three all survived, but by the narrowest of margins, Swank by only 45 votes. It was a good year for newcomers, as E. W. Marland of Ponca City easily captured the nomination to oppose the Eighth District's Republican incumbent, Milton Garber. One old-timer did very well, too. Jack Walton was successful in competition with a half dozen seasoned vote getters seeking the open post on the Corporation Commission, beating W. C. McAlester, C. C. Childers, I. L. Cook, Charles West, and George S. Long in the first primary—the last named a Tulsa dentist and brother of the Louisiana "Kingfish," Huey P. Long. In the runoff, Walton edged State Treasurer A. S. J. Shaw, 221,509 to 212,847.

In the race for the senatorial nomination, Senator Elmer Thomas found himself in a fierce struggle with Gomer Smith, a young Oklahoma City criminal attorney who brought the old-age pension issue to the forefront; R. W. McCool, former state chairman and Norman city manager; and Judge Albert C. Hunt, as well as three unknowns. Thomas eliminated Smith in the second round, 251,248 to 161,594,[57] but not before the dynamic lawyer had introduced himself to his first statewide audience, many of whom would remain his devoted admirers through future campaigns.

The general election of 1932 was only a formality in Oklahoma, where resentment against President Herbert Hoover and his party was exceptionally bitter. Except for last-ditch Republicans and a few drys, Hoover had no friends in Oklahoma, despite his recent appointment of the state's first Cabinet member, Patrick J. Hurley, as secretary of war. Sentimental considerations, like the governor's lack of ardor for the national ticket, were of small moment against the people's utter contempt for the Republican party and its representative in the White House, who was saddled with all their miseries. Roosevelt swept every county, all but unanimously in the south and west, to win an unprecedented electoral majority: 516,468 votes to Hoover's 188,165. Only in Tulsa County, where the *Tribune* remained the last metropolitan apologist for Hoover, was the Democratic steamroller slowed, though even there, the Roosevelt majority was still seven to five. Except for the Garber-owned papers of the northwest and a few other rock-ribbed Republican organs, the state's press was rewarded for its surprising unanimity in urging a straight Democratic ticket. Both the *Daily Oklahoman* (Oklahoma City) and the *Tulsa World* blessed the Roosevelt cause, and many of the small county seat weeklies found no accusation against Hoover too incredible to believe and print. Whether jack rabbit stew was ever a staple item of diet on the state's dining tables, it was certainly the favorite dish of the rural editorialists.

The landslide carried every Democrat to victory in the major races, and it was a matter of note when a Republican was elected constable

[57] *Directory of Oklahoma, 1977,* pp. 556-57.

*Disgraced former Governor Jack Walton's successful campaign for the cor-
poration commission affirmed the claim that any Democrat could win in 1932.
Courtesy Western History Collections, University of Oklahoma.*

or justice of the peace in a remote district. For the first time, the Democrats won every congressional district. Marland ousted the Republican
incumbent from the previously inpregnable Eighth District. In addition,
the Democrats elected the state's new congressman at large (a seat made
possible after the 1930 census) and returned Elmer Thomas to a second
Senate term with a 207,000-vote majority over Wirt Franklin, the Republicans' stand-in. In the Democratic sweep, even Jack Walton found vindication. His election to the State Corporation Commission proved that

it really was true that any Democrat could win in 1932.[58]

Despite the massive Democratic majority, the governor's legislative strength had actually declined. Except to differentiate themselves from the despised Republicans, the winners' Democratic party affiliation often meant very little, at least in the way of a coherent strategy for government. With virtually no Republican opposition to force them into common cause, the state's Democrats were moving into an every-man-for-himself free-for-all, with the Murray program its first victim. In the house, perhaps only forty-nine of the members supported the governor, while some forty others actively opposed him. The balance of power rested with an unstable, independent faction. Meanwhile, the senate was still poised to resist Murray's assertions of executive power.[59]

When the Fourteenth Legislature convened in January, 1933, the state's fiscal situation, serious in 1931, had become urgent. The state debt had increased by a third since 1931, with no end in sight. Desperate, the legislature cut appropriations by more than a third to $21,642,000, a niggardly sum but still nearly $2 million above the governor's biennial recommendations. Searching for new sources of revenue to offset the $30 million drop in property tax collections, the legislature and the governor fought each other to a standstill. A sales tax of 1 percent—half of Murray's request—was finally approved, but with ample exemptions. The governor's proposed three cents cigarette tax was finally passed by the legislature, only to be overturned by referendum in August, 1933. For his part, the governor angrily vetoed legislative bills taxing chain stores, establishing an old-age pension system, and granting property tax exemptions on homesteads. Meanwhile, the frustrated governor had to contend with zealous legislators who turned the summer's special session into an embarrassing inquiry into the operation of the School Land Commission.[60]

Murray's stalemated battles with the legislature eventually took a rear seat to his struggles with the national administration, especially after the New Deal's first tentative efforts at relief for the destitute. The governor's own concern for the impoverished was genuine enough, but it was soon submerged in a personal struggle with a power greater than his own.

The enormity of the depression quickly overwhelmed the primitive structure of relief in the state. Aside from special cases like its pensions to Confederate veterans, the state left relief a responsibility of local authorities as late as 1930. Barely adequate in the best of times, county aid was always inadequately funded and usually grudgingly given. In the crisis of mass need, private contributions supplemented county efforts, but never sufficiently. As late as 1933, for example, relief officials in Pittsburg County spent only $4,500, including private donations, to aid the elderly and the infirm. About 70 percent of the total went to main-

[58] Ibid., pp. 557-58; Benson et al., *Oklahoma Votes,* p. 49.
[59] Bryant, *Alfalfa Bill Murray,* p. 239.
[60] Ibid., pp. 240-41.

tain the county poor farm. Nothing at all was allowed the able-bodied unemployed.[61]

In 1931 the legislature appropriated $300,000 for immediate, direct relief—a miserly figure to be sure, although Oklahoma thereby became one of only four states granting direct relief at all.[62] That money was quickly exhausted, whereupon Murray exacted "voluntary" contributions of 1.5 percent of the salaries of state employees to replenish the relief fund and ordered the Highway Department to use gasoline tax collections in excess of $1 million to hire the unemployed for public work. Eventually spending $1.2 million for state relief during his administration (plus another $6,000 of his own money), the concerned governor sponsored projects that ranged from the distribution of a million free textbooks for the children of the poor to allowing ten unemployed men to plant gardens on the unused land between the governor's mansion and the state capitol.[63]

Despite such humanitarian sympathies, Murray was determined to resist the new federal relief projects that followed Franklin Roosevelt's inauguration in March, 1933. Superficially, his stance was determined by constitutional scruple, especially the traditional belief that public welfare was beyond the strict limitations of federal authority. Likely more important, however, was his quite realistic belief that federal relief could not be controlled from the governor's office. In large part, his obstinacy was also one of personal distrust of the president. Bill Murray was lastingly wounded by Roosevelt's easy destruction of his presidential ambitions in 1932. Worse than merely defeating him, Roosevelt had ridiculed him with loose charges of demagoguery. Ridicule to a man like Murray was answered by undying hatred.

Because the New Deal's Federal Emergency Relief Administration (FERA) channeled the first relief funds through state governments, Murray was initially able to follow a consistent policy of control or obstruction. While the governor forbade counties and cities to accept relief loans from the federal authority, he refused to fill the state's quota for emergency employment under the new Civil Works Administration. Meanwhile, the expenditure of FERA funds was closely supervised by the governor and county relief committees subject to his appointment.[64]

Murray's critics almost immediately began to charge that his handling of federal funds was riddled with corruption and political favoritism. Washington soon dispatched Aubrey Williams, FERA liaison officer, to Oklahoma City for a conference with the governor. Perhaps deliberately, Alfalfa Bill was on his worst behavior. Wearing dirty socks and no shoes, the governor met Williams and offered his guest a cup of tea strained

[61] County Relief Files, W. W. Redwine Collection, Western History Collections, University of Oklahoma, Norman, Oklahoma.

[62] Henry J. Bitterman, *State and Federal Grants-in-Aid* (New York and Chicago: Mentzer, Bush, & Co., 1938), p. 155.

[63] Bryant, *Alfalfa Bill Murray,* pp. 205, 246.

[64] FERA Files, Murray Collection.

through a filthy handkerchief. When he compounded those insults by cursing Roosevelt, Williams stalked out, reporting to the administration that he found "thieving and favoritism on all sides. I found that every Tom, Dick, and Harry in the state was getting relief whether they were unemployed or not." Patience finally exhausted, national authorities took the administration of relief from the governor's hands in early 1934, giving Oklahoma the dubious honor of joining Huey Long's Louisiana with a federalized relief program. Murray protested impotently as Washington compounded the insult by coolly denying him a voice in federal patronage, further isolating the enraged governor.[65]

Murray's feud with Roosevelt had hardly ended. After leaving the governor's office, he spent the last twenty-one years of his life consumed by a hatred of everything that Roosevelt represented to him.[66] His feud with the president was only too typical: a personal struggle born of immense ego, for which the state's needy suffered most.

In fact, Murray's entire administration became an object lesson in the hazards of politics grounded in personality. From the moment of his startling triumph in the Democratic primary of 1930 to the federal takeover of relief in 1934, the central issue in Oklahoma politics was "Murrayism." Less a program than a personality, it had inspired the best of his administration—the farsighted tax proposals, the ending of the impeachment mania, and the imaginative actions to relieve distress. But the worst in his administration—the defeat of the firebells initiatives, the unrestrained patronage system, the constant bickering with any who crossed him—also flowed from the excesses of that same personality.

In a similar way, the state's Democratic party, despite its two recent and impressive triumphs, was victimized by the politics of personality. Rather than a unified instrument for the exercise of power, the party was little more than a leaky umbrella for hostile factions opposing and supporting the headstrong executive. Lesser leaders carved out their own fiefdoms, independent of the party's titular heads in Washington or Oklahoma City. If one symptom of that was the centrality of Murrayism in the early 1930s, another was registered in the strange aftermath of the 1932 race for congressman at large.

Population gains measured in the 1930 census entitled Oklahoma to a ninth congressman, to be elected on a statewide basis in 1932. In that year's Democratic primary, a host of long-established politicians crowded the ballot. Former Congressmen Claude Weaver[67] and E. B.

---

[65] The story is recounted in James T. Patterson, *The New Deal and the States: Federalism in Transition* (Princeton, N.J.: Princeton University Press, 1969), p. 54.

[66] Murray's declining, postgubernatorial years were consumed with rage at the New Deal and modern liberalism. After two later tries for office, he eventually fell in with such extremists as Gerald L. K. Smith and wrote a series of books upon the menaces of the New Deal, communism, and "International Jewry"—all of which he came to see as one. That pathetic period is covered in Bryant, *Alfalfa Bill Murray*, pp. 256-76.

[67] Weaver was the author of a pamphlet, "Why I Go to Church," that had a circulation of a million copies. He said later that he had not been to church since. Lyle H. Boren

Howard; Commissioner of Charities and Corrections Mabel Bassett; the indefatigable Campbell Russell—these and sixteen others fell victims to a schoolteacher from Moore who was so obscure that his name had been left off the tally sheets prepared by newspaper offices. More than 56,000 voters marked their ballots for Will Rogers, surely most of them out of confusion, for this Rogers was no kin to the famed humorist. Despite ample newspaper notice that his was a mistaken identity, Rogers went on to defeat Mabel Bassett by two to one in the runoff primary and led the state ticket in the subsequent general election. Four more times, until the office itself was abolished in 1943, voters would reelect him to a full decade in Congress.[68] During that time he contributed no humor whatever to congressional proceedings.

During his years of service, Rogers would have to turn back a series of equally bogus challengers. These included Robert E. Lee, Sam Houston, William Cullen Bryant, Wilbur Wright, and Brigham Young. After Rogers's success, a plethora of famous or suggestive names splashed the ballot through the 1930s. In 1938 alone, such worthies as Oliver Cromwell, Daniel Boone, Huey Long, Brigham Young, Wilbur Wright, and Patrick Henry all sought preferment, though none came close to equaling Mae West's 67,607 votes in the race for commissioner of charities and corrections[69]—Mrs. West probably appearing to offer more charity than correction. One can surmise the appeal of one of the most durable of the "shadow name" candidates, T. Bone McDonald, who ran well for various posts over the years. It was perhaps fortunate that T. Bone had given up by 1946, the year of the great meat famine.

If the famous name filings owed much to Oklahoma's notoriously long ballot, the success of a Will Rogers or a Mae West also testified to the incoherent nature of Democratic party politics in the depression era. Having obliterated their Republican opposition, the state party fell victim to the fragmentation of personality cults, even as its national counterpart was evolving into a disciplined, if diverse, body. It remained to be seen if that transformation could be effected in the Sooner State. In early 1935, outgoing Governor William H. Murray conferred with his successor, a man determined to do just that. E. W. Marland patiently listened as Alfalfa Bill rambled and fumed before turning over his office. Until he did, Marland sat in a chair chained to a radiator.

---

and Dale Boren, *Who is Who in Oklahoma* (Guthrie: Co-operative Publishing Co., 1935), p. 518.

[68] *Directory of Oklahoma, 1977,* pp. 556, 560, 564, 568, 571, 575.

[69] Ibid., pp. 567-68.

CHAPTER 10

E. W. Marland: The New Deal's Pale Imitation

I N ITS first hundred days of emergency legislation, the New Deal broke the tension of the economic crisis, but the depression was still the inescapable reality in Oklahoma as the time came to choose a successor to Governor Murray. Agriculture was still in the doldrums. Industrial disintegration continued to take its toll in human suffering and frustration in public affairs. The early New Deal experiments, like the limited efforts closer to home, could hardly arrest the galloping economic disease that afflicted the whole country. The disorders were nowhere more serious than in Oklahoma, where a savage drought, coming in the midst of the 1934 primaries, punctuated the people's strident demands for government help. No political effort that failed to reckon with the economic distress of the people, one-third of whom were near destitution, could hope for success in such a time. All candidates for all offices were quick to perceive the popular mood. Subtly but perceptibly, the discontented had come to look to the federal government as the instrument of their deliverance from misery, and all politicians, of whatever persuasion, agreed that the battle against the depression was the paramount issue.

Under those circumstances, there was nothing listless about Oklahoma's Democratic primary of 1934, where voters were confronted with a record 531-square-inch "bedsheet ballot."[1] Hardly a prominent public

---

[1] As in other states, the massive ballot was only one reflection of the political turmoil unleashed by the depression. In fact, the Oklahoma ballot of 1934 was only slightly larger than the *average* state ballot of two years earlier, which was 505 square inches. The national record was probably taken in the New York Democratic primary of 1912 with a ballot fourteen feet long. See Walter L. Gray, "The Long Ballot in Oklahoma" (M.A. thesis, University of Oklahoma, 1952), pp. 31-32.

figure since statehood neglected to enter his name in the filing period. Charles Haskell and Lee Cruce were dead, and Robert L. Williams was on the federal bench, but three other former governors were in the midst of the contention. Without jeopardizing his current post on the Corporation Commission, Jack Walton sought to better himself and win a triumphant comeback race as governor. Henry S. Johnston wanted to be congressman at large, and J. B. A. Robertson, a supreme court judge.

Of course, the sitting governor, William H. Murray, attempted to make himself the irrepressible issue in the race for his succession. Although he was anathema to the national administration and had earned the hatred of most of the state's daily newspapers, the retiring chief executive still retained a considerable popular following, especially in the rural areas. Moreover, he continued his stranglehold on the party machinery.[2] All of this he hoped to transfer to a handpicked slate of candidates for ten major state offices. Leading the slate, and thereby bearing the stigma of Murrayism, was Holdenville's Tom Anglin. He had earned the governor's endorsement when he had served as the Fourteenth Legislature's speaker of the house and had kept the assembly from a searching investigation of the administration. Although of unquestioned ability and scarcely disliked by anyone, Anglin proved to be a colorless and unconvincing campaigner. Worst of all, his pleasant image was contaminated by the taunts that he was Murray's "Crown Prince." Still, in a fifteen-man field in the first primary, the governor's choice was almost certain to win one of the runoff slots.

Murrayism affected most of the other candidacies as well as Anglin's. Virtually all the remaining gubernatorial aspirants attempted to claim the anti-Murray banner. Among them, Attorney General J. Berry King seemed to enjoy the advantage at the outset. King had been the most vocal enemy of the governor within the statehouse and not infrequently had claimed credit for thwarting Murray's designs, most notably in the firebells campaign. King enjoyed the trumpet support of the *Tulsa World* and of his own paper, the *New Star*.[3] "Oklahoma needs, not a Governor who would be King, but a King who would be Governor" was the attorney general's slogan. Clever enough in his play on words, King only emphasized the force of Murray's personal rule in shaping the state's politics.

Few candidates were able to evade the shadow of Murrayism. One of the few to escape was Gomer Smith, who had shown unusual vote-getting power in his maiden race for Elmer Thomas's Senate seat two years earlier. Smith's 1934 platform incorporated a host of radical proposals, including the public ownership of utilities, the use of marginal lands for relief families, a complete reorganization of state government, and the writing of a new state constitution. Nor did he neglect his familiar

[2] *Harlow's Weekly,* February 17, 24, March 3, 1934.
[3] The *New Star* at times read as though Berry's only opponent was Murray himself. See issues of May 10, May 31, June 14, and June 28, 1934, for especially searing indictments of the current administration.

demand for ample old-age pensions. Jack Walton offered a predictable hard-hitting campaign, ignoring Murray's regime and his own failures in the governor's office, to promise aid to veterans, equal rights for women, and state encouragement to "honest" business and "honest" oilmen, along with the standard old-age pension and homestead tax-exemption planks.[4]

One final candidate mounted a campaign that sharply contrasted with Smith's and Walton's flamboyant appeals as well as with the sins and virtues of the Murray regime. Congressman E. W. Marland was not seriously regarded when he announced for the governorship in August, 1933. While he stayed in Washington until a few weeks before the primary, an efficient organization, centering in Ponca City, was quietly reaching out to take his message across the state. His manager, Howard B. ("Pete") Drake, an investment counselor, age thirty-eight, enlisted all but unanimous support from the former employees of the once mighty Marland Oil Company. A number of political professionals, including R. H. Wilson, Hubert Bolen, and Scott Ferris, signed up for the Marland cause, as did two rising new politicians, Ed Falkenberg of Medford and Robert S. Kerr of Oklahoma City. Although the Marland headquarters circulated little campaign material, store windows and service stations soon blossomed with Marland's picture alongside his single slogan: "Bring the New Deal to Oklahoma." With those six simple words, the Marland candidacy offered to transcend the prevailing politics of personality.

Of all the aspirants, E. W. Marland was best suited for that approach.[5] Dignified to the point of aloofness, Marland was also free from the rancorous old controversies that raged around the heads of Anglin, King, Smith, and Walton, for he had never held office until his election to Congress in 1932. Although a newcomer to public life, he had long been a subject of considerable public attention. The way he had built a fortune and then lost it to the conniving denizens of Wall Street was already a Sooner legend, and it struck a responsive chord among thousands of citizens who shared his rage and sense of loss. The powerful testimony of his neighbors recounted his humanitarian enterprises, and the onetime philanthropist reaped a harvest of gratitude from the beneficiaries of his past largesse. Most significantly, Marland's campaign was tuned to the phenomenal popularity of the New Deal. Although his speech-making fell short of the extravagant standard of Oklahoma political oratory, his promises were as generous as those of any of his rivals. Coming from such

[4] During the filing period another Jack Walton, this one a farmer from Turley, attempted to enter the race. Denied a place on the ballot, the farmer responded with this tongue-in-cheek pronouncement: "I see no reason why I should not aspire to this high office. I have never been convicted with a serious crime. I am in no way related to the J. C. Walton who was impeached while governor." *Harlow's Weekly,* May 5, 1934.

[5] For an admiring portrait that emphasizes Marland's business career, see John Joseph Mathews, *Life and Death of an Oilman: The Career of E. W. Marland* (Norman: University of Oklahoma Press, 1951).

a man, they only seemed more sincere, more dignified, and more possible of achievement.

While Marland successfully appropriated the New Deal label for his own campaign, there was little evidence that Washington was overtly involved in his efforts. Except for National Committeeman Scott Ferris, none of the Oklahomans who had won positions of responsibility in the administration took an active part in the state's internal struggle. Every Democratic candidate, whatever his personal views, paid tribute to Roosevelt, for none dared risk any other course in 1934. The president's own choice—if, indeed, he had one—was unknown.

The Marland campaign ignited in the final days before the June primary and confounded the predictions of the newspapers' political prophets, who generally had looked to Anglin and King to battle for executive position. In fact, the Ponca Citian easily led all other contenders by gathering 156,885 votes, some 55,000 more than Anglin, a distant second in the large field.[6] With the air of one eager to forget the recent unpleasantness, Anglin withdrew from the runoff race in a generous tribute to Marland's popularity and thereby struck the first blow at the runoff primary. Walton, who placed a very distant third, attempted to have the State Election Board declare him eligible for a runoff with Marland; but the board refused to permit the substitution of third place for second.[7] It was a fortunate decision, for the state was spared three weeks of Walton's firebrand campaigning, and the result could hardly have been changed in any case.

Otherwise, the chief results of the Democratic primaries were the defeat of most of Murray's presumptive slate and major changes in the party's congressional ticket. Of the ten candidates who carried the banner of Murrayism through the primaries, only two managed to emerge with nominations. Hugh Harrell, tapped for state treasurer, and John Rogers, Murray's favorite to keep his position as state examiner and inspector, were both victorious, though each was forced into a runoff election. Otherwise, none of the other eight—including, of course, Anglin—was able to do better than second, and three of them did even worse than that.[8] The results could be interpreted as a stinging rebuke of Murrayism. More likely, they measured the inability of any incumbent governor to influence the nominations within his own political party.

Changes within the congressional ticket had been in the making for some time. In 1934 they resulted in the defeat of three veteran congress-

---

[6] State of Oklahoma, State Election Board, *Directory of Oklahoma, 1977,* p. 558.

[7] *Oklahoma City Daily Oklahoman,* July 7, 1934.

[8] The Murray slate and its record: Governor—Tom Anglin (second); Secretary of State—J. T. Jones (third); State Auditor—Sam M. Bounds (fourth); State Treasurer—Hugh Harrell (first); Superintendent of Public Instruction—John Murray (second); Commissioner of Charities and Corrections—Jessie E. Moore (second); Commissioner of Insurance—Sharpe W. Philpott (second); State Examiner and Inspector—John Rogers (first); President State Board of Agriculture—Ben R. Cook (second); Corporation Commissioner —Sam Hawks (third). *Directory of Oklahoma, 1977,* pp. 558-59.

men in the Democratic primary and the replacement of two other incumbents who did not seek reelection. Since Marland was yielding his Eighth District seat after one term, his place on the ticket was taken by Phil Ferguson, a Woodward rancher. The Second District's W. W. Hastings, who had narrowly escaped defeat in 1932, declined another contest, and his place went to the youthful Jack Nichols of Eufaula. In an exciting three-way race in the Fourth District, the colorful District Judge Percy L. Gassaway of Coalgate unseated the veteran Tom McKeown and stopped a strong bid on the part of Wewoka's longtime party wheelhorse, Joe Looney. Booted and spurred, Gassaway would be granted one wild term in Washington before his outraged constituents had a chance to replace him.[9] In the Fifth District, Professor Josh Lee of the University of Oklahoma won a clear majority over four contenders, including Campbell Russell and the incumbent, F. B. Swank. Elsewhere, the Democratic incumbents won renomination, including Will Rogers, the congressman at large who was forced into a runoff with the deposed former governor, Henry S. Johnston. Johnston's turgid speeches, lachrymose tributes to the pioneers, and stirring recitations of the "Battle Hymn of the Republic" provided most of the entertainment in the otherwise boring runoff campaign that, after Anglin's withdrawal, had been deprived of its leading attraction.

In spite of all the recent contention, the Democrats approached the November general elections with unguarded optimism. Marland's victory seemed momentarily to have united all factions of the party, and outside the state, the Democrats' choice was everywhere applauded. Walter Harrison, the veteran writer for the *Oklahoma City Times,* caught much of the prevailing sentiment with the satisfied verdict that "this much is certain—Oklahomans will not have to apologize for the conduct of their governor after the first of January."[10] The obvious butt of Harrison's comment sounded one of the few sour notes in an editorial in the *Blue Valley Farmer:* "I know what they will say after four years of Marland, with increased appropriations, greater expenses of government and corresponding deficits, resulting in greater bond issues. The extravagant man in public office, while spending money, is applauded, but after the money is gone the people kick him until the debt is paid."[11] For all its spleen, it turned out to be an accurate prophecy.

Against the obvious portents of doom, the state's Republicans fought the general election with spirit. Former Senator William B. Pine carried the tattered Republican banner into November with optimistic—and clearly deluded—forecasts of victory. The *Blue Valley Farmer* was

---

[9] Other than his bizarre appearance, Gassaway's only contribution to public affairs was a verbal feud with Louisiana Senator Huey Long, whom the Oklahoman described as "the greatest gob of human filth that ever made a decent tumblebug vomit up his meal." Radio Address of April 8, 1935, Percy L. Gassaway Collection, Western History Collections, University of Oklahoma, Norman, Oklahoma.

[10] July 6, 1934.

[11] July 12, 1934.

strongly for Pine, and although Murray did not take the stump himself, it was plain that the retiring administration wanted the defeat of the New Deal's advocate. Ross Rizley, the Republican state chairman, and Lew Wentz, the party's favorite son, orchestrated the GOP's attack on Marland and the entire Democratic ticket. Rizley tried without much success to identify the state Democrats with the federal patronage machine of Postmaster General James A. Farley, the Republicans' favorite bogeyman in the early stages of the New Deal. The *Tulsa World,* then cultivating Roosevelt's favor, correctly analyzed the basis of the Republican attack upon Marland as "largely actuated by a desire to disturb and discredit President Roosevelt." The paper accurately observed that "the Republican campaign in this state cannot be dissociated with malice toward the New Deal."[12]

With one party firm in its opposition to the national administration and the leading candidate of the other pledged to bring its benefits to the state, the election returns rolled in with predictable results. Marland won by a majority that was unprecedented up to that time, 365,992 to 243,841. Although Pine took the worst drubbing yet accorded a Republican gubernatorial nominee, he still ran 60,000 votes ahead of the remainder of his ticket. Everywhere, the Democratic victory was as nearly total as in 1932. Once again, the Democrats took every statewide office and every seat in the nine-member congressional delegation. They even improved on their earlier record performance in the state legislative races to win 111 of the 120 house seats and all but one in the state senate.[13] As leader of the ticket, E. W. Marland read in the victory a certain mandate: "The New Deal has come to Oklahoma. There's no other question. . . . I am going through with it, and those who object will be saved in spite of themselves."[14]

Ernest Whitworth Marland was sixty years old when he assumed the governorship in January, 1935.[15] A native of Pennsylvania, he was the son of moderately well-to-do parents who had him educated in private schools, the University of Pittsburgh, and the law school of the University of Michigan. Marland was a precocious student who earned his law degree at nineteen and passed his bar examination long before he was legally eligible to practice. After his twenty-first birthday, he joined a Pittsburgh firm specializing in mining litigation. The better to prepare himself for his legal duties, he also studied metallurgy and earth formations and, within a few years, was an acknowledged expert in the science of geology.

Gradually, he abandoned his first profession to give his full devotion to locating and developing oil deposits in West Virginia. After the Panic

[12]October 25, 1934.

[13]*Directory of Oklahoma, 1977,* pp. 562-63; Oliver L. Benson et al., *Oklahoma Votes, 1907-1962* (Norman: University of Oklahoma, Bureau of Government Research, 1964), p. 49.

[14]*Oklahoma News,* November 7, 1934.

[15]For biographical details, see Mathews, *Life and Death of an Oilman.*

of 1907 wrecked his first large-scale venture, he followed reports of soaring production in the Bartlesville, Red Fork, and Glenn Pool fields and moved west. Confident that the initial discoveries represented only a fraction of the petroleum reserves to be found in the new state, he began to explore north and west of the existing centers of production. Without financial resources of his own, he first prospected on the 101 Ranch, located about fifteen miles from his future home in Ponca City. Within four years, he and the investors who had the prescience to join him were reaping rich rewards from the new Cushing Field, and the Marland Oil Company had been born.

At its peak, the Marland empire reached into most of the United States and part of Mexico from its nerve center at the beautiful Marland estate in Ponca City. Its founder became rich and his philanthropies numerous: churches, hospitals, schools, and uncounted individuals knew him as their benefactor. But early in 1930 the $85 million empire collapsed, the victim, as Marland put it, of the "wolves of Wall Street"—the investment bankers who took control of the company and unceremoniously deposed its founder.[16] As the familiar green, triangular "Marland" signs were repainted to a red "Conoco," the man who had lost more than any Oklahoman turned his legendary humanitarianism—and new vengefulness—to politics. As the first Democrat ever to win election from the Eighth District, he helped launch the New Deal in Washington before returning to bring its promise to Oklahoma. In a brief preinaugural speech, Marland outlined the meaning of that promise:

We are coming to a new thought. It is the duty of government to provide every man able to work and willing to work with employment and to take care of those unable to work. . . . Every man in this state who wants to work can be put to work and we can take care of all the poor who cannot work. We can give everyone a decent living and a good home in which to rear a family.[17]

For all the splendor of his background and all the spaciousness of his vision, E. W. Marland soon proved one of the most disappointing public men in Oklahoma history. Almost immediately, his presumed mandate failed him, and the Marland administration came to grief. Despite his record majority and his humane sympathies, the governor was miscast as a political leader. Cold, aloof, quarrelsome, and incredibly naive, he was utterly unfit for the give and take of bruising statehouse politics. As governor, he sought to run the state as he would a corporation— a benevolent and farsighted executive who dispatched general commands, the specifics to be worked out by faithful employees who dared

---

[16] Marland's account of the collapse of his empire to the machinations of Wall Street was given voters as an effective campaign tract in his 1932 congressional race. See E. W. Marland, "My Experience with the Money Trust," copy in E. W. Marland Collection, Oklahoma State Archives, Oklahoma City, hereafter cited as Marland Collection.

[17] *Oklahoma News,* January 8, 1935.

Future Governor E. W. Marland as Ponca City's princely oilman. Courtesy Western History Collections, University of Oklahoma.

not question his wisdom. Perhaps only after his ruin would he come to realize that independent department heads and legislators were very much inclined to dispute his judgment and sabotage his designs, for they owed him neither their jobs nor their salaries.

Marland's failure to bring the New Deal to Oklahoma was caused by more than his own personal inadequacies. At every turn, his plans encountered insurmountable obstacles. Legislators refused to limit their own prerogatives to the higher cause of efficient state planning. Local officials declined to relinquish their powers to appointed experts in Oklahoma City or Washington. Grandiose schemes for expanded public welfare stumbled on the rock of fiscal crisis. At bottom, Oklahomans were psychologically unprepared for the swift transition of an agrarian, patronage-minded commonwealth to a social welfare state supporting vast new agencies and requiring a high degree of administrative skill.

Finally, the Marland dream crumbled before the realities of political power. Despite its recent impressive triumphs—perhaps, indeed, because of them—the Oklahoma Democratic party of the 1930s fitted almost exactly V. O. Key's classic definition of affairs in the one-party South. By the mid-1930s, the party was actually "a holding-company for a congeries of transient squabbling factions, . . . which fail by far to meet the standards of permanence, cohesiveness, and responsibility that characterize the [ideal of a] political party."[18] For Marland to have succeeded in bringing the New Deal to Oklahoma demanded that he do precisely what Franklin Roosevelt was doing on a larger scale: assert his authority over a broad-based but disciplined coalition of voting blocs committed to the pursuit of liberal goals.

The new governor was unable to appreciate the necessity for building such a constituency and unprepared to articulate the goals for dramatic action. But even if he had possessed the president's own political gifts and instincts, Marland would have failed. Oklahoma, like most states that vainly attempted their own "little New Deal" experiments in the 1930s, lacked a tradition of disciplined voter blocs, at least since the demise of the Farmer-Labor Reconstruction League. No urban political machines, no politically conscious ethnic communities, no powerful labor unions stood ready to train their followers in the systematic use of their ballots. The new groups called forth by the depression, e.g., the business lobby or the old-age pensioners, were most effective in obstruction or in embarrassing Marland's cause. At the polls, most Oklahomans cast their ballots on the basis of temporary emotions and fleeting preferences—a Bill Murray here, a Will Rogers there, and an E. W. Marland in 1934. Each would win an election, but none could claim a mandate. Because none could depend upon a constituency that was either permanent or cohesive, none could force party responsibility upon his fellow Democrats. In the end, the New Deal changed state

---

[18]V. O. Key, *Southern Politics in State and Nation* (New York: Random House, Vintage Books, 1949), p. 16.

politics, but the changes were forced by national necessity. Governor Marland became a mere bystander in unhappy attendance.

The clearest measure of Marland's failure was the fate of the comprehensive agenda that he laid before the Fifteenth Legislature.[19] The new governor implored the legislators to appropriate $5 million, immediately to be distributed by existing federal social workers to Oklahoma's 35,000 needy citizens ineligible for continued federal assistance. If relief was the imperative in crisis, Marland felt that state planning was needed for the long road to recovery. He proposed the creation of five new, professionally staffed agencies to coordinate the war on the depression. A planning board would survey the state's resources and oversee their efficient use and conservation. A housing board would build 115,000 subsistence homesteads for the needy and direct future construction. A flood control board, modeled on the New Deal's Tennessee Valley Authority, would supervise reclamation of depleted soil and build a network of dams for irrigation, power, and recreation. A new industries board would establish state-owned factories to process native products and supply the indigent with necessities. A highway board would disburse state and federal funds to inaugurate a massive public works program and restore one-third of the state's wage earners to productivity.

The price of Marland's proposals was breathtakingly expensive. The five proposed superboards would require an initial appropriation of $7.5 million. When that sum was added to his other requests, Marland was proposing a total state outlay of $35 million. Moreover, that budget would be for a single year, because the governor promised additional recommendations after the completion of a report by the Brookings Institution on the modernization of Oklahoma government.[20] That the previous legislature had spent the state $4 million deeper into debt while struggling with a *two-year* budget of only $21 million underscored the magnitude of Marland's ambitions.

To help meet those newly assumed obligations, Marland also urged a comprehensive series of new taxes that featured new levies on the petroleum industry: severance taxes on crude oil, natural gas, and gasoline, along with an increased gross production tax. Oilmen would not be alone in bearing the cost of this vast expansion in state services. The new governor also recommended tripling the one-cent sales tax to finance his relief proposals. A battery of emergency taxes would also tap insurance premiums, inheritances, cigarette sales, salaries, and rental income.

[19] The following paragraphs are taken from *Governor Marland's First Message to the Fifteenth Legislature, January 15, 1935,* copy in Oklahoma Governors Collection, Oklahoma State Archives, Oklahoma City.

[20] Prior to his inauguration, Marland had privately commissioned the Brookings Institution to compile a report on the operations of Oklahoma government with recommendations for their thorough overhaul. *The Report on a Survey of Organization and Administration of Oklahoma* was finally issued in mid-1935. The 483-page text was a thoughtful analysis of state and county government, including a battery of proposals for their improved operation. The proposals, like the *Report* itself, were conspicuously ignored by all save a few political scientists and, later, historians.

No governor had ever demanded such thoroughgoing changes, but none had ever been elected with such a commanding majority. Yet, only a week after the inaugural, the veteran correspondent Lee Hills was writing in the *Oklahoma News,* "One week out at sea, the Marland Ship of State is rolling in rough legislative waters, with motors idling."[21] In short order, the Marland motors were silenced and his ship scuttled.

As Marland's momentary majority dissolved, a frightened and determined business community, from which the necessary tax increases must come, rose in powerful indignation. The Mid-Continent Oil and Gas Association, the state's oil lobby, hurled its considerable weight against the gross production and severance tax proposals. Similarly, the insurance interests and the state's chambers of commerce, the latter organized under the name of Associated Industries, lined up opposition to the gross premium and income tax increases. The Oklahoma Retail Merchants, representing the state's small businessmen, bitterly resisted an increase in the state sales tax. Indeed, that group took the offensive and fired a barrage of publicity directed at eliminating the existing one-cent rate.[22]

All these interests found their champion in the person of the contentious speaker, Leon C. ("Red") Phillips. A powerfully built, humorless, and conservative representative from Okemah, Phillips quickly emerged as the governor's most formidable critic. With his conservative allies, Phillips threw up an impassable roadblock in the lower chamber. While the inexperienced governor napped, Phillips and his supporters altered the house rules to give the Rules Committee (headed by the speaker and packed with his allies) arbitrary control over the house calendar. Infinitely better suited to legislative infighting than the lordly governor, Philips used that power to consolidate his position as the strongest figure in the capitol.[23] Without the new forms of revenue, the administration's visionary plans would come to nothing. Red Phillips and his allies, both within and without the legislature, made sure that there would be no dramatic tax increases. The fate of the Marland utopia was decided then and there.

For the first few weeks, Phillips and Marland sparred for power, and the speaker won every skirmish, dismantling the governor's proposals one by one. By the second month of the session, Phillips was able to launch his own counteroffensive. Promising to balance the budget, the speaker moved to slash appropriations by a third of their existing level, oblivious to the governor's barely remembered recommendations. Damning Marland's superboards with his contempt, the speaker brusquely explained that: "If the revenue is available for the extra things, we shall adopt such parts as are practicable. . . . The present House of Representatives is progressive enough to care for the needs of the destitute . . . and

[21] January 23, 1935.

[22] Cecil L. Turner, "Oklahoma's New Deal: Program and Reaction" (M.A. thesis, University of Oklahoma, 1963), pp. 26–28; *Oklahoma News,* April 21, 1935.

[23] *Oklahoma News,* January 13, 1935.

Still dignified but no longer happy, Governor Marland watched his "Little New Deal" go down in legislative flames. Courtesy Western History Collections, University of Oklahoma.

conservative enough to save the people from the hallucinations of the dreamers."[24]

By the legislature's adjournment, the state's chief dreamer had been awakened to the realities of political power. The proposed five executive boards had been reduced to the most innocuous two. Only a limited flood control measure with a weak supervisory board, along with a hollow state planning board, won final approval; their combined annual appropriations were only 12 percent of Marland's original requests. One-sided compromises had reduced most of the governor's tax proposals by half — no increase over the old rates in most instances. The major exceptions, like the new cigarette tax, fell safely on consumers.[25] The appropriation for relief was 75 percent under Marland's recommendation; in fact, it fell short of matching available funds under the Federal Emergency Relief Administration (FERA). Over-all, appropriations were barely 60 percent of the governor's initial request. Once the Marland program was decently buried, the legislators turned their energies to spectacular investigations of the Banking Commission and the School Land Commission, coming just short of impeaching three state officials before exhaustion set in.[26]

Although its output bore little resemblance to the original Marland program, the 1935 session was not altogether unproductive. Where the governor's self-presumed mandate had failed, necessity often moved even the least liberal to accept new responsibilities in the midst of depression. For example, the precipitous drop in local property tax receipts compelled a record biennial appropriation of $16.4 million to the common schools, the first step toward the state's replacing local school boards as the dominant agency in public education. Similarly, the unprecedented $2.5 million biennial relief appropriation drew the state ever closer to enlarging and assuming the welfare obligations of the financially strapped counties. Marland's liberal mandate was unavailing. So was the rigid orthodoxy of the economy bloc.

Necessity compelled other changes as well. Federal law required the creation of minimal state planning authorities as a condition for receiving vital grants from the FERA. The Oklahoma State Planning Board, only advisory and underfinanced, was the result. It was only a faint version of Marland's original idea, but it was also an example of the lure of federal money in establishing state foundations for future economic planning.

Marland's one undisputed achievement was likewise the child of necessity. At the time of Marland's election, industrial chaos and uncontrolled production had brought the oil industry to its knees and state militiamen

[24] *Harlow's Weekly,* February 16, 1935.
[25] Ibid., May 4, 1935.
[26] State of Oklahoma, Legislature, House of Representatives, *Journal,* 15th Leg., reg. sess., April 29, 1935, pp. 2:3745-48.

to its fields. The specter of drastic federal regulation hung over the industry. Marland found a ready audience when he took the lead in seeking a common solution with the executives of the other oil-producing states. Four of those states, led by Oklahoma, signed the "Treaty of Dallas" in February, 1935, establishing the Interstate Oil and Gas Compact, with Governor Marland its first chairman. Approved by Congress and the president within a year, the compact grew to include eighteen states (including all of the oil-producing states except California) by 1945. The oil compact's commission promoted standard legislation and the coordination of state allowables to fit production to predictable market demands. Although state compliance was not mandatory, the commission's influence was bolstered by the certainty of harsh federal action should the arrangement fail. Oilmen quickly perceived the advantages of that rational system over the individualistic chaos they had exploited for temporary advantage at the certain risk of their ultimate common ruin. The first such interstate agreement, the oil compact soon became a model for similar industrial and state planning arrangements.[27]

Within the state, the impasse that had blocked Marland's program in the legislature made it certain that late 1935 would bring a torrent of attempts at direct legislation. Six state questions appeared on the special election ballot of September 24, 1935.[28] Two of them—the perennial proposal to open the executive offices to women and a reorganization of the School Land Commission—were fairly routine. The others represented a new theater in the continuing war between Marland and the legislative leadership, for listed on the ballot were rival forms of two unquestionably popular issues. When the governor had extended his endorsement to an initiative petition for homestead exemption from property taxes, the legislature had responded with its own, more conservative, referendum. The chief difference was that the legislative version would exclude tax exemption from existing school levies, while the governor's option would permit it. An even clearer difference was apparent in the two versions offered for old-age pensions. The Marland proposal was considerably more generous, both in coverage and the level of benefits.[29] For example, the governor's plan made eligible all elderly citizens who had been residents of the state for any five of the previous ten years and lacked "a reasonable subsistence compatible with decency and health." The hastily prepared legislative alternative limited eligibility to the elderly (defined as five years older than Marland's minimum) who had resided continu-

---

[27] The most convenient summary of the background and significance of the oil compact is in George B. Tindall, *The Emergence of the New South, 1913-1945,* History of the South, vol. 10 (Baton Rouge: Louisiana State University Press, 1967), pp. 433-72, especially pp. 438-40.

[28] A thorough treatment is William S. Harmon's "Oklahoma's Constitutional Amendments: A Study of the Use of the Initiative and Referendum" (Ph.D. diss., University of Oklahoma, 1951), pp. 44-47.

[29] Identified with the governor, the proposal's impetus had come from Ira Finley and his "Veterans of Industry."

ously in the state for the past fifteen years and received less than $350 annual income. Similarly, while the legislators' version was silent on financing (giving the governor's allies a chance to accuse them of "offering the old people an empty sack"), the Marland initiative specified funding by heavy levies on gross business income.

The governor's pension proposal drew the greatest fire. The conservative press and his legislative critics assailed the proposal, and the Associated Industries used delaying tactics, especially challenging the sufficiency of signatures on the pension initiative. Although the petition contained 180,364 signatures (twice the number necessary for a place on the ballot), the desperate businessmen found a valuable ally in Secretary of State Frank Carter, the official whose ministerial function included the heretofore routine certification of petitions. Deliberately, Carter dragged out the process by constant delay in hearings on every conceivable technical point. Only seven days before the scheduled special election, Marland, ignoring the endless hearings, asserted gubernatorial prerogative to order the question placed on the ballot.[30]

In a direct test of the governor's and the legislature's popular support, Marland emerged the easy victor. Voters rejected the legislative form of homestead exemption in favor of a two-to-one approval of the governor's more generous option. Similarly, they overwhelmingly repudiated the legislature's version of old-age pensions in favor of the Marland initiative, which passed with a crushing majority of 204,626 to 78,783.[31] The governor's victory proved to be short-lived, however. Responding to a suit filed by Associated Industries, the state supreme court swiftly overturned the election results by voiding the pensions election, holding that Marland had exceeded his constitutional authority in bypassing the obstructionist secretary of state.[32]

It was another year before pensions became a reality in Oklahoma, and then the credit was not Marland's. Again, it belonged to the federal government. The national Social Security Act of 1935 held out the lure of federal matching grants to the states for welfare payments, but on the condition that each state establish a central agency to administer the state-federal payments to the elderly, as well as to needy dependent children and to the blind. In creating the State Department of Welfare, Oklahoma merely accepted the minimal demands of that federal law. Where the state was allowed flexibility, in setting benefit levels and providing for its share of the financing, it revealed the limits of its new commitment. Recipients were allowed a maximum of thirty dollars a month, a sum that had to include all other sources of income and that could not be increased even if the federal contribution should exceed thirty dollars. Financing was linked to the regressive sales tax, which

---

[30] Harmon, "Oklahoma's Constitutional Amendments," pp. 50–51.

[31] *Directory of Oklahoma, 1977,* pp. 644–65.

[32] *Associated Industries* v. *Oklahoma Tax Commission,* 176 Okla. 120 (1936); Harmon, "Oklahoma's Constitutional Amendments," pp.. 54–55.

was doubled (to two cents) and earmarked for the new welfare department.[33]

Approved by voters as a constitutional amendment at the 1936 primary elections,[34] the new welfare measure suggested the state's reluctant
acceptance of new responsibilities. Other results of the same elections
also reflected Oklahoma's ambiguous response to the depression and the
New Deal.

Thomas Pryor Gore's seat in the United States Senate was the main
attraction in the 1936 primary. The old progressive's ingrained distrust
of power, whether in the hands of corporations or of the federal government, had turned him into a bitter foe of what he took to be the dangerous
unconstitutional usurpations of Franklin Roosevelt's New Deal. By 1936,
Gore, the old agrarian reformer, clearly occupied the conservative ground
of the Democratic party.[35]

Three candidates vied for the open space to Gore's left. Governor
Marland, defying the tradition that the state executive does not yield
the office to which he has been elected, relied on the state party organization to reproduce his triumph of 1934, which had been the work of
amateurs. Once more, Marland unfurled the banner of loyalty to President Roosevelt. Fifth District Congressman Josh Lee asserted the same
claim, and his own complete identification with the president could not
be disputed. Arguing his absolute loyalty to Roosevelt, Lee was invading
Marland's preserve. Unlike the governor, he was not embarrassed by an
awkward record of attempting to imitate the New Deal in state government. Gomer Smith stood conspicuously to the left of both challengers.
Smith had first sought a Senate seat in 1932, embracing the pension issue
before losing the nomination in a runoff with Elmer Thomas. Four years
later, he appeared to have been a prophet. By then, he had also risen
to the vice-presidency of the nationwide Townsend Clubs, the group that
agitated on behalf of Dr. Francis Townsend's scheme of granting every
old person $200 monthly. Easily the most radical candidate of the four,
Smith entertained the electorate with rabble-rousing assaults upon entrenched wealth and appealed to the downtrodden from that new and
noisy campaign weapon, the sound truck.[36]

Because preelection polls registered a heavy voter preference for the

[33] Harmon, "Oklahoma's Constitutional Amendments," pp. 61-62. See also *Fourth Annual Report of the Oklahoma Department of Welfare*, copy in Clayton H. Hyde Collection, Western History Collections, University of Oklahoma, Norman, Oklahoma, for a
comprehensive survey of the evolution of the state's welfare system.

[34] The margin of approval (340,438 to 229,542) was much smaller than for the more
generous but invalidated Marland initiative of the previous year. *Directory of Oklahoma,
1977*, p. 646.

[35] For Gore's growing opposition to the Roosevelt administration, see Monroe Lee
Billington, *Thomas P. Gore: The Blind Senator from Oklahoma* (Lawrence: University
of Kansas Press, 1967), pp. 159-75.

[36] The senatorial contest is discussed ibid., pp. 175-78, and in Royden J. Dangerfield
and Richard H. Flynn, "Voter Motivation in the 1936 Oklahoma Democratic Primary,"
Southwestern Social Science Quarterly 27 (1936):97-99.

president,[37] Gore's best hope rested upon a division of the liberal vote. That apparently realistic possibility proved to be impossible, for the election turned less on issues than on personality. A new political star was in the ascendancy, and Josh Lee, with his polished speech-making and smoothly efficient organization, was that star. In a campaign surprisingly free of the personal abuse that usually characterized primary stump speaking, Lee put on a dazzling performance. His promises were generous: "A Farm for Every Farmer, and a Home for Every Family." His practiced wit never deserted him as he glad-handed his way across the state, ignoring his opponents and slashing the "Old Deal" Republicans. In the first primary, Lee took a tremendous lead, surprising the most seasoned forecasters, to win 168,030 votes. Governor Marland barely qualified for a runoff; his 121,433 ballots were far behind Lee's total and only 1,848 ahead of Gomer Smith's. Thomas Gore paid for his apostasy in opposing Roosevelt in 1936 as he had for opposing Wilson in 1920. His 91,581 votes left him dead last. Too proud to follow Tom Anglin's sensible example of 1934, Marland doggedly continued the contest through to the bitter end, and Lee won the runoff election convincingly, 301,259 to 186,899.[38]

Gore's dismal performance revealed the folly of opposition to Roosevelt's New Deal at the crest of its popularity. The more specific lessons of the dramatic Senate primary were less certain. Political scientists comparing the election returns discovered that, of the four contenders, only Gore, the conservative, appeared to have drawn his support from identifiable voting blocs, in particular, the urban, propertied, and high-income sectors of the electorate. If a recognizable constituency for conservatism was already evident, however, nothing of the kind was apparent for the three more liberal contenders. Neither Marland, Lee, nor Smith had established a firm base with any identifiable social or economic group. In each case, voters had apparently decided, not from the substance of social or economic interests but out of preference for their personal styles—Marland's ingrained dignity, Lee's steady charm, or Smith's calculated inurbanity.[39]

In view of Gore's fate, Democrats of every stripe were moved to proclaim their devotion to the president in the 1936 general election. The lone prominent exception was Alfalfa Bill Murray, who warmly introduced Alf Landon on the Republican's campaign tour.[40] Most of

---

[37] A Gallup poll of November, 1935, identified Oklahoma as a "Definitely Democratic State" in any election involving Roosevelt. A follow-up poll in January, 1936, showed 60 percent of the state's voters supporting the president against any challenger. George H. Gallup, ed., *The Gallup Poll: Public Opinion, 1935-1971*, 3 vols. (New York: Random House, 1972), 1:3, 11.

[38] *Directory of Oklahoma, 1977*, p. 563.

[39] Royden and Flynn, "Voter Motivation," pp. 98-100.

[40] Though not a candidate himself, Murray eagerly enlisted in what he described as a crusade for "Liberty, law and Landon opposed to Russian red revolution." Keith L. Bryant, *Alfalfa Bill Murray* (Norman: University of Oklahoma Press, 1968), pp. 258-59.

the campaign noise was furnished by the Republicans and three of the state's major dailies. The *Daily Oklahoman,* the *Oklahoma City Times,* and the *Tulsa Tribune* submitted the president to scathing attacks, although he retained the support of the *Tulsa World* and the qualified endorsement of the Scripps-Howard *Oklahoma News.* As far as the local ticket went, the anti-Roosevelt forces were decidedly outclassed. Josh Lee, crisscrossing the state a dozen times in his punishing itinerary, streamed the Roosevelt banner wherever he spoke. Senatorial nominee Herbert K. Hyde, a rabidly anti-New Deal Oklahoma City lawyer, headed the weakest Republican ticket since statehood. The staple content of the GOP attack in four successive presidential elections became something of a compendium of Hyde's 1936 speeches, which charged the Roosevelt regime with dictatorship, regimentation, bureaucracy, communism, vote buying, suicidal spending, waste, and corruption[41] — words that swiftly became Republican cliches to be parodied and ridiculed by Democratic funmakers in the succeeding decade. In 1936, as later, the very extravagance of the Republican indictments probably reacted in the president's favor.

Although Roosevelt could not equal his smashing state triumph of 1932, his 1936 margin over Landon was convincing enough. The president carried every Oklahoma county except Major in beating Landon by more than two to one. The Democratic sweep touched every corner of the state and nearly every public office. The house returned only three Republicans to 114 Democrats, and the state senate became unanimously Democratic for the first and only time in its history. Nearly as popular as the president himself was the state's new junior senator, Josh Lee, who crushed Hyde with a 264,000-vote majority, the largest yet received by an Oklahoman.[42]

Joshua Bryan Lee — as a boy he had supplied his own middle name after hearing the Great Commoner — was born at Childerburg, Alabama, in 1892, the son of a country doctor with the unimpeachable Democratic name of Thomas Jefferson Lee. The family moved to Greer County, near Rocky, in the late territorial days, where the youthful Lee first tried his unusual talents as a public speaker and rural schoolteacher. While a student at the University of Oklahoma, he won a national oratorical contest and, upon receiving his degree in 1917, joined the faculty as an instructor in speech. Two years later, he was head of the department.

Politics remained the unsatisfied interest of the young professor, and in 1924 he took a master's degree in political science from Columbia University, followed by a law degree from Cumberland University in 1925. Back home, he became the state's most popular after-dinner speaker, and his wide acquaintance among educational, religious, and fraternal groups was underestimated by the professional politicians who dismissed the "elocution professor" contemptuously when he decided to file for

[41] *Oklahoma City Daily Oklahoman,* October 1-November 2, 1936.
[42] *Directory of Oklahoma, 1977,* pp. 565-66; Benson et al., *Oklahoma Votes,* p. 49.

Oklahoma's New Deal senators with the state's first senators; Josh Lee, Thomas Gore, Robert L. Owen, and Elmer Thomas. Courtesy Western History Collections, University of Oklahoma.

Congress in 1934. Throughout his house term and the Senate term that followed the 1936 landslide, Lee followed Roosevelt without deviation and demanded that his party colleagues do the same.

By the time of his startling senatorial victory, Lee had built up an effective organization of his former students. The so-called "Rover Boys," young men of the depression generation, would soon be harvesting the rewards of power. Alfred Murrah, Luther Bohanon, and Royce Savage engineered Lee's senatorial triumph, and the Young Democrats organization, never very useful in the scheme of party government, became an adjunct of his Washington office. The aggressive methods of his subordinates in distributing federal patronage, especially their tendency to bypass old-line politicians, earned the orator many enemies and the abiding hatred of the metropolitan press.

Among the major cities' dailies, neither Roosevelt nor the New Deal had many friends by 1936. E. K. Gaylord's *Daily Oklahoman* and *Oklahoma City Times* continued to describe themselves as Democratic newspapers, but they featured the most virulent anti-New Deal opinion. Similarly, the *Tulsa Tribune,* under the able editorship of the Wisconsin Republican, Richard Lloyd Jones, preferred to think of itself as independent, but its Republican sympathies were plain. No Democrat since Jack

Walton in 1922—the same Jack Walton who later imposed military censorship on its pages—had earned the *Tribune's* endorsement. Only the *Tulsa World* was staunchly pro-New Deal in 1936, and its publisher, Eugene Lorton, made a permanent break with the national administration the next year.

Despite the stout conservatism of the state's major newspapers, the acclaim of Oklahoma voters for the president and his party could not be denied. Neither could it be translated into success for Marland and his "little New Deal." Still smarting from the personal rebuke delivered in his Senate race, the governor was able to claim only one real victory after 1936, when the Democratic caucus narrowly ousted Red Phillips as house speaker for the Sixteenth Legislature. Marland's plans for a Sooner New Deal got nowhere. The legislators who repudiated the leadership of Phillips rejected that of Marland as well. Thereafter, real power lay with the powerful chairmen who commanded the assembly's major committees. The inept Marland, his pathetic messages to the legislature routinely ignored, was reduced to the status of the state's chief clerk.[43]

Two matters required the convening of a special legislative session three weeks after the general election. The state faced a deadline of January 1, 1937, to establish an unemployment insurance program that would make Oklahoma eligible to receive federal grants under the Social Security Act of 1935. The simple expedient was the adoption of a model state bill the New Deal had handed down from Washington. Implementation of the recently approved homestead exemption measure required more effort. After a series of compromises, the legislature finally agreed to exempt the first $1,000 of home assessments from property taxes. It was a generous and popular move, except to local governments and school districts, which thereby stood to lose an estimated $2,394,877 in sorely needed tax collections in the first year alone.[44]

The legislature's generosity continued unabated during the regular session. To offset the decline in county and school revenue, the lawmakers appropriated massive amounts of state aid, including $7.6 million for emergency relief and $25.6 million for the common schools. The educational appropriation alone equaled the entire state budget of only four years earlier, and it was clear that such unprecedented money bills would earn the 1937 session the eternal label, the "Spending Sixteenth." The major revenue act was the expansion of the recently doubled sales tax to include, for the first time, food and other items of universal consumption. The one exception was the purchase of petroleum products. The legislature chose to enlarge the regressive sales tax rather than increase gross production taxes on the ever attentive oil and gas interests.[45]

The oil and gas lobby was not the only pressure group to win the legis-

---

[43] Mathews, *Life and Death of an Oilman,* pp. 251-52; Legislative Messages File, Marland Collection.

[44] Turner, "Oklahoma's New Deal," pp. 64-70.

[45] Ibid., pp. 76-84.

lature's attention. After years of struggle, the organized medical profession finally won its battle to close the low-cost hospital at Elk City with legislation that ended the cooperative threat to physicians' incomes. The Retail Merchants Association barely lost the fight to end the competition of chain stores by taxing them out of existence; but it did win the alternative—price-fixing in the guise of a fair-trade law.[46]

Amidst the barest pretense of executive leadership, the legislators also were able to turn policy to their own narrow political interests. The most revealing example involved the fate of the massive emergency relief appropriation. Bypassing the new state department of welfare, the legislative leaders insisted that the money, which was matched by federal grants, be turned over to their loyal allies on the patronage-ridden and notoriously inefficient county welfare boards. Within a year, the distribution of welfare funds, including the federal contribution, became a national scandal. Federal investigators discovered that no fewer than 20,766 of the 69,222 citizens receiving pensions as needy old people were ineligible, many because they were not needy, others because they were not old. In most counties, administration was shaped by local political interests, never anxious to turn down a worthy voter or party worker. In three counties, the consequent roll-padding was so excessive that the number of "needy" recipients of old-age pensions was actually greater than the county's total elderly population in all income brackets. The legislators feigned great indignation at the "intervention" of the "sorority sob sisters"—as they derisively called professionally trained federal social workers—and raged at the prospect that university graduates would replace loyal partisans back home. All passion spent, the legislature eventually bowed to federal accounting and personnel standards only after the temporary suspension of all federal relief funds to Oklahoma by an appalled Social Security Administration.[47]

The highway building program thereupon became the richest patronage lode to be mined when the senate took control of the Highway Commission from the fumbling governor. Looking to the creation of thousands of "make work" jobs to be distributed through traditional channels of patronage, the legislature approved a $35 million road bond issue pushed by Senate President Pro Tempore Al Nichols of Wewoka. It was stopped only by the state supreme court's ruling it improper, as it clearly was, since the measure would have obligated the state without a vote of the people—an unconstitutional, if fully understandable, omission.[48]

---

[46] Ibid., pp. 100-106.

[47] *Harlow's Weekly*, February 12, 1938; Buelah Elizabeth Amidon, "Sooners in Security: What is Happening in Oklahoma," *Survey Graphic*, April, 1938, pp. 203-207. The sweeping federal indictment of the corrupt distribution is available in "Transcript of Hearings Before the Social Security Board," copy in Clayton H. Hyde Collection, Western History Collections, University of Oklahoma, Norman, Oklahoma.

[48] *Boswell* v. *State et al.*, 181 Okla. 435 (1937). The bond issue was invalidated under the constitutional prohibition of debts in excess of $600,000 without a popular vote. The

Without including the road bond issue and the earmarked taxes, the Spending Sixteenth fully earned its name with biennial appropriations that totaled nearly $64 million, triple the state budget when Marland had first taken office and nearly $40 million greater than projected tax collections for the next two years.[49] It was that record of extravagance that forever destroyed the hapless Marland's reputation. To be sure, the legislature's deeds had been well beyond his control. It was also the record that became the immediate springboard for a conservative counterattack. The *Tulsa Tribune,* ever ready to take up arms against New Deal extravagance, was not alone in thinking the Sixteenth Legislature "the worst in the history of the state." Even the moderate *Oklahoma News* expressed shame and shock at the "legislative chiselers and manipulators who have made a farce of representative government."[50]

To its credit, the legislature had something to show for its generosity. The Marland administration ended the fruitless obstructionism of the Murray regime. It allowed thousands of Oklahomans some relief by taking part in the Civilian Conservation Corps (CCC) camps and Works Progress Administration (WPA) projects in every county. Such landmark programs as unemployment compensation and public welfare were adopted and placed within the structure of government. Planning had become a visible duty of the state, embodied (after a 1937 reorganization) in the State Planning and Resources Board.[51] Meanwhile, the state's responsibility for what had always been purely local obligations was now accepted—in welfare, in education, and, after the creation of the highway patrol in 1937, in law enforcement.[52]

On the other side, it was equally clear that Marland's bright promise of bringing the New Deal to Oklahoma had gone the way of the defunct Marland Oil Company. As often as not the most important changes of the past four years had been determined in Washington, not Oklahoma City, and sent to the state as gifts wrapped in federal regulations. The state's new roles were often unavoidable, usually reluctant, and always minimal.

Politically, the state's dominant party was more amorphous than ever. None could gainsay Oklahomans' devotion to the president, but within the state, no one—not the inept Marland, not even Josh Lee—had been able to fashion a permanent coalition of liberal support. Gore's defeat

---

legislature's argument that the $35 million bond issue technically was not a "debt" was rejected, five to four. The issue is discussed in Turner, "Oklahoma's New Deal," pp. 89-93.

[49] Untitled typescript, Leon C. Phillips Collection, Western History Collections, University of Oklahoma, Norman, Oklahoma.

[50] *Tulsa Tribune,* May 10, 1937; *Oklahoma News,* May 9, 1937.

[51] The reorganization combined the earlier State Planning Board with the existing Conservation Commission and State Forestry and Parks Department with an initial operating budget of $600,000. Turner, "Oklahoma's New Deal," pp. 94-96.

[52] Bob L. Blackburn, "Law Enforcement in Transition: From Decentralized County Sheriffs to the Highway Patrol," *Chronicles of Oklahoma* 56 (1978):194-207.

demonstrated to alarmed conservatives the hazard of outright assault upon the hallowed FDR, but events also suggested the potential of a more circumspect counterattack on extravagance and experimentation. The counterattack would be directed at an urban, propertied audience of business and professional people who had grown suspicious of the New Deal.

The performance of the Sixteenth Legislature made conservative counterreformation all the more possible. A militant metropolitan press stood ready to trumpet its advance. In the person of the governor's foremost critic, sullen Red Phillips, the cause had a likely champion. In fact, it was his one victory against the spenders of the 1937 legislature that gave them their certain opportunity. Phillips and his minority "economy bloc" had won repeal of the runoff primary. That change would allow a sufficiently determined minority to win Democratic nomination and, all but inevitably, election in 1938.

CHAPTER 11

To the Right, March! Leon C. Phillips and Conservative Reaction

T HE high promise offered by Governor E. W. Marland at the beginning of his administration had faded into despair and disillusionment before his term was half ended. By the end of the second biennium, an attitude of cynicism pervaded public life, while a carefree legislature mortgaged the state to indulge favored departments and contractors. Weak leadership in the executive branch, coupled with the indifference of too many legislators, hastened the state along the road to bankruptcy. Except for the stout assistance of the national government, Oklahoma would have suffered even more. The depression had scarcely been eased when the severe downturn of 1937-38 threatened further disasters. A near breakdown in essential state services resulted.

In this dreary impasse, the people demanded a strong governor, untainted by association with the discredited officials. The Republican party, never nearer total annihilation than it had been in 1936, was in no shape to provide it. Indeed, by 1938, Republicans seriously considered the formal abolition of their party in favor of a "grass-roots" coalition of all anti-New Dealers.[1] Even though the party eventually agreed to go through the motions of formal participation, its weakness was accurately measured in the choice of its gubernatorial nominee, Ross Rizley of Guymon.[2] The veteran of a single state senate term under Murray,

[1] *Harlow's Weekly,* March 26, 1938.

[2] The voters' disinterest in the GOP was indicated by the poor primary turnout of 52,548. That figure represented a drop of 26 percent from the average level of Republican primary participation in the three previous gubernatorial primaries. State of Oklahoma, State Election Board, *Directory of Oklahoma, 1977,* pp. 547, 554, 561, 569.

Rizley was the originator of the forlorn idea of disbandment. His candidacy was doomed to inevitable defeat, the certain sacrifice to whoever emerged from the large field of Democratic aspirants.

Understandably, the Democratic primary became the supreme test in 1938. It registered new highs of political interest, gauged by the number of voters (590,695) and the number of candidates for state jobs (1,007). For the fifth successive time, the primary fell in a year of industrial and agricultural depression, with its attendant cycles of hope and misery, promises and disappointments. State government was reeling under a debt mounting at the rate of $21 million a year.

For all the hazards of statesmanship, many formidable contenders joined the Democrats' gubernatorial primary, and most of them met the seemingly hopeless situation almost jauntily. Former governor and incumbent Corporation Commissioner Jack Walton, still undaunted by his 1923 impeachment and subsequent failures, entered in January. Ira M. Finley, a three-term veteran of the state legislature, former head of the State Federation of Labor, and, since 1932, champion of the pensioners, did likewise. State Treasurer Hubert Bolen, trusted adviser to many a governor and senator, entered in the same month, along with former House Speaker Leon C. Phillips and William S. Key, past adjutant-general, warden of the State Penitentiary at McAlester, and state administrator of the Works Progress Administration.

One final contender had already entered his well-remembered name a full year before the general election. William H. Murray, constitutionally ineligible to succeed himself in 1934, had announced his return to the political wars in the resurrected *Blue Valley Farmer* of November 19, 1937. Against a badly divided opposition, Murray seemed to have an excellent chance to return to the governor's mansion. He was the best known living Oklahoman, still popular with farmers because of the tax relief credited to his administration, attractive to anti-New Dealers for his opposition to the New Deal, and the idol of the courthouse lawn debating societies, which admired his contrariness. When the runoff primary had been eliminated in 1937, no one had foreseen the likelihood of yet another Murray comeback. By 1938, however, that prospect emerged in the belief held by many voters that the state needed an executive who would not yield his prerogatives to the legislature. A hasty attempt to force a return to the double primary failed. An effort to enlist another candidate of the same name in the governor's race deliberately to befuddle Murray's legions was abandoned after the old veteran countered with a demand that he be identified on the ballot as "Former Governor William H. 'Alfalfa Bill' Murray."

As irascible as ever, Murray ran a typically vigorous campaign. Although he kept his habit of ignoring national matters to lecture his audiences on purely state issues, there was no doubt that his candidacy had national overtones: he was the state's most prominent critic of the New Deal. It appeared that many state Republicans, as well as anti-Roosevelt Democrats, were contributing heavily to his cause, for the

Blue Valley Farmer went to 350,000 boxholders. Admittedly, Murray was handicapped by the rigidity of his mind and his refusal to compromise the principles fixed by decades of political observation and practice. The constitution-maker, now sixty-eight years old, had lost none of his fire, and his campaign accentuated the eccentricities that had earned him a dubious fame during his term as governor. Nonetheless, the large field and the absence of a second primary made Murray the leading contender as late as six weeks before the preferential voting, when the straw polls agreed on his likely nomination.[3]

Of the anti-Murray candidates, General William S. Key had the upper hand, at least in the campaign's early stages. The personable Wewokan was both the New Deal's firmest advocate and its most obvious beneficiary. Senator Lee's "Rover Boys," his old allies from the national guard, and his fellow federal officeholders could deliver a sizable vote, and all were prominent in Key's camp. Moreover, as the state's first WPA administrator, he could expect the support of thousands of voters, their numbers approaching a majority in some counties, who were grateful for the sustenance given them by the New Deal through the worst years of the depression. Drys and churchmen also rallied to his standard, and, except in Tulsa and Oklahoma City, he enjoyed a favorable reception from the state's press. From a well-organized headquarters, staffed by seasoned political professionals, Key launched a campaign marked by a systematic approach to the issues, remarkably free from the personal vituperation indulged in by other contenders.

Predictably, the most vituperative among them was Jack Walton. Unable to use the Ku Klux Klan as a whipping boy, Walton began the campaign as the leader of the pack demanding increases in relief checks and old-age pensions, increases that would amount to $24 million, magically administered without snooping social workers. Ora Fox, president of the Old-Age Pension Association (and a Walton appointee to the Corporation Commission) endorsed the deposed governor, as did "Cyclone" Patterson, a dynamic agitator and publisher of the *Security Age*.[4] A strong, radical showing in Walton's behalf was conceivable. But the entry of Ira Finley, who was second to none in his ardor for pensions, badly cut into Walton's new preserve and doomed the former governor's chances. The radical vote, unstable at best since Walton's victory of sixteen years earlier, scattered in the frenzied campaign.

In the end, Walton joined a number of less colorful contenders as a spectator in what became a three-cornered contest, as former house speaker Phillips, Murray, and General Key emerged as front-runners. The big, red-haired Phillips had been the most powerful speaker since Murray presided over the house in the First Legislature. Ousted from that capacity by the ill-fated Sixteenth Legislature, Phillips had earnestly sought a federal judgeship in 1937, only to see Senator Josh Lee inter-

---

[3] *Harlow's Weekly,* May 28, 1938.
[4] Ibid., April 2, 1938.

vene to ruin his chances.[5] Phillips had then thrown his considerable weight (all three hundred pounds of it) into the race for governor. Murray dismissed the former speaker's chances on the grounds that Alfalfa Bill's pseudoscientific study of the relationship between mental and physical attributes proved that Phillips "had too much avoirdupois and suet to be a deep thinker."[6] Phillips's opposition to the Marland administration had been legendary; in fact, it was likely his greatest campaign asset. His was also the best-financed campaign; E. W. Smartt, secretary of the Retail Merchants' Association, rallied the commercial interests, and Robert S. Kerr, president of the Mid-Continent Oil and Gas Producers' Association, handled the money. Literally hundreds of thousands of his campaign folders blanketed the state, while probably a majority of his old legislative colleagues rushed to climb aboard his bandwagon. They were joined by a relative latecomer but vital ally, Dr. Henry G. Bennett, the politically active president of Oklahoma A. and M. College. Bennett's influence with the state's agricultural institutions and the federal farm agents and crop control supervisors was no small factor in any candidate's calculations, and in 1938 that influence was solidly behind Red Phillips.

Although Phillips was the leading critic of Marland's aborted "little New Deal," his legislative record had included a number of quiet votes in labor's behalf, and he also won the support of several American Federation of Labor locals in his gubernatorial bid. Moreover, he never neglected to proclaim his loyalty to the president and the national administration. A dedicated foe of Marland's spurious New Deal in Oklahoma City, Phillips repeatedly affirmed his loyalty to Roosevelt's version in Washington.[7]

While selecting a new governor, Oklahoma voters would also choose a United States senator in 1938. As in the gubernatorial race, the Republicans all but gave up the ghost. In fact, they came close to nominating one when they named the unheralded Harry O. Glasser as their latest senatorial sacrifice. Again, the real choice was made in the Democratic primary, where three candidates sought preferment. After thirty years of service in both houses of Congress, Elmer Thomas was seeking a third term to the Senate. Although the Thomas record was hardly one of legislative brilliance, he was counted as a dependable ally of the New Deal, and he had been remarkably diligent in serving his constituents' requests in Washington.[8]

[5] A detailed study of Phillips's public career is available in Robert Arthur Bish, "Leon C. Phillips and the Anti-New Deal Agitation in Oklahoma" (M.A. thesis, University of Oklahoma, 1966). Phillips's failure to win the coveted judgeship and the beginning of his consuming vendetta against Senator Lee is covered at pp. 37-42.

[6] Murray, *Memoirs of Governor Murray and True History of Oklahoma,* 3 vols. (Boston: Meador Publishing Co., 1945) 3:237.

[7] Bish, "Leon C. Phillips," pp. 45-60.

[8] Eric Manheimer, "The Public Career of Elmer Thomas" (Ph.D. diss., University of Oklahoma, 1953), pp. 134-41.

The senator's challengers were Governor Marland and Gomer Smith. Marland's was largely a futile candidacy, for his record in the governor's office was an insurmountable liability. His campaign was an object lesson in an Oklahoma governor's inability to generate and maintain a consistent base of electoral support. As in 1934 and 1936, Marland attempted to tie his candidacy to the New Deal, but his futile attempts to fashion a miniature gave him very little chance against Thomas, whose own credentials as a New Dealer were impeccable. In addition, Gomer Smith, still the darling of the old folks, was asserting his own claims to the banner of liberalism. Following the death of Fifth District Congressman R. P. Hill, Smith had been elected to the unexpired portion of Hill's House term, and his only deviation from the Roosevelt program had been to the left.

Without a candidate of their own, the party's conservatives, particularly the group who took their opinions from the Tulsa dailies, turned to Smith against the more bitterly despised New Dealers, Thomas and Marland. Smith, who could always make the transitions of expediency with a minimum of difficulty, thus went into the campaign with the dual support of extreme conservatives and extreme radicals. Neither the *Tulsa Tribune* nor the *Tulsa World* was notably disturbed about the odd arrangement. Both endorsed Smith as the best candidate able to dislodge the Josh Lee-Elmer Thomas cabal of New Dealers and their patronage appointees.

According to the conservative press, the instrument of these liberal conspirators was their control over the "vote slaves" of the relief rolls. The theme of WPA coercion was labored in daily "revelations" that usually managed to link Key, the former state administrator, with a scandalous federal ring led by Senator Lee with the dual intent of re-electing Senator Thomas while also taking control of the state capitol.[9] Harry Hopkins, the national relief administrator, added fuel to the fire on June 25, just seventeen days before the primary election, when he authorized a WPA wage increase for thirteen southern states, including Oklahoma. The 65,843 state relief workers thereby received an increase in the minimum wage of about $10 a month to $32.50. Whatever the effect on their votes, Senator Thomas was prompt to claim the credit in congratulatory letters to the WPA workers: "It's up to you, friend. I have kept the faith. Will you?"[10]

With both the gubernatorial and the senatorial campaigns revolving around federal policy alignments, it was only fitting that the resolution of the major races came at the hands of the president. As part of his famous attempt to "purge" conservative elements from the Democratic party,[11] Franklin Roosevelt visited the state three days before the July 12

[9] *Tulsa Tribune,* June 14, 1938; *Tulsa Daily World,* June 11, June 29, 1938.
[10] *Oklahoma News,* June 27, 1938.
[11] The best treatment of the 1938 "purge" is in James McGregor Burns, *Roosevelt: The Lion and the Fox* (New York: Harvest Books, Harcourt, Brace, and World, 1956), pp. 358-80.

primary election. At various stops of the presidential train, one of every five Oklahomans turned out to view the most popular politician of his time. Seventy-five thousand attended his concluding appearance at the Oklahoma City fairgrounds, where leading candidates in both races—with the stout exception of Bill Murray—hoped ardently for the presidential blessing. In the senatorial contest, Roosevelt could deny none of the three contenders with the indictment that they were "'yes, but' Democrats." All three were staunch New Dealers, but it was "my old friend, Senator Thomas" who received the presidential anointing. As for the governor's contest, neither Key nor Phillips received blessing by name. The president limited his remarks to one quick jab. With unmistakable reference to Alfalfa Bill, Roosevelt observed that "some are not even 'yes, but' people. . . . One of the candidates for a place on the Democratic state ticket in Oklahoma this year is nationally known as a Republican."[12]

No label from any other source could have been so damaging. Murray's political death warrant was signed with the presidential seal, and his consistent lead over the past months withered in the final three days of the campaign. Murray, like the conservative metropolitan press, worked himself into a lather of resentment against what the *Daily Oklahoman* called "this gratuitous advice from the throne."[13] In fact, the *Oklahoman* was still incensed about it the morning after the election:

Three days ago, Oklahoma was the political highway of a political Napoleon. He came in his capacity of party leader to tell the freemen of Oklahoma how their ballots should be cast in their own election. He came to choose a senator for a sovereign state. He came to select a governor for an independent commonwealth. He came with his shalts and his shalt nots.[14]

Murray's resentment lasted even longer, and for good cause: after the president's brief comment, his hopes for an unprecedented return to power were crushed. In the voting, he received fewer than 25 percent of the ballots, and his total was nearly 31,000 below that of Phillips, who won the nomination with the thinnest of victories, 3,105 votes over Key. The vote distribution was fundamentally sectional. Murray carried twenty-one counties, all but two of them south of the Canadian River. Key and Phillips each took twenty-eight, Key winning a solid bloc of eastern counties from Ottawa to Pottawatomie (and only three in the west), while Phillips made his strongest showing in the sparsely populated western counties. The real difference between the two leaders was that Phillips supplemented his sectional strength with big leads in the state's largest cities—Oklahoma City, Tulsa, Enid, and Ponca City.[15]

[12] *Oklahoma City Daily Oklahoman,* July 10, 1938.
[13] Ibid., June 18, 1938.
[14] Ibid., July 13, 1938.
[15] *Directory of Oklahoma, 1977,* p. 567; Oliver L. Benson et al., *Oklahoma Votes, 1907–*

Franklin Roosevelt's final public ridicule of Alfalfa Bill had retired the old warrior and left Phillips and Key to battle it out from their sectional bastions. So close was the result that it seemed certain that a Roosevelt endorsement would have won the contest for Key, that is, had Phillips not carried out the threat that prevented such an endorsement: to withdraw from the race and throw his support firmly behind Murray.[16] Because there was no endorsement, there was no withdrawal, and Phillips was left the Democratic gubernatorial nominee with a little more than 30 percent of the primary vote. What Roosevelt did *not* say in the governor's contest was much more important than what he did say in the Senate race. Thomas won easily, as he would have done in any event. The only apparent contribution of Roosevelt's endorsement was to swell the incumbent's margin to nearly 45 percent of the total vote— some 62,000 ballots ahead of Gomer Smith and nearly 137,000 beyond the shopworn, discredited E. W. Marland.[17]

The Democrats triumphed in the general election by default. There was no organized fight on Phillips, although the incumbent administration was frigidly cool to his candidacy. If his was not the sort of personality to evoke wild enthusiasm, there was comfort in his hulking presence and in his roaring indictments of spendthrift, inefficient government. His legislative record was generally beyond serious attack, for despite his attacks upon the worst excesses of the Sixteenth Legislature, he had supported the successful constitutional amendment for old-age pensions as well as the record school aid appropriation, the two areas where too much economy might have proved disastrous. Against the feeble efforts of the GOP's Ross Rizley, Phillips, for the third successive time, smashed the existing record for a gubernatorial victory by burying the Republican with a 207,000-vote margin. The Democrats' electoral invincibility was present in every race, as Elmer Thomas destroyed Harry Glasser by an equally comfortable margin; and every Democratic candidate for reelection was returned to Congress, along with the Fifth District's new representative, A. S. ("Mike") Monroney, and the Fourth District's Lyle Boren, both Democrats. In the legislative races, the Democratic unanimity was only technically broken when a single Republican survived the deluge to be sent to the senate, while the Democrats took 102 of the 115 seats in the lower house.[18]

In personal appearance, Oklahoma's eleventh governor was almost a caricature of the familiar American image of the politician, at least as portrayed by political cartoonists.[19] Tall, red-faced, red-haired, and

---

1962 (Norman: University of Oklahoma, Bureau of Government Research, 1964), p. 89.

[16]Robert A. Bish interview with Irvin Hurst, May 23, 1966, cited in Bish, "Leon C. Phillips," p. 57.

[17]*Directory of Oklahoma, 1977,* p. 568.

[18]Ibid., pp. 570-71; Benson et al., *Oklahoma Votes,* p. 49.

[19]Phillips's biography is taken from the *Oklahoma City Daily Oklahoman,* May 5, 1935, November 13-14, 1938.

enormously fat, Phillips did little to dissipate the traditional impression. His manners were bucolic; the black cigar was never missing. He had been born in Worth County, Missouri, December 9, 1890. The family came to a farm near Clinton late in the territorial days. In 1909 the strapping youth entered Epworth University (now Oklahoma City University) to prepare for the ministry. After two years, his professional interests shifted to the law, and he transferred to the University of Oklahoma, where he played on the college football team and took his law degree in 1916. In the same year, he formed the law firm of Row and Phillips at Okemah.

After brief military service as a private in the artillery, he returned to his legal practice in Okemah and plunged into the various church and fraternal activities expected of rising young lawyers. In 1932 he won his first election to the state legislature as part of the Roosevelt landslide. By his second term, he served as speaker of the house of representatives, where his deep growl exceeded in volume and fury anything the legislature had known for years. His dismantling of the Marland program measured his mastery of legislative infighting, but he carefully aligned himself with both labor and business interests and constantly asserted his loyalty to the true New Deal in Washington, if not the misguided Marland version in Oklahoma City. Unceremoniously deposed as speaker in 1936 and denied a coveted federal judgeship in the next year, he retained his patent on financial solvency. The excesses of the Sixteenth Legislature opened the door for his triumphant vindication in 1938.

The new governor's inaugural address was as straightforward a commentary on the woes of state government as had yet been heard. Although he disclaimed any reproach for his predecessor—"I have no word of censure for Governor Marland"—his pledges to reform a host of state functions, to eliminate extravagance, and not to seek another office during his term did not miss their target. One observer noticed that the outgoing governor "flinched under the verbal lashing and drew his overcoat around him as if to ward off the blows."[20]

The new administration departed from its predecessor in far more than a verbal repudiation. Marland's monumental ineptness in dealing with headstrong legislators (most notably, of course, Phillips himself) gave way to the new executive's absolute domination over the legislature. Asserting his will with the force of a sledgehammer, Phillips set ruthless retrenchment as his chief target, and the new governor overlooked no possible source of influence in pushing his economy program into law. His care ranged from dictating the organization of each chamber to placing J. Z. Armstrong on the state payroll as an "Investigator with the Executive Department." The zealous Armstrong was the governor's personal agent, reporting only to Phillips such politically useful data

[20] Ibid., January 12, 1943.

Leon C. "Red" Phillips brought bulk and determination—but neither good humor nor liberalism—to the governor's mansion. Courtesy Oklahoma Historical Society.

as the campaign plans of his opponents, as well as the business and marital problems of would-be independent legislators.[21]

Phillips's command was evident even before his formal inauguration, when the Seventeenth Legislature unanimously approved his reorganization proposals for the Highway Commission and the Tax Commission. Once he formally assumed his gubernatorial duties, the legislature also meekly followed his call for drastic retrenchment in state government and undertook the spartan task of restoring the state's public credit. Throughout his term, the major legislative bills were prepared in the governor's office, and their progress was duly charted to final adoption. The custom of allowing department heads to exceed their prescribed budgets by contracting for expenses to be met by later supplemental appropriations was terminated immediately by legislation making executives financially liable for such excesses. A strong companion bill that authorized the governor to reduce appropriations on his own orders if he judged state funds to be inadequate to cover them was adopted by the compliant legislature, although later voided by the courts as unconstitutional. Largely the same effect was realized, however, by a joint legislative "yardstick" committee, which met constantly with Phillips, measuring every budget request by the governor's standards. According to this yardstick, departmental and institutional spending was slashed by about 20 percent.[22]

Education was probably the chief victim of the governor's obsession with economy. The 1939 reduction of the biennial education appropriation to less than $25 million—still large by predepression standards—was accompanied by a continuing loss in local revenues for the support of the public schools. The consequence was that total school spending by the end of the 1930s was actually less than the meager sum expended at the decade's beginning. School leaders raged at the governor's limit but were powerless before his threat to veto any larger sum, a move that likely would have closed the state's schoolrooms.

Despite the relentless economies, poor tax collections and the diversion of money to service the debt still left the state with a deficit after the first biennium of Phillips's term. Convinced that new taxes would be necessary if the state's books were ever to be balanced, the governor demanded of the Eighteenth Legislature a series of tax increases. The 1941 assembly meekly complied by approving large increases in the state's motor-use taxes, including automobile licenses, truck excises, and gasoline tax. The cigarette tax was also increased from three to five cents a pack. Meanwhile, school aid continued to suffer, although there was a fractional increase in the biennial appropriation. Even that figure would not have been possible except for the diversion of four million dollars of road use taxes to the education fund.

[21] Armstrong's reports and memoranda are available in the Leon C. Phillips Collection, Western History Collections, University of Oklahoma, Norman, Oklahoma, hereafter cited as Phillips Collection.

[22] The retrenchment work is fully recorded in an untitled typescript, Phillips Collection.

In the 1941 legislature, like that of 1939, major bills were promulgated from the governor's office, and the lawmakers passed their idle time in the futile discussion of less urgent business. Exhausting days were filled with debate on such questions as a barbers' price-fixing law, the regulation of commercial juke boxes, and the revenue potential of natural gas and oleomargarine, both of which escaped the tax searchers. Repeal of prohibition was vigorously debated, but to no end, because Phillips declared that there would be no special election on the matter as long as he was governor. On the other hand, he did nothing to encourage a stringent enforcement bill that would have made local officials responsible for prohibition law violations. The bill, aggressively pushed by the redoubtable Ila Huff of Oklahoma County, the legislature's lone woman member, declared that county attorneys, sheriffs, and constables must have "prima facie, guilty knowledge" of illicit operations if public places sold alcoholic beverages to the certain knowledge of the remainder of the community. Though reasonable enough, the bill came to nothing. Through it all, both the Seventeenth and the Eighteenth legislatures were notably dull, the most remarkable commentary being that Phillips maintained his unchallenged control throughout.

The most enduring work of either legislature was the 1941 session's dutiful support of the capstone of the Phillips retrenchment, the "budget balancing" amendment to the state constitution. The legislature temporarily adjourned to allow members to stump loyally for the measure, which directed the State Board of Equalization to furnisn each succeeding legislature with an estimate of total state revenue for the following biennium. In effect, deficit spending was prohibited because appropriations exceeding those estimates were automatically voided. Presented to the voters at a special election of March 11, 1941, the amendment encountered only the half-hearted opposition of some educators and was approved by a crushing majority, 163,886 to 85,752.[23] In one mighty stroke, the determined governor had struck a permanent blow against the mindless expansion of state spending that had ruined Marland's reputation.

That implicit rebuke to his New Dealish predecessor in Oklahoma City was more than matched by the governor's steadily souring relations with the administration in Washington. Despite his repeated avowals of loyalty to the president, Phillips's support for the New Deal was never more than verbal, an unavoidable expediency with an electorate enthralled by Roosevelt's magic. Beneath the words lay a decided hatred of government spending, centralization of power, and political realignment—in sum, everything that the New Deal represented.

A clue to the new governor's future relations with Washington was written into the 1938 Democratic state platform that Phillips dictated before the general election. Above the two leading planks (promises to pay the state's debt and to balance the budget) was the coolest praise

[23] *Directory of Oklahoma, 1977,* p. 649.

for the president's policies, coupled to a self-described "demand": that "all emergency and experimental legislation be repealed" upon the return of prosperity. The platform, again showing Phillips's hand, affirmed Oklahoma Democrats' continuing adherence "to the general principles of government as stated by Thomas Jefferson, . . . 'the least governed people is the best governed people.'"[24]

New Dealers who had mistakenly supposed that, as governor, Phillips would be friendly to the national administration got a rude shock on the day after his inauguration, when he addressed the legislature for the first time. Amid scattered remonstrations toward various New Deal programs, the governor launched into a tirade directed at the administration's most prominent Oklahoma project: the construction of the $54 million hydroelectric Denison dam on the Red River. A stunned audience heard Phillips devote a third of his speech to denouncing the project in ever shriller tones. He took the position that valuable Oklahoma bottomland was being flooded, costing farmers and state and county treasuries dearly, without consent of the people or the state, to "enrich Dallas and Fort Worth merchants." Since the dam would be, in his eyes, worthless in meeting the constitutional object of flood control, he also pronounced the project to be an unconstitutional usurpation of state sovereignty, "the most shocking disregard of states' rights that has yet occurred."[25]

The unexpected assault on the Denison project pitted Phillips squarely against the national administration. It also set the stubborn governor at odds with the entire Oklahoma congressional delegation (except for the Fourth District's Lyle Boren), Senators Josh Lee and Elmer Thomas, and his own planning and resources board. The state legislature, however, stood solidly behind the governor and his handpicked house speaker, Don Welch of Madill, whose bailiwick would be largely inundated by the project. The speaker and the governor forced condemnatory resolutions through the legislature and systematically altered Oklahoma statutes to throw up every conceivable roadblock to federal authority. Meanwhile, the governor fought the president, and any other New Dealers behind the project, in protracted lawsuits that twice reached the United States Supreme Court before his quixotic crusade was ended in a memorable decision by Justice William O. Douglas. In the end, the Court waved aside convoluted arguments about state sovereignty to reaffirm explicitly the federal government's authority to build dams to provide public electrical power.[26]

Undaunted, the governor renewed the war with Washington in a similar dispute involving the damming of the Grand River. Again posturing as the stout champion of states' rights against the bureaucratic dictation of the New Deal, Phillips involved the state in protracted and futile court

[24] The printed platform and original typescript are in the Phillips Collection.
[25] *Oklahoma City Daily Oklahoman,* January 11, 1939.
[26] The entire fight is exhaustively covered in Bish, "Leon C. Phillips," pp. 71-111.

proceedings. Even his 1940 declaration of martial law to prevent the completion of the Disney dam was unavailing. Although the state eventually received increased federal compensation for its flood losses, the judicial dispute ended in a victory for federal authority, leaving the governor to fulminate against the New Dealers and their steady aggrandizement at the expense of the states.[27]

Phillips's fruitless fights with the federal dam projects were rooted in many motives. Publicly, he emphasized concern for the loss of government revenue as rich farmland was flooded and removed from the tax rolls, a motivation consistent with his administration's obsession with fiscal matters. Probably more important to the obstinate governor was his continuing vendetta against the projects' most vocal supporter, Senator Josh Lee. A man capable of consuming personal hatreds, Phillips saw in his obstructionist stance a chance to take vengeance on the senator who had cost him a federal judgeship in 1937 and who, by turning his organization to William S. Key, had almost put the governor's chair beyond reach in 1938. Personalities aside, it must be conceded that Phillips was motivated by principles, all of them conservative, against federal domination of states, against public electrical power, and against massive deficit spending. Phillips's obsession with state retrenchment was, after all, only one thread in his negative philosophy, so quickly and so thoroughly revealed that the president must have regretted his failure to destroy the Phillips candidacy when the chance had come in 1938.

Perhaps the ugliest of Phillips's reactionary policies was the antiradical crusade the governor sanctioned throughout his term. As in other states, conservative suspicions of the New Deal's liberalism easily flared into extremist fears that dedicated radicals, especially Communists, were using the façade of reform to mask their calculated subversion of American institutions. To timid minds, those fears were beyond a doubt sincere, if misplaced. Those fears also were exploited by more sophisticated persons to make reckless charges of communism to silence the New Deal's advocates. In either case, Phillips added his voice to the alarm when, in December, 1938, he publicly warned all Communists to get out of Oklahoma.[28] Just after his inauguration, the governor repeated his warning and charged the University of Oklahoma with harboring subversives on its faculty, demanding that they be fired.[29]

The Communist issue furnished the governor with a club against the university's president, Dr. W. B. Bizzell. Although Phillips was an illit-

---

[27] Ibid., pp. 142-74.

[28] *Oklahoma City Daily Oklahoman,* December 6, 1938. At the time, the total Communist following in the state was variously estimated at about six hundred, and that number may well have been exaggerated. *Harlow's Weekly,* March 26, 1938; *Oklahoma City Daily Oklahoman,* May 27, 1938.

[29] The early charges against the university are presented in James Arthur Robinson, "Anti-Sedition Legislation and Loyalty Investigations in Oklahoma" (M.A. thesis, University of Oklahoma, 1955), pp. 40-45.

Governor Phillips, appropriately clad for a metaphorical pose as the symbol of rugged individualism. Courtesy Western History Collections, University of Oklahoma.

erate in the field of political theory and his evidence that Communists were connected with the university was really nonexistent, he knew that he was replenishing his arsenal for an assault on the university's budget. It was not an unpopular tactic; he was appealing to that segment of public opinion that is always suspicious of increased spending for higher education. The financial basis of his attack was implied two months later when Representative John Hallinan, the governor's choice as chairman of the house appropriations committee, renewed the allegations and named a list of likely subversives. The list included the state's three most able students of government—Cortez Ewing, H. V. Thornton, and Royden Dangerfield. The esteemed and quite astonished professors demanded a chance to answer the preposterous charges, but they received none. The university's budget was then cut by more than 25 percent.[30]

The 1941 legislature took up where its predecessor had left off. In addition to slashing the university's appropriations by another 17 percent, the legislators also made Oklahoma an early pioneer in legislative investigation of communism. A select committee under the direction of Senator Joe Thompson vigilantly worked to drive Communists from their pulpits, especially at the university. The committee's chief targets were Dean Nicholas Comfort (head of the School of Religion), Dr. W. C. Randels (professor of mathematics), Dr. Maurice Halperin (professor of linguistics), and a Norman minister unconnected to the school, John B. Thompson. Their liberal brand of Christianity—or "freak theories," as the governor put it—brought Comfort and Thompson to the committee's attention. Professors Randels and Halperin were brought under its searching gaze after they had publicly opposed a pending bill to ban Communists from office.

Accompanied by much favorable publicity in the *Daily Oklahoman,* the commitee pressed its inquiry into the suspects' political and religious beliefs, organizational affiliations, and voting habits—with warnings against "hiding behind the [secret] ballot." The diligent investigators even examined samples of the professors' scholarship. If Dr. Randels's scholarly contribution to higher mathematics bore a dubious relation to the point at hand, equally dubious was the members' capacity to judge it. Examining one of Randels's articles, a puzzled Thompson admitted that "this stuff may be mathematics, [but] I wouldn't know. It doesn't look like anything I ever studied, but I only went to the third grade."[31]

Despite their diligence, one of the committee's members, Senator Paul Stewart of Antlers, confessed during the hearings that they had probably failed to locate a single Communist at the university. True enough: their final report admitted that they could discover no conclusive evidence of communism at the Norman campus, although the committee did point to the four suspects' involvement in civil rights organizations as suspi-

[30] Ibid., p. 43.
[31] Ibid., pp. 59–74. See p. 66 for Thompson's judgment on higher mathematics and lower politics.

cious evidence of "fellow traveling." The committee closed by urging speedy adoption of the pending antiradical proposals and added another of its own: the creation of detention camps to hold "subversives" in the event of "emergencies." Despite the sensationalism of its investigations, the committee was able to claim only one scalp, when the university subsequently canceled the teaching contract of Professor Halperin. Ironically, he left Norman to take a job, at triple his former salary, with the Office of Strategic Services, the World War II forerunner of the Central Intelligence Agency.[32]

The Eighteenth Legislature passed the pending bills that the Thompson committee had endorsed, although no action was taken on the gratuitous recommendation of concentration camps. With the slightest shadow of dissent, the lawmakers did forbid Communists and other advocates of violence from holding public office, required elected officials to take an antiradical oath (exceeding in length the existing oaths of office), and denied a place on the Oklahoma ballot to any party advocating the political use of violence. Adjournment prevented the legislators' consideration of a final bill, a loyalty oath for educators, but the test would not be forgot.[33]

While the governor stayed in the background during the senate investigation, his incautious public statements probably lent encouragement to those who, deliberately or otherwise, blurred the distinction between political liberalism and subversive radicalism. Certainly, his was the major influence in halting Oklahoma's compliance with New Deal requests on the states. Under his command, the Seventeenth Legislature all but annulled the state wage-and-hour law that had been summarily adopted when it was handed down from Washington in 1937. The same legislature did approve a measure that prepared the state for participation in the federal government's new housing program by creating an unpaid board to administer a federal grant of $8 million for slum clearance and new construction. Haughtily rejecting the federal largesse, Phillips killed the bill by pocket veto, serving notice that Oklahoma would no longer march to Washington's drumbeat.[34]

The gap between the governor and the president widened to an unbridgeable chasm with the election of 1940. Prior to that time, Phillips, even in his most obstructionist poses, had lashed out at several of the president's programs but had not yet attacked Roosevelt himself. The president's quest of an unprecedented third term forced the governor to drop any remaining pretense of support. As the third term drive mounted, Red Phillips eagerly accepted the role of Franklin Roosevelt's foremost conservative foe in Oklahoma.

The opening shot of Phillips's anti-Roosevelt campaign came in a

[32] Ibid., pp. 76–79. Presumably, the OSS would be as free from Communist taint as the American Legion, which the diligent committee absolved of any Communist infiltration.
[33] Ibid., pp. 81–84.
[34] *Harlow's Weekly,* May 6, 1939; Bish, "Leon C. Phillips," p. 114. Administration representatives pleaded personally but unsuccessfully for state compliance in both cases.

nationally publicized speech that he delivered before the American
Petroleum Institute in late 1939. The speech was a trenchant attack
upon the "crackpot schemes and impractical utopian desires" of unnamed, but unmistakable, leaders who, "under the guise of advanced
and streamlined Americanism, . . . would destroy this country and the
institutions we love."[35] By early 1940, the governor was both more vitriolic and more precise. Speaking directly of the president, Phillips
charged that a third White House term was unthinkable for an executive who was guilty of attempting to coerce the Congress, enlarge the
Supreme Court, and purge loyal "Jeffersonians" from his own party.[36]

While the governor's shrill leadership of the anti-third-term movement
pitted him against a still popular president, it also set him once more
against his inveterate state foe, Josh Lee. An always dependable source
of New Deal support, the senator was also a leading advocate of the
"draft Roosevelt" cause, which, under the president's coy direction, was
pushing the Democratic party in the precedent-shattering direction of
another term for Roosevelt. Anxious state party leaders exacted pledges
from Phillips and Lee that neither would publicly split the party by
attempting to dictate the membership of the Oklahoma delegation to
the Democrats' national convention. The two continued to snipe at
each other in an escalating war of words, while encouraging their allies
to control the vital precinct and county conventions that would decide
the shape of the state's delegation. Those critical meetings, held in the
spring of 1940, ended in a general sweep for the Roosevelt-Lee forces,
and the resulting state convention instructed Oklahoma's forty-four delegates to support Roosevelt at the national convention, should he "offer"
his candidacy.[37]

As the governor, Phillips was named an at large delegate to the historic
and ill-tempered Chicago convention. Bound by the unit rule, which required that the state's entire convention vote be cast according to the
wishes of the delegation's majority, Phillips officially added to the history
of the event by casting his ballot for Roosevelt's renomination. He also
contributed to the ill humor, sulking in splendid bitterness as Oklahoma
climbed aboard the Roosevelt bandwagon. The governor and his anti-
New Deal minority were able, however, to align the Sooner delegates
with the party's conservative wing in resisting the surprising vice-presidential candidacy of arch-New Dealer Henry A. Wallace. Even when
the battle was over and the conservatives routed, Phillips and the Oklahomans stubbornly refused to join in the traditional conciliatory motion
of granting Wallace's nomination by acclamation.[38]

Oklahoma's conservative Democrats returned from Chicago less chastened by defeat than angered to vengeance. With the silent support

[35] Speech files, Phillips Collection.
[36] Untitled ms., ibid.
[37] The battle between Phillips and Lee is fully discussed in Bish, "Leon C. Phillips,"
pp. 112-33.
[38] Unidentified press clippings, Phillips Collection.

of Phillips, Ed Moore, a wealthy Tulsa oilman and disgruntled anti-Roosevelt delegate, organized a disaffected band supporting the presidential candidacy of the Republican nominee, Wendell Willkie. Amply financed by the state's oilmen, the bolting Willkie Democrats screamed the tocsin of extreme conservative ideology, for they saw themselves as rallying "men of every party who would save the establishments of freedom" from the "Marxistic New Deal, [which] will seal the doom of liberty."[39] In contrast to the vigor of the Willkieites, the state's Democratic leaders seemed generally subdued in their support of Roosevelt. Robert S. Kerr, who had been named national committeeman while still in Phillips's favor at the previous state party convention, was one of the few praising the president with anything like the old-time ardor.

Despite the hysteria of the Willkie forces and the notable coolness of most of the state's Democratic party hierarchy, Oklahoma kept its familiar place in Roosevelt's column in 1940, when the president carried the state by the still comfortable margin of 474,313 to 348,872. The total vote established a new record for the state, but it also indicated a considerable decline in Roosevelt's electoral appeal. Compared to 1936, Roosevelt's percentage of the ballots had dropped by a full ten points, and the anti-Roosevelt total had climbed by nearly 104,000. In 1936 the president had carried seventy-six counties (all except Major); in 1940 he led only in fifty-six, losing both in the First and the Eighth congressional districts, and losing especially heavily in Tulsa County. In addition, the Democrats' congressional monopoly was broken after four terms when the Eighth District returned to the Republican fold by sending Ross Rizley to Congress.[40]

None of the notable Republican gains of 1940 translated into an improved showing within the state. In fact, the GOP's share of state legislative seats actually suffered a net loss of five, from fourteen to nine in the two houses.[41] For that reason, the 1940 returns hardly signaled an imminent resurrection of the Republican party at the grass roots. They did, however, point to an increasing national and conservative orientation of Oklahoma Republicans, moving away from matters of local culture and inherited voting habits to defend a conservative view of proper national policy against the detested heretic they found in the White House.

Of course, the conservative reaction to the New Deal went well beyond the GOP, as the formal Democratic affiliations of the bolting Willkieites and Governor Phillips demonstrated. By 1940, Oklahoma politics had developed a strong strain of conservative ideology, defined in opposition to New Deal "waste," "regimentation," and "bureaucratic dictation." It was heartily endorsed by a militant metropolitan press and politically

[39] *Jeffersonian Voice of Oklahoma* (n.p., n.d.), copy in R. B. Morford Collection, Western History Collections, University of Oklahoma, Norman, Oklahoma.

[40] *Directory of Oklahoma, 1977,* pp. 573-74; Benson et al., *Oklahoma Votes,* p. 65.

[41] Benson et al., *Oklahoma Votes,* p. 49.

championed by Governor Phillips. The result was that state politics, as it responded to national issues, was becoming less a biennial donnybrook of personalities. It remained to be seen, however, if the emergence of a conservative cause could be matched by an equally vigorous and coherent rival. The administration of Phillips's successor began to provide an answer, as ambiguous as it was effective.

CHAPTER 12

The Wartime Administration of Governor Kerr

A S THE elections of 1942 approached, the country had been at war only a few months. Political interest was slack. Applications to candidacy dropped sharply from 1940, for the war overshadowed state political activity. The party in power, benefiting from appeals to unity behind the commander-in-chief, also suffered from the consequences of wartime privation, anxiety, and battlefield reverses. Recruitment under the draft was daily taking young men from their homes and making every family sensitive to public issues. Resentment against organized labor was exceptionally deep. Strikes of whatever dimension in defense and war plants were highlighted in the newspapers. Exploiting the issue of labor's role in the crisis, a strong antiadministration movement appeared. Its leadership fell to the remnant of the Willkie Democrats, who seized upon the Roosevelt administration's "coddling" of unpatriotic "labor bosses," a symbol of liberalism's inadequacy before the challenge of total war.

The immediate object of the conservative counterattack was the United States Senate seat occupied by Josh Lee. The president's faithful ally since their massive joint victory of 1936, Lee consistently endorsed the most advanced New Deal programs. His leadership in the thinly disguised "draft Roosevelt" movement of 1940 made him the most convenient administration target within the state. Trusting his renomination campaign to the "Rover Boys" and his patronage appointees at home, the senator remained in Washington, where he urged the expansion of the New Deal's domestic programs, even amid the unprecedented military crisis. His election-year bill proposing a power authority similar to the Tennessee Valley Authority for the Arkansas River basin demonstrated his steady determination to enlarge the liberal agenda,[1] but it also raised questions

---

[1] *Oklahoma City Daily Oklahoman,* January 27, 1942.

of the senator's understanding of his constituents' priorities. The New Deal's quest for social justice meant little at a time of unequaled foreign challenge.

Even more troublesome for his reelection chances was Lee's stout refusal to allow the recent gains of organized labor to be sacrificed to war hysteria. Resentment against trade unions ran deep in rural Oklahoma, and the arch-conservative metropolitan press had never been reconciled to the power wielded by "the bosses." That smoldering animosity was ignited by the *Daily Oklahoman* in a mid-March ultimatum to the state's congressional delegation: their political careers would be ruined unless the forty-hour work week were repealed and antistrike legislation adopted for defense plants.[2] Picked up by the country weeklies and ambitious political challengers, the loose charges against "labor racketeers" and "appeasers in Congress" provided ready explanations for the grim news from the war front. To the credit of Lee's liberal principles, if not his political sagacity, the embattled junior senator refused to yield to the publishers or an obviously disturbed public opinion.[3]

It was the labor question that provided the ammunition in the Democratic primary fight against Lee's renomination. Lee returned to the state only on hurried trips to call for loyal and unanimous response to Roosevelt's war leadership to match the British devotion to Churchill. His vulnerability was concealed, however, by his weak primary opposition. In the August primary, Lee received 188,279 votes, well below Elmer Thomas's winning total of 1938, but enough to take an outright majority in a ten-man field of nine unknowns and one cranky old man, William H. Murray.[4]

The gubernatorial contest provided the real fireworks in the Democratic primary. Governor Phillips, publicly neutral, privately endorsed the claims of Gomer Smith, hardy perennial of the Sooner hustings, as his successor. Phillips's former ally, Robert S. Kerr, however, was the leading contender; and, as Democratic national committeeman, Kerr enlisted the support of county organizations across the state. Judge Frank P. Douglass, a longtime party wheelhorse, was the third strong contender. The issues were personal, the product of a fierce internal quarrel within the Phillips administration that had produced a new alignment of party leaders. Control of the state party rested on the outcome.

Kerr had become the chief spokesman for the national administration

[2] Ibid., March 10, 1942.

[3] For numerous excellent examples of public concern over labor unions in defense and war, see the correpsondence files in the Leon C. Phillips Collection, Western History Collections, University of Oklahoma, hereafter cited as Phillips Collection.

[4] Murray's last campaign for public office netted him a mere 10 percent of the vote. Lee's closest primary challenger was Orel Busby, a district judge from Ada, whose campaign on the senator's "coddling" of organized labor presaged the future strategy of the GOP. Nonetheless, the listless Busby candidacy claimed only slightly more than half of Lee's primary total. State of Oklahoma, State Election Board, *Directory of Oklahoma, 1977*, p. 575.

in Oklahoma following Phillips's indignant break with the president at the Chicago convention of 1940. While Phillips had sat out the campaign, party workers naturally turned to Kerr, who did not feel obliged to consult the obviously indifferent titular head of the party during the presidential race. The resulting differences between the two were aired publicly in the 1942 governor's race, as Phillips threw the weight of his administration behind Gomer Smith, the one man he felt capable of denying Kerr's long-planned bid for the governorship. Turning against his former ally with an unreasoning loathing, the incumbent governor also purged Kerr supporters from the state payroll and toyed with the idea of enticing Oklahoma A. and M. President Henry G. Bennett to enter the race. The well-known educator and prominent Baptist layman was a considerable threat to Kerr. It was widely believed that he would withdraw from the race rather than take on Bennett and the legion of alumni and A. and M. Agricultural Extension Service agents.[5] When Bennett refused to leave his comfortable college presidency, the race settled into a three-man affair and one of the most dramatic personal feuds in Oklahoma's political history.

The candidates and their string bands set out on an exhausting campaign tour that *Life* magazine appropriately satirized as "the corniest primary in the United States."[6] Oklahomans had come to expect a free show as part of an election year's entertainment, and they were not disappointed. Kerr had the obvious early advantage, for his organization had been perfected in anticipation of the race, and the expected light wartime vote made organization a critical factor. The danger lay in his role as favorite that made him the focus of criticism and the fact that Judge Douglass, like Kerr, was campaigning as a loyal supporter of the president and his policies. While the two pro-New Deal candidates threatened to split the vote of Roosevelt's supporters, Gomer Smith stood to reap the harvest of dissatisfaction that was being cultivated in the senatorial race. In addition, he enjoyed the quiet but obvious support of the Phillips administration to enlarge his dependable constituency; the pioneer pension advocate maintained a loyal following among the poor and the old. Finally, his latent talent for demagoguery was fully aroused by the irresistible temptation to denounce Kerr, the well-to-do oilman. Douglass's calm discussion of issues was quickly drowned out by Smith's oratorical fireworks, and Kerr was compelled to resort to his own considerable talent for showmanship, appealing to the masses with a twangy baritone delivery of "Take Me Back to Tulsey, I'm Too Young to Marry."

In the end, the election was decided by personality, as Kerr put together a winning mosaic of allegiances that he had polished over the

[5] Anne Hodges Morgan, *Robert S. Kerr: The Senate Years* (Norman: University of Oklahoma Press, 1977), pp. 12–14; J. Z. Armstrong to Leon C. Phillips, June 6, November 17, 1941, both in Phillips Collection.

[6] *Life,* July 13, 1942, pp. 21–27, quotation from p. 21.

years. A former state American Legion commander and renowned contributor to Baptist causes (Kerr reputedly gave 30 percent of his vast
income to the church), he drew upon the votes of veterans, churchmen,
oilmen, party workers, and New Deal followers. He needed them all.
He barely overcame "Ole Gomer" and the motley crowd of pensioners
and New Deal critics who wanted to destroy any friend of FDR. In the
lightest primary voting since World War I, Kerr edged Smith by a count
of 147,169 to 136,842. Douglass and four other also-rans divided 110,381
ballots.[7]

Without a runoff primary to solidify his hold on the Democrats, Kerr's
minority nomination by a still divided party might have presaged difficulty in the general election against the Republican nominee, William J.
Otjen. Governor Phillips's hatred of his party's new nominee had hardly
cooled, and except for naval victories in the Pacific, the military situation worsened in the summer and fall of 1942. By November, the constantly reiterated Republican charges of bungling in the conduct of the
war seemed to have some foundation. Moreover, unpredictable turns in
the race for the Senate seat added to the Democrats' uncertainty.

Former Senator W. B. Pine, nominated in the spring to make a race
generally regarded as hopeless, died suddenly on August 25, six weeks
after the primary. After a long delay, the Republican State Central Committee finally certified its substitute nominee: Ed H. Moore of Tulsa,
seventy-one years old and an anti-New Deal Democrat who had led the
Willkie bolters in 1940. The committee's choice of such a candidate
would have been a mystery in any other year, too baffling to contem-
plate during the depression. Moore still retained his Democratic party
registration.[8] In 1942, though, Moore was ideal—an aging patriot sternly
demanding an end to the peacetime frills of the New Deal's social planners. Although the GOP's choice of a registered Democrat suggested
the party's bankruptcy, this modern Cincinnatus offered one undeniable
virtue: there would be no financial worries in his campaign.

It was quickly apparent that Moore was unconvinced of the futility of a
campaign. Though he had never sought public office and pretended that
his candidacy was a spontaneous draft, he launched his campaign with
the zeal of a religious crusade. The inspired fire-eater called forth a "coalition" crusade of Republicans and "Jeffersonian Democrats" against
the "New Deal administration." From the first shot he stressed two popular campaign themes: opposition to Roosevelt's labor policies that permitted "treasonable strikes" by "irresponsible labor unions" and outrage
at the pensions that the Democratic congressmen had recently voted
themselves.[9] As for his immediate opponent, Moore lashed out at Lee

[7] *Directory of Oklahoma, 1977,* p. 576.
[8] *Oklahoma City Daily Oklahoman,* September 4, 1942.
[9] *Tulsa Daily World,* September 12, 1942. A retirement plan for public servants in the
legislative branch had long been advocated by political scientists, but its adoption in 1942
was badly timed. It was shortly repealed—too late to save many Democratic members,
some of whom had not voted for it.

as the president's "number one henchman," a "mediocre, rubber-stamp congressman." Moore also included Kerr for a dose of strong medicine, describing the gubernatorial candidate as Senator Lee's "Charlie McCarthy."[10] Kerr was bearing the brunt of the Democratic fight in Lee's absence from the state. By the close of the campaign, Moore admitted to no doubts that "Josh Lee is a positive menace to our American government,"[11] and Moore's rhetorical excesses were fully echoed by the incumbent Democratic governor. In a radio address of October 8, Red Phillips combined a frank endorsement of Moore with a slashing attack on "Little Josh" and Kerr as "Gimmecrats," unworthy of conservative Democratic support.[12]

The reactionary salvos of Moore and Phillips were countered by the worst political blunder of Lee's political career. Always an earnest dry, Lee ignored the urgent danger in Oklahoma to remain in Washington to press his amendment to the youth draft bill—an altogether useless attempt to ban alcoholic beverages from army and navy installations and their adjacent areas. His entirely sincere but quixotic effort was inevitably defeated. Lee returned to Oklahoma a scant ten days before the election to find the farmers, the newspapers, and the corporate interests united in a massive assault on the New Deal and his own reelection. The Rover Boys, scattered throughout the federal service and the armed forces, had been unequal to the challenge. Moore's campaign newspaper reached every boxholder, and the variety and ingenuity of his charges regularly stole headlines.[13]

William J. Otjen, the colorless but able Enid attorney who was Moore's running mate in the gubernatorial contest, was almost the forgotten man in the campaign. His chief argument was the customary Republican claim that one-party government was baneful; short of a change of party, no effective housecleaning was possible. Otjen also echoed, more grammatically but less spectacularly, the charges made by Moore in the Tulsan's violent speeches against the New Deal.

The final two weeks of the campaign deepened the gloom of the Democrats. Kerr, resisting the whirlwind almost unaided, sustained the shock of two critical bolts. In his radio address of October 8, retiring Governor Phillips included virtually the entire leadership of the state Democratic party in his indictment. Not long after, Gomer Smith, Kerr's close competitor in the recent Democratic primary, added his name to the prominent Democratic bolters. Against a background of organ music and wartime urgency, Smith pleaded for the conservative coalition ticket of Moore and Otjen in the most effective radio speeches of a brilliant oratorical career.

The apostasy of Phillips and Smith provoked a desperate frenzy in

[10] *Okmulgee Daily Times,* October 16, 1942; *Shawnee Morning News,* October 4, 1942.
[11] *Miami News-Record,* October 30, 1942.
[12] The typescript of the speech is available in the Phillips Collection.
[13] Robert Arthur Bish, "Leon C. Phillps and the Anti-New Deal Agitation in Oklahoma, 1935-44" (M.A. thesis, University of Oklahoma, 1966), pp. 193-96.

the Democratic camp. Kerr, equal to any challenge to personal debate, declared that "abuse from Red Phillips is a recommendation of good character" and described "Possum Red's" dramatic radio address "as full of falsehoods as the streets of Stalingrad are full of holes."[14] Other Democratic victims of Phillips's accusations responded with equal spleen. Trying to emphasize the necessity of party loyalty, State Chairman France Paris shrugged off the governor's position by reminding voters that Phillips was "born a Republican," was chairman of the University of Oklahoma's Republican club during his student days, and had refused to support the national ticket in 1940. To Paris, Phillips's radio tirade was merely the "rigor mortis of his political death."[15] Moman Shepard, the Grady County Democratic chairman whom Phillips had called the "water-carrier" for the school bloc, responded with equal vigor and greater wit that "Phillips is serving the Republicans in a less desirable capacity."[16]

The unexpected bolt of Gomer Smith called for greater delicacy. Smith, after all, had been a loyal partisan up until 1942, and he still commanded a sizable following, especially in the traditional Democratic bastion of Little Dixie, the southeastern quarter of big-voting Democratic counties. Anxious lest "Ole Gomer's" loyal supporters follow him into the Republican camp, Kerr chose to downplay Smith's desertion and to reduce his own campaigning in Little Dixie to hold down the region's turnout and, thereby, reduce the likelihood of a strong Republican showing.[17]

The lightest voting since the adoption of woman's suffrage gave the general election results a puzzling ambiguity. The Democratic ticket for the lesser state offices won handily, but Kerr led Otjen by only 16,000 votes—the narrowest gubernatorial majority since Robert L. Williams had overcome the combined challenge of Republicans and Socialists in 1914. In the congressional races, the Democrats held their seven seats, all by reduced majorities. Incumbent Representative Jack Nichols of the normally impregnable Second District won by only 385 votes. Even the First District's Wesley Disney, who was by now a Republican in all but name (enough so that Ed Moore had endorsed him), saw his margin dwindle from 37,000 votes in 1940 to fewer than 8,000 two years later. The Republican rebirth carried into the state legislative races, in which the party tripled its share of the seats, its best showing since the Hoover landslide in 1928.[18]

The most stunning news of the election, however, was the defeat of Senator Josh Lee, who only six years earlier had been sent to Washington

---

[14]The mutual recriminations among Kerr, Phillips, and Smith can be followed in the *Oklahoma City Daily Oklahoman,* October 9-19, 1942.

[15]Ibid., October 10, 1942.

[16]Ibid.

[17]Morgan, *Robert S. Kerr,* pp. 16-17.

[18]*Directory of Oklahoma, 1977,* pp. 576-77; Oliver L. Benson et al., *Oklahoma Votes, 1907-1962* (Norman: University of Oklahoma, Bureau of Government Research, 1964), p. 49.

with the greatest majority ever given an Oklahoman. Moore won Lee's seat by 37,510 votes. The incumbent's total of 166,653 votes was only 36 percent of what he had gained in his record 1936 performance. More remarkable, his general election showing was nearly 22,000 below his primary vote—a singular performance without precedent or sequel in Oklahoma elections.[19]

To the senator-elect and his rabid anti-New Deal following, the meaning of the election returns was obvious; as Moore said, it was "a result of popular resentment against the Roosevelt party, which has bungled the prosecution of the war and placed politics above the welfare of the nation." Moore also read in the returns a mandate to end the "infiltration of bureaucrats," the "encouragement of labor racketeers," and the "bungling interference with industry [by the] unnecessary regimentation" of price controls.[20]

There was an element of truth in that obviously colored analysis. Oklahomans' reception of the New Deal had cooled perceptibly since the worst years of the depression, and in that respect they were not unlike other Americans. Ed Moore's new Senate post was only one of fifty-one gains made by the GOP in the 1942 elections. The national Democratic leadership recognized the dimensions of the setback and its chief causes: dismal news from the battlefronts, resentment at the expense and power of bureaucracy, and the president's labor policy.[21] Moore's hard-hitting, not to say intemperate, attacks on precisely those issues were as decisive as they were timely.

In that respect, Moore had the great support of the metropolitan press, particularly the *Tulsa World* and the *Tulsa Tribune,* never more immoderate in their anti-Democratic prejudice. Typical was the introduction to a solemn news account in which the *World* described a routine meeting of state Democrats: "Oklahoma's Democratic party, which has ridden the state governmental saddle until it developed a callousness to misconduct of elected officials and the theft of public funds, . . ." The same issue ran pictures of Kerr and Lee in which both were laughing, with the latter portrayed in an unusually silly "candid shot," alongside photos of a sober Otjen and a stern (if somewhat youthful) Moore above the caption: "Two of them Know War is Nothing to Grin About."[22]

Nevertheless, the real meaning of the astonishing Republican resurrection in Oklahoma was less certain than Moore's claims. His victory was no clear popular mandate against the New Deal; rather, it rested upon a record low Democratic turnout. Fewer than 30 percent of the potential voters of the state actually reached the polls, and only 45 percent of those who had voted in the presidential election two years earlier returned in 1942. Worse still, from a Democratic standpoint, was the distribution of

---

[19] *Directory of Oklahoma, 1977,* pp. 575-76.

[20] *Tulsa Daily World,* November 5, 1942.

[21] John Morton Blum, *V Was for Victory: Politics and American Culture During World War II* (New York: Harcourt, Brace, Jovanovich, 1976), pp. 231-33.

[22] *Tulsa Daily World,* September 27, 1942.

the vote. Strongly Republican Tulsa County, which gave Moore a 14,000-vote majority, registered its second highest turnout in an off-year election. By contrast, the election boards in Little Dixie had a dull day. In the traditionally Democratic banner counties of Bryan, Choctaw, Jackson, Johnston, and Love, turnout averaged a mere 17.8 percent of the electorate. The percentage voting in Garfield, Ellis, Grant, Major, and Tulsa counties—historic Republican strongholds—was nearly twice as great: 37.3 percent.[23] Josh Lee's later assertion that his meteoric political career ended with the election day's beautiful cotton-picking weather[24] was somewhat fanciful. Sunshine had little to do with the difference, for, after all, it fell on Democrat and Republican alike. The difference was that Republican voters were stirred by their strongest campaigner in memory, while Democrats were lulled to indifference by Lee's belated efforts and Kerr's calculated decision not to campaign in Little Dixie.

The election returns permit another interpretation: poor voter turnout can be attributed to private indecision. Unable to choose between rival candidates, voters often resolve their dilemma by not voting at all.[25] Quite likely, that is what happened in Oklahoma in 1942. Preoccupied by a war that was not going well and disenchanted with the New Deal at home, normally Democratic voters sat out the election. If unable to bring themselves to vote for a Republican, neither could they muster the resolve to vote for the most consistently liberal Democrat in the state. The result, indecision mixed with indifference, allowed a stunning victory by the state's most reactionary forces.

Those who were moved to vote sent to the Senate a man virtually unknown before his fiery seven weeks' campaign. Born in Missouri and equipped with a law degree from the Kansas City School of Law, Ed Moore had come to Indian Territory in 1901. Like many another early pioneer, he taught school, practiced law, and dabbled in the oil business. Unlike most of the others, he prospered enormously from holdings in the Seminole and Cushing fields, as well as from holdings in Kansas and California. After his first oil company was sold to the Phillips Petroleum Company for a reported $40 million, Moore formed new but smaller firms related to the industry, while also overseeing his 10,000-acre ranch near Okmulgee. It was not until Roosevelt's second term that he became seriously interested in politics as a determined foe of the New Deal and all its works.

Once in the Senate, Moore dropped all pretense of independence or bipartisan sponsorship. His allegiance was strictly Republican, and he

[23]Benson et al., *Oklahoma Votes,* p. 129. General election turnout usually runs lowest in Little Dixie during nonpresidential years because the local and congressional races have usually been decided in the Democratic primary. Nonetheless, the region's poor participation was striking in 1942: turnout was only 63 percent of the level of 1938.

[24]Bish cites his 1966 interview with the former senator for Lee's easy explanation. See "Leon C. Phillips," p. 169.

[25]Angus Campbell et al., *The American Voter: An Abridgement* (New York: John Wiley and Sons, 1964), pp. 49–64.

Senator Ed Moore, the aging reactionary who won a United States Senate seat for the GOP and Democratic anti-New Dealers. Courtesy Oklahoma Historical Society.

confessed to hating "every vestige of the New Deal." His few speeches stung his Democratic colleagues with the tireless recitation of the alarming parallels between the "Roosevelt party" and the Communists of Russia, which he pronounced "Roosha."[26] On domestic issues, his record was an unblemished 100 percent opposition to the New Deal, extending even to federal spending for Oklahoma projects.[27] Although his views on the folly of subsidies for special interests did not, of course, include those to the oil industry, he completely fulfilled the expectations of his supporters and most of his critics. In only one respect were the latter confounded: Moore lived out his term to retire in 1948 at age seventy-seven.

While Moore sounded the trumpet of arch-conservatism in Washington, his ally, Red Phillips, waited only briefly before making official his switch to the GOP. In one of the bitterest attacks yet made on the New Deal, in June, 1943, Phillips announced his decision to change his party registration in a long public letter that was then admiringly published by the fiercely anti-Roosevelt *Manufacturers' Record.* The former governor managed to hit every note in the right wing jeremiad as he assailed the "New Deal party" with charges of reckless extravagance, mindless bureaucracy, and unnecessary regimentation, as well as the usurpation of authority unconstitutionally seized from the Congress, the courts, and the sovereign states.[28]

Stunned by their Senate loss and the desertion of Gomer Smith and Red Phillips, Oklahoma's Democrats gratefully turned their attention to Oklahoma City, where Robert Samuel Kerr was inaugurated as the state's twelfth (and first native-born) governor. Born on a Pontotoc County farm, Kerr was the son of a Texas mother and a Missouri father, who served as a county clerk of the early statehood era. His natural ebullience was fortified by several priceless political assets: a farm boyhood, college and legal training that gave three Oklahoma institutions the right to claim him as an alumnus, a small business background in Ada, ardent church and fraternal leadership, and a fortune made in oil. Although he had been a party worker in Pontotoc County and later served in a minor capacity during the Marland administration, he had never been a candidate for elective office before running for governor in 1942. It was his role as Democratic national committeeman and as state spokesman for the national administration after 1940 that established his leadership and earned him the public recognition that made possible his gubernatorial race. More cautious politicians had shown little ardor for Roosevelt's quest of a third term. Once in the campaign, Kerr ignored the ideological barbs of his chief opponents to put together

---

[26] For example, see Ed H. Moore, "Americanism versus Communism," speech of October 19, 1944, copy in Phillips Collection.

[27] Robert Lewis Taylor, "Dear Constituent: Go Fly a Kite," *Saturday Evening Post,* July 17, 1943, pp. 9-10, 78-80.

[28] Phillips, "A Southern Democrat Renounces the New Deal Party," *Manufacturers' Record,* August 1943, pp. 32-33, 60.

New Governor Robert S. Kerr takes his oath of office to a notable lack of enthusiasm from his predecessor and political foe "Red" Phillips. Courtesy Western History Collections, University of Oklahoma.

a personal victory that drew upon his past associations. Clad in red suspenders and an ever-present "feedsack blue" shirt, "Smiling Bob" told his listeners, "I'm just like you, only I struck oil," with just enough sincerity to make it believable.[29]

In notable contrast to the stormy rule of his predecessor, Kerr was determined to make good on his inaugural promise to cultivate harmony and end the habit of "smearing the reputation of persons who do not agree with the administration."[30] His chief appointments, reflecting a nice balance between the demands of party organization and the needs of administrative efficiency, were one indication of his insistence on a more mature approach to public administration. Carefully staffing the offices under his control, Kerr soon proved his capacity as an organizer and fiscal manager. In addition, the governor's loyal party work and the

[29] Morgan, *Robert S. Kerr,* pp. 3-17.
[30] *Oklahoma City Daily Oklahoman,* January 12, 1943.

earlier legislative service of his brothers, Aubrey and B. B., gave him a nucleus of legislative support, which he constantly enlarged. In the end, the new governor secured as effective control as Phillips had ever exercised. Free of the bitterness and consuming distractions of personal vendettas, Kerr stayed relaxed. Phillips had driven the lawmakers to do his bidding; Kerr's method was salesmanship and persuasion. The patronage whip was convenient but usually kept out of sight.

The climate of the statehouse was refreshingly different. On one issue, Kerr and his predecessor were alike: both were determined to reduce the state's debt, which at the beginning of 1943 totaled $37 million. The governor stopped far short of the previous retrenchment, which had severely damaged existing services and the public schools, but he stoutly resisted pressures to reduce taxes or increase appropriations beyond normal needs until the debt was paid. Of course, the times were propitious. Revenues soared with wartime inflation and income increases, and expenditures for public works were necessarily curtailed as the military monopolized building materials. Within three years, reserves in the carefully guarded sinking fund were more than adequate to clear the debt that had loomed as all but insurmountable only a few years before.[31]

The debt vanished, and the governor could then oversee a rapid but carefully planned expansion of state services, especially in his second biennium. Under Kerr's administration, common school appropriations increased by just under 84 percent; the average amount of the old-age pensions rose from $21.92 to $49.16 per month; and total welfare expenditures climbed by almost 112 percent to nearly $62 million annually. The new spending levels were accompanied by fresh assertion of the state's authority. For example, increased allocations to the schools were conditional upon the local districts' acceptance of state-mandated minimum terms and teachers' salaries. The record expenditures of Kerr's final biennium still left surpluses of around $20 million. Wartime prosperity was no small factor in Kerr's good fortune that he could combine Phillips's fiscal prudence with Marland's sincere humanitarianism without risking the political recriminations that had engulfed them.[32]

The governor's able stewardship was born of his businesslike conviction that state solvency was a prerequisite for future industrial expansion. As a private businessman, Kerr was renowned (and amply rewarded) for his willingness to risk indebtedness, but public business was another matter: he believed that a responsible financial record would be a major

[31] "Report and Recommendations of the Joint Legislative Taxation Committee Twentieth Legislature," copy in Gubernatorial Files, Robert S. Kerr Collection, Western History Collections, University of Oklahoma, Norman, Oklahoma, hereafter cited as Kerr Collection.

[32] *Enid Events,* Robert S. Kerr Special Edition (1954), copy in Roy J. Turner Collection, Oklahoma State Archives, Oklahoma City, Oklahoma; Morgan, *Robert S. Kerr,* pp. 19-23. Kerr's legislative record is summarized in Walter L. Gray, "Legislation Passed During 1943 and 1945," Departmental Correspondence, Kerr Collection.

selling point in his drive to attract industry to Oklahoma—a drive that would free the state from its bondage to oil and agriculture.

The memory of the state's misery at the hands of those boom-and-bust masters inspired Kerr to become Oklahoma's leading salesman. Ever willing to appear foolish in a good cause, he constantly dramatized Oklahoma, whether in the role of pecan peddler, party orator, or drumbeater for the musical comedy, *Oklahoma!*—a show that he himself saw more than a dozen times. He brought the National Governors' Conference to the state in the summer of 1946, and he traveled more than 400,000 miles, promoting the agricultural and industrial possibilities of his favorite state wherever he went. He flew to New York or Chicago or Dallas or San Francisco to extol such native products as Oklahoma's sorghum molasses—likely as not, with samples of the merchandise. His travels and unabashed showmanship were derided by his political enemies, but even they could not question the governor's command of data on resources, labor, and taxes as he wooed prospective industrialists.[33]

Kerr's vision of economic modernization was paralleled by his commitment to political change. He had learned that the day of frontier-style factional politics and personal rule was over. Economic growth demanded expert planning. The clearest expression of that resolve was Kerr's gift of life to the State Planning and Resources Board. What had been, at best, a paper agency of no discernible influence suddenly bustled with activity, its reports and recommendations becoming persuasive exhibits in the governor's appeals to potential employers. After 1943, its work was supplemented by a postwar planning commission, which coordinated the development of rural water policy and transportation, especially aviation. Under the governor's farseeing eye, the state and local planning agencies were directed by men qualified neither by party affiliations nor their campaign contributions but by their shared understanding of the need for professional competence to avoid the economic chaos that had followed the First World War.[34]

In a similar way, Kerr sponsored what none of his predecessors would have countenanced: the curtailment of his own executive prerogatives. In 1944 voters approved constitutional amendments, heartily supported by the governor, that authorized independent boards of regents for the University of Oklahoma as well as for the seven regional agricultural colleges. Though subject to gubernatorial appointment, the new boards were freed from the executive's direct authority, for they were granted seven-year terms with removal only for clearly defined causes. Thus ended a politically potent but educationally disastrous form of gubernatorial power. A second long-standing abuse was likewise terminated by

[33] Morgan, *Robert S. Kerr,* pp. 21-22.
[34] Don McBride to Mrs. Lawrence Smith, March 13, 1944; "Minutes of Planning and Resources Board Meetings," both in Departmental Correspondence, Kerr Collection.

the electorate's approval of the Kerr proposal to establish a pardon and parole board. The ultimate power of clemency was left in the governor's office, but the granting of pardons—a perennial source of political mischief—was thereafter done upon the recommendations of the independent board.[35]

None of these changes should obscure Kerr's own ambitious political calculations. With one eye on his party's fortunes and the other on Ed Moore's Senate seat, Kerr urged that the voting age be lowered to eighteen and the election process be eased for servicemen. Both were expected (not least by Republican opponents) to increase the Democrats' share of the ballots, but the first was never adopted, and the approval of the second made no apparent difference. More successful was the governor's demand to restore the runoff primary. Undoubtedly influenced by his own close call when a minority nomination had nearly cost him the general election, Kerr won restoration of the double primary by a constitutional amendment in 1944.[36]

Equally inspired by recent events was the 1943 requirement of multiple ballots for future elections. Anxious to avoid the danger of local Democrats' being buried in a statewide Republican landslide, the legislature ordained that voters be handed one ballot for county races, a second for state offices, and a third for congressional posts. Since presidential electors were already separated from other candidates, voters would confront four ballots in presidential election years, more if also deciding on initiatives and referenda. Citizens would thus be less inclined to let their vote in the "glamor" races determine choices for lesser offices.[37]

While striking at the threat of straight Republican balloting, the governor and legislature provided further insurance for Democrats. The end of "famous name" filings was long overdue. Josh Lee's renomination bid in 1942 had been seriously threatened when a Craig County farmer of the same name had tried to enter the Democratic primary. Although Vinita's Josh Lee had been denied a ballot slot on a hastily discovered technicality, the prospect of two Josh Lees on the same ballot had caused Democrats more consternation than amusement. They detected in the move an ingenious plot to deny the incumbent's renomination through deliberate voter confusion.[38] A 1943 law ended that danger by empowering the State Election Board to deny listing to any candidate whose name was identical or similar to that of an incumbent or any previously announced candidate. Going a step farther, the law also struck at one source of the state's reputation for political immaturity when it denied as prima facie frivolous the candidacy of an individual who "adopts, appro-

---

[35] *Directory of Oklahoma, 1977,* p. 651; William S. Harmon, "Oklahoma's Constitutional Amendments: A Study in the Use of the Initiative and Referendum" (Ph.D. diss., University of Oklahoma, 1951), pp. 244–49.

[36] Gray, "Legislation Passed," Departmental Correspondence, Kerr Collection.

[37] *Session Laws of Oklahoma, 1943,* Chap. 7, sec. 1, Title 26; Irving Dillard, "Oklahoma Makes Ready for 1944," *New Republic,* August 9, 1943, p. 194.

[38] Typescript radio address of October 8, 1942, Phillips Collection.

priates, uses or purloins the name of any person of State or National reputation, living or dead, or of any hero, public official, military general, or any well-known individual or celebrity." The law could not exclude a future race by a Will Rogers or a Huey Long, but it did require that the names be theirs from birth.[39]

Not even the governor's acute political sensitivity kept him from being trapped in the one disaster of an otherwise successful administration. One of Kerr's first acts was to approve a sweeping legislative authorization to investigate "all past administrations." The activities of the legislative investigating committee, headed by Senator Guy A. Curry of Stigler and Representative R. M. Mountcastle of Muskogee, were fully expected to bring forth all sorts of revelations about the indiscretions of public men. However, the governor insisted that the rights of an accused person be fully protected, an insistence that served as a brake on the more zealous legislators, and the inquiry ended with no charges being brought.

Outside the capitol, the matter was not allowed to die for want of agitation. Governor Phillips, in the waning days of his reign, had authorized Gomer Smith to bring suit in the federal court at Oklahoma City against members of E. W. Marland's textbook commission, including Oklahoma A. and M. College President Henry G. Bennett and State Superintendent of Public Instruction A. L. Crable. The charge was that the accused had conspired to fix prices on state-adopted textbooks and sought an indemnity of $5 million. After the federal court dismissed the charges, George Miskowsky, Oklahoma county attorney, countered with his own criminal charges of bribery against Phillips and his parole investigator, Robert Fitzgerald. Fitzgerald was eventually convicted, and Phillips won his freedom only after two trials, the first of which ended in a hung jury. For a time, it appeared that all Oklahoma officialdom, past and present, would be drawn into the maelstrom of litigation.

While the former governor was fighting criminal charges, the most spectacular of all investigations got under way in Tulsa County, where the ambitious county attorney, Dixie Gilmer, secured grand jury indictments against Bennett and others as co-conspirators in the alleged attempt to rig textbook prices. The political implications were reverberating and the question of jurisdiction crucial. Kerr, arguing that the charges, if true, properly belonged to the state, ignored Gilmer's sum-

---

[39] *Session Laws of Oklahoma, 1943,* Chap. 5, sec. 1, Title 26. Huey Long, no relation to the late Louisiana Kingfish, placed third in the 1946 balloting for Democratic nomination as state treasurer. After the abolition of his at-large seat, Will Rogers tried and failed to win nomination for the Fourth District congressional seat in 1944. Whether because of increased voter sophistication or a smaller constituency, his career was decidedly terminated when he received 2,942 votes, 9 percent of the total.

In the most recent "famous name" case, Wilbur Wright won Democratic nomination in 1974 over Will Rogers, a retired highway patrolman and kin to neither the humorist nor the former congressman. Wright's general election triumph was a major embarrassment to state government. He had been elected to the same post in 1970 and forced to resign it to escape certain impeachment over seemingly fraudulent travel claims. The Wright affair was a compelling argument for making the position appointive.

mons to appear before the Tulsa County grand jury. Moreover, he publicly defended Dr. Bennett as innocent of any wrongdoing, and in the midst of the furor, accepted the presidency of the state Baptist convention, with the besieged educator as his vice-president.[40]

Upholding the governor's position, a Tulsa district court dismissed Gilmer's indictments for lack of jurisdiction, and the 1945 legislature immediately jumped into the fray with its own investigation of the "machine" of Dr. Bennett. In a serious blunder, Kerr fought the proceedings with such vigor that his chosen house speaker, Johnson Davis Hill, resigned the speakership to protest the governor's meddling. In the end, the investigations of 1945 came to nothing, except to tarnish the governor's reputation and to repay Bennett for his refusal to become part of the Phillips attempt to block Kerr's candidacy in 1942.[41]

Considerably wiser was the governor's acceptance of a fight that offered much better odds and much greater rewards. Early in 1944, the resignation of Jack Nichols from the Second Congressional District created a vacancy, which was to be filled by special election. At the time, the Roosevelt administration was on the defensive, for the Democratic majority in the House of Representatives, only nominal since 1942, was even more precarious after party reversals in recent by-elections. The border state of Kentucky had gone Republican in the elections of November, 1943. The Republican high command, inspired by Nichols's razor-thin victory of 1942, reasoned that the trend was in their favor. Advised by Senator Moore, the GOP chose to make the special election a national battleground;[42] the administration, obliged to restore its tottering prestige, joined the fight, making the largely rural district a testing place of national proportions.

Although both parties dispatched nationally prominent campaigners to the scene, the key combatants were Governor Kerr and Senator Moore. Almost unnoticed in the pyrotechnics of the more celebrated statesmen were the actual candidates for office: William G. Stigler, the Democrat, and E. W. Clark, the Republican. The voters of eastern Oklahoma, somewhat astonished and pleased by the attention lavished upon them, kept their heads and voted normally, which in that district was

[40] This defiant gesture was decidedly unwise for other than the obvious reason. It also appeared to offer graphic proof of John Gunther's subsequent charges of a "covert political power" exercised by the Baptist churches. (Gunther, *Inside U.S.A.,* rev. ed. [New York: Harper and Brothers, 1951], p. 971). Except for an occasional highly publicized figure like "Baptist Bob," the religious preferences of candidates are seldom an issue in Oklahoma statewide elections, perhaps not even known by the mass of the voting public. The two-party system and, even more, Democratic factionalism, cut across all religious lines, making church affiliation a minor irrelevancy in most cases.

[41] Kerr's successful but damaging intervention in Bennett's behalf is recounted in Morgan, *Robert S. Kerr,* p. 20. While Bennett's career, if not his reputation, survived legislative scrutiny, Crable escaped impeachment by only four votes. He was subsequently retired by the electorate in the 1946 Democratic primary.

[42] Senator Moore had a special grievance: the Democratic nominee, William Stigler, had been Josh Lee's campaign manager in 1942.

Democratic.[43] The GOP had made a strategic error in making a full-dress fight for a district that had sent but one Republican to Congress (Alice Robertson, in 1920). For the Democrats, the victory was advertised as evidence of the president's recuperative powers and a prelude to the 1944 national elections. The real victor in the contest was Governor Kerr, for his standing in the national party and administration soared with Stigler's election.

As a reward for the governor's demonstrated party loyalty and newly discovered talent for stem-winding oratory, Roosevelt named Kerr to deliver the keynote address at the 1944 Democratic National Convention. Sensing the political potential of his appearance, Kerr scrapped the national committee's proposed draft and, with Henry Bennett, wrote a new speech. The keynote, a splendidly delivered tribute to the New Deal and the president's war leadership, also dredged up reminders of "Hooverism." Kerr's practiced wit inspired the lagging Democrats. Not least, his speech brought heaping individual honors to the beaming governor. Amid rumors that the address would surely win him a Cabinet post—perhaps even the vice-presidency—Kerr bathed in the attention paid himself and his state.[44]

Although Kerr received no Washington assignment, his access to the White House was considerably widened by his convention appearance and the yeoman work he performed for his party in the 1944 campaign. Within the state, most political attention was fixed on Elmer Thomas's bid for a fourth Senate term. If less fervent than the ill-fated Josh Lee, Thomas's dependable support for Roosevelt's policies was undeniable. Like Lee's, his renomination was bitterly contested by the antilabor, anti-Roosevelt Democrats who had contributed to the Moore victory two years earlier. Most of their support—particularly that of the Tulsa "oiligarchy"—clustered around Wesley Disney, the First District representative who finally relinquished his impregnable House seat for a long-anticipated Senate bid. Recalling the successful attack upon Lee, Disney ran a negative campaign against the incumbent and the "CIO goon squads" of "foreigners" alleged to be supporting Senator Thomas's re-election.[45]

Eight other Democrats competed with Disney, all as anti-Thomas candidates of one sort or another, while the senator comfortably posed as an elder statesman above the battle, but not above identifying himself with the most glamorous federal projects. Thomas also relied upon his efficient campaign organization and his long record as errand-boy for constituent requests to Washington. Disney's ideological campaign was

---

[43]Stigler defeated Clark by a margin of 22,036 to 18,502. *Directory of Oklahoma, 1977,* p. 577.

[44]Kerr, "Aims and Purposes: Democratic Keynote Address," *Vital Speeches,* August 1, 1944, pp. 611-16. The favorable reception of the address is witnessed in the *Oklahoma City Daily Oklahoman,* July 14, 1944.

[45]The renomination battle is recounted in Eric Manheimer, "The Public Career of Elmer Thomas" (Ph.D. diss., University of Oklahoma, 1953), pp. 189-91.

unable to overcome that record. The incumbent was renominated with 36 percent of the primary vote to Disney's 26 percent.[46] Since the runoff primary had not yet been restored, Thomas took the nomination into the November election against William J. Otjen, the Republicans' senatorial candidate.

Otjen had run a strong race against Governor Kerr two years earlier, and he seemed to have a good chance against Thomas, for he appropriated Disney's tactic of belaboring the incumbent with charges of dangerous and extreme liberalism. State Republicans also made a determined fight on behalf of their national ticket of Thomas Dewey and John Bricker. Dewey had some claims to local affections, for his wife was Frances Hutt of Sapulpa, and his September address in Oklahoma City was one of the highlights of his race. While Dewey ran a dignified race, Bricker, his running mate as the vice-presidential candidate, took the low road. Bricker's speeches in the state's smaller cities—Ardmore, Pauls Valley, Shawnee, El Reno, Kingfisher, and Enid—were savage attacks on bureaucracy, federal aid to education, and the New Deal's wartime alliance with communism. Otjen's Senate campaign reflected those attacks on the "alien" New Deal with pale copies of Bricker's tirades.[47]

Kerr, in his dual capacity as governor and Democratic national committeeman, shouldered his party's burden in the 1944 race. It soon became plain that the Republican ideologues' evangelistic fervor was most effective with the already converted. Greatly improved reports from the battlefronts and the uncertainties of denying Roosevelt's leadership in the war helped the Democratic ticket to victory once more. For the third consecutive time, however, Roosevelt's winning majority in Oklahoma declined. His 401,549 ballots and 56 percent in 1944 were quite enough, but both were diminished reflections of 1932's 516,468 votes and 73 percent.[48]

In losing the Senate race, Otjen got 105,000 votes more than Ed Moore's winning total of 1942. The vastly improved turnout, some 94 percent above 1942, still left him more than 81,000 votes short of Thomas. Other than increasing their vote totals, the GOP was able to claim only one improvement over 1942. With Disney out of the way, the First District went Republican for the first time since 1928. By sending George Schwabe to Congress along with the Eighth District's Ross Rizley, the GOP increased its share of the state's congressional delegation to one-fourth.[49]

[46] The vote totals were: Thomas, 85,672; Disney, 64,322. Lieutenant Governor James E. Berry received 62,244 votes, and the remaining 23,761 ballots were scattered among seven other candidates. *Directory of Oklahoma, 1977*, p. 577.

[47] Details of the Republican campaign, particularly that of Otjen, are available in Manheimer, "The Public Career of Elmer Thomas," pp. 190-94.

[48] *Directory of Oklahoma, 1977*, pp. 557, 579.

[49] Ibid., p. 558. The improved Republican performance did not carry over to state legislative races. The 1944 GOP gain of two senate seats was offset by the loss of two in the lower chamber. Benson et al., *Oklahoma Votes*, p. 49.

Winning the presidency and the Senate race while containing Republican gains elsewhere, the Democrats were heartened by the results. The 1944 campaign also strengthened Kerr's growing reputation in national circles. In that election and the years that immediately followed, the governor filled more out-of-state speaking engagements than any politician except the president himself.[50] As his stature grew, Kerr was able to win increasing federal support for his efforts to lift Oklahoma's economy from its unhealthy dependence on oil and agriculture. Quickly reversing the obstructionism of his predecessor, the governor proved the benefits of state cooperation with Washington to get federal money for roads, dams, and other projects beneficial to the state, without the accompaniment of useless bickering over state's rights.

Of course, timing once more proved right for Kerr. The state's central location and generally mild climate won it more than its share of Washington's billions in defense dollars. Twenty-eight army camps were either built or enlarged to train men for the emergency. In addition, the state received thirteen naval bases (the largest on the prairie north of Norman) and several Army Air Corps training centers to pump millions into Oklahoma's stagnant economy. The largest of the air bases, Tinker Field, was built on the empty flatlands east of Oklahoma City to cover 3,600 acres at a cost of $100 million.[51] The emergency also allowed the governor to call upon Washington to finance public works less directly tied to the war effort. By early 1945, fifty-three such projects were under construction at a total cost of $5.8 million, nearly three-fourths of which was federal money.[52]

Anticipating the end of the war, Kerr also moved to advance the state's interests in the era of postwar recovery. The focus of the governor's efforts grew out of the disastrous 1943 floods in eastern Oklahoma, where torrential spring rains drove the Arkansas, Verdigris, and Grand rivers beyond their banks to inundate nearly 1.5 million acres. Twenty-six people had died as a result, and property losses totaled more than $31 million. Kerr swiftly mobilized every available federal and state agency for relief.[53] He saw in the swirling muddy waters an omen for the state's future, and also his own. Years later, he would remember the flood for awakening him to a "ready-made issue which no one in politics was using" and which he could make his exclusively.[54] Eventually that vision would move him to the United States Senate, but as governor, Kerr was already acting on the issue. Within months of the raging flood,

[50] Morgan, *Robert S. Kerr*, p. 23.

[51] Edward Everett Dale and Gene Aldrich, *History of Oklahoma* (Edmond: Thompson Book Co., 1969), pp. 368-70.

[52] Don McBride to Mrs. Lawrence Smith, March 13, 1944, Departmental Correspondence, Kerr Collection.

[53] Kerr, *Land, Wood, and Water* (New York: Fleet Publishing Corporation, 1960), pp. 159-67.

[54] Kerr is indirectly quoted by Joseph E. Howell in William A. Settle, Jr., *The Dawning, A New Day for the Southwest: A History of the Tulsa District Corps of Engineers, 1939-1971* (Tulsa: U.S. Army Corps of Engineers, Tulsa District, 1975), p. 45.

Kerr broke the logjam of $200 million in Oklahoma water projects then approved by the Army Corps of Engineers and the Bureau of Reclamation.[55]

Whether war expenditures or civilian public projects, the federal largesse that Governor Kerr diligently sought finally helped end Oklahoma's long depression. As the war and his term were ending, Sooners found themselves better off, not just in absolute terms but also relative to their fellow Americans. In 1929, Oklahoma's annual per capita income had been $454, only 64 percent of the nation's average; and as late as 1940, the Oklahoma total was only 62 percent of the national figure. The first real improvement in both measures came with the war boom. By 1944, the state's per capita income had climbed to 78 percent of the national average, en route to a 1948 level of $1,140—80 percent of the national average and 2½ times the level of 1929.[56]

Oklahoma's new prosperity coincided with the end of Governor Kerr's term and the state's experience with the depression and the New Deal, a paradoxical victim of its most successful programs. As Oklahomans watched the final days of the Kerr administration, they must have been impressed by the changes of sixteen years. It was, after all, only that interval which separated them from old Alfalfa Bill Murray's "cheese and crackers" campaign, its stunning success born of the conviction that running a government was just like running a farm.

In those sixteen years, Oklahomans had moved generations away from Bill Murray and his rustic values. The most visible difference was in the size and responsibilities of their government, a difference symbolized in the State Department of Welfare. Sixteen years earlier, the agency had not even existed, and "relief" had been an obligation only barely accepted by county authorities. By 1946 that one agency spent nearly three times the total state outlay of Murray's final year in office, twelve years before. As in social welfare, the state's new activities in public education and economic planning had forever ended any resemblance between modern public administration and running a farm.

Politics, too, had changed. Politicians were less flamboyant, farther removed from the immature personal struggles of the frontier era. The old attacks on entrenched wealth and personal sin had generally given way to a calmer, more mature political style, and consensus in favor of orderly economic growth submerged the raucous exchanges that had passed for statesmanship for most of the past quarter century. Kerr provided an interesting bridge between the old and the new breeds of politicians. The Oklahoma Democratic party, though hardly transformed by the national "Roosevelt revolution," was less divided by powerful personalities and rival ideologies than before. Their nonideo-

[55] Kerr to A. W. Zelomek, July 6, 1943, Departmental Correspondence, Kerr Collection.
[56] U.S. Department of Commerce, Bureau of the Census, *Historical Statistics of the United States, Colonial Times to 1970,* 2 vols. (Washington: Government Printing Office, 1975), 1:245; Paul A. Brinker and Kehar S. Sangha, "Manufacturing, Value-Added, and Wages in Oklahoma," *Southwestern Social Sciences Quarterly* 38 (1957):121-22.

logical commitment to growth, directed by an efficient state administration and stimulated by federal spending, readied state Democrats to turn back future challenges from the conservative ideologues sheltered in the Republican party.

One final change was less tangible but, for all its abstraction, probably most important. The depression, the New Deal, and World War II had awakened in Oklahomans an awareness of the inevitability of change. From the dusty cotton fields to the booming cities, Oklahomans could look back to the Murray-Gore campaign against the rich boys, certain that things would never be so simple again. Change had become the single certainty, and government—both state and national—was the catalyst.

CHAPTER 13

Roy J. Turner and the Politics of Modernity

WORLD WAR I wrecked the surge of socialism, and the end of World War II blunted the reform thrust of the New Deal. Even in the immediate postwar elections of 1946 and 1948, most Oklahoma Democratic politicians were unwilling to hazard more than passing reference to Franklin Roosevelt and his liberal legacy. Of the politicians who had clambered aboard the New Deal's bandwagon a decade earlier, only retiring Governor Robert S. Kerr and Fifth District Representative A. S. ("Mike") Monroney still paid open and generous tribute to the late president. Doctrinaire liberalism of the E. W. Marland and Josh Lee variety was nowhere apparent. The phrase "New Dealer" was commonly employed as a hostile label, never a self-description, by candidates of both parties, who routinely advertised themselves as conservative, "safe and sound," practical businessmen, economical of the tax dollar, and stalwart foes of bureaucracy. Feeding upon mounting postwar discontents, some spoke ominously of the federal government's "interference" in state affairs and complained of the centralization of power in Washington. The most opportunistic, quick to scent a shift in the prevailing winds, shouted against "regimentation" and reached for the previously discarded banner of "state's rights."

The change in popular mood accompanied the politicians' more conservative posturings. If suspicious of modern liberalism's efforts at social engineering, the electorate was determined that every level of government, including the state government, would extend services long denied by depression and wartime privation. The public mood was notably materialistic. Voters looked to Oklahoma City to provide costly improvements, while they simultaneously waited expectantly for tax reductions or, at least, a shift in the tax burden to others.

All through the postwar era, those contradictory attitudes defined the agenda of state affairs. Gone were the old crusades against great wealth and its presumed inequities. In their place were a limited series of mundane issues, no less complex and no less challenging for all their fundamental conservatism. If none embraced sweeping social or economic reform, all did raise the perennial questions of modern politics: Who gets what and who pays for it?

As early as 1946, in the first electoral contest of the postwar era, those issues had asserted the centrality that they would keep for years thereafter. Roads, schools, pensions, and taxes were the staple items of Oklahoma's modern politics. Finally freed from the grinding burden of depression-era deficits, the state's budget, already approaching $50 million annually, became the prime arena of political combat.

Highways were a burning issue, not merely to contractors and their political agents but to the general public. New construction had never kept pace with the constantly increasing traffic even before the war, and maintenance was shamefully inadequate. In the rural areas, the farm-to-market roads built under the New Deal accounted for only a fraction of the state's mileage. The vast majority of country roads remained dust choked in the dry summer months and muddy, impassable quagmires during much of the spring and winter. At the same time, commercial interests and urban spokesmen were demanding better constructed and more durable major highways to link the state's growing cities. Both needs were acute, and advocates of both sides perforce looked to the state's road-user taxes, especially the 5.5-cent state gasoline tax, for the immediate solution.

As urban and rural interests wrestled over the division of road money, they also battled over its control. Industrial and metropolitan spokesmen argued for further centralization of road building authority in the State Highway Commission, to the end that the state would get a unified system emphasizing the main arteries. On the other side, farmers joined county officials to hold out for the more locally attuned—and much less efficient—authority of the county commissioners to decide a major portion of public spending.

The school question took similar shape. Again, the need was undeniable. Institutions of higher learning, always a state responsibility, had to have more money. Their funding had been barely adequate in the best of times, and they were now challenged by skyrocketing postwar enrollments. Already, the university's medical school was threatened with the loss of accreditation. At the same time, the common school system was struggling to retain a level of mediocrity, at best. In addition, the stability of the public school system was disturbed by the departure of hundreds of able teachers annually. Local school revenues, dependent upon a farcical and uncoordinated county assessment system, fell from the late 1920s onward, and the state gradually had been compelled to take up the slack. The state's supplement had never been adequate to achieve a uniformly high standard of instruction, yet the more favored districts looked with disfavor upon any attempt to equalize educational opportunities in poorer places.

Both the road and school issues had grown to maturity during the depression and the destruction of local tax bases. The third central issue of modern politics was likewise a child of the 1930s. In little more than a decade, Oklahoma's reluctant acceptance of welfare had grown to become a major responsibility of state government. By 1946, the State Department of Public Welfare was spending $44.4 million annually, an increase of 562 percent from its modest level of only nine years earlier.[1] A major portion of that money went to the state's needy old people. Because of their unusually large number (a demographic quirk of Oklahoma's peculiar settlement forty or fifty years earlier), and because of their continuing poverty, more than half of Oklahoma's population over 65 were receiving Old-Age Assistance (OAA) grants. Those pensioners were thoroughly disgruntled, for the size of their monthly checks barely kept pace with the advancing cost of living. Measured in constant, 1940 dollars, the average monthly OAA grant of $17.63 in 1940 had increased to a little more than $20 in 1946.[2] A sizable bloc of voters, especially in the eastern counties, the pensioners were also well organized. Ora J. Fox and his Oklahoma Welfare Federation, both faithfully supported by the pensioners' mites, represented the demands of the elderly in every campaign and before every legislative assembly.

While the road, school, and pension forces scrambled for postwar tax dollars, a powerful but vocal segment of the population wanted tax reduction. Businessmen argued that industry was leaving or avoiding Oklahoma to seek a more benevolent sovereignty. The charge, more assumed than proved, was echoed in virtually every political campaign that followed the war. The Oklahoma Public Expenditures Council, a conservative research organization formed in 1946 and joined by most of the business leaders of the state, supported the notion; and only the rarest of politicians dared to break publicly with the presumed consensus of "no new taxes," remission of local levies as an incentive for industrial relocation, and the reduction of other levies thought to be injurious to business.

In candid moments, most politicians probably would have agreed with the more measured assessments of students of state government: the Oklahoma tax system was less a problem of level than of structure. The irresponsibility of independent local tax collectors had forced state taxes upward to cover the grossly inadequate but politically popular low local tax levies. Much of the state's archaic tax system had been embedded in the cumbersome constitution. Significant tax revision, therefore, would demand major—and unlikely—constitutional amend-

---

[1] State of Oklahoma, Department of Public Welfare, *Annual Report of the Department of Public Welfare for Fiscal Year Ending June 30, 1954* (Oklahoma City, 1954), p. 45.

[2] Ibid., pp. 43, 47. The proportion of Oklahoma's elderly citizens who received OAA grants was more than triple that of the nation as a whole.

ments. That problem had been compounded by the tendency over the years to assure the voters' constitutional approval for proposed new taxes by reserving the levies for specified popular public projects. The best example was the most reliable and most lucrative source of state revenue, the 2 percent sales tax, which produced more than $40 million annually, virtually all of it earmarked for the use of the state Welfare Department. A diminishing fraction of total state revenue was thus subject to legislative appropriation through the general fund; and much of that had to be used to meet the obligations that local governments had passed to the state. By 1946, it was clear that the entire chaotic system demanded drastic overhaul, but it was equally clear that such would be impossible without politically explosive alterations in the governmental machinery.[3]

No modern candidate would attempt E. W. Marland's old effort to import a liberal revolution to public affairs. None would try to resurrect Bill Murray's legions of the rural unwashed against the haughty "establishment" of the cities. None would attempt the progressive or Socialist rally of the "producers" against the "parasites." All eschewed such crude appeals in favor of a unanimous endorsement of better roads, better schools, and better treatment of the needy aged. Given the complexities of the question, only the bravest of contenders dared specify who would get the new roads or who would pay for the improved schools. During campaign season, promises were vague. To the victor would fall the burden of specificity.

For all of its hazards, politics still attracted swollen lists of aspirants. If rarely divided by issue, each tried to put together the momentary coalitions that resulted in election. Organization became critical to electoral success. Election canvasses became ever more intensive and ever more costly, the statutory limitations of statewide campaign expenditures ($3,000) ever more absurd. Everything cost money: county managers and field workers, headquarters staffs, the young and ambitious agents who drove the dusty caravans of string bands and stump speakers. Letters from "education managers," "labor managers," "farm chairmen" and "women's directors" appealed to the special interests of their respective groups. Reams of newsprint were consumed in garish red, white, and blue advertising for a smiling candidate and his brief slogan. Radio and later television air time consumed massive chunks from campaign budgets. By 1946, when each of the three leading Democratic gubernatorial contenders needed upwards of a million dollars, the day of the professional had arrived. Assessing that campaign, Bill Murray, the retired Sage of Tishomingo, wryly observed that "Oklahoma is going to have the best governor money can buy."[4]

---

[3]The most objective discussion of the creaking tax machinery is in John J. Klein et al., *The Oklahoma Economy,* OSU College of Business Economic Research Series, no. 1 (Stillwater: Oklahoma State University, 1963), pp. 95-107.

[4]*Oklahoma City Times,* June 11, 1946.

No less important was the candidate's public image. In most contests, a statehouse veteran emerged to stress his long experience in state affairs, the very experience that allowed his rivals to brand him as "Old Guard." At least one contender would emerge as the "fresh face," the inspired newcomer pledged to "clean up the mess" left by the "politicians" in Oklahoma City. All would dramatize themselves with rallies, slogans, and string bands, all of which somehow confirmed their fitness for office.

In many ways, the 1946 campaign was typical of most of those to follow. Nine contenders crowded the Democratic primary ballot, but only four entertained serious prospects. H. C. Jones, onetime Carnegie druggist and subsequently an Internal Revenue collector, resigned his federal job to make the race. Jones was widely regarded as Governor Kerr's candidate for succession. It was believed that the governor had induced Jones to enter; but Kerr, more concerned with his own certain United States Senate bid two years later, scrupulously avoided an outright endorsement or a public display of administration pressure in Jones's behalf. Jones thus suffered the liabilities and earned none of the assets of administration support.

A second major candidate came forward to champion all those who nursed grievances against the Kerr administration and the "mess" in Oklahoma City. Dixie Gilmer, the fiery county attorney from Tulsa, enjoyed the worshipful support of the Tulsa dailies. Gilmer had a flair for sensational charges against the "textbook racketeers" and other rascals in Oklahoma City, but he had failed to prosecute the alleged textbook ring in his own jurisdiction.

While Jones and Gilmer struggled over the merits and demerits of the Kerr administration, two newcomers emerged as serious candidates. William O. Coe, who had previously served as an Oklahoma County legislator, made his maiden statewide race as a naval veteran of the recent war. Coe pitched his appeal to veterans and their families in a race against the "professional politicians" of the older generation. Ironically, Coe was also the candidate of one of the most durable of those professionals, Gomer Smith. It would tax an expert in political bookkeeping to draw a balance sheet of the worth of Smith's lush radio endorsements and stump speeches for Coe. While the veteran bad boy of the Oklahoma Democrats made many voters aware of Bill Coe's name, Smith was simultaneously driving away thousands of others who disliked the sponsor.

Roy J. Turner had no such liability. A self-made oil millionaire from Oklahoma City, Turner ably put together a strong personal following. Except for Tulsa's would-be kingmakers, most businessmen looked with favor on his promise of a "business administration." At the same time, his homespun qualities overshadowed suspicions of his oil background. A successful rancher and renowned sponsor of 4-H Club projects for rural youth, he was also given to composing and singing country music. Politically, he enjoyed the endorsement of Ora Fox of the Welfare

Roy J. Turner, "All Oklahoma's Candidate" in 1946 and like the other post-World War II executives a "safe and sound" businessman. Courtesy Oklahoma Historical Society.

Federation as well as most of the Democratic courthouse officials. Turner's party record was regular. He had contributed to Roosevelt's fourth term campaign when most southwestern oil magnates were apoplectically denouncing the president. Yet he was never identified with the New Deal, and his relations with Governor Kerr were distant. Like every other contender, he favored "improved" roads and schools, "adequate" pensions, and a program of strict economy.

Turner's strong primary performance entitled him to his campaign billing as "All Oklahoma's Candidate." His managers surely had not overlooked any sizable group in their calculations, for when the ballots were counted, he registered a comfortable plurality of 36 percent, more than 53,000 votes ahead of the runner-up, Dixie Gilmer. The Tulsan, riding a stunning hometown endorsement, came from behind to displace H. C. Jones by 5,000 votes to win second place and a spot in the runoff primary. Coe finished a strong fourth, well enough to assure future campaign appearances.[5]

The brief runoff campaign produced a speedy realignment. Governor Kerr clearly favored and actively supported Turner in preference to Gilmer, whose strong showing was a stinging rebuke to the current administration. On the other side, Gomer Smith could not resist the temptation to instruct the voters who had ignored his previous appeal, this time for Gilmer. Smith and Gilmer combined the fire that they had separately directed at Jones in the first primary and redirected it toward Turner as the candidate of a nefarious statehouse "machine" and the ancient textbook scandal. This facile attempt to identify Turner with affairs dating back to 1937, when Turner had been a stranger to politics, finally prompted the *Daily Oklahoman* to an unusual front-page endorsement of Turner on the Sunday before the election. "Voters are Being Deceived," it warned. "The present textbook commission," the *Oklahoman* reminded Gilmer, "is one of unquestioned integrity," headed by President George L. Cross of the University of Oklahoma. The Tulsa prosecutor was accused of making "false and hysterical charges" to smear indiscriminantly anybody in public office.[6]

The *Oklahoman*'s judgment was largely accurate, for Gilmer's campaign did play upon the public's unease with prevailing conditions. Not the last to make such an appeal, Gilmer showed something of its early potency by reducing Turner's first primary margin by half, before losing 194,311 to 169,397. In other races, the electorate's inchoate rebellion against incumbents exploded against dozens of established administrators and legislators. Only those state officers who had won renomination in the first primary survived the insurgent spirit of the runoff and the demand for new faces. The two most prominent casualties in the state-

[5] State of Oklahoma, State Election Board, *Directory of Oklahoma, 1977,* pp. 579-80; Oliver L. Benson et al., *Oklahoma Votes, 1907-1962* (Norman: University of Oklahoma, Bureau of Government Research, 1964), p. 94.

[6] *Oklahoma City Daily Oklahoman,* July 21, 1946.

wide races were A. L. Crable and Mabel Bassett. Crable, state super-intendent of public instruction for ten years and a leading figure in the alleged corruption of 1937, lost to Dr. Oliver Hodge, then the Tulsa County school superintendent, by more than two to one in a headline race. For twenty-four years Mabel Bassett had served as commissioner of charities and corrections, her talent for publicity earning the enmity of successive governors, sheriffs, jailers, and legislators. Her 88,000-vote plurality in the first primary melted before Buck Cook, a former highway patrolman and veteran of the recent war. Voters did not know Cook, but they had tired of Mrs. Bassett and her incessant feuds with any who crossed her majestic path.[7]

Other races indicated that 1946 was the year of the war veteran. Each of the three congressional incumbents who was forced into run-offs was retired, each by a military veteran. Lyle Boren ended ten years of service to the Fourth District in giving way to Glen D. Johnson, a youthful veteran from Okemah. In the Sixth, Jed Johnson lost after twenty years to Toby Morris of Lawton, a district judge and World War I veteran whom Johnson had twice beaten before. By a much closer margin, Preston Peden, a young Altus attorney and World War II veteran, ousted incumbent Victor Wickersham in the Seventh District. The Third District's incumbent, Paul Stewart of Antlers, opportunely decided against seeking reelection in 1946. His place was taken by yet another combat veteran, Carl Albert, whose birth in the modest community of Bugtussle was no handicap to his later status as a Rhodes scholar and eventual speaker of the United States House of Representatives.

Two bruising intraparty fights in a year of national Democratic decline augured ill for the success of Turner and the ticket that he headed into November's general election. While the Democrats were quarrelling as usual, the Republicans sat quietly and all but unanimously chose the former mayor of Tulsa, Olney F. Flynn, as their nominee. The son of the GOP's territorial congressional delegate, Flynn was an able administrator, who was credited with restoring the fiscal soundness of Tulsa's municipal government. A conservative lawyer and oilman, he shared most of Turner's campaign virtues, and Republicans could claim, with some justification, that he was more experienced in public affairs. His bulwark was Tulsa County, which was also his greatest handicap. Other sections of the state resented the pretensions of the northeastern metropolis whose fabled "moneybag Republicans" at times seemed so impatient with the fate that deposited them in such a backward state, so benighted that it did not share the enlightenment of the Oil Capital.

In the general election campaign, the state GOP played in a minor key the refrain sounded by the national party in its slogan of disarming calculation: "Had Enough?" Accumulated frustrations and resentments against thirteen years of national Democratic supremacy were

---

[7] *Directory of Oklahoma, 1977*, p. 580.

Carl Albert as a young soldier (left) and as Speaker of the United States House of Representatives (above). Courtesy Western History Collections, University of Oklahoma.

focused on the unpopular price controls of the embattled Office of Price Administration. However irrelevant to the party battle within the state, Oklahoma Republicans tried to consolidate the support of the meat packers, real estate men, and lumbermen who were fighting for the elimination of the OPA. Their major Democratic target was the Fifth District's Fair Deal congressman, Mike Monroney, who was gravely threatened despite his 1946 *Collier's* award as the nation's outstanding House member. At the same time, they linked detested price controls to the state's "oppressive" taxes, echoing the businessman's conviction that the system "prevents industries entering Oklahoma and invites [the] industries you have to leave."[8]

On the opposite side, Democratic party leaders quickly patched over their differences in the face of an inspired Republican challenge. Gilmer and Coe, both of whom had further ambitions, endorsed the Turner ticket. True to his promise, outgoing Governor Kerr went to the state convention to affirm the party's choice as his successor. For the first time in years, the Democrats suffered no prominent party bolt, though their campaign was widely regarded as unusually listless. The party largely counted upon established voting habits for a victory, leaving the underdogs in the GOP to provide most of the fireworks.

The chief effect of the Republican campaign was to increase greatly the voter turnout, which increased by more than 115,000 over the 1942 race. The heightened voter interest still left the GOP behind, but by only 32,000 votes in the governor's race. One definite improvement was the party's victory in Oklahoma County, which deserted the Democratic ticket for the first time since 1930. In less glamorous races, the Democrats did better, sweeping the secondary races by familiar margins and preserving the one-sided legislative party division, thirty-seven to seven in the senate, ninety-five to twenty-three in the house. Despite the national Republicans' first clear-cut congressional victory since 1928, the state delegation remained six-to-two Democratic. George Schwabe and Ross Rizley retained their First and Eighth District seats, but Monroney turned back the strong challenge of Carmon C. Harris 47,173 to 43,508, to preserve the preponderant Democratic majority.[9]

Four state questions, all pushed by the Oklahoma Education Association, added to voter interest in the election and foretold the teachers' growing political muscle.[10] Attempting to prevent a recurrence of the often aired but never resolved textbook scandal, the voters approved a system of multiple adoptions for state-purchased texts. They also authorized an increase in local school levies to fifteen mills (subject to local referendum) plus an additional mill to support segregated school

[8] *Tulsa Daily World,* October 29, 1946.

[9] *Directory of Oklahoma, 1977,* p. 582; Benson et al., *Oklahoma Votes,* pp. 49, 98.

[10] The battle over school amendments—a battle that pitted the education bloc against critical taxpayers—is briefly recounted in William S. Harmon, "Oklahoma's Constitutional Amendments: A Study of the Use of the Initiative and Referendum" (Ph.D. diss., University of Oklahoma, 1951), pp. 110-15.

construction. In addition, a minimum appropriation, $42 per student, was required of the legislature. Within two years that fixed-dollar goal would appear to be inadequate. Faulty assessments continued to rob the schools of their basic resource, the general property tax. Increased state aid and local ad valorem levies both were meaningless without a thorough overhaul of local assessment practices. As demands for new construction, equipment, and decent teacher salaries multiplied, many already overburdened districts were too poor in taxable property to sustain quality schools. Abnormal population shifts, accelerated by the war boom in several communities, added to the burden.

Understandably, the educators did not wait long before taking their demands to the Twenty-first Legislature. Although the schools could count on increases in the revenues from taxes earmarked for education (primarily, a major portion of the annual motor license fees), they insisted upon general fund appropriations greatly in excess of the new governor's cautious recommendation of $18 million annually. Turner's figure remained firm in the senate, where President Pro Tempore Jim Nance beat back the efforts of the school bloc, ably led by Senator Furman Phillips of Atoka. The aroused teachers were more successful in the lower chamber, whose final appropriation added some $8 million to the governor's allotted figure. The governor's influence prevailed, however, in the conference committee, and the ultimate sum was set at $18,599,981. When added to the earmarked educational revenues, the total annual state contribution was a little more than $29 million, enough to tide the schools over another year and leave the teachers angry enough to fight another day.

While the schools battled for their share of tax dollars, road advocates struggled against other claimants to state revenue, as well as among themselves. After months of wrangling and logrolling, the legislature committed $39 million to road construction in the following biennium, with $11.9 million of that set aside for country roads. A bold move to shift road funds from rural to urban counties was turned back by Turner's veto. Urban forces did win one principal victory—the reorganization of the Highway Commission. The fifth such reorganization since the Trapp administration, it set the commission's membership at eight, each representing approximately equal population areas, since the districts were defined by the current congressional district lines. Moreover, the new board's decisions were partially insulated from political manipulations, since the members were granted staggered, eight-year terms to free them from the most immediate gubernatorial and legislative pressures. Finally, actual administration was left to an appointed expert. H. E. Bailey, a trained engineer, became the first highway director, his annual salary of $12,000 making him the highest paid state employee.

The most bitter road fight of the assembly involved Governor Turner's proposal for a $54 million toll road connecting Oklahoma City and Tulsa. Allied with the governor were the business interests of both major cities, who argued that the superhighway was necessary to relieve congestion on dangerous U.S. 66. The immediate opposition centered around the legislative representatives of the towns that would be by-passed by the new road. Aware that their Main Street trade would be eroded by the toll road, the legislators and their hometown chambers of commerce mixed the medicine of suspicion of powerful contractors and bond firms. Over strong protest, the 1947 legislature gave initial approval for an Oklahoma Turnpike Authority to begin the task of selecting a route and securing right-of-way and financing. The fight was renewed in 1949, when the authority barely survived an attempt at abolition. The issue remained alive through many a day in court, but the opponents could not halt the project. They did, however, exact a compromise that required the creation of toll booths within a half mile of the major affected towns—Chandler, Stroud, Bristow, and Sapulpa. Construction finally began in December, 1949. Delays continued as the federal Reconstruction Finance Corporation failed to buy turnpike bonds, forcing the state to turn to private bond firms. In May, 1950, a consortium of three firms purchased the bonds at under 4 percent annual interest, the repayment pegged to the $1.40 full-distance toll which was to be eliminated once the bonds were paid off. Further con-struction delays eventually required a supplemental $7 million bond issue before the highway was open to traffic in May, 1953. Appropriately christened the Turner Turnpike, the four-lane superhighway became the monument to a moderate governor's sensible approach to state administration.

While the toll road agitation mounted, Turner ended his relations with Ora J. Fox, the professional pension promoter whose endorsement had unquestionably bolstered the governor's 1946 race. Turner incurred the enmity of his former ally by vetoing two 1947 pension measures that provided for a mandatory minimum pension of $50 monthly (more than a third above the average at that time), as well as a rental allow-ance for those on the steadily lengthening welfare rolls. Fox responded with an initiative petition to secure the recall of elected state officials; its certain target was the governor himself. The secretary of state, Wil-burn Cartwright, refused to certify the measure's place on the ballot. Fox was more successful in mobilizing his forces to prevent a flank attack on his own activities: legislation designed to restrict pension agitators. Fox demonstrated his political prowess by killing the bill.

The final major piece of the governor's 1947 program was a $4 million reduction in the state income tax. Although exemptions were raised to excuse thousands in the lowest income brackets, most of the relief went to large taxpayers. Other schedules were mildly revised, but the basic tax system, securely lodged in the constitution, remained un-changed. The formula for distributing gasoline tax receipts was altered slightly to guarantee county distribution according to mileage, area, and population, each to have equal weight. The reformed formula did nothing, however, to limit the discretion of county commissioners in their road spending.

Nonetheless, the tax changes bolstered Turner's stock with the sensitive business interests, as did the governor's rock-willed stance on fiscal matters. He had a capable adviser and close friend in patronage adviser H. W. McNeil, whom the legislators referred to as "Coach." The governor quickly asserted his mastery of the unruly house rebels who threatened his leadership on taxation, highway, and school questions.

Turner also continued his predecessor's personal promotion of Oklahoma's industrial potential. He traveled almost as often as Kerr, advertising the state's advantages. Under his auspices, a three-car railroad traveling exhibit toured the midwestern and eastern states in the summer of 1947, proudly displaying its "Made in Oklahoma" materials and advertising the state's commercial assets: low-cost fuel, central location, access to transportation, and "the right governmental attitude toward industry." In an era of record-shattering postwar strikes, the industry-hunters emphasized Oklahoma's manpower, which they described as "industrious, war-trained workers, ambitious, loyal, lots of energy, NOT MAD AT ANYBODY and not taking orders from any Communist leaders." Only slightly less subtle was the tour's frank acknowledgment of Oklahoma's prevailing low industrial wages, justified on the imaginative grounds that the state's workers could supplement their meager salaries by raising their own chickens![11]

Like Kerr, Turner also used the Planning and Resources Board as a valuable staff agency to encourage further industrial location in the state. Its work was supplemented by a series of citizens' panels, filled with the state's most prominent businessmen, collected by the governor to win Oklahoma its share of the defense contracts parceled out by the air force as part of the massive military-industrial buildup of the early Cold War period.[12] The experience of McAlester was one example of local industrial development committees' work. The Naval Ammunition Depot there had laid off 4,000 of its 5,000 employees. The city established an industrial foundation, surveyed its resources, and altered its zoning requirements. Fully equipped for an industry-hunting campaign, the McAlester planners focused their efforts on clothing manufacturers likely to be attracted by the city's large surplus of women workers. In 1947 the campaign bore its initial fruits when the Seamprufe Company established a plant in McAlester, the company's first west of the Mississippi.[13]

The net effect of such efforts escapes precise measurement. The

[11] *Handbook for the Oklahoma Industrial Tour*, copy in Industrial Research Commission File, Roy J. Turner Collection, Oklahoma State Archives, Oklahoma City, Oklahoma, hereafter cited as Turner Collection.

[12] Industries Mobilization Commission File, Turner Collection.

[13] Speech File, Raymond Gary Collection, Western History Collections, University of Oklahoma, Norman, Oklahoma.

state's per capita income continued to climb, but measured in constant dollars, the increase was a modest 5 percent during the four Turner years, hardly matching the 54 percent increase between 1941 and 1947. Much of that gain was deceptive, for it was the result of the exodus of low-income marginal farmers. Agriculture continued the decline that dated to the depression. In 1940 the state's farms were still the largest single provider of state income, contributing nearly 22 percent of the total. By 1950, agriculture's long domination had ended, its contribution (14 percent) ranking behind wholesale and retail trade (23 percent) and just ahead of government employment (11.6 percent), manufacturing (11.5 percent), and personal services (11 percent).[14]

The 1948 presidential election, combined with an especially bitter fight over Oklahoma's choice for the United States Senate, provided the state more than its share of electoral fireworks. Because President Truman's defeat seemed all but certain in the summer of 1948, most local interest centered on the race for the Senate seat occupied by Ed Moore. Republican leaders, aware of Moore's extreme vulnerability as an aging reactionary, were relieved when Moore declined to seek renomination. The Republican captains turned to Ross Rizley, Guymon's four-term congressman, as their choice. Nominated over only token primary opposition, Rizley led a united Republican campaign into November, fortified by a million-dollar war chest and confident of repeating Moore's victory as a coalition candidate of Republicans and conservative Democrats.

On the Democratic side, former Governor Kerr was always recognized as the leading contender, but his nomination first had to overcome the usual intraparty bloodletting. In the first primary, Kerr drew nine opponents, six of them highly regarded vote-getters. The pensioners' darling, Ora J. Fox, was expected to run a strong race, particularly in the southeastern region, with its legions of elderly. Fourth District Representative Glen D. Johnson had already spent a considerable portion of his single House term campaigning for promotion. Three statehouse veterans—Attorney General Mac Q. Williamson, Lieutenant Governor James E. Berry, and Secretary of State Wilburn Cartwright—announced for the post. None, of course, jeopardized his state job while seeking elevation to Washington.

All of these were doomed by the entry of Gomer Smith. Always the shrewd opportunist, Smith capitalized on the opposition to Truman's civil rights program, magnified by current black challenges to Oklahoma's segregated education, to campaign on the revived doctrine of state's rights. In addition, he linked Kerr to every other unpopular Truman policy, denouncing modern liberalism with such vigor that he earned the warm if perhaps unwelcome embrace of Gerald L. K. Smith, the professional fear monger who had recently moved his "Christian Nationalist" headquarters to Tulsa. From his electoral base in Little

[14]Klein et al., *The Oklahoma Economy,* pp. 7, 39.

Dixie, Gomer Smith demonstrated once again that he was the best endowed natural orator and most dangerous foe of party regularity on the Oklahoma hustings.

Kerr, the target of all attacks, remain unruffled. Never deigning to mention his opponents, Kerr endorsed the bipartisan foreign policy of the early Cold War, skirted the civil rights issue, and never tired of expounding federal soil and water projects to "build Oklahoma."[15] His well-cultivated political network reached into virtually every community, and his showman's instincts were highlighted by his joint appearances with Gene Autry and his standard rally opening, the Daughters of the Pioneers "singing the songs you love best." His lavishly financed campaign forces erected hundreds of billboards, purchased thousands of dollars of newspaper space and radio time, and employed numerous functionaries to staff local headquarters. In some ways, Oklahoma elections had become biennial auctions, but Kerr's spending was so visible that it seemed to confirm his opponents' charges against the "millionaire candidate."

The returns of the first primary suggested that the massive expenditures might have been necessary. Though Kerr had entertained a faint hope of a first primary majority, he fell short by 46,000 votes, taking 135,878 ballots (37 percent) to Smith's 73,511 (20 percent). None of the remaining candidates came close.[16]

Smith and Kerr, renewing a bitter feud, squared off for the second primary. The former governor stuck to his well-organized campaign of economic uplift, his greatest danger that his overconfident supporters would be unmoved to vote. Smith grew ever more desperate, damning Kerr for alleged improprieties in the statehouse, denouncing the Truman civil rights program as designed by the Communist party, and defending his defections from Democratic regularity. The two Tulsa dailies dipped into their pools of bile to endorse Smith against "the vanguard of paid political healers" supporting the "millionaire corporation president," a quality not previously thought to be much of a liability by the Tulsans.[17]

In the end, Smith was unable to overcome the Kerr organization or his own reputation as an opportunist and party bolter. In a remarkably light turnout, Kerr maintained most of his initial advantage to win 168,861 to 124,519. Smith's only real strength was in the Tulsa metropolitan area and nine scattered southern counties. His insistence that opposition to federal civil rights was somehow befriending blacks was stonily rebuffed by black voters. With some justice, blacks could claim that they provided Kerr his victory margin, since nearly all the state's

---

[15]The Senate campaign, emphasizing Kerr's role, is covered in Anne Hodges Morgan, *Robert S. Kerr: The Senate Years* (Norman: University of Oklahoma Press, 1977), pp. 26-29.

[16]*Directory of Oklahoma, 1977*, p. 583.

[17]*Tulsa Daily World,* July 24, 1948.

70,000 black votes went in a single bloc to the former governor.[18]

The GOP presidential nominee was again Thomas E. Dewey. He had won 45 percent of the vote against the immensely popular Roosevelt in 1944. Oklahoma's Republicans, whose national convention delegation had been aggressively pro-Dewey from the start, had high hopes of carrying the state in 1948. Against this threat, the state Democratic hierarchy, commanded by Governor Turner and State Party Chairman James H. Arrington, forced a surprisingly united front upon the party. Oklahoma became a real electoral battleground for both national parties, its Senate seat as bitterly contested as its presidential electoral votes. Alone of the forty-eight states, Oklahoma had neither a Dixicrat nor a Progressive ticket to cloud the issue: both Strom Thurmond's southern state's righters and Henry Wallace's forces were denied places on the ballot, since neither met the mandatory primary requirements of the state's constitution and statutes.

In a whirlwind two-day appearance in late September, Truman delivered twenty-two speeches to Oklahoma audiences. The pugnacious Missourian grittily defended his policies and lambasted the "do nothing" Republican Eightieth Congress, particularly for its inadequate farm policies. Kerr tied his campaign to the president's and eagerly assaulted the "grisly record of Ross Rizley" in the powerful House Rules Committee.[19] For their part, Republicans counted upon Democratic disaffections to put Dewey in the White House, while they unabashedly appealed to conservative ideologues, anti-Kerr Democrats, and assorted race-baiters to retain their Senate seat.

The election eve prediction of James Arrington that the embattled president would carry the state by 100,000 votes was heavily discounted. Yet when the returns were in, Truman's majority over Dewey was an awesome 183,000 ballots, more than double Roosevelt's margin of 1944. Only the landslides of 1932 and 1936 exceeded the Democrats' 63 percent showing in Truman's behalf. The Democratic tide swept through all of the southern counties by top-heavy margins and spilled over into the traditionally Republican areas along the Kansas border. For all its confidence, the GOP carried only nine counties for Dewey, each by a narrow margin.[20]

Turner's insistence upon a united Democratic effort proved to be wise. The amazing Harry Truman led Kerr by 11,000 votes and carried seven counties that the Senate nominee lost. Indeed, it was Truman who carried Democrats to victory everywhere in Oklahoma. The congressional delegation became unanimously Democratic for the first time

[18]Benson et al., *Oklahoma Votes,* p. 132; Morgan, *Robert S. Kerr,* p. 28.

[19]According to Morgan, it had been Kerr's decision to run an independent campaign, for he believed Truman's efforts were doomed. The decision to unite his candidacy with that of the embattled president—a decision that proved to be surprisingly fortunate—was forced upon him by the governor and party hierarchy. For that decision and the united senatorial and presidential campaigns, see Morgan, *Robert S. Kerr,* pp. 28–32.

[20]Benson et al., *Oklahoma Votes,* p. 67.

in ten years. In the First District, it was no surprise that the popular Dixie Gilmer retired Republican Congressman George B. Schwabe by 10,000 votes, but the loss of Rizley's old seat in the rock-ribbed Eighth District was startling. Distrust of the Republican farm policies that Truman had so effectively denounced allowed the little-favored Democratic nominee, George H. Wilson of Enid, to carry eleven of the district's twelve counties and bury Milton Garber's hopes to win the seat long held by his father. At the local level, dozens of Republican county officials were washed away by the Democratic tide. The state senate's Republican delegation fell from seven to five, and the GOP's house membership shrank by nearly half, from twenty-three to twelve.[21]

The results confirmed the governor's wisdom in forcing common cause upon the state and national campaigns. The margin for Truman, his second highest percentage in the nation, was especially gratifying, since Turner had raised some conservative eyebrows in accepting the leadership of the national Truman-Barkley Clubs. More than anything else, the election demonstrated that Oklahomans were only superficially moved by the emotional issue of civil rights or the more distant implications of foreign policy, even amidst the Berlin airlift. Sooners feared Dewey and depression more than the assorted hobgoblins of the Republican ideologues. They wanted their share of postwar prosperity, and they followed the party that seemed most likely to offer it, unmindful of the frightened talk of communism, bureaucracy, and federal dictation.[22]

For the severely disappointed Republicans, it was a bitter lesson. The *Tulsa Tribune* reached for Shakespeare to record its feelings ("Oh, what a fall was there, my countrymen!") In an editorial as nearly Democratic as its readers were likely to see, the *Tribune* lapsed from its customary habit of inveighing against the "socialistic" New Deal to rage at the shortsighted reactionary principles of the discredited Eightieth Congress. Its conclusion that the election returns must stand as "a warning to the Republican leadership that it cannot stray too far to the right of center"[23] was advice that the most astute state Republicans would eventually accept.

Governor Turner's work for the national ticket had the more immediate effect of his being offered a Cabinet position as secretary of agriculture. Refusing the offer, the governor explained that he preferred to stay in Oklahoma to complete the program that he would lay before the legislature. In time, he might have regretted the decision, for the 1949 assembly proved to be notably unruly as well as surprisingly cool to many of his key proposals.

The Twenty-second Legislature gave some promise of being a smoothly efficient operation. Leadership of both houses rested firmly with the

---

[21] Ibid., p. 49; *Directory of Oklahoma, 1977,* pp. 584–85.
[22] Morgan, *Robert S. Kerr,* p. 32.
[23] *Tulsa Tribune,* November 3, 1948.

governor's allies, Bill Logan of Lawton, senate president pro tempore, and Walter Billingsley of Seminole County, speaker of the house. In addition, Jim Nance headed the critical Senate Revenue and Taxation Committee. Nance had previously served both chambers as their presiding officer, and he "knew the ropes." The members were to be the highest paid in state history. The electorate's habitual niggardliness had been temporarily overcome in July, 1948, when a constitutional amendment raised legislators' pay by 250 percent. Despite all these portents for a harmoniously efficient and professional session, the 1949 legislature established a record for length (eighty-six days) exceeded only by the First Legislature and a record for wrangling matched by few previous meetings. The main reasons were two weary but explosive issues: appropriations and prohibition.

In the end, the governor's fiscal leadership was severely tried. Appropriations were held to the level prescribed by the governor, but they were divided more to the liking of the powerful school bloc. Fifty million dollars, far more than Turner had recommended and 35 percent above the previous biennial appropriation, were allotted to the common schools.

An increased gasoline tax appeased the highway lobby, and the huge general fund allocation to the public schools was a morale booster, but they left meager sums for other state functions, most notably higher education and mental hospitals. College walls were straining from the unprecedented postwar enrollments, and the state's mental health system bordered on disgrace. Under the circumstances, the single solution was the one that Turner proposed to the legislators: a bond issue to finance the sorely needed construction and repair of college and mental health facilities. Closely following the governor's recommendations, the legislature approved a constitutional submission for an immediate $36 million bond issue, the debt to be retired by an additional two-cent cigarette tax.[24] Governor Turner ordered the referendum measure placed on a special election ballot of September 27, 1949.

A second question appeared on the same ballot. Inspired by the overthrow of prohibition in Kansas in 1948, repeal's advocates in the Twenty-second Legislature demanded a referendum on the subject. Long and fruitless hours were exhausted before legislative leaders finally shelved the move, preferring a popularly initiated measure. A new "wet" organization, the Oklahoma Economic Institute, prepared the petition that took the heat off legislators. As its name implied, the institute was composed chiefly of businessmen, who offered a new tactic, appropriate to the postwar era, for repeal. Refusing to debate the morality of alcohol use, the group argued that prohibition was simply an economic question, "a practice that is financing the underworld and depriving the

---

[24] Earmarking the proposed cigarette tax revenue and its attachment to the constitution was yet another example of the steadily more awkward tax structure. It was also an example of the government's reliance upon consumption levies, particularly upon items of disputed moral value, rather than other forms of taxes.

state of revenue from taxation."[25] More than 100,000 voters signed the petition.

In ordering submission, the governor incurred the wrath of the state's ever vigilant dry forces. Although this was the fourth time that repeal would be voted upon, Turner was the first governor to place the issue on a special election ballot, depriving dry forces of the power of the silent vote. Moreover, the proposed amendment was easily the best yet offered by the many wet groups. Unlike earlier submissions, this would have repealed prohibition outright, commanding the legislature to "enact laws for the strict regulation, control, licensing and taxation of the manufacture, sale and distribution of intoxicating liquors." In addition, it explicitly outlawed open saloons and the sale of alcohol to minors.

No doubt inspired by the repeal question, 590,000 Oklahomans—nearly twice as many as had voted on the previous three state questions—marched to the polls. Prohibition was given a ringing endorsement; repeal was voted down, 323,270 to 267,870. Only eleven of the state's seventy-seven counties registered approval, and of those, all but three were in the Tulsa or Oklahoma City metropolitan areas. Most voters stayed in the voting booths long enough to approve the $36 million bond issue, which won by a count of 343,900 to 239,190.[26]

Victory for the institutional bond issue gave the state some breathing room in its battle for decent state services within tight budgetary restraints. The actual allocation of revenue required a brief special session that met in December, 1949, and routinely approved Turner's recommendations. The largest part of the new money ($18.8 million) went to capital construction for the state's penal institutions and the hard pressed mental health and other cleemosynary facilities. In addition, $10.7 million went for the construction of new college buildings, including a new medical school at Oklahoma City. Another $4.4 million was set aside for the repair and modernization of the campus buildings throughout the state.

Turner cautiously introduced a series of reform proposals during his second biennium, but they stumbled on the rocks of legislative opposition and local intransigence. The governor's attempt to consolidate schools would have reduced the number of local districts from 2,600 to 680. It died a quick death in the legislature. County commissioners and their legislative allies beat back a similar effort to require that the commissioners share their road-building equipment. With that bill's defeat, each commissioner was left free to purchase whatever he might choose for his private fiefdom, a power that was central to the commissioners' local influence. A similar proposal, endorsed by the governor and tax-efficiency experts, would have required integrated state

---

[25] The recurrent prohibition controversy is fully treated in Jimmie Lewis Franklin, *Born Sober: Prohibition in Oklahoma, 1907-1959* (Norman: University of Oklahoma Press, 1971). The 1949 repeal effort is covered in pp. 150-53, quotation from p. 151.

[26] *Directory of Oklahoma, 1977*, p. 653. Of course, the two metropolitan counties heavily favored repeal.

purchasing for all departments through one central agency. It also lost. In the end, the one reform accomplishment was the long overdue reorganization of the State Board of Agriculture to remove the board's presidency from the long, archaic list of elected state offices.

A series of investigations completed the work of the Twenty-second Legislature. Nine investigations were sponsored by the house. Two confirmed recent journalistic charges of primitive conditions at the state mental hospital located at Norman; they became persuasive and vital elements in the popular approval of the 1949 bond issue. Investigation into the activities of Ora Fox ended with the denunciation of the professional pension advocate for his personal use of the old folks' contributions. Fox's standing with the pensioners suffered hardly at all.

Amid national fears of Communist influence, the state also saw a brief revival of red-hunting. Students of the University of Oklahoma boldly protested a proposed loyalty oath for college students and teachers. The indignant house of representatives named a committee to investigate Communist activity at the university. D. C. Cantrell, a poorly schooled member from Haskell County, headed the probe, which brought ten university officials under its searching gaze.[27] The committee found no evidence of communism, and its activities quickly became an embarrassment. Oklahoma County's young J. D. McCarty urged Cantrell to extend his inquiry into the school's football team, which had been seen wearing red jerseys, and House Speaker Walter Billingsley added that the marching band should be equally suspect. Representative Cantrell himself hardly contributed to the committee's prestige. His standard opening question of witnesses—"Where was you borned at?"—confirmed his confession that he "never went to school very much," as well as the educators' distrust of publicity-seeking legislative yahoos. Within a week, the committee quietly dissolved, its only apparent casualty its own chairman. Cantrell was firmly retired by voters at the next election.

The most critical public question of the Turner administration was debated not in legislative committee or the governor's office but in the highest courts of the land. Since the adoption of the territorial school code of 1897, Oklahoma's schools had been operated on a racially segregated basis. Mandated by the state constitution of 1907, segregation had since been reinforced by a variety of statutes that left little doubt of the state's intention to maintain segregated schools at all levels.

Of course, Oklahoma had not been alone in practicing educational segregation. At mid-century the system was either required or permitted in seventeen states and the District of Columbia, and its legality had been repeatedly affirmed by the United States Supreme Court since the landmark *Plessy* v. *Ferguson* decision of 1896. Beginning in the 1930s, *Plessy*'s "separate-but-equal" justification had been under legal assault,

---

[27] The 1949 investigation is covered in James Arthur Robinson, "Anti-Sedition Legislation and Loyalty Investigations in Oklahoma" (M.A. thesis, University of Oklahoma, 1955), pp. 86–97.

most notably by the Legal Defense Fund of the National Association for the Advancement of Colored People. The NAACP's dedicated if poorly paid staff of black attorneys resolved to break down the Jim Crow system by attacking it at its point of greatest vulnerability: graduate and professional education. That initial attack offered the advantage of hitting separate schools where inequality was most demonstrable, while minimizing public sensitivity, because the students directly affected would be adults. For the same reason, the NAACP chose to open the front in the border states, where segregationist sentiment was presumably weaker than in the Deep South.[28]

The first notable break in the segregationist wall came in one of those border states in 1938, when the United States Supreme Court ordered Lloyd Gaines's admission to the all-white University of Missouri. Responding to an NAACP lawsuit, the High Court ordered Missouri to provide Gaines the legal education that was not otherwise available within the state, since the state's separate college at Jefferson City offered no legal training to blacks.[29]

Despite the clear portents of the *Gaines* decision, Oklahoma did nothing to prepare itself for the inevitable challenge to its own segregation laws for higher education, though they were substantially identical to Missouri's.[30] In January, 1946, the inevitable came in the person of a bright, quiet young woman, Ada Lois Sipuel. A native of Chickasha and an honors graduate from Langston, the state's one college for blacks, Miss Sipuel applied for and was denied admission to the law school at the University of Oklahoma by university officials, who acted under state law. Amos T. Hall, a respected Tulsa attorney, appealed the decision to the District Court of Cleveland County on the basis of the *Gaines* case. When the state court denied the petition, Hall, joined by the NAACP's Thurgood Marshall, took the case before the United States Supreme Court. In January, 1948, the Court affirmed its *Gaines* decision and ordered the state to provide Miss Sipuel legal training.[31]

Inasmuch as the state's segregation laws had not been explicitly overruled, Oklahoma's answer was the overnight creation of a separate law school for Langston University, the black college. Operating out of a corner of the state capitol with a faculty of three Oklahoma City attorneys, the hastily improvised school asserted Oklahoma's fidelity to separate but equal—or, at least, separate—education. To no one's surprise,

[28]Richard Kluger, *Simple Justice: The History of Brown v. Board of Education and Black America's Struggle for Equality* (New York: Random House, Vintage Books, 1977), pp. 71-172.

[29]Ibid., pp. 202-13; Missouri *ex rel. Gaines* v. *Canada,* 305 U.S. 337.

[30]Oklahoma's critical role in the school integration cases is admirably treated in Kluger's *Simple Justice*. A briefer treatment is available in John T. Hubbell, "The Desegregation of the University of Oklahoma, 1946-1950," *Journal of Negro History* 62 (1972): 370-84. A detailed primary account is George Lynn Cross, *Blacks in White Colleges: Oklahoma's Landmark Cases* (Norman: University of Oklahoma Press, 1975).

[31]*Sipuel* v. *Board of Regents of the University of Oklahoma,* 332 U.S. 631.

Miss Sipuel and her lawyers refused to have anything to do with the new school and returned to court. The Cleveland County District Court certified that the separate school afforded blacks a substantially equal legal education and thus met the Supreme Court's initial mandate. Marshall again appealed to the Supreme Court, this time striking at the heart of the segregation issue: the Jim Crow law school was not only a poor imitation of the legal education afforded whites, but segregated education was, itself, inherently unequal education. Unwilling to go all the way, the High Court, by a seven-to-two decision, allowed the state court's judgment to stand. On that basis, Miss Sipuel was again denied admission to the Norman school.[32]

While the *Sipuel* case was moving through the courts, six black Oklahomans applied for admission to graduate programs at the University of Oklahoma in January, 1948. In keeping with state statutes, all were rejected for admission. The following month, as the state once more readied for certain legal assault, the governor and legislature endorsed the segregation laws and instructed the State Regents for Higher Education to plan for separate graduate facilities at Langston. The regents thereupon named a special committee of deans from the Norman and Stillwater campuses to study the feasibility of establishing and maintaining segregated graduate facilities.

The deans' report, issued in March, 1948, was a straightforward statement of the difficulties of trying to maintain segregated graduate education. If Oklahoma were to provide equal as well as separate graduate schooling, the deans said, the cost to the state for physical facilities alone would be at least $12 million. Moreover, staffing would be virtually impossible, regardless of the monetary outlay, since only a handful of black Ph.D.'s were then available to provide a faculty to approach the quality of those at the state university and the agricultural college. Finally, the deans estimated that no more than twenty-five or thirty blacks would enroll in the graduate courses in any single semester, leaving the expensive departments and buildings unused most of the time, silent monuments to the folly of segregation. The deans' conclusion was inescapable: blacks should be admitted at once to the "graduate and specialized programs in all institutions of the state."[33]

Logic and urgency from academicians annoy politicians. State officials continued to mark time, vainly hoping that the problem would fade away miraculously. The NAACP's Thurgood Marshall guaranteed that it would not. From the six rejected black applicants of January, 1948, Marshall chose George W. McLaurin for a test case. Sensitive to the segregationists' claims that the ultimate end of integrated education was the horror of racial intermarriage, Marshall, as he later confessed, selected McLaurin deliberately; at age sixty-eight, McLaurin was not likely to intermarry with anybody.[34] In September, 1948, a special three-judge

[32] Kluger, *Simple Justice,* pp. 258-60; Cross, *Blacks in White Colleges,* pp. 52-65, 73-74.
[33] Cross, *Blacks in White Colleges,* pp. 65-71, 74-76.

federal district court ordered McLaurin's admission to the university.[35]

The court's order finally compelled state officials to act, although it also granted them considerable leeway. Because the cautious decision had not explicitly overturned the state's segregation laws, the university regents accepted McLaurin as a student but insisted that his schooling be on a segregated basis within the university. On October 13, when McLaurin first attended university classes, he discovered that all his courses had been scheduled for the same room, Carnegie 104. The shape of the room accomplished McLaurin's physical separation from the white students: he was assigned a separate seat in a small anteroom that adjoined the main room. In addition, he was also assigned separate tables in the library and school cafeteria, as well as separate (but equal) toilet facilities. The judgment of the leading historian of the school integration battles must surely apply: it was "Oklahoma's most inventive contribution to legalized bigotry since the adoption of the 'grandfather clause.'"[36] In any case, the regents' decision was soon buttressed by an act of the 1949 legislature. As shaped by Senate President Pro Tempore Bill Logan, the statute allowed the admission of blacks to any of the state's colleges if the courses they sought were not offered at Langston. However, their instruction was to be, like McLaurin's, "given in separate classrooms or at separate times."[37]

An angry Thurgood Marshall immediately returned to Oklahoma to represent McLaurin before the same three-judge district court. He argued that the state's behavior was in direct violation of the Fourteenth Amendment's guarantees of equal protection of the laws. That argument, which would ultimately prevail, was rejected by the court. Holding that the amendment "does not abolish distinctions based on race and color," the court affirmed the university's internal segregation as "having its foundation in the public policy of the state."[38]

Appeal to the United States Supreme Court followed automatically. For the NAACP's strategists, McLaurin's case potentially represented a new beachhead in the struggle against segregation. Unlike the previous landmark school cases, *McLaurin* seemed to force the Court to rule directly on the constitutional legitimacy of segregation. McLaurin unquestionably had been afforded equal educational facilities. At issue was the question, as Justice Robert Jackson phrased it in oral argument, of whether "there can be no separate treatment of Negro and white

[34] Kluger, *Simple Justice,* p. 266. McLaurin, a professor at Langston University, was a poor candidate for intermarriage for another reason: he was already married. Ironically, his wife, in 1923, had been the first black to apply (unsuccessfully) for admission to the university. Marshall's sensitivity to the "race-mixing" charges was not unrealistic. Indeed, George L. Cross, then president of the university, reproduces several hysterical letters raising just that claim in *Blacks in White Colleges,* pp. 120–21.

[35] *McLaurin* v. *Oklahoma State Regents for Higher Education,* 339 U.S. 637.

[36] Kluger, *Simple Justice,* p. 268.

[37] Cross, *Blacks in White Colleges,* p. 111.

[38] Quoted ibid., pp. 105–106.

students that is equal." A unanimous but cautious Supreme Court answered only on narrow grounds. Without overturning *Plessy*'s separate-but-equal formula, the Court ruled that the state had acted unconstitutionally in its forced separation of black and white students, specifically that "the equal protection clause of the Fourteenth Amendment is violated when a state, after admitting a Negro student to graduate instruction in its state university, affords him, solely because of his race, different treatment from other students."[39]

The effect within the state was the quiet, desegregated admission of blacks to Oklahoma colleges. Only a handful were affected, however, for the Court left standing the major portion of the 1949 revision of the segregation statutes that allowed black admission to colleges only in those cases in which Langston offered no training—primarily in graduate and professional education. Untouched were the vast majority of undergraduate students, not to mention students in Oklahoma's elementary and secondary schools. All continued to operate on a segregated basis.

Like so much else in the immediate postwar years, the status of school desegregation was unresolved at the moment but portentous for the future. Braced by the *McLaurin* decision, the advocates of school desegregation prepared to press the attack against Jim Crow at all levels of education. The Turner administration had taken the first blows of that advance, but only the most shortsighted thought *McLaurin* to be Oklahoma's last confrontation with old injustice and newly asserted federal judicial authority. Similarly, the conflicting demands for ever-expanding state services that had shaped legislation in the late 1940s were certain to be reopened. An archaic tax system, operating within the awkward machinery of a frontier government, would not always be equal to the problems of a contemporary society.

[39]Kluger, *Simple Justice,* pp. 280-84.

CHAPTER 14

"Just Plain Folks": Johnston Murray Holds the Line

B Y mid-century, Oklahoma politics had assumed its postwar shape.
The central elements in every gubernatorial campaign and successive administrations were the level of state spending and the distribution
of state services. Rival contenders bid for the support of powerful voting
blocs—teachers, pensioners, road contractors—amid otherwise vague
pledges calculated not to antagonize the remaining constituents. Public
administration became a hazardous balancing act in which the chief executive attempted to mediate conflicting claims upon the state treasury.
At the same time, governors would be compelled to work with strong-
minded legislators, whose smaller constituencies often gave them publicity as champions of one parochial group against rivals from other
districts. Under the circumstances, the only thing more difficult than
gaining the governorship was leaving it with an untarnished reputation.

The mounting costs of modern statewide campaigns—television was
a factor for the first time—limited the 1950 Democratic gubernatorial
field to three serious aspirants. William O. Coe, who had made an excellent showing in his 1946 "get acquainted" race, had been preparing his
campaign for nearly four years before making a formal announcement
in April. By that time, he had created what most observers thought was
the best organization of all candidates—one that drew upon the quiet
support of Senator Robert S. Kerr's followers. Despite his alliance with
the state's most professional politician, Coe assiduously campaigned as
the war veterans' champion against the professionals. It was the veterans
who provided the backbone of Coe's organization, and their support
was repaid by the candidate's pledge to support a $700 state "bonus"
for participants of the late war.[1]

[1]Unidentified clippings, Governor's Campaign Scrapbook, Johnston Murray Collec-

267

Former Judge Frank P. Douglass resigned his current position on the Federal Mediation Board to return to the state and campaign as a "true Democrat" seeking the gubernatorial nomination. Linking himself to Harry Truman and organized labor, Douglass offered the closest thing to a liberal campaign that Oklahoma saw in 1950. The bulk of Douglass's support came from the state's thin ranks of organized labor, particularly the political action committees of the Congress of Industrial Organizations (CIO) unions. Attempting to broaden his appeal, Douglass looked to the elderly, whom he sought to woo with a plan of greatly enriched pensions, entirely financed by a two-cents national sales tax. The proposal's chances for adoption were dim at best—as dim as Douglass's attempt to generate a state coalition on behalf of Fair Deal liberalism.[2]

The most likely Democratic candidate of 1950 made no such effort. Johnston Murray's campaign was initially one of nostalgia, for the son of William H. Murray never let voters forget that he was "Bill's boy." As his father had done twenty years earlier, Murray announced his candidacy in January, on his mother's birthday. The aging Alfalfa Bill endorsed him as the best contender, "even if he were not related to me." According to the state's best known public man, his son, "if elected . . . , will be as diplomatic and careful as his mother's uncle. . . . Otherwise, he is a Murray. 'A chip off the same block.'"[3]

The *Daily Oklahoman*'s veteran political commentator, Otis Sullivant, observed that the Murray name was the candidate's greatest asset; as Johnston Smith or Johnston Anything-Else he would hardly have been regarded as a serious contender.[4] His personality was never the sort to inspire wild enthusiasm, and his public background was extremely limited. He had never before sought elective office, and his political experience was confined to perfunctory county and district party posts and a single year as secretary of the School Land Commission. Indeed, many of his closest friends doubted that he had the taste for the bruising political combat that the governorship demanded. They felt, perhaps rightly, that the quiet, unassuming man was being pushed beyond the limits of his ambitions, and perhaps his talents, by his vibrant, red-haired wife, Willie.[5]

The Murray campaign became an odd amalgam of the old and the new in Oklahoma politics. The candidate's public appearances were standard fare. Under the initial direction of John Steele Batson, a "Na-

---

tion, Western History Collections, University of Oklahoma, Norman, Oklahoma, hereafter cited as Johnston Murray Collection.

[2] *Oklahoma City Daily Oklahoman,* May 19, 1950.

[3] Campaign Circular of January 9, 1950, William H. Murray Collection, Western History Collections, University of Oklahoma, Norman, Oklahoma. Johnston's "mother's uncle" was the able and dignified Chickasaw Governor Douglas H. Johnston.

[4] *Oklahoma City Daily Oklahoman,* January 6, 1950.

[5] Martin Hauan, *He Buys Organs for Churches, Pianos for Bawdy Houses* (Oklahoma City: Midwest Political Publications, 1976), pp. 49-50.

"Just Plain Folks": Johnston and Willie Murray. Courtesy Western History Collections, University of Oklahoma.

tionally Famous Square Dance Caller," the Murray caravan daily made the rounds of Oklahoma's small towns. After a few hillbilly songs by Charlie Huff and his string band had drawn a crowd, Murray would make a brief talk—never failing to mention his mother and father— and pass out campaign leaflets to the faithful before moving on.[6] His campaign slogan was simple: "Just Plain Folks," a phrase used three decades earlier by the Hardings and with the same uncertain meaning. It was an apparent pledge to be a good ol' boy, just like the voters.

The Murray candidacy eventually reached beyond mere nostalgia. William C. Doenges, who owned automobile dealerships in Tonkawa, Tulsa, and Bartlesville, became Murray's financial "angel," in charge of raising campaign funds, chiefly from Doenges's fellow businessmen. Doenges did his work well, and the campaign never suffered for lack of money.[7] Businessmen liked Murray's pledge to "hold the tax line" and cut back on "unnecessary, wasteful, and inefficient" state spending. They certainly preferred that to Coe's budget-busting veterans' bonus and Douglass's suspicious alliance with the CIO's "labor dictators," as Murray always called them.[8]

Two other critical groups had moved under the Murray banner by early summer. Óra Fox, still enjoying his role of kingmaker with old folks' ballots, threw the considerable weight of his Oklahoma Welfare Federation behind Murray's pledge to increase pensions by reducing the spending on "snooping" caseworkers. The United Dry organization, fresh from success in defeating a special election on repeal in 1949, also gave Murray a ringing endorsement. The drys were preparing a counterattack to close taverns and restrict the sale of beer by local option. Though Murray stopped short of endorsing those extreme demands, he was the only Democratic candidate to bid openly for the prohibitionists' support, and he made clear his support of the state's existing antiliquor laws. More- over, the more zealous drys recalled that seventeen years earlier, Bill Coe, then a representative from Oklahoma County, had voted to submit the Twenty-first Amendment (repealing national prohibition) to popular vote—enough to condemn him as an uncertain ally in their ongoing battle with Demon Rum.[9] Thus the Murray campaign moved into midsummer, fortified by business, pensioner, and prohibitionist support, with Alfalfa Bill's heir proclaiming that "by the Grace of God and the help of the plain folks, we will make something of Oklahoma besides a place to be from."[10]

While Johnston Murray was assembling his gubernatorial coalition, Senator Elmer Thomas was fighting for his political life. Thomas was

[6] Assorted clippings, Governor's Campaign Scrapbook, Johnston Murray Collection.

[7] Hauan, *He Buys Organs for Churches,* pp. 17-29.

[8] Unidentified clippings, Governor's Campaign Scrapbook, Johnston Murray Collec- tion.

[9] Ibid.; *Oklahoma City Daily Oklahoman,* April 23, May 7, 1950.

[10] Murray statement of September 18, 1950, Political Campaign Correspondence, John- ston Murray Collection.

completing his fourth United States Senate term in 1950. By virtue of his seniority, he had risen to commanding heights in Washington. As the third-ranking Democratic senator, Thomas was chairman of the Agricultural Committee, as well as the Appropriations Committee's vital Armed Forces Subcommittee. From those powerful posts, Thomas had kept his record of faithful service to his constituents, overseeing the allocation of defense contracts and water projects, as well as the voters' personal requests upon the Washington bureaucracy.

By 1950, however, Thomas was clearly vulnerable. His once invincible political network had atrophied over the years. His sponsorship of farm legislation was no longer decisive in a state where scores of thousands of farmers had moved to town. New issues—particularly, those involving America's new global commitments—often left him fumbling for responses. Most of all, Thomas was seventy-four years old and no longer equal to the challenge of a vigorous young opponent.[11]

That opponent was the Fifth District's Representative Mike Monroney. A former newsman and a six-term congressman, Monroney had carefully groomed himself for the Senate bid. By 1950, he was ready, and he launched an energetic campaign against the aging incumbent. Through the summer, each candidate blasted the other with issues generated by their years of congressional service. Thomas criticized Monroney's opposition to the president's loyalty program, while Monroney pointed to the senator's vote to cut air force appropriations on the eve of the Korean War as an invitation to the subsequent aggression. At bottom, however, the contest was one of image and personality—Thomas, the aging champion of farmers, versus Monroney, the young advocate of industry and city.[12]

The primary voting of July 4, 1950, produced few surprises. As had been freely predicted, Johnston Murray led the short gubernatorial field, taking 240,991 votes, only 13,000 fewer than an outright majority. His lead over Bill Coe, the second-place finisher, was a little more than 88,000 votes. Frank Douglass finished a distant third. Monroney's lead over Senator Thomas was much smaller—15,000 ballots—but it was enough to make the runoff's outcome all but certain. John Jarman, a state senator from Oklahoma City, led the large field for the seat Monroney was vacating. Among the other congressmen, only the first District's Dixie Gilmer and the Fourth District's Tom Steed had any real primary opposition. Both defeated previous incumbents, Wesley E. Disney and Glen D. Johnson, respectively.[13]

---

[11] Eric Manheimer, "The Public Career of Elmer Thomas" (Ph.D. diss., University of Oklahoma, 1952), pp. 195–209.

[12] Ibid., pp. 210–17.

[13] State of Oklahoma, State Election Board, *Directory of Oklahoma, 1977,* pp. 585–86. A fourth gubernatorial aspirant, Phil Ferguson, received 22,621 votes, less than 10 percent of Murray's total. In the subsequent runoffs, Monroney's margin over Thomas grew to 27,000 ballots; and John Jarman and Victor Wickersham defeated second-place finishers. Dixie Gilmer was spared a runoff when Wesley Disney withdrew after the first primary. Ibid.

A. S. "Mike" Monroney, 1950 victor over Elmer Thomas and three-term United States senator. Courtesy Western History Collections, University of Oklahoma.

In the face of Murray's commanding first primary lead, Coe's withdrawal from the runoff would not have been surprising. Never had a second-place candidate edged the initial front-runner in a second gubernatorial primary, and certainly none had after starting with a near-90,000-vote disadvantage. Coe had won only eight counties to Murray's sixty-eight,[14] including Coe's own Oklahoma County—in fact, including Coe's home precinct. Surely, Murray's position was unbeatable, Coe's concession inevitable.

The concession never came. With the now visible support of the Kerr organization, Coe promised to "jerk the mask off Johnston Murray" and took to the airwaves. In a statewide radio address of July 10, he launched a vicious personal attack upon Murray as a "just plain phoney," unworthy of public office because he was a child deserter and a draft dodger. His opponent's previous marriage gave Coe the ammunition for the first charge. In 1931 a Cleveland County district judge had granted Murray's first wife a divorce on the ground of his failure to support her and their son. A second court order of 1938 had been necessary to compel Murray to provide overdue child support payments. In newspaper advertisements, Coe reproduced the two court decrees, dramatically underscoring the judge's declaration of Murray's unmet financial obligations to his first family. Murray's resignation from the national guard before Pearl Harbor and his failure to enlist during the war were the basis of Coe's draft dodger charge, a serious allegation as American troops were departing for Korea.[15]

Fresh personal indictments brought a daily barrage to the reeling Murray campaign. Hastily, Murray offered his defense. He had resigned from the national guard, but in 1938, nearly four years before the Japanese attack. After Pearl Harbor, he had tried to enlist but was rejected because of his age. As for the child desertion charge, Murray ignored the court's formal legalisms. But he did produce the "deserted" child, Johnston Murray, Jr., to campaign by his side, always introduced with "I love him, and he loves his daddy." His former wife, now remarried, announced that she intended to vote for him and, for good measure, that her present husband did too. The Murray forces even produced W. G. Long, the Cleveland County judge who had granted the Murrays their divorce, to announce that he also intended to vote for Johnston Murray.[16]

Meanwhile, a number of politicians, many cool to Murray but appalled by Coe's tactics, made their choice for the front-runner. Frank Douglass announced his support and urged his recent followers to turn back the "unjustified and unwarranted personal attacks" that would shatter the Democratic party should Coe take the nomination.[17] Jim Nance, the powerful legislator who had presided over both chambers, promised to

[14] Douglass carried Cherokee County.
[15] *Oklahoma City Daily Oklahoman,* July 11, 1950.
[16] Ibid., July 17, 18, 19, 1950.
[17] Ibid., July 22, 1950.

answer Coe's "fire with fire," and immediately did so by pointing to the challenger's dubious moral record on prohibition and a past filled with "mysterious connections of a shady nature."[18]

Still, it was Coe who was on the offensive, generating new charges faster than his opponent could answer the old ones. He also moved to attract new blocs of dissidents. Blacks, whose votes had been critical to Robert S. Kerr's Senate nomination two years earlier, were reminded of Alfalfa Bill's least enlightened racial views and cautioned that, in that respect, Johnston probably was a "chip off the same block." Similarly, Coe pointed to the senior Murray's recent fondness for Republicans, hinting that his son was a secret Republican hiding in Democratic robes. Both arguments were expected to be especially effective in rural eastern Oklahoma, where the black population was relatively large and the number of Democratic hardliners particularly strong. In that same region, Coe was invading Murray territory and proselyting Murray stalwarts for increased old-age pensions, without jeopardizing his unique call for ample veterans' bonuses.[19]

After three weeks of unprecedented gubernatorial bloodletting, the voters returned to the polls on July 25. By that time, Murray's 88,000-vote first primary lead had withered to virtually nothing. Coe swept nearly the entire eastern half of the state, but Murray's strong western vote gave him a final lead of fewer than a thousand votes in a total of more than 470,000. Coe immediately charged fraud and demanded a recount, which was granted after legal maneuverings. The recount benefited only Murray, however, and the final vote stood at 235,830 to 234,870.[20]

The razor-thin Murray victory and his obviously tarnished "just plain folks" image heartened only Republicans. Their own primary had been a model of decorum and boredom. Jo O. Ferguson, a veteran party leader, took the GOP nomination over four unknowns. The total Republican primary vote—55,411—was not even 11 percent of the Democratic turnout, a sure sign of the impotence of organization Republicans.[21] An even more certain sign was the GOP's choice of its senatorial nominee, W. H. Bill Alexander. A famous evangelist and minister

[18]Unidentified clippings, Governor's Campaign Scrapbook, Johnston Murray Collection.

[19]Speech File, Political Campaign Correspondence, Johnston Murray Collection.

[20]*Directory of Oklahoma, 1977,* p. 586. Martin Hauan, who served as Murray's press secretary, has asserted that "campaign managers for both sides" later told him that an unnamed political operator from southeastern Oklahoma had, in fact, added just enough paper ballots at the last minute to swing the election to Murray. The allegation can be neither proved nor disproved. However, the fact that Murray was reported leading by 591 votes with fifty-seven Oklahoma County precincts uncounted (but the Little Dixie vote already tabulated) on the morning after the election suggests that either the charge is untrue or the unknown manipulator was remarkably prescient. Murray's final margin was 970 votes. Hauan, *He Buys Organs for Churches,* p. 30; *Oklahoma City Daily Oklahoman,* July 26, 1950.

[21]*Directory of Oklahoma, 1977,* p. 586.

of Oklahoma City's First Christian Church, Alexander was a political amateur. As late as four months before the primary, he was also a Democrat who was considered a probable Democratic contender until his astonishing decision to seek the Republican nomination. His campaign as a Republican was riddled with irony, for although he ran with conservative blessing, he was personally considered a liberal; and though a renowned churchman, he opposed prohibition. Finally, his campaign manager retained his own Democratic registration and gave no indication that he would vote for, much less support, the Republicans' gubernatorial nominee.[22]

Under the circumstances, the best the GOP could hope for was that Democratic dissension would redound to their favor, and it did. While Coe refused a public break with the party, his supporters organized a "Democratic Veterans for Jo O. Ferguson" movement and sponsored full-page newspaper announcements that "Murray Topples in Shame: Records Reveal Child Desertion"—advertisements all but identical to those that Coe had run before the second primary.[23] The general election campaign thus followed long familiar lines: a disaffected Democratic faction spitefully abetting a party powerless in its own behalf.

The November general election established a new record for gubernatorial voting, as nearly 650,000 Sooners went to the polls. Democratic habits, spurred by Murray's reminders of "soup kitchens and breadlines,"[24] held just well enough to give him the thinnest Democratic victory (51.1 percent of the total vote) in thirty-six years. Ferguson's strong showing in the normally Republican areas and in the two metropolitan counties, which gave him a 33,000-vote lead, was overcome only by Murray's three- and four-to-one majorities in the southern counties. The Republican strength barely extended beyond the governor's race, however. Monroney bested Alexander to take the Senate seat, 345,953 to 285,224, a margin roughly equal to those in the other statewide races. The state legislature remained closed to the GOP; the senate split (40 to 4), and the house division (99 to 9) represented only a marginal improvement over the last election. The Republicans did regain the two congressional seats they had lost in the surprising 1948 Truman landslide. George B. Schwabe returned to his old First District post, beating incumbent Dixie Gilmer, and Page Belcher took the Eighth District seat from George H. Wilson. The remaining Democratic incumbents, like the new Fifth District congressman, John Jarman, had no trouble turning back Republican challengers.[25]

Five state questions added to the length of the ballots. Each was decisively rejected, including two considered important. Educators ral-

[22] *Oklahoma City Daily Oklahoman,* March 12, 1950.
[23] Ibid., November 1, 1950.
[24] Ibid.
[25] *Directory of Oklahoma, 1977,* pp. 586-87; Oliver L. Benson et al., *Oklahoma Votes, 1907-1962* (Norman: University of Oklahoma, Bureau of Government Research, 1964), p. 49.

*Nostalgia and perhaps an unfortunate contrast: "Alfalfa Bill" administers the
oath of office to son Johnston Murray. Courtesy Western History Collections,
University of Oklahoma.*

lied to bury the road builders' attempt to forbid the diversion of road-
user taxes to the public schools. Voters also decisively rejected the latest
constitutionally mandated referendum on the call of a new constitutional convention, 347,143 to 159,908. More than a year's study by
political scientists and civic groups was thus canceled, the victim of
voters' ingrained resistance to change and the particular suspicions of
urban voters that any convention would be controlled by rural interests:
the legislature had decreed that the convention be apportioned on the
basis of the existing lower house districts.[26]

The pervasive negativism on the referenda, like the pessimism of
recent political campaigns, was an appropriate backdrop for Johnston
Murray's term of office. Oklahomans who anticipated that the new
governor would exercise the forceful leadership that his father had
given twenty years earlier were totally disappointed. Indeed, the contrast between father and son was startling. The older Murray had been
unmovable in his convictions; the younger was given to indecision and

---

[26] *Directory of Oklahoma, 1977,* pp. 654-55. The remaining questions, also defeated,
called for a reorganization of the Highway Commission, the appointment of separate
regents for Oklahoma Military Academy, and strengthening the United Nations.

vacillation at critical moments. The elder had dominated his administration with an iron hand; his son left affairs of state to drift. Alfalfa
Bill had eschewed the ceremonies of office; Johnston seemed more
absorbed with the trappings of power than its exercise. His father had
advanced bold new programs, but Johnston Murray was content to hold
the line. If the first Murray was strong, the second was merely stubborn.

In accord with the state's custom, the legislators allowed the new
governor to select the leaders for the 1951 assembly (Ralph Bullard of
Duncan as speaker of the house and Boyd Cowden of Chandler as senate
president pro tempore), and they listened politely as Murray announced
his brief legislative program. In essence, that program was to avoid new
taxes and hold state spending to the lowest possible level. With no more
executive guidance, the Twenty-third Legislature began its biennial struggle over the state budget. Appropriations became the assembly's chief
preoccupation, the allocation of money its only real accomplishment.

In the end, the state budget established a new record for state spending, $144.8 million over the next two years. The figure was deceptive,
however, for virtually all of the increase was due to the artificial increase in state revenue from the continuing inflation that followed the
end of postwar controls and the beginning of the Korean War. The
same inflation limited actual increases in state services. The small real
improvement that was made, mostly in behalf of the common schools
and mental hospitals, came from the single breach in the governor's
no-new-tax policy, a three-dollar per gallon increase in the state's beer
tax.

Without significant increases in spending, every major state responsibility began to show the strains of the administration's obsession with
economy. Road building slowed appreciably, as the Korean War drove
construction costs well beyond the earmarked funds. Improvements
already planned were eventually made, but the shortage of money forced
the Highway Department to take eighteen months to complete work
that had been scheduled for twelve. At the same time, work slowed
on the nearly completed Turner Turnpike, not for lack of money but
because of the governor's indecision. By the time Murray had finally
decided on the relative merits of asphalt and concrete, changing his
mind almost daily, the state was forced to supplement its initial indebtedness with another $5 million bond sale.

As the first of the postwar babies prepared to descend upon the state's
classrooms, educators appealed for dramatic increases in state aid. The
governor had responded with adamant insistence that the common
school appropriation not be increased at all above the previous biennium's $50 million. The eventual $58.6 million appropriation owed nothing to him and hardly satisfied the schools' demands.[27]

Murray yielded on the final increase because he had no choice. His
original plan had been to hold state aid constant while forcing local

[27] *Oklahoma City Daily Oklahoman,* May 16, 1951.

governments to increase their contributions to the schools. Murray had sponsored a bill that would have compelled county assessors to place property on the tax rolls at a minimum of 35 percent of its fair cash value. Since assessments averaged only 25 percent of true value, the forced increase, still well distant of the constitution's toothless mandate of 100 percent, would have added some $18 million to county treasuries. Half of that would have gone to the local schools. Unfortunately, the governor's persistence was unequal to his insight.

After the bill's introduction, county officials raised such howls of protest that Murray's own floor manager, Bill Logan, reported that he could not find a single supporter for the measure, presumably including himself.[28] The governor refused to press the fight and accepted a cosmetic change in county tax boards with no penalty at all for underassessment. Reluctantly, he signed the appropriation for increased state aid, at the same time urging that the schools tighten their belts by reducing salaries and increasing class size.

Murray's negative economic obsession was best revealed after the 1951 legislature's adjournment. A record flood of vetoes (nearly forty) slashed almost $1 million from the appropriated budget. The largest cut was the $425,000 voted for the care of mentally and physically handicapped children. In killing the bill, Murray turned their problems over to the already hard pressed local school districts. At the same time, he also vetoed bills that would have liberalized eligibility for Old-Age Assistance payments, empowered counties to collect a quarter-mill levy to provide hospital care to the indigent, and assigned one dollar from OAA grants to group insurance for the needy elderly. The last two were rejected as the first steps to socialized medicine, the first as part of the governor's struggle with the welfare bloc.[29]

That struggle, setting the governor against his campaign ally Ora Fox, had broken open in a rare mid-session message in which Murray had declared war on the expensive welfare system. Citing the abnormal and growing state cost of Old-Age Assistance, Murray declared his opposition to Fox's proposed increase of the sales tax to 3 percent to finance larger grants for the meager pensions then paid. He was determined to cut total welfare spending.[30] The governor had no trouble on the first because most legislators were equally leery of a major tax increase. His close control of the Welfare Department allowed his victory on the second as well. OAA grants, which had averaged $50.15 per month when Murray was elected, were reduced to $45.80 per month during his first year in office. Moreover, tighter scrutiny of recipients steadily reduced the proportion of the elderly receiving state aid by roughly 10 percent during Murray's first biennium.[31]

[28] Ibid., March 28, 1951.
[29] Ibid., June 2, 1951.
[30] Ibid., March 7, 1951.
[31] State of Oklahoma, Department of Public Welfare, *Annual Report of the Department of Public Welfare for Fiscal Year Ending June 30, 1954,* pp. 43, 47.

The governor's leadership of the Twenty-third Legislature had been loose, at best. Murray was obviously much more at ease with the ceremonies of office than with bruising contests of power. He enjoyed sitting at the head table. Highly publicized tours of Latin America and attendance at various national conferences—Murray would spend one-fourth of his term out of state—repeatedly took him away from the capitol and its conflicts. His spirits visibly soared with the weekly open houses at the governor's mansion, an idea initiated by the vivacious Willie Murray. The open houses displayed the glamor and the prestige of the governorship, which he always preferred to its pressures.

While the governor relished his brief celebrity status, the legislators had a free hand in the more demanding work of politics. The 4 percent decrease in state population recorded in the 1950 census would cost the state two congressmen after 1952. The 1951 legislature reapportioned the congressional districts, without gubernatorial interference and with predictable partisan intent. The two traditional Republican strongholds along the Kansas border—the First and the Eighth Districts—were combined into a single district that would pit the GOP's two congressmen against each other in 1952.[32] Forced to sacrifice similarly one Democratic congressman, the legislators chose to combine Toby Morris's Sixth District with Victor Wickersham's Seventh. The two were considered the weak men in the state delegation, their maverick ways contributing little to Democratic fortunes. For the fifth time since statehood, the legislators refused to permit significant changes in their own district lines, thereby increasing once more the overrepresentation of declining rural areas at the expense of the growing urban centers.

It was also the legislature, not the governor, that was responsible for the revival of anticommunist concern. The 1949 assembly had embarrassed itself by its inept investigation of alleged radicalism at the university. But subsequent events—the perjury conviction of Alger Hiss, Senator Joseph R. McCarthy's daily sensations "disclosing" subversion in high places, and the outbreak of war in Korea—raised the specter of communism once more. The legislators' response was a new loyalty oath, replacing the earlier model and extending its coverage to all governmental employees as well as public officials. Without a single dissenting vote, the 1951 legislature required all employees and officeholders to affirm their allegiance to the United States, willingness to take up arms in the nation's defense, and nonmembership (present, future, and for five years past) in the Communist party or any organization blacklisted by the United States Attorney General as a Communist front. The governor approved the oath despite his conviction that it was unconstitutional, particularly in its "guilt by association" principle and denial of employment to those whose religious scruples forbade

---

[32] The two Republican incumbents never faced each other; Representative Schwabe died at the end of his term. Second District Representative W. G. Stigler also died before the 1952 elections.

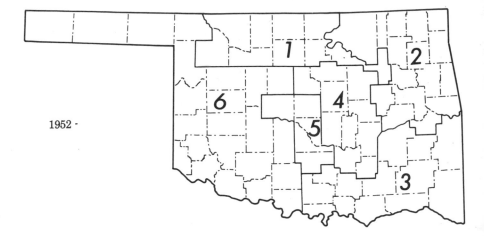

Oklahoma Congressional Districts, 1952-61. From Historical Atlas of Oklahoma, *First Edition, by John W. Morris, Charles R. Goins, and Edwin C. McReynolds.*

bearing arms. The governor justified his approval "to keep us in line with the thinking of the rest of the country."[33]

Murray's misgivings proved to be well founded. When eight professors at Oklahoma A. and M. College refused to sign the oath, seven as conscientious objectors and one, an Iranian exchange professor, unwilling to affirm American allegiance, the oath was challenged in court. A state district court upheld the act, Judge W. A. Carlisle declaring, "It's an outrage for people like that to draw public funds."[34] That decision was upheld unanimously by the state supreme court, but in December, 1952, the United States Supreme Court voided the measure. The High Court's decision, also unanimous, struck at the penalties visited upon those whose only guilt was their past membership in organizations that they might have joined in innocence. Justice Hugo Black filed a separate opinion that boldly assaulted the fundamental principle involved. "Test oaths," Black observed, "are notorious tools of tyranny. When used to shackle the mind they are, or at least they should be, unspeakably odious to a free people."[35] His point was lost, however. The 1953 assembly promptly replaced the voided oath with a second and more carefully drafted version to meet the Court's specific objections.

[33] *Oklahoma City Daily Oklahoman,* January 13, 1951. The entire story of the loyalty oath is told in James Arthur Robinson, "Anti-Sedition Legislation and Loyalty Investigations in Oklahoma" (M.A. thesis, University of Oklahoma, 1955), pp. 133-71.

[34] Quoted ibid., p. 163.

[35] Quoted ibid., p. 170.

The elections of 1952 separated the enactment of the two loyalty oaths. Ray C. Jones's Corporation Commission seat was the only state-wide office subject to contest, but the presidential race aroused enormous interest. For the third time an Oklahoman offered his presidential candidacy to the national Democratic party. Robert S. Kerr, though still in his first term, had become a major figure in the United States Senate. Within months of his arrival at the Capitol, the *Saturday Evening Post* expressed the nation's marvel at "the big boom from Oklahoma: the richest—and loudest—man in the Senate."[36] Allied with the acknowledged master of senatorial power, Georgia's Richard Russell, Kerr had quickly displayed talents and influence rare for a freshman senator. His leadership in the Senate's rejection of Leland Olds's renomination to the Federal Power Commission and his sponsorship of the bill that denied the FPC's authority to regulate interstate natural gas prices were measures of Kerr's incisive legislative mind. Both fights, critical to the Fair Deal's fate in Congress, established his national reputation. They also raised the specter that would haunt the Oklahoman throughout the remainder of his fabled career, of a special-interest, oil-and-gas senator whose public resolves reflected his personal business interests.[37]

Despite that image, Kerr entertained serious hopes for the Democratic presidential nomination in 1952. Since his rousing convention address of 1944, Kerr had been an intimate of presidents and national party leaders. Surveying the other possibilities, he concluded that Tennessee's Estes Kefauver was too independent, Vice-president Alben Barkley too old, Russell too southern, New York's Averell Harriman too rich, and Illinois Governor Adlai Stevenson too coy. Robert S. Kerr was just right—the happy orator, able to unite a divided party in a fresh campaign against the party of depression and Hooverism.

The Kerr candidacy was not without its detractors, particularly in Oklahoma. Few prominent Democrats shared the senator's sanguine estimates of his prospects. Moreover, Kerr and his growing organization within the state had made many enemies. Former Governor Roy J. Turner, perhaps the most popular Democrat within the state, was already preparing his own bid for Kerr's Senate seat in 1954 and understandably resisted any effort to increase his rival's prestige. The state's new junior senator, Mike Monroney, had won his own position without any help

---

[36] Marquis Childs, "The Big Boom from Oklahoma," *Saturday Evening Post,* April 9, 1949, pp. 22-23, 118-20, quotation from p. 22.

[37] Leland Olds, first appointed to the FPC in 1939, had asserted the commission's right to regulate interstate gas prices under the Natural Gas Act of 1938. Kerr split with the Truman administration in blocking Olds's reappointment and with his subsequent bill denying FPC authority over interstate gas sales. That bill was vetoed by President Truman. At the time of the controversy, liberal journalists asserted that the effect of the bill would be to increase consumers' gas bills by as much as $200 million per year and net the Kerr-McGee Company $50 million additional profit. The entire story, including Kerr's response to those charges, is well told in Anne Hodges Morgan, *Robert S. Kerr: The Senate Years* (Norman: University of Oklahoma Press, 1977), pp. 55-105, p. 93 for Kerr's self-defense.

from Kerr in 1950, and his philosophical differences with Kerr were well known. The critical figure was, however, the governor, the customary leader of the state's delegation to the national convention. Johnston Murray was in a position to get revenge for Kerr's support of Bill Coe's ugly gubernatorial campaign of two years earlier.

The consequence was a quick compromise between the governor and the senator. In exchange for a delegation pledged to Kerr's presidential candidacy, Murray received a free hand in dictating the state party's organization. Bill Doenges, the governor's campaign financier and chief adviser, took the national committeeman's post that Elber Harber had vacated to join the Reconstruction Finance Corporation in 1951. Smith Hester, another Murray ally, replaced James Arrington, Kerr's longtime confederate, as state party chairman. Murray thus acquired a power within the party beyond all proportion to his electoral or legislative influence. Kerr was guaranteed the support of his own state's delegation.[38]

In the end, Kerr had little else. Months of campaigning and heavy expenditures netted the senator just sixty-five votes in the national convention. Estimates of his spending ran to a quarter of a million dollars. An elaborate campaign headquarters at the Chicago convention included a facsimile of the Pontotoc County log cabin in which Kerr was born. An organist played songs from *Oklahoma!*, which Kerr had practically appropriated as his theme song. The Kerr candidacy collapsed, the victim of the senator's image as a brash wheeler-dealer. Publicly, Kerr was philosophical, commenting, "I've drilled dry holes that cost me a lot more . . . and had less fun." Privately, he was a chastened and changed man. In the words of his biographer, "unable to shed the stereotype of a parochial, special interest politician, Kerr now determined to exploit it."[39]

While Oklahoma Democrats were recovering from their last favorite-son presidential candidacy, the state Republicans had been stirred to unfamiliar vigor. Except for recurrent Democratic divisiveness, Republicans had few illusions about their party's electoral prospects. While popular Republican participation steadily dropped, the party's leadership had fallen ever more securely to a series of oil millionaires whose activities centered around Tulsa—successively, Jake Hamon, William G. Skelly, Lew Wentz, and Bailie Vinson. As Republican national committeemen, they dispersed federal patronage and campaign funds to build a party of unflinching conservatism, promoting their own brand of ideological orthodoxy at the conscious expense of a broad-based party of diverse popular appeal. The 1948 Dewey candidacy, which they pursued in Oklahoma as a holy crusade against socialism, federal regimentation, and other hobgoblins, had been a sign of their intent. Its dismal performance was the measure of their success. So too was the

---

[38] Ibid., pp. 121-25.
[39] Ibid., pp. 125-39, Kerr quoted p. 137, Morgan's judgment, p. 139.

steady decline in the number of offices, particularly county and legislative posts, that the GOP even bothered to contest.

The 1948 debacle had taught many Republicans the folly of their
party's self-imposed ideological straitjacket. In 1952 they were ready
to act. The presidency suddenly seemed within their grasp. The Korean
War, allegations of domestic subversion, and twenty years of one-party
rule and accumulated frustrations gave them their chance. In Dwight
D. Eisenhower, a candidate of such uncertain principles that he had
been considered a serious Democratic possibility for Truman's inheritor,
they had their candidate. Their greatest hazard was the still obstinate
fixation upon simon-pure conservatism.

The result was a rare contest for control of the state GOP, a contest
that pitted the self-styled "grass-roots" people against the "oil crowd"
leadership. The former were led by C. E. Barnes, an Oklahoma City
attorney, and drew their greatest following from the rural wheat belt of
traditional Republican counties, although they were also strong in Oklahoma City. The latter, led by former National Committeeman Skelly,
were based in Tulsa, the self-proclaimed "Oil Capital of the World."
At stake were Oklahoma's votes in the Republican National Convention.
The Barnes element favored Eisenhower. The Skelly band resolutely
promoted Ohio's conservative Senator Robert A. Taft, the beneficiary
of generous campaign donations collected from Tulsa's oilmen.[40]

The struggle raged through the normally somnolent precinct and
county conventions and into the district conventions of early 1952.
Only in the conventions held in Bartlesville and Ponca City—the First
and Second District conventions, both dominated by the so-called "oil
crowd" and the party leadership—did the Taft forces prevail. In every
other convention held outside the shadow of the state's oil derricks,
the grass-roots faction made strong showings for Eisenhower, reflecting
Ike's two-to-one edge over Taft among the Republican rank and file.[41]

The subsequent state convention, attended by 1,344 delegates, was
easily the largest and the liveliest that Oklahoma Republicans had ever
seen. Taft's and Eisenhower's followers were deadlocked, and there
were enough favoring other candidates to preclude endorsement for
either. The leadership was therefore forced to compromise with the
aroused insurgents. Though named the chairman of the delegation to
the national convention, Skelly and his six fellow supporters of Taft
had to admit Barnes and three other Eisenhower followers to their
circle, along with four who favored General Douglas MacArthur. That
division continued even as the national convention broke for Eisenhower. Four delegates stayed with Taft to the bitter end, and another
four supplied MacArthur's only last-ditch strength in the entire convention.[42]

[40] Paul T. David, Malcom Moos, and Ralph M. Goodman, eds., *Presidential Nominating
Politics in 1952*, vol. 3, *The South* (Baltimore: Johns Hopkins Press, 1954), pp. 296-97.
[41] Ibid., pp. 297-99.
[42] Ibid., pp. 299-302.

Unmindful of the GOP's internal troubles, the Eisenhower campaign compelled a desperate and temporary unity upon the state Democratic leadership. Kerr graciously lent his oratorical talents to Adlai Stevenson and spoke in typical rousing fashion in favor of the man who had taken the Democratic nomination from him. Governor Murray also stumped for the nominee, while former Governor Turner headed the national committee's agricultural division, and Senator Monroney directed the party's national speakers' bureau. Stevenson appeared in the state in October to deliver a witty attack on the GOP "Old Guard" and to remind Sooners of their past sufferings under Republican presidents. In support of the most literate leader since Wilson, the Democratic campaign could muster no better theme than weary reminders of the depression:

> *When Hoover was in I lived on a farm.*
> *A dollar bill was as long as my arm.*
> *I never saw a ten dollar bill.*
> *If Ike is elected, I never will.*[43]

Democrats could no longer convince voters that Herbert Hoover was the enemy. Neither could they present Stevenson as anything other than a liberal in the Roosevelt-Truman tradition. The metropolitan press made the Democratic nominee the tool of "labor bosses," "big city machines," and other sinister forces.[44] A large bloc of Democrats identified themselves as "Jeffersonians" and enlisted in the "Citizens for Eisenhower" organization, which appeared in sixty of the state's seventy-seven counties. The Eisenhower campaign was not one of inflexible conservatism, though, as the candidate himself demonstrated in his October visits to Tulsa and Oklahoma City. Denying that he intended to abolish Social Security or otherwise erase the New Deal's achievements, Ike promised only a decent and honest administration.[45]

Both sides and seasoned political forecasters predicted a close vote, but they were all wrong. A record 68 percent of eligible Sooner voters went to the polls to give General Eisenhower 518,045 ballots, 54.6 percent of the total. Eisenhower carried forty-three counties in all, including both Tulsa and Oklahoma counties, which combined to give him a 52,000-vote lead over Stevenson, about 60 percent of his statewide winning margin. The Democrats' presidential strength was confined entirely to their rural bailiwicks of the south. Even there Stevenson drew nothing like the six- and seven-to-one majorities commonly accorded Democratic candidates.[46]

---

[43]"Republican Nightmare," copy in Oklahoma Democratic Party Collection, Western History Collections, University of Oklahoma, Norman, Oklahoma.

[44]For a particularly good example, see *Oklahoma City Daily Oklahoman,* October 10, 1952.

[45]Ibid., October 13, 1952.

[46]Benson et al., *Oklahoma Votes,* p. 16.

To a remarkable degree, the Eisenhower victory was a purely personal tribute. While taking Oklahoma's electoral college vote, the GOP won only a single congressional seat in the new, six-member delegation. Page Belcher was the choice of his traditionally Republican constituents in the newly defined First District, but the Democratic nominees in the remaining districts rolled up 63 percent of the vote to take the other five seats handily. That result was strikingly at odds with the consequences of the two other Republican presidential victories. In both 1920 and 1928, the GOP had been able to pull congressional nominees into office via Warren Harding's and Herbert Hoover's coattails. Even more arresting were the results of the state legislative races. In both 1920 and 1928, the GOP had captured a large share of the seats in the lower house, 60 and 45 percent, respectively. But in 1952, the party that won the presidential contest took only 16 percent of the posts in the lower chamber, fewer, in fact, than they had won in 1942, 1944, or 1946.[47]

Ike's personal victory thus signaled no imminent resurrection of Oklahoma's Republican party. On the contrary: the conservative Taft element, led by oilman William G. Skelly and National Committeeman Bailie Vinson, refused to acquiesce in their convention defeat. Rather than use the Republican victory to build a strong state organization, the oilmen and the grass-roots factions continued their battle, with patronage and campaign funds the major weapons. The pro-Eisenhower group generally had Washington's ear in the distribution of federal appointments, but the unrepentant Taft group kept its stranglehold on campaign funds within the state. The GOP's leadership continued to operate at cross-purposes, and their rare presidential victory only widened internal differences.[48]

Among Democrats, the election returns were interpreted as a caution against the expansion of government services.[49] The three state questions that had been placed on the 1952 general election ballot each went down to crushing defeat. Ora Fox's Welfare Federation's initiative petition to increase the sales tax to 3 percent was defeated, 727,540 to 115,592. Nearly as large a majority rejected a proposed $125 million bond issue to pay state bonuses to veterans of World War II and the Korean War. A third question, endorsed by liberal Democrats since Kerr's administration, would have lowered the voting age to eighteen. It, too, was rejected, 639,226 to 233,094.[50]

The electorate's apparent endorsement of the status quo only encouraged Governor Murray's conservative inclinations. His required opening message to the Twenty-fourth Legislature reinforced his in-

[47] Ibid., p. 49; *Directory of Oklahoma, 1977*, p. 587.

[48] David, Moos, and Goodman, eds., *Presidential Nominating Politics*, p. 302; Stephen Jones, *Oklahoma Politics in State and Nation, 1907-1962* (Enid, Oklahoma: Haymaker Press, 1974), pp. 68-69.

[49] *Oklahoma City Daily Oklahoman*, November 6, 1952.

[50] *Directory of Oklahoma, 1977*, pp. 655-56.

dolent program of "keeping the lid on for economy and no new taxes."[51] Murray called for holding total appropriations to $158 million in order to save approximately $7.5 million that was available as new revenue. He made a series of recommendations to allow a cautious expansion in state services within that limited budget. These included such money-saving reforms as reducing the number of counties through consolidation, upgrading local property assessments, eliminating the homestead exemption from property taxes, and abolishing or consolidating state boards and departments.[52]

Those proposals were not without merit, but they were also without hope. The governor lacked the will to overcome, or even to meet, the legislative opposition to each. As statehouse observer Otis Sullivant wrote in the *Daily Oklahoman,* "It takes more than a speech, holding open houses, and performing the routine of being governor to drive through a legislative program."[53] In failing to exert executive muscle—control over state patronage, for example—or even to make his recommendations specific—which departments and counties should be consolidated?—Murray fell far short of that necessary "more." The result was that as the governor retreated to his public appearances, the legislature wandered without executive direction.

What leadership there was fell to the commanders of the separate chambers, House Speaker James Nance and Senate President Pro Tempore Raymond Gary. Although both were experienced in legislative procedures, neither was able to overcome the absence of executive concern. The two houses, moreover, were bitterly divided over the allocation of state revenues. The governor's figure was immediately scuttled in favor of funding decent support for public services, but while the senate favored highways, the house sought to award the increment to the schools and mental hospitals. The struggle ran through the entire meeting, prolonging the legislature to a grueling ninety-day session, the longest since the First Legislature. Fist fights and scratching matches erupted in the chambers as each house threatened the other with investigations. The governor refused to intervene, and the logjam was broken only after the legislators' pay dropped, after seventy-five days, to the minimum of $3.33 per day. After nearly a month of earning less than their own clerks, the exhausted members settled on a $166 million budget, just $1,000 less than was available. Included in the figure was $8.5 million from the general fund to the Highway Department, which had received none in 1951, and $62.1 million for common schools, an increase of $3.5 million.

The governor's vague economizing proposals had been junked altogether. For all the talk of consolidation and retrenchment, the only

[51] *Oklahoma City Daily Oklahoman,* March 20, 1952.
[52] Ibid., January 7, 1953.
[53] Ibid., January 11, 1953.

change that Murray saw through to completion was an innocuous measure to provide a central telephone switchboard for the capitol. His one success was approval for a turnpike system, already popular in the legislature, to authorize new superhighways between Tulsa and Joplin, Missouri, and between Oklahoma City and Randlett on the Texas border near Wichita Falls. Otherwise, his major legislative activity was a series of strongly worded veto messages over minor appropriations, many of which were summarily overridden.[54] So weak was his authority that veteran legislators strained to recall Governor Marland's fate with the "Spending Sixteenth" as the closest parallel.[55]

As poor as the governor's legislative relations were, his political ebb came after adjournment. As his own term drew to a close, his wife, Willie, began to run for the governorship in her own right. Johnston Murray had no illusions regarding his wife's, or any woman's, gubernatorial prospects, but he found himself unable to withstand her constant badgering that he mobilize his administration in her cause. No Oklahoma governor had been able to dictate his successor, but Johnston Murray reluctantly tried, despite his deep personal misgivings. His efforts to line up state employees and contractors in Willie's behalf[56] gained her nothing. The vivacious first lady was an energetic hostess, a piano teacher, and a competent performer, but she was not to be the nominee for governor in 1954. The effort cost both of them dearly. Johnston Murray lost most of his public reputation before an amused electorate. Willie Murray lost Johnston. After the debacle he finally summoned the courage to divorce her and free himself from her overweening ambitions, but not without a dramatic and humiliating fight, which Willie insisted upon waging in the state's newspapers.[57]

By the time of the humiliating divorce fight, Murray had already ended any hope of future political honors for himself. On his last day in office, Murray had addressed the legislature. Most governors had used the occasion as a final summing up of their administration's achievements, ignoring past battles with the solons. Murray, however, gave the legislature a "rawhiding," summoning all of the bile that he had previously used in his ignored (and unpursued) recommendations and veto messages. One last time, the governor scored the legislature for an "oppressive" tax system, "bloated" welfare expenditures, "queer assessment" practices, and hopelessly inefficient state and county administration. That said, he left Oklahoma for Texas, where he went to work for the Lone Star State's Republican party, and submitted his final comments to the *Saturday Evening Post.* "Oklahoma's In a Mess!" headlined the magazine's article by "Ex-Governor Johnston Murray," who

[54] Ibid., June 7, 1953.
[55] Ibid., April 16, 1953.
[56] Ibid., December 9, 1955.
[57] Hauan, *He Buys Organs for Churches,* pp. 56–70.

told a national audience of the "staggering maze of unsolved problems which shame my state and hold it in the category of the retarded."[58]

Murray's critics rose in righteous indignation, their bluster obscuring the possibility that much of what he had written was true. Apparently, many did agree, for the magazine reported that nearly three-fourths of the letters that it received in response to the article seconded the former governor's observations.[59] Long after his one serious study could do any good, Murray helped define the problems of contemporary Oklahoma government. In doing so, however, he had only magnified his own inadequacies. His administration had addressed those very problems with little more than speechmaking. His had been a "don't-rock-the-boat" governorship, and his final confession did nothing to change that. It only demonstrated that the boat was leaking badly.

---

[58] Murray, "Oklahoma's in a Mess!," *Saturday Evening Post,* April 30, 1955, pp. 20-21, 92, 96-97.

[59] Ibid., June 4, 1955. One letter of dissent came from Senator Kerr, who scolded Murray for selling his "birthright for a 'mess' of pottage." The fullest rejoinder subsequently was offered by Murray's successor: Raymond Gary, "I say Oklahoma's OK," ibid., July 9, 1955, pp. 27, 67-78, 80.

CHAPTER 15

Raymond Gary: Master of the Old Guard

O NLY in his flamboyant exit did Johnston Murray recall the drama of his father. Well before that time, the governor was a spent force, his standing probably higher with the remnant of state Republicans than with his own party. By the opening of the 1954 election season, those Democratic factions had become a bewildering patchwork of temporary alliances aimed at the two major political positions to be filled that year.

The senatorial contest, matching two popular former governors, was fought with heavy artillery. At least in the early skirmishes, the gubernatorial battle was waged with small arms. Sixteen candidates officially announced for the Democratic nomination for the governorship, and the resulting campaign was one of the liveliest in decades. The Murray administration was represented by two contenders. Willie Murray, the governor's wife, was the first woman to seek the chief executive's office. Fittingly, her platform included the pledge to place at least one of her sex on every state board. She also promised air conditioning and television to the public schools.[1] Her husband's reluctant efforts on her behalf were largely futile; most Oklahomans regarded her candidacy as a curiosity. The chief effect of her campaign was to deny the administration's full support to William C. Doenges, Johnston Murray's financial chairman four years earlier, and later the Democratic national committeeman. The Murray administration's influence, such as it was, thus did not affect the campaign.

Several of the contenders tied their candidacies to issues they hoped could generate a plurality in the divided field. Professional pension advocate Ora J. Fox made the predictable pledge to raise the monthly stipends

---

[1] *Oklahoma City Daily Oklahoman,* July 4, 1954.

289

granted the elderly to $100, to provide their medical care, and to double their homestead exemptions and thus lower their taxes. Promising to eliminate the Welfare Department's caseworker system, Fox also tossed out a series of bizarre proposals to attract random dissidents. State construction of bomb shelters in every city, the abolition of capital punishment, and the establishment of a newspaper in Oklahoma City to compete with the *Daily Oklahoman* headed the list. Given the generosity (and imaginativeness) of Fox's platform, his most incredible promise was the simultaneous commitment to lower state taxes.[2]

William Gill and Bill Logan were much more direct with their appeals, for each attempted to ride a single issue into the governor's mansion. For Gill, a former city manager of Oklahoma City, that issue was a state right-to-work law to limit the power of labor organizations and appeal to the mid-century Sooners' distrust of "labor bosses" and "union racketeers." Logan, a legislative veteran from Lawton, pledged to repeal the state's "unworkable" and "unenforceable" prohibition statutes.[3]

William O. Coe was the Murray administration's chief critic, as might have been expected after his razor-thin defeat in the runoff of 1950. Coe wasted no time in assaulting the "machine" of professional politicians, who were blamed for denying the champion of the little people four years before. No candidate surpassed Coe in his ability to play upon popular frustrations with the passion and speaking style of an itinerant evangelist. Coe promised to rid the statehouse of every employee, specifically to fire all welfare commissioners and fill their places with pensioners. Still the advocate of veterans' pensions, he once more advanced the notion of a soldier's bonus, to be financed by luxury taxes on the wealthy.[4] Through the long summer, Coe demonstrated his mastery of the Gomer Smith style of politics: dramatic, populist attacks upon the political establishment in the name of all those who nursed grievances against the government. His was a campaign deplored by most of the daily press and discounted by the more sophisticated voters; but it also had strong appeal, certain to end in the runoff primary, when again Coe could unleash his demonstrated talent for invective against a single opponent.

Most experienced observers agreed that the runoff opponent would be Raymond Gary, one of Coe's principal supporters of 1950. Gary announced his candidacy in January, and in the months that followed he stuck to the themes that testified to long experience in state government. A fourteen-year veteran of the state senate from Madill, two-term president pro tempore, and three-term chairman of its appropriations committee, Gary offered a reasoned and informed, if undramatic, analysis of state finance. His campaign offered a comprehensive five-year, $250 million road-building project to add 2,500 miles to the state system. At the same time, he also endorsed increased financing for education, mental

[2] Ibid.
[3] Ibid.; Martin Hauan, *He Buys Organs for Churches, Pianos for Bawdy Houses* (Oklahoma City: Midwest Political Publications, 1976), pp. 71-72.
[4] *Oklahoma City Daily Oklahoman,* July 4, 1954.

facilities, and the welfare system. Expected growth in state revenue, he insisted, would allow such improvements without adding to the tax rates.[5] His stump speeches, delivered in a straightforward, no-nonsense way, were no match for Coe's fireworks; but his campaign organization, which drew upon his legislative and courthouse allies across the state, was easily the best in the race.[6] In addition, his candidacy gradually drew the support of voters who came to recognize him as the most likely alternative to Coe.

As the gubernatorial race became a two-man affair, it came to resemble the United States Senate campaign. There, former Governor Roy J. Turner was clearly the only serious challenger to the incumbent, his predecessor in the executive's chair, Robert S. Kerr. Turner was a powerful candidate. His conservative and able stewardship in Oklahoma City gave him the support of the businessmen and others who distrusted Kerr's affiliations with Franklin Roosevelt and Harry Truman. Kerr's prestige had also suffered considerably from his ill-fated presidential candidacy of 1952, a debacle that many Sooners saw as evidence of the senator's "swimming beyond his depth."[7]

If accurate, that lesson had not been lost upon Kerr. Following his 1952 defeat, he deliberately deemphasized national matters to concentrate upon issues central to Oklahoma, particularly the development of the state's water resources and the farmers' struggle with the restrictive farm policies of the Eisenhower administration. Kerr was thus fortified for the showdown with another popular former governor. Refusing to mention his chief rival by name, Kerr emphasized the benefits of seniority in winning federal water projects for Oklahoma. The object of his special scorn was Agriculture Secretary Ezra Taft Benson, the contemporary version of his favorite whipping boy, Herbert Hoover.[8]

Although Turner was the early favorite in the race, he was unable to match the senator's incomparable appeal on the stump. Nor did he have Kerr's well-cultivated connections with churchmen, educators, and blacks. As his lead withered, Turner resorted to personal attacks, gleefully orchestrated by his campaign director, Gomer Smith, perennial foe of Kerr. Turner charged Kerr with excessive absenteeism in Congress and a voting record that made him one of the five "biggest spenders in the Senate." Increasingly desperate, the challenger's well-financed campaign churned out literature suggesting the incumbent's lust for power and resurrecting allegations of various conflicts of interest.[9] Kerr remained unruffled and never deigned to answer a single charge, content

[5] Ibid., January 21, 1954.

[6] Political Campaign Files, Raymond Gary Collection, Oklahoma State Archives, Oklahoma City, Oklahoma.

[7] Otis Sullivant, "Rich Man's Race," *Nation,* June 26, 1954, p. 542.

[8] Anne Hodges Morgan, *Robert S. Kerr: The Senate Years* (Norman: University of Oklahoma Press, 1977), pp. 139-40, 176-79.

[9] Senate Campaign Files, Roy J. Turner Collection, Oklahoma State Archives, Oklahoma City, Oklahoma.

Senator Robert S. Kerr poses with typical ebullience. Courtesy Western History Collections, University of Oklahoma.

to promote the development of Oklahoma's "wood, water—and wampum."[10]

Several intense local races added to the drama of the gubernatorial and senatorial campaigns. In fact, rumors of vote-buying in several of those races led Governor Murray to call out the national guard to oversee the balloting in five counties, an unprecedented step that *Time* magazine reported as evidence that "there's always an aroma in the State of Oklahoma" at election time.[11]

Despite the scattered presence of guardsmen, voting proceeded regularly and with predictable results. Kerr rolled up a huge rural vote to lead Turner by 33,000 ballots. Seven minor candidates drew well enough to deny Kerr a first primary victory, but he fell just short, with 49 percent to Turner's 42 percent. That was still good enough to force Turner's withdrawal from a runoff. In the governor's race, Coe used a strong rural vote, particularly in the extreme eastern and western counties, to take first place with 159,122 votes, 30.4 percent of the total. Gary, a native of Little Dixie's Marshall County, cut into Coe's former strength in the southeast and showed enough vote-getting ability across the state to place a close second with 156,376, or 29.9 percent. Only Bill Logan was anywhere near the two leaders. His 68,955 votes—nearly half of which came from urban Oklahoma, Tulsa, and Comanche counties—netted his single-issue candidacy just 13.2 percent of the votes, but it did suggest a growing sentiment for repeal of prohibition. Willie Murray could do no better than seventh, falling 5,000 votes behind Ora Fox.[12]

Turner's withdrawal ended their senatorial contest, but Democrats still expected a bitter fight in the Gary-Coe runoff. They were not disappointed. Recalling his tactics of four years earlier, Coe immediately pledged to open up on "the machine and the money hogs backing Gary."[13] During the three weeks that separated the two elections, Coe charged that his opponent was the creator of the undefined "mess" at Oklahoma City, a draft dodger, and the puppet of the powerful *Daily Oklahoman.* (His rival was labeled Raymond "Gaylord" Gary.) Seizing upon Gary's failure to vote on the latest loyalty oath, Coe added that there was "something maybe a little funny about his patriotism."[14]

But Raymond Gary was no Johnston Murray. The gentle-going Murray had fallen on the defensive, almost fatally so, Gary fought back, matching Coe allegation for allegation. Each candidate took to television to slash the other with the latest startling disclosure, and Sooners enjoyed a welcome break from the monotony of summer reruns. Following Coe's

[10] 1954 Campaign Speech File, Robert S. Kerr Collection, Western History Collections, University of Oklahoma, Norman, Oklahoma.

[11] "Aroma in Oklahoma," *Time,* July 19, 1954, p. 18.

[12] State of Oklahoma, State Election Board, *Directory of Oklahoma, 1977,* pp. 589-90; Oliver L. Benson et al., *Oklahoma Votes, 1907-1962* (Norman: University of Oklahoma, Bureau of Government Research, 1964), p. 99.

[13] *Oklahoma City Daily Oklahoman,* July 8, 1954.

[14] Ibid., July 14, 1954; Hauan, *He Buys Organs for Churches,* p. 79.

charges came Gary's counterattacks: that Coe had deposited in a personal account the $12,000 his supporters had put up for the 1950 recount; that Coe had introduced bills repealing prohibition and legalizing gambling during this brief legislative stint; that he had once sponsored a bill mandating the lash for juvenile offenders. Whatever its value as television entertainment, the state's political discourse reached its nadir when each candidate dramatically held up photographs of the other's expensive home, to prove somehow his rival's unfitness to govern common folks.[15]

The second primary results closely followed the first. Coe continued his hold on the extreme east and west, but Gary consolidated most of the support that had gone to the other contenders to keep the margin close in the rural areas and ride to victory on a 14,000-vote majority from populous Oklahoma and Tulsa counties.[16]

In the other feature race, James E. Berry's twenty-year tenure as lieutenant governor was finally ended by Caddo rancher Cowboy Pink Williams. Born James Pinckney Williams sixty-two years earlier, he recently had achieved notoriety when the Post Office Department refused to mail his printed postcards that invited Democratic farmers to a public kicking of Republican posteriors, determining that the cards were obscene. Just before the 1954 filing period, he legally changed his name to Cowboy Pink, and his new name and fame enabled him to overtake Berry's nearly two-to-one lead in the first primary and retire the incumbent by 19,000 votes in the runoff.[17]

Amidst the typical Democratic furor, the tattered remnants of the GOP held their own nominating primary with equally typical lethargy. Two years after Eisenhower's presidential landslide, state Republicans could muster no candidates at all for eleven of the twenty-three statewide elective offices, and in only three instances did they have as many as two. With barely 10 percent of the Democrats' primary turnout, the Republicans nominated Reuben Sparks, a Woodward attorney, for the governorship and Fred M. Mock, former United States Attorney for Oklahoma's Western District, for the Senate. Kenneth W. Gray won the dubious privilege of contesting Cowboy Pink for the lieutenant governorship.[18]

The obvious disinterest in Republican party fortunes testified to the failure of the grass-roots movement of 1952. By 1954, the conservative Tulsa oilman and National Commiteeman Bailie Vinson ousted the grassroots faction's leader, Floyd Carrier, as state party chairman and once again monopolized both party finances and patronage. Both powers were used to maintain the party's simon-pure ideology at the expense

[15] *Oklahoma City Daily Oklahoman,* July 20, 24, 1954; Hauan, *He Buys Organs for Churches,* pp. 86-87.
[16] The final margin favored Gary 251,920 to 233,079. *Directory of Oklahoma, 1977,* p. 589.
[17] Ibid.; *Oklahoma City Daily Oklahoman,* July 28, 1954.
[18] *Directory of Oklahoma, 1977,* p. 591.

of a broader electoral appeal.[19] Under those circumstances, the GOP's chances still rested on the decisions of its rivals, particularly embittered Democratic bolters. In 1950, Coe's supporters had played that role. In 1954, Coe joined them. In major radio addresses, Coe announced his support of Sparks in preference to Gary and his presumed machine.[20] At the same time, Roy Turner conspicuously refused to campaign in Kerr's behalf, although he stopped short of an actual party break.

Neither Turner's coolness nor Coe's fire had much effect. In the November general election, Gary won the largest majority that any Democratic nominee had won since Leon Phillips's depression-era victory of 1938. Kerr was reelected by a smaller but still comfortable margin. Even in these glamour races, the results demonstrated the aberrant nature of the Eisenhower victory. Pre-1952 voting habits remained unchanged; Sparks and Mock were strong only in the traditional Republican counties of the northern belt, while the southern half of the state returned to its accustomed top-heavy Democratic majorities. The congressional delegation remained unchanged, and every Democratic nominee for the lesser state offices, including Cowboy Pink Williams, won with about 60 percent of the vote. The Republicans failed even to contest roughly half the legislative seats, hence the division of the two bodies revealed a familiar Democratic preponderance, 102 to 19 in the house and 39 to 5 in the senate.[21]

Raymond Dancel Gary, Oklahoma's fifteenth governor, was born to a family of Marshall County tenant farmers on January 21, 1908. After a typical farm boyhood, he attended the teachers' college at Durant and taught in the county's schools before being elected school superintendent. In 1940 he left that post for the state senate, and served six years as chairman of the critical appropriations committee and four as president pro tempore. Gary retained his farming and ranching interests during his political rise and, after 1945, developed the Sooner Oil Company, a small distributing firm. Politics was his passion, however, and his was the politics of the Little Dixie tradition. A confirmed dry, he was also an active Baptist layman who served as a trustee of the Oklahoma Baptist Convention.[22] Gary never became a polished public speaker, and his efforts were delivered in a bucolic twang with many grammatical lapses. But few, if any, governors matched his intimate knowledge of public affairs and understanding of the legislative process.

Both were revealed at the very start of his term. Gary delivered the governor's traditional legislative message extemporaneously, his lack of notes underscoring his thorough familiarity with the state's business. In broad strokes, he sketched his program: a vastly improved highway system; a major overhaul of school financing; a new water authority; a

[19] *Oklahoma City Daily Oklahoman,* January 4, 1955.
[20] Ibid., October 1, 1954.
[21] *Directory of Oklahoma, 1977,* pp. 591-92; Benson et al., *Oklahoma Votes,* p. 49.
[22] *Oklahoma City Daily Oklahoman,* October 3, 1954.

Governor Raymond Gary, the acknowledged master of traditional state politics. Courtesy Western History Collections, University of Oklahoma.

proposed department of commerce and industry; and a limit of state spending to $170 million.[23] Unlike Johnston Murray's visionary demands, Gary's recommendations did not risk futile confrontations with legislative blocs or local interests. Unlike his predecessor, Raymond Gary had the power—and the determination—to push them through.

Under the governor's guidance, the Twenty-fifth Legislature solemnly went about its tasks, avoiding most of the tomfoolery that had prolonged the previous assembly. One by one, Gary's recommendations became law. Within a month, the Department of Commerce and Industry was approved, to assume the search for new industries, neglected by the overburdened Planning and Resources Board. A Water Study Commission laid the groundwork for the promised water authority that would be created in 1957.

As in every postwar session, appropriations generated the most wrangling. Again, Gary's control remained firm. An expanded road system had been his chief campaign promise and high on his list of legislative priorities. The complacent legislature approved his specific proposals. Ten million dollars of general fund money was added to the Highway Department's regularly earmarked revenues and growing federal matching funds, for a total of nearly $84 million in the biennium, a 50 percent increase achieved without strain. At the same time, Gary's Highway Commission developed a system of "sufficiency ratings" to improve coordination and establish priorities in road construction. A legislative act, endorsed by the governor, also placed the first, if loose, restrictions on the county commissioners' use of road funds.[24]

The developing highway system not only redeemed the governor's campaign promises but also raised his power over the legislature. Gary knew from experience that the route to a legislator's heart often ran along the roads of his district. Gary acted virtually as his own highway commission, carefully approving projects most likely to bring the recalcitrant lawmakers to terms. If one result was a criticism from the metropolitan press over "political" roads in favored rural areas, another was an executive direction rare to postwar politics.[25]

The surest test of the governor's leadership was the final shape given the state budget. Total appropriations squared almost exactly with Gary's initial recommendations. At $168 million, a slight increase of $1.5 million over the previous biennium, the budget required no increase in general taxes,[26] but neither did it allow any great expansion of services. Mental hospitals and other social service institutions received $25.5 million, no real gain. Although continuing enrollment increases had forced college operating expenses up by 12 percent and compelled the state regents to request an additional $21 million, Gary's higher education figure pre-

[23] Ibid., January 12, 1955.

[24] Ibid., February 3, May 29, 1955.

[25] Ibid., January 4, 1959.

[26] The fee for drivers' licenses was increased by fifty cents, the proceeds devoted to making the Department of Public Safety self-sufficient.

vailed; the final appropriation for colleges increased by only $1 million, to about $37 million for the 1955-57 biennium.[27]

Common school financing was the sternest test of Gary's leadership. By declaring all segregated schooling unconstitutional, the United States Supreme Court's epochal *Brown* decision of May, 1954, extended the principles tentatively advanced in the earlier *Sipuel* and *McLaurin* decisions. At the same time, the decision threatened not only the state's traditional racial policies but the entire structure of public school finance. Alone of the segregationist states, Oklahoma had provided constitutionally for different financing methods of its white and black public schools.[28] For white schools, taxes were levied and budgets were planned on a district basis, with the state supplementing the local collections. Black schools, however, were funded by a four-mill countywide levy, which was also enriched by the state. The probable Supreme Court-ordered prohibition of the separate funding arrangements, therefore, would imperil the financing of the entire public school system.

To Gary's credit, his administration did not hesitate. As a candidate, he had pledged acceptance of the High Court's 1954 decision, and as governor he did not wait for the Court's final implementation decree of 1955. While other governors prepared to resist school desegregation, Gary reaffirmed his commitment to the *Brown* principle, refused to countenance schemes of resistance or "contravention," and presented the legislature with a thoroughgoing proposal to ease the state's acceptance of the inevitable. The governor carefully shepherded an omnibus amendment that removed the constitution's separate financing mandate; transferred the existing county levies for black schools to the local districts; authorized up to ten additional mills for school support; raised district debt limits for construction; and provided a $15 million bond issue for capital improvements at state colleges and mental hospitals.

Tagged the "Better Schools Amendment," the proposal was diplomatically silent on its long-term effect, the financial emasculation of the state's segregated school system. But that purpose was not denied when the governor took the stump in the April, 1955, special election. Aided by school forces and his legislative allies, Gary underscored the amendment's significance, particularly in those counties with sizable black enrollments. His emphasis was financial: the amendment's failure could cost the state millions of dollars in local revenue and federal aid; its adoption could save at least $1 million from the closing of small, inefficient black schools.[29] Coupled with that economic appeal, however, was the governor's avowal of simple justice. "I grew up in 'Little Dixie,'" he confessed, but as "an active Baptist and believer in the scriptures. . . , I have never understood how persons can call themselves Christians and believe that God made them superior because they were born with white skin."[30]

[27] *Oklahoma City Daily Oklahoman,* April 1, May 29, 1955.
[28] Art. 10, sec. 9.
[29] *Oklahoma City Daily Oklahoman,* March 21, 1955.

Gary's firm endorsement of the amendment met virtually no organized opposition. In the April balloting, voters approved the change, by a three-to-one majority, 231,097 to 73,021.[31] Following approval, the legislature adopted the final school code, preparing the state to accept the Supreme Court's final orders, while also allocating $60.5 million to the public schools and $13.75 million of new bond money to ease the pressures on college operating budgets.[32]

Within a week of the legislature's adjournment, the Supreme Court handed down its final decree in the *Brown* case, ordering the desegregation of the public schools with "all deliberate speed." Under Gary's continuing leadership, Oklahoma prepared for good-faith compliance.[33] Although the State Board of Education agreed to allow the local systems a year's grace, the governor publicly warned school boards against unreasonable delay in accomplishing full desegregation. In that first year, 273 schools, including those of Oklahoma City and Tulsa, voluntarily dropped their racial barriers.[34]

In January, 1956, the state board moved directly against segregation by altering the formulas for the distribution of state aid to local schools. The effect of the changes was to place a severe financial penalty on those local districts that continued to maintain separate facilities. At least partially because of that pressure, an additional 167 schools opened their doors to blacks in September, 1956, when 3,177 black students attended classes with 88,990 whites. More than twice as many black students—a total of 6,583 —attended mixed classes at the start of the following term. When the school doors opened in September, 1958, the last year of Gary's term, the number had risen to 8,351.[35]

By later standards, that number was hardly awe-inspiring. Because the State Board of Education had stopped short of denying all state aid to segregated local districts, a large number of school systems, particularly in the southeastern corner of the state, continued to maintain separate facilities. Moreover, even those districts that had abolished de jure segregation usually continued to assign children to schools on a geographic basis. Such assignments, because of prevailing residential segregation, resulted in a minimum of integration. Thus, only about a fourth of the black students in the "integrated" districts actually attended classes with whites.[36]

For all its slowness, Oklahoma was at least moving toward full integration. In the same years that federal troops would be required to escort

[30]Quoted in Hauan, *He Buys Organs for Churches,* p. 121. See also Raymond Gary, "The South Can Integrate Its Schools," *Look,* March 31, 1959, p. 21.

[31]*Directory of Oklahoma, 1977,* p. 657.

[32]The remainder of the bond money financed the remodeling of Central State Hospital in Norman and a new school for the retarded at Pauls Valley.

[33]The state's early response to the historic decision is well covered in Monroe Billington, "Public School Integration in Oklahoma, 1954-1963," *The Historian* 26 (1964):521-31.

[34]Ibid., pp. 526-27.

[35]Ibid., pp. 527-29, 531.

[36]Ibid., p. 530.

nine children to Little Rock, Arkansas, classrooms and other public schools were closed out of spite, Oklahoma never joined the exhausting and destructive campaign of "massive resistance." Emotions were kept in check. District by district, the state's progress toward desegregation was enviable.[37] The dominant theme was compliance, not defiance. That record was chiefly the work of a state administration that never encouraged the possibility that the fateful decision would be reversed.

The 1956 elections were the quietest since World War II. Only two statewide offices were listed on the primary ballots. In an even poorer turnout than in 1954, the Republicans nominated Douglas McKeever for the United States Senate and Robert L. Kinkaid for the Corporation Commission. On the Democratic side, Mike Monroney was renominated to a second Senate term over token opposition. Andy Payne had served as clerk of the supreme court since 1934 on the strength of his victory in the 1928 cross-country "bunion derby" race. Attempting to move up to the Corporation Commission, he lost the Democratic nomination to Harold Freeman. In a match of two congressional veterans, Toby Morris won nomination to the Sixth District seat over incumbent Victor Wickersham. Before the 1951 redistricting, Wickersham had represented that portion of the district that was the old Seventh, Morris the part that was the old Sixth.[38]

The most explosive primary contest was an otherwise obscure, purely local race for the state senate seat representing Wagoner and Okmulgee counties.[39] Incumbent Senator John Russell, a strong Gary ally, was challenged by Tom Payne, who had backed Coe in the recent governor's race. Payne led in the balloting until Wagoner County's abnormally large number of absentee ballots were tallied to give Russell a narrow edge. Payne then filed a court protest aimed at invalidating the more than eleven hundred absentee ballots. At that hearing, evidence surfaced that twenty of Russell's campaign workers each had been paid with $20 relief checks issued by the State Emergency Relief Board. That board, independent of the State Welfare Department, was directed by Frank Easley, a Gary appointee and fellow native of Madill. Its purpose was to provide temporary support to the indigent until their relief applications could be certified by the Welfare Department. The board's local field representatives provided lists of the needy, who were routinely granted emergency relief checks. In this case, however, the Wagoner County field agent was Earl Johnston, Senator Russell's patronage appointee, and the "needy" included some very well-heeled Russell supporters. Their checks, approved by Easley, had been cashed by and

---

[37] Those impatient with Oklahoma's progress should compare its record to that detailed in Numan V. Bartley, *The Rise of Massive Resistance: Race and Politics in the South During the 1950's* (Baton Rouge: Louisiana State University Press, 1969).

[38] *Directory of Oklahoma, 1977,* pp. 592-93.

[39] This complex story is taken from Hauan, *He Buys Organs for Churches,* pp. 124-31. A more impartial account is available in Wayne F. Young, "Oklahoma Politics with Special Reference to the Election of Oklahoma's First Republican Governor" (Ph.D. diss., University of Oklahoma, 1964), pp. 194-98.

deposited in the account of Bob Jeffrey, Russell's campaign manager. Confronted with such evidence, the local court invalidated the absentee ballots. Russell then appealed that decision to the state supreme court. During that appeal, Wagoner County grand juries issued indictments against Russell, Easley, Johnston, Jeffrey, and Jeffrey's secretary, as well as Jenks Craig, Governor Gary's administrative assistant and patronage adviser.

The protracted criminal cases extended into 1957 and finally ended with Jeffrey and Easley pleading guilty on conspiracy charges. Johnston was granted immunity in exchange for his testimony. Russell's trial ended in a hung jury. Charges against the others were dropped.

Through the long court fight, underscored by the dramatic coverage of the *Tulsa Tribune,* Gary acted with credit. Though never charged himself, he could not escape the taint of political scandal that touched close associates. Nonetheless, the governor issued an executive order placing the Emergency Relief Board under the Welfare Department's supervision, suspended the issuance of emergency relief checks, and ordered a full investigation. His boldest move was an executive order of dubious constitutionality that declared the senate seat vacant and called for a new election while Russell's original appeal was still before the supreme court. Payne won the second contest handily.

The public furor over the Wagoner County relief scandal provided the state GOP a weapon in the general election contests. It was one that the state party desperately needed. Early omens of trouble in the presidential race, stemming from a severe drought and a marked decline in farm income, had been overcome by the voters' reluctance to replace President Eisenhower in the midst of the international crisis in the Middle East.[40] State Democratic leaders briefly pulled together to put 500 speakers on the stump for Adlai Stevenson in the final week, but few believed that Oklahomans would end their infatuation with their genial president.[41] Nonetheless, the GOP was clearly in the role of the spectral Wizard of Oz: all head and no body. Douglas McKeever, senatorial nominee and state ticket head, bravely posted election ads that were "paid for by the Republican state committee, not your WELFARE dollars."[42] Still, the party hardly anticipated any real gains.

They were right. In a smaller version of the 1952 campaign, Eisenhower carried Oklahoma by a margin of 473,769 to 385,581 over Stevenson. Nearly 90,000 fewer votes were cast than in 1952, yet Eisenhower's majority of 55.1 percent was slightly better than his earlier margin, 54.6 percent. Eisenhower's second victory rested on the same electoral base as the first: a huge lead in metropolitan Oklahoma and Tulsa counties and greatly reduced Democratic totals in the southern counties. For all of Eisenhower's personal strength, his Oklahoma partisans could muster only 44 percent of the vote against Senator Monroney and barely 40

[40] *Oklahoma City Daily Oklahoman,* November 6, 1956.
[41] Ibid., November 2, 1956.
[42] Ibid.

percent in the Corporation Commission contest. They had not even bothered to contest the four openings on the state supreme court, and their congressional candidates were all smothered, except for the First District's safe incumbent, Page Belcher.[43] The decline in Republican party fortunes could be measured the following February, only three months after their second decisive presidential victory, when the Republican State Committee called a meeting to plan the next gubernatorial contest. They failed to draw a quorum.[44]

The token Republican contingent in the Twenty-sixth Legislature[45] generally joined the massive Democratic majority in bowing to the governor's will. No executive since Leon Phillips was as secure in his legislative leadership as was Raymond Gary in 1957. House Speaker Bill Harkey and Senate President Pro Tempore Don Baldwin served as his dutiful agents, and the smoothly tuned session routinely approved virtually all Gary's initiatives.

The first of the governor's requests was directed at the still smoldering Wagoner County affair. The legislators quickly ratified Gary's earlier executive order that placed the Emergency Relief Board under the Welfare Department. They also approved the governor's proposals to tighten the distribution of absentee ballots, update voter registration, and grant the state courts jurisdiction over primary contests involving allegations of fraud. The first of those measures corrected the long-standing problems that made the Wagoner County case possible. The last was in response to the supreme court's recent decision denying jurisdiction in the Russell-Payne contest.[46]

The legislature then turned to the heart of Gary's recommendations for the second biennium: roads and schools. A record $18 million appropriation from the general fund to the Highway Department, record receipts from the gasoline taxes, and the new federal interstate program combined to make these the golden years for roads. The administration awarded $152.4 million in new road contracts its final two years. That awesome figure completed the construction or resurfacing of 3,519 miles of state highways under Gary's administration.[47]

More than $48 million of the federal money was allocated to Oklahoma's share of the new interstate highway system. As the slate planned the construction of the superfreeways, it shelved earlier proposals to expand the toll road system with new routes stretching north, south, and southwest from Oklahoma City and linking Tulsa to Dallas. In the end, only one new toll road, connecting Oklahoma City to Lawton, won final approval.[48]

---

[43] *Directory of Oklahoma, 1977,* pp. 593-94; Benson et al., *Oklahoma Votes,* p. 68.
[44] *Oklahoma City Daily Oklahoman,* February 26, 1957.
[45] The partisan split was 101 to 20 in the house, 40 to 4 in the senate.
[46] *Oklahoma City Daily Oklahoman,* May 26, 1957.
[47] State of Oklahoma, State Highway Department, *Biennial Report of the State Highway Commission and Director to the Governor of Oklahoma, January 1, 1957-December 31, 1958,* pp. A-14, A-20, A-51.

The unprecedented expansion of the road system, while one of Gary's greatest accomplishments, again opened the governor to attack for "political" road building. Critics pointed to the $6 million Willis bridge spanning Lake Texoma and the $2.4 million highway connecting the bridge to Gary's hometown as examples of projects whose most certain merit was to put Marshall County "in handsome shape."[49] Some even suggested that certain routes were laid out to benefit the economic interests of the governor and his closest political associates. The most prominent of those critics was H. E. Bailey, the powerful highway engineer whom Gary inherited from the Murray administration. When Bailey openly protested the elimination of new toll roads and alleged corruption in the sale of land to the Highway Department, Gary fired Bailey, who was immediately hired as a "road consultant" for the Tulsa Chamber of Commerce. Gary's response was to order the Highway Commission to "lock the desk" on all road projects for Tulsa County until the Tulsans dismissed Bailey. They did so, one day later, depriving Bailey of a forum but hardly silencing the suspicions of politics in Gary's road program.[50]

While defending his personal integrity, Gary also insisted that most of the talk about "political" roads came from the metropolitan press and its own fully political insistence that road funds be channeled away from the rural counties to their own urban areas. There was truth both in Gary's defense and in the metropolitan complaints. Although Oklahoma and Tulsa counties led the state in total road contracts, their share of the spending was nowhere nearly proportional to their volume of traffic. Moreover, the Highway Department's sufficiency studies in 1958 showed Oklahoma County ranking seventieth among the seventy-seven counties in the average quality of its state highways. Tulsa's rating was even worse: seventy-sixth. In both counties, the average state highway was officially classified as "inadequate," and Tulsa County's barely achieved even that ranking. In contrast, rural Pushmataha, Major, Cimarron, Blaine, Texas, and Marshall counties had the state's best roads. In fact, thirty-three rural counties each had highways ranked two categories above those of either of the urban counties.[51]

In some measure, politics did, indeed, account for the difference. Nearly five decades of malapportionment had given rural interests the dominant voice in the state legislature. Ever the realist, Gary had accepted that reality and allowed the distribution of road funds to mirror legislative power. He had used the same distribution to augment his own power.

The best example was the 1957 struggle over educational appropria-

[48] Ibid., p. A-51; *Oklahoma City Daily Oklahoman,* May 29, 1957.

[49] *Oklahoma City Daily Oklahoman,* January 4, 1959.

[50] Ibid., September 20, 1957; Hauan, *He Buys Organs for Churches,* pp. 116-18; Raymond Gary, "News and Opinions, October 16, 1958," Speech Files, Raymond Gary Collection, Western History Collections, University of Oklahoma, Norman, Oklahoma, hereafter cited as Gary Collection.

[51] *Report of the State Highway Commission, 1957-1958,* p. A-58.

tions. The Oklahoma Education Association and the legislature's school bloc insisted on increasing "starting teacher" salaries by $600, to $3,000 per year, with proportional increases for experienced educators. Determined to avoid a tax increase, the governor initially called for increases of half that amount. He eventually worked out a compromise with the house leadership: the full increase, financed by the savings derived from new legislation closing 200 inefficient school districts. Those who resisted compromise, like Jefferson County's Bill Bradley, eventually acquiesced when the governor revealed the cost of their independence—exact, district-by-district lists of the road projects to be cancelled should the compromise fail.[52]

In this case, the final result was an education bill in complete accord with the governor's desires. The final appropriation of $71 million was the largest single sum ever voted by the legislature. It allowed for increases in the average teaching salary to $4,700 by the end of Gary's term, an increase of nearly one-third over the four-year period. In addition, the Twenty-sixth Legislature added more than $4 million annually to the teachers' retirement fund by earmarking a portion of the gross production tax. Approval of the Better Schools Amendment in 1955 also provided increased local support for the schools, as well as the construction of 4,200 new classrooms through 1958. Altogether, Gary had redeemed the educational commitments he made as a candidate.[53]

At the same time, noticeable improvements were made in the welfare system and mental health program. Steady increases in earmarked sales tax receipts sent total welfare spending to nearly $100 million by 1958. In the meantime, the number of the elderly requiring state aid continued to decline as an increasing proportion began to qualify for federal Social Security benefits.[54] The result was an increase in average Old-Age Assistance benefits from $58.50 a month in 1954 to $65.32 in 1958. In addition, the 1957 legislature also approved a program of medical care for the needy, making Oklahoma the first state to provide medical treatment for its indigent citizens. That same assembly also granted Gary's request for a $4 million appropriation to the state's eleemosynary institutions, which allowed the administration to boast that the mental health system, a national scandal only a decade earlier, had reached the status of a national model by 1958.[55]

The governor's leadership, decisive over state spending, faded at those few points where it encountered entrenched political interests. Gary won approval of a general personnel act that provided standardized salary

---

[52] *Oklahoma City Daily Oklahoman,* May 26, 1957; Hauan, *He Buys Organs for Churches,* pp. 268–70.

[53] *Oklahoma City Daily Oklahoman,* May 26, 1957, January 4, 1959.

[54] In 1951 only 14.3 percent of the state's elderly citizens received Social Security benefits. By early 1959, that proportion had increased to 58.3 percent. State of Oklahoma, Department of Public Welfare, *Annual Report of the Oklahoma Department of Public Welfare for the Fiscal Year Ending June 30, 1959,* p. 10.

[55] Ibid., p. 1, table 4, table 5.

classifications for all state departments. The statute prevented legislative discrimination against the employees of the least favored departments, but it still left virtually all state employment dependent upon legislative patronage. Moreover, the legislature adopted nearly 200 local bills that altered county officials' salaries on an individual and often seemingly whimsical basis. Similarly, the legislators effectively emasculated the recently adopted amendment establishing a constitutional wildlife department. Approved by voters at the 1956 primary elections, the amendment's promise had been to remove the Wildlife Department from politics. In vitalizing the amendment, however, the legislature retained its full control over the department's rules and regulations.[56]

Gary was no more successful in restricting the powers of the county commissioners. Although he pushed through a bill requiring the commissioners to use 20 percent of the road income derived from commercial vehicle license fees to match federal funds, his bolder move to limit their total annual road funds to $29 million failed. Veteran capitol observers agreed after the session that the commissioners' grip on the legislators was so complete that only the most forceful of future governors could successfully challenge their influence and inefficiency.[57]

The succeeding administration would address just that point. It would also confront two other issues raised during Gary's second biennium: reapportionment and prohibition. Neither was part of the Gary official program; in fact, he opposed the first. When the urban Democrats and Republicans successfully circulated an initiative petition to call an election to force more equitable congressional districting, Gary used his prerogative to place the measure on the November, 1956, ballot, calculating that the large presidential turnout would doom the proposal by the silent vote. He was right. Although voters favored the measure by a margin of 391,453 to 297,628, it failed by 42,000 to win a majority of all votes cast.[58] An even more unlikely effort to equalize state legislative districts appeared in the 1957 legislature, under the sponsorship of Oklahoma City's George Miskovsky. Rural forces voted it down in a festival of derision. A private lawsuit, filed by Tulsa attorney Sid White and directed at the same end, also languished in both the state and federal courts.[59]

Unlike the reapportionment attempts, the latest battle over alcohol enlisted the governor's personal concern. In 1955, militant drys launched an initiative petition aimed at prohibiting beer sales on a county option basis. With Gary's blessing, the petition won 137,500 signatures; and after exhaustive legal challenges, he placed the question on a December, 1957, special election ballot. Understandably leading the opposition was the beer industry, organized under the name of Oklahoma United. The brewers' defense was an appeal to self-interest, typical of the postwar

[56] *Oklahoma City Daily Oklahoman,* May 26, May 29, 1957.

[57] Ibid., May 26, May 30, 1957.

[58] *Directory of Oklahoma, 1977,* p. 659.

[59] *Oklahoma City Daily Oklahoman,* February 2, February 27, 1957.

era: the prohibition of the sale of beer would jeopardize business, cripple tax revenues, and wreak havoc on all those groups dependent upon state spending. Thousands of letters to businessmen, teachers, and state employees cautioned them to "consider carefully the impact on [your] profession" should the measure pass.[60]

Gary, a devout Baptist who had sponsored an identical county option plan while in the state senate, emerged as beer's most prominent foe. The governor admitted to no doubts that alcohol was a greater threat than Sputnik, the recently launched Russian satellite. He also denied that the state budget had any great need of beer taxes. But his major point was the moral one, and it put him "happy to stand on the side of 3,500 churches in opposition to a commodity that is causing [destruction to homes] and . . . young people to wind up in a life of crime."[61]

Despite the governor's concern, the measure failed, 275,528 to 214,012, losing especially heavily in the more urban counties. The voting pattern suggested that the drys were the victims of loosened personal attitudes toward alcohol, attitudes that held the evils of beer less than the state's need for revenue. Disappointed as the drys were at the moment, they soon would be even more so, for their defeat revealed their first weakness since the statehood election and stiffened their foes' resolve to counter-attack in the name of total repeal.[62]

Because Gary had been too shrewd to make his personal preference a part of his official program, defeat of the beer measure left no mark of failure on his administration's remarkable record. In the last month of his tenure, he was able to survey its accomplishments: a record road-building program, "peaceful integration" of the public schools, an improved local base for education along with enriched state supplements, and marked improvement in the state's care of the needy. Privately, Gary confessed the source of those achievements: his administration had "absolutely controlled" the legislature.[63]

It truly had, and the consequences could be measured in the contrast with Johnston Murray's lack of that control and his subsequent failures. Unlike his predecessor, Raymond Gary was himself a legislative veteran, one of the fabled Old Guard, who was fully aware of the mechanics of political power. Eschewing hopeless confrontations, he had deliberately charted a conservative course that, for all its success, rarely challenged the legislature's ultimate sources of strength: its rural domination, its patronage prerogatives, and its alliance with powerful local interests. Those were the limits within which Gary achieved his success. They were also the limits that would define both his successor's campaign and the critical test for the subsequent administration's fortunes.

[60] Jimmie Lewis Franklin, *Born Sober: Prohibition in Oklahoma, 1907-1959* (Norman: University of Oklahoma Press, 1971), pp. 154-65, quotation from p. 164.

[61] Quoted ibid., pp. 166-67.

[62] Ibid., pp. 171-72.

[63] Radio Speech of December 20, 1958, Speech Files; and Letter of Transmittal, both in Gary Collection.

CHAPTER 16

The Big Red E: J. Howard Edmondson
and the Old Guard

THE 1950s passed into most history textbooks as a decade of drift, an era in which America enjoyed its prosperity free from the political rancor of the New Deal-Fair Deal period. Through most of the decade, Oklahoma fully shared that quality. For all the momentary tempests of the Murray and Gary administrations, Sooners took their share of postwar abundance in relative political comfort. Despite Eisenhower's personal popularity, the Democrats had never been more firmly in charge of state and local affairs. Political leadership rested in the familiar hands of party professionals, especially veterans of the legislature and county courthouses. It was they who still defined the conservative agenda of the postwar years: moderation, frugality, and cautious growth. Conspicuous by its absence was any threat of substantial change, especially any that might jeopardize the party professionals and their traditional sources of influence.

Between the gubernatorial elections of 1958 and 1962, nearly every element of that postwar political pattern was tested. New men, new forces, and new issues challenged those elements of tradition. By the early 1960s, one era of state politics had come to a sudden and surprising close. Neither its passing nor the uneasy emergence of its successor had been free of conflict.

For all of its unsettling subsequent effects, the 1958 governor's race began routinely enough. Bill Coe once more tried to play to the resentments of the disaffected, and half a dozen political veterans once more entered the lists, all stressing their experience in government. No less routine was the consensus that assigned the favorite's role to a self-made millionaire of conservative persuasions, W. P. Bill Atkinson. Seeing Atkinson a certain winner, most party professionals, including Governor Raymond Gary, signed up in his cause.[1]

The quiet support of a governor who yet retained most of his popularity, particularly among rural voters, was only one of Atkinson's assets. Probably more important was the candidate's personal wealth, amply displayed by a surfeit of billboards, television spots, and newspaper advertisements, all proclaiming Atkinson's drive to "Build Oklahoma." A former journalism teacher at Oklahoma City University, Atkinson had supplemented his modest salary by selling real estate at nights and on weekends. When the federal government announced plans to build a wartime air base in the vicinity of Oklahoma City, he had shrewdly bought several farms in the area he expected to become the final location of the base. His guess had been right. When Tinker Field was placed east of the capital city, Atkinson began the development of Midwest City, which overcame its prosaic name and uninspired design to become the state's largest wartime suburb. Further enlarged by postwar building, Midwest City and nearby Del City blended into the metropolis. Atkinson moved into the upper ranks of the state's economic elite, cultivated ties with businessmen and political figures, and prepared for a governor's race.[2]

By 1958, nearly every forecaster agreed that Atkinson was the man to beat for the governorship. With a cautious platform calculated to offend no one, Atkinson put together a formidable coalition that included businessmen, labor leaders, educators, and a host of powerful rural legislators. It was the same coalition that had elected nearly every Oklahoma governor since the Great Depression.

In 1958, however, their calculations were upset from a surprising source. A young, urban-oriented candidate doggedly concentrated on a few issues new to political debate and outflanked the experts by his adroit use of the instruments of modern politics: opinion polls, television, and professionally packaged campaigning. J. Howard Edmondson exploded on the professionals seemingly from out of nowhere to ambush their favorite and knock political alignments askew.

He was not altogether unknown. His older brother, Ed, was completing his third term as the Second District's congressman, and Howard was serving with some distinction as county attorney for Tulsa County. Still, his name had never appeared on a statewide ballot and, only thirty-two years old, he was the youngest candidate ever to seek the governorship. It was little wonder that the capital city's *Daily Oklahoman* buried the first news of his announcement on its third page under the one-column headline: "Cleanup Asked by Edmondson."[3] Neither was it surprising

[1] Wayne F. Young, "Oklahoma Politics With Special Reference to the Election of Oklahoma's First Republican Governor" (Ph.D. diss., University of Oklahoma, 1964), pp. 201-202.

[2] Ibid., pp. 228-29.

[3] *Oklahoma City Daily Oklahoman,* January 8, 1958.

that the most experienced political forecasters continued to expect his withdrawal from the hopeless venture as late as April. They, like the party leaders, remained enthralled with the more accustomed maneuverings of the Democratic officialdom.

With few initial advantages beyond the Tulsa newspapers' encouragement and his brother's contacts, Edmondson stuck to a consistent theme of modernizing state government.[4] A highway commission given constitutional status, he pledged, would build roads where the traffic was, not where political pressures dictated. A merit system for state employees would promote more professional service. Central purchasing would save taxpayer dollars then being wasted by separate and inefficient requisition. A shorter ballot would remove minor offices from the election list and relieve voters of the quadrennial guessing game of passing upon candidates whose qualifications they seldom knew. Removing the constitutional limits upon legislative representation while guaranteeing each county at least one seat would give the urban electorate a fair voice in government and also protect rural interests.[5] Finally, Edmondson endorsed neither the certain repeal nor the blind continuance of prohibition, but he did promise a public referendum on the matter within ninety days of his inauguration.

Although Edmondson depicted himself as a candidate of issues, not personality, it is unlikely that the electorate fully understood the promises that quickly became catch phrases. It was even less certain that voters comprehended the obstacles likely to impede each proposal. But they could not escape the candidate's considerable personal attributes: a ruggedly handsome face beneath a shock of brilliant red hair, a deep speaking voice, a charming demeanor, and the youthful vigor of a man barely in his thirties. Edmondson's personal magnetism was revealed in the medium revolutionizing American politics and perfectly suited to his own candidacy: television. While he was not the first Oklahoma politician to use television, Edmondson was the first to master it. Both Governor Gary and Bill Atkinson were obviously uncomfortable before the camera, and even Bill Coe's talent on the stump faded before the more intimate medium. Edmondson was its perfect practitioner—always at ease, always seeming to address each viewer personally, always the confident spokesman for modern government, and many observers believed, the most charismatic candidate in memory.

Ironically, Edmondson virtually stumbled into television. His early campaign was never adequately financed, and almost out of desperation he had started buying television time from KOCO-TV. Then operating

---

[4] On Edmondson's platform, see Young, "Oklahoma Politics," p. 203.

[5] The existing constitutional formula, contained in Article 5, section 10, prescribed a limit of seven representatives per county, and required that each county have at least ½ percent of the state's total population in order to elect a representative. Had that formula been enforced, twenty-six counties would have been ineligible for representation. Removing the limit of seven representatives would have approximately doubled Oklahoma and Tulsa counties' share of the lower house.

Young, handsome, and charismatic, J. Howard Edmondson led the Democratic party to victory and left it in shambles. Courtesy Western History Collections, University of Oklahoma.

out of Enid, the struggling American Broadcasting Company affiliate
sold daytime spots at bargain basement rates. After a few performances,
Edmondson's private polls showed remarkable gains and, more important, small campaign contributions began to come in. The candidate
began to buy more air time whenever he had the money, and by the
early summer he had made a full commitment to the use of television.[6]
By that time, he also had perfected his campaign symbols, soon to be
an indelible part of the state's political lore: the "prairie fire" that was
sweeping Oklahoma; the catchy jingle "E-D, M-O-N-D, S-O-N spells
Edmondson" (to the tune of "Harrigan"); and the "Big Red E," a clever
combination of the name recognition, distinctive hair color, and a play
on the nickname of the mighty University of Oklahoma football team.

His campaign artistry was discovered slowly. Edmondson long remained buried in the pack battling for a runoff slot against the potent
Atkinson candidacy. The well-financed Atkinson campaign maintained
its confidence as other contenders concentrated their fire on the front-
runner. Fearing controversy, Atkinson straddled such issues as reapportionment and prohibition and stressed his financial orthodoxy in bland
television addresses, delivered with the aid of an expensive teleprompter.
To the star-studded Atkinson camp, the only real question in the first
primary seemed to be the selection of the Midwest City developer's
final foe.

That confidence evaporated with the election returns of July 1. Riding
a stunning hometown endorsement from Tulsa County, J. Howard Edmondson showed enough strength across the state to lead Atkinson into
the runoff by 742 votes. The two leaders combined to account for nearly
half (42 percent) of the total ballots, leaving the remainder of the field
scattered far behind. Each of the other candidates drew well only from
his own immediate bailiwick, if at all.[7]

The brief runoff campaign was anticlimactic, more entertaining than
dramatic. In stiff television addresses, Atkinson repeated his pledges of
economy and businesslike administration. He was, however, decidedly
on the defensive, because Edmondson had all the momentum of a winner.
The runoff results established a record margin. Edmondson carried
seventy counties to bury the hapless Atkinson, 363,742 to 158,780. The
day belonged to youth. George Nigh and William A. Burkhart joined
Edmondson in primary victories. Nigh, a former schoolteacher and state
representative from McAlester, took the lieutenant governorship from
the aging Cowboy Pink Williams. Burkhart finally retired State Treasurer
A. S. J. Shaw, who had held secondary offices since 1922. In the only
other notable primary contest, Toby Morris and Victor Wickersham
renewed their struggle for the Sixth District's Democratic nomination

[6]Martin Hauan, *He Buys Organs for Churches, Pianos for Bawdy Houses* (Oklahoma
City: Midwest Political Publications, 1976), pp. 89–90.

[7]Oliver L. Benson et al., *Oklahoma Votes, 1907–1962* (Norman: University of Oklahoma, Bureau of Government Research, 1964), p. 101.

for the third time since the congressional redistricting of 1951. Morris, the incumbent, led in the initial returns by 53 votes. A recount increased the final margin to 81.[8]

The results of the general election campaign were never in doubt. Edmondson's stunning primary victory left no room for a major Democratic bolt, and for campaign purposes, the party seemed to be more united than at any time since 1932. On the other side, the GOP's cause was never more hopeless. Only 61,500 Republican stalwarts bothered to vote in their party's primary, and they chose a former Democrat, Phil Ferguson, to head their ticket. That choice was hardly auspicious, for Ferguson had emphasized his determination to end the popular homestead tax exemption. Like Edmondson, he was identified as a "wet," thus neutralizing a divisive issue and sacrificing the considerable "dry" support he might have won. Finally, Ferguson was tainted in Republican eyes by his three congressional terms as a Democratic congressman under the New Deal.[9]

The virtual wipeout of the GOP was evident in the November balloting. Edmondson became the only candidate to carry every county since the Roosevelt landslide of 1932, and his final percentage (74.1 percent) exceeded even FDR's previous record, 73.2 percent. Edmondson's personal strength was demonstrated in the rare fact that his candidacy rolled up a larger margin than that of his party's routinely elected candidates for the secondary state offices. Although Eisenhower had carried the state twice since 1952, the Republican gubernatorial vote had declined by more than 200,000 between 1950 and 1958, and the party's misfortunes carried over into every other race. A strong ticket and the electoral consequences of the 1957 recession gave the Democrats five of the six congressional seats, and they barely failed to oust Page Belcher in the normally rock-ribbed First District. The Democratic proportion of the total congressional vote was exceeded only in the 1932 sweep. Similarly, the Republicans dropped half their legislative seats, including all those from Tulsa County—their poorest showing since the Great Depression.[10] In the subsequent Twenty-seventh Legislature, the tiny Republican contingent advanced no candidates for leadership, voted for the Democrats' designated officers, and generally tried to escape identification as Republicans.[11]

Thirty-three years old at his inauguration, James Howard Edmondson was the state's youngest governor and the youngest in the nation at the time. His family had been active in Democratic politics for years. His father had been a Muskogee County commissioner, and his brother Ed had represented the Second Congressional District since 1953. Hoping

[8] State of Oklahoma, State Election Board, *Directory of Oklahoma, 1977,* pp. 594-95.

[9] Ibid., p. 595; *Oklahoma City Daily Oklahoman,* November 2, 1958.

[10] *Directory of Oklahoma, 1977,* pp. 595-96; Stephen Jones, *Oklahoma Politics in State and Nation, 1907-1962* (Enid: Haymaker Press, 1974), pp. 69-70.

[11] Samuel C. Patterson, "Dimensions of Voting Behavior in a One-Party State Legislature," *Public Opinion Quarterly* 26 (1962):186.

to establish his own base outside his older brother's shadow, he had moved to Tulsa County and, after brief service as county attorney, launched the campaign that took him to the governor's chair.[12] His astonishing triumph testified to new forces in Sooner politics: the power of television, the appeal of youth, and the urban voters' dissatisfaction with the Old Guard politics entrenched in the rural-dominated legislature and the county courthouse "rings." Using those themes to such an extent that he came to personify them, Edmondson advanced a program so revolutionary that it left permanent marks upon the state's political history.

The Edmondson administration began as a continuation of the campaign. The governor surrounded himself with youthful advisers fresh to politics. The so-called "crewcuts" shared the governor's eastern Oklahoma upbringing, his university law class of 1948, or his Phi Gamma Delta fraternity ties. J. Leland Gourley, Whit Pate, Sam Crossland, Max Genet, Mike Pedrick, Mack Burks, and the ever-present Joe Cannon became the central figures within the inner circle. Their lack of political experience was frequently shown by insensitive if not ruthless action. They scorned the prerogatives accorded legislators and made enemies unnecessarily by their abrasive behavior.[13]

In the governor's own eyes, a new executive-legislative relationship had been established in his record-setting primary and general election victories. The lawmakers were bound by his pledge of a "fresh breeze" constituting a "mandate," a term often heard in the early days of the administration. The legislature's tenuous acceptance of the Edmondson mandate was revealed early in the session. Legislative veterans, conceding the governor's popular support, granted him the familiar privilege of naming their formal leaders—Marietta's Clint Livingston as house speaker and Duncan's Harold Garvin as senate president pro tempore.[14] They listened coolly, however, to the program he outlined at the beginning of the 1959 session.

That program was an unflinching reaffirmation of his campaign promises: a referendum for repeal of prohibition, central purchasing for state agencies, and a merit system for state employees. He repeated his call for a constitutional highway commission and added a proposal to replace the county attorney system with a more centralized district attorney plan. Legislative reapportionment under his campaign formula (at least one seat for each county but no upper limit for the most populous) completed the list of major reforms. On the more routine business of appropriations, Edmondson proposed an austere budget of approximately $200 million. To ease the state's growing financial squeeze, he recommended the transfer of several institutions and functions from the hard-pressed general fund to the more secure Welfare Department, the constitutional bene-

---

[12] "The Oklahoma Kid," *Saturday Evening Post,* May 16, 1959, pp. 36-37, 70-75.
[13] *Oklahoma City Daily Oklahoman,* December 16, 1962.
[14] Ibid., July 25, 26, 1958.

ficiary of the growing sales tax revenue. A state income tax withholding system was also proposed for short-term relief. Longer range solutions, particularly regarding highway financing, he left to the legislature, which he offered the equally unpleasant alternatives of raising taxes, submitting a bond issue, or ending the common schools' sharing of road-user taxes.[15]

Nearly all these proposals were destined to encounter roadblocks that most voters had never foreseen. None had been formulated in consultation with powerful legislators or political blocs. Surveying the governor's proposals, the *Daily Oklahoman's* Ray Parr could liken his position only to that of a football coach who deliberately scheduled one awesome opponent after another. At one stroke, Edmondson was taking on the militant drys with his proposed repeal referendum; institutional and department heads with central purchasing; patronage-oriented legislators with a merit system; road contractors and their allies with the reformed highway commission; the county courthouses with the district attorney bill; pensioners with the plan to tap welfare revenues; retail merchants with a withholding proposal; and college and public school employees with an inelastic budget. Parr's conclusion was fundamentally correct: "by totalling up [Governor Edmondson's] list of political opponents, that doesn't leave much of anybody left, except the people, and they don't count for much in the overall political maneuvering."[16]

The arena for that maneuvering was the Twenty-seventh Legislature. Particularly in the upper chamber, veterans like Ray Fine, Joe Bailey Cobb, Clem McSpadden, Frank Mahan, and Everett Collins exercised power beyond all proportion to the prominence of their hometowns — Gore, Tishomingo, Nowata, Fairfax, and Sapulpa, respectively. Neither house had ever been seriously reapportioned to reflect the population shifts of the previous half century — indeed, the senate remained exactly as it was in 1907. The result was that legislators, often elected from rotting boroughs, had built up a network of power that reflected the interests of their rural constituents and courthouse allies, who looked to them for favor and protection. As a group, they had been conspicuously absent from the Edmondson bandwagon; in fact, they were the essence of the Old Guard that had been his campaign foil. Edmondson's record-shattering nomination and election had left them unconverted: he might propose, but it was they who would dispose, mandate or no mandate.[17]

The first test came with the attempted overhaul of the existing Highway Commission. Each of the eight Gary appointees was to be replaced by Edmondson men. In a move that surprised even his critics, the governor nominated Jenkin Lloyd Jones to the politically powerful board. Jones was not only a Republican but also, as editor of the *Tulsa Tribune,* he had made something of a career of baiting the rural-dominated, Demo-

[15] Ibid., January 14, 1959.
[16] Ibid., April 26, 1959.
[17] A good and very critical appraisal of senatorial power is available in Jones, *Oklahoma Politics,* pp. 159-74.

cratic legislature. When the senate refused to confirm Jones's appointment, Edmondson doggedly resubmitted it, dispatched his crewcuts to remind the recalcitrant of his mandate, and appeared on television to call forth a popular outpouring against the resisting senators. It was all to no avail. The senators curtly rejected Jones a second time and pointedly advised the governor not to embarrass himself by trying again. It was a symptomatic defeat for the governor, for it was the first time that the upper chamber had rejected such an appointment since 1927, when Henry Johnston suffered a similar loss at the hands of an impeachment-bent legislature.[18]

The Jones appointment demonstrated the young administration's lack of acumen and its misplaced faith in its mandate. It also opened a deep rift with the proud and powerful senate. To most of the public, however, the defeat was more than erased by Edmondson's successful handling of the explosive repeal question.[19] The governor carefully shepherded through the legislature a referendum measure that embodied the recommendations of a special citizens' committee he had appointed to study the repeal question. The plan called for: (1) privately owned liquor stores in towns of more than 2,000 people, county seats, and state lodges; (2) a 2 percent sales tax plus special liquor taxes to be determined by the legislature; (3) a division of revenue with affected localities receiving one-third and the state general fund two-thirds; (4) stringent control under an alcoholic beverage commission to be established by the legislature; and (5) possible county option two years after the beginning of repeal. Compromise between Edmondson and legislative leaders, including George Miskovsky, who had threatened to circulate an independent and different initiative, changed the last feature to allow a second state question providing for immediate county option in the same referendum measure. In mid-February both chambers approved submission of the referendum, wets joining drys who feared that rejection would result in an even more distasteful proposal by the initiative route.

The battle shifted to the public forum. While the United Drys concentrated their campaign among churchmen, a new repeal organization, United Oklahomans for Repeal, chose to reach for the support of a new generation of the uncommitted. Headed by "Coach" H. W. McNeill, legislative liaison for Governor Turner, the U.O.R. emphasized the revenue potential of liquor and contrasted the strict controls of repeal with the problems of the existing "unenforceable" prohibition law. Although Edmondson remained publicly neutral on the issue, his adviser, Whit Pate, served as an ex-officio member of McNeill's executive committee. Joe Cannon, Edmondson's thirty-four-year-old commissioner of public safety, played a more visible and more important role in the pro-

[18] *Oklahoma City Daily Oklahoman,* January 28, 29, February 1, 1959.
[19] The full account of the repeal fight is well told in Jimmie Lewis Franklin, *Born Sober: Prohibition in Oklahoma, 1907-1959* (Norman: University of Oklahoma Press, 1971), pp. 173-95.

repeal campaign. Highway patrol roadblocks, well-publicized raids of expensive clubs, and relentless pressure on county sheriffs were Cannon's weapons to give the voters the strong medicine of total law enforcement and thus a clear alternative: legal liquor or none at all. Of course, Cannon's activities fell short of drying up the entire state, but they did emphasize the lackadaisical, if not hypocritical, enforcement of the liquor laws. They also had the effect of stirring up public interest in the metropolitan counties whose votes would be critical if repeal was going to win.

More than 700,000 Oklahomans voted in the special election of April 7, 1959, and the repeal amendment won, 396,845 to 314,380. Somewhat surprisingly, the separate county option proposal was voted down even more decisively; drys joined determined wets to defeat it by well over two to one.[20] Another five months passed before Oklahomans had their first legal drink. Only near the end of the session did the legislature finally approve the control measure, which coupled a high liquor tax of $2.40 per gallon[21] with an enforcement commission subject to gubernatorial appointment and senate confirmation. A belated senate amendment to the bill mandated a minimum age requirement of thirty-five for commission members—five years above the constitutional requirement for the governor and high enough to eliminate the Edmondson crewcuts, Joe Cannon in particular.[22]

Repeal of prohibition stood as Edmondson's best-remembered achievement. At the time, however, the spiteful senate action was indicative of the worsening relations between the administration and its legislative critics. Once the repeal question was resolved, the legislature considered the reform proposals that were the heart of the new governor's program. After unprecedented wrangling, Edmondson was able to claim but two major successes, the merit system and central purchasing. Both were approved by the thinnest of margins in the final moments of the session. The merit bill was surprisingly strong, allowing the governor to place state agencies under the system at his discretion and, in most cases, making future employment subject to competitive examination. Only employees who already had more than two years of continuous service were exempted from its application. The program was administered by a seven-member personnel board, all subject to senate confirmation and three to be ex-officio representatives of the legislature. Many correctly anticipated that the system, approved by a one-vote margin in the senate, would be subject to attacks in the succeeding legislature.[23]

[20] *Directory of Oklahoma, 1977,* p. 660.

[21] The resulting revenue from liquor sales was never anywhere close to that predicted by repeal's proponents. In the first year of legal sales the state collected $8.25 million in alcohol taxes as suppliers filled their inventories. The figure fell to $5.4 million in the third year. *Oklahoma City Daily Oklahoman,* December 16, 1962.

[22] Ibid., May 26, 1959.

[23] Ibid., March 18, May 21, 1959; Jean Graves McDonald, "Oklahoma Patronage, the Political Parties, and State Elective Officials" (Ph.D. diss., Michigan State University, 1972), pp. 68-71.

The central purchasing bill, the governor's only other unqualified success, limped through at the session's end when Edmondson enlisted the help of higher education. Desperately fighting for revenue above the governor's recommended figure, the college forces threw their weight behind the bill after Edmondson made central purchasing the price for more college money—and exempted higher education from most of its provisions.[24] The compromise was one legislators understood.

The remainder of Edmondson's proposals were maimed or killed outright. The withholding tax plan, for example, was finally approved but conspicuously without the attachment of the emergency clause, a deliberate legislative oversight that delayed its enforcement for ninety days and gave aroused merchants time to organize the campaign that overturned the act in a November, 1960, referendum. Similarly, the governor's recommendation to transfer specified activities to the Welfare Department and its earmarked revenue was diluted to keep the Whitaker Orphans Home and the school at Taft dependent upon general fund appropriations. Other proposals—most conspicuously, the district attorney system and legislative reapportionment—were buried intact.

The stormiest contest of the 1959 session involved Edmondson's highway proposals. Early in the session the administration considered a total overhaul of road financing as recommended by another of the governor's study committees which, like the repeal committee, did not include a single legislative member.[25] In the end, however, the governor scrapped that drastic change to focus on his campaign pledge of a constitutional highway commission. In mid-April he added another proposal—the transfer to the State Highway Department of the $29 million of road money assigned to the county commissioners.[26]

If of less popular interest than the liquor question, the road proposals, even in their scaled down forms, were the most explosive matters that Edmondson laid before the legislature. One senator metaphorically described them as "the hottest thing since the Chicago fire."[27] The superficially innocuous elevation of the Highway Commission to constitutional status actually struck close to the heart of state political power. To its advocates, the bill's chief effect was the removal of politics from road planning and construction. But its critics fully understood that the politics to be removed was the legislature's influence over the most expensive activity of state government. Road building, moreover, traditionally generated sizable campaign contributions from contractors and provided local voters with the most direct measure of their representative's effectiveness. Raymond Gary had understood the political significance of

---

[24] *Oklahoma City Daily Oklahoman,* July 5, 1959.

[25] Ibid., December 14, 1958, January 11, 1959.

[26] The road-fund transfer proposal had originated with two young senators—Keith Cartwright of Durant and Fred Harris of Lawton—who had studied a similar plan then used in North Carolina. Edmondson's endorsement of the reform fully committed his administration to the bill.

[27] *Oklahoma City Daily Oklahoman,* April 21, 1959.

highways and had catered to it. J. Howard Edmondson understood it, too, and he aimed to eliminate it.

The transfer of county road money to the State Highway Commission involved similar issues. The money in question was, at the time, roughly $29 million raised by road-user taxes and distributed by the State Tax Commission to the county commissioners. The roads in question were those not designated as state or federal highways—83,510 miles of the state's total mileage of 93,646.[28] To the advocates of transfer, the issue in question was the county commissioners' notorious inadequacy and inefficiency. Acting with only a minimum of state supervision, the commissioners had managed to pave less than 5 percent of their roads, and their critics found little wonder in that. The independent Oklahoma Public Expenditures Council, an often snarling watchdog of commissioner practices, estimated that the commissioners routinely paid friendly contractors an average of 55 percent above market prices for road material. More objective State Highway Commission experts repeatedly deplored the failure to match available federal funds and refusal to follow modern engineering and accounting practices. They also criticized the commissioners' sporadic repair practices, which apparently were grounded less in objective need than in random public complaints, particularly those of worthy groups and their own friends. A special legislative investigating committee led by Hugh Sandlin of Holdenville agreed and scored the commissioners for their deliberate evasion of bid requirements, payment for materials never delivered, maintenance of incomprehensible records, and other misuse of state tax money.[29]

Opponents of the transfer saw the central issue differently. To them, the question was one of dubious centralization purchased with the currency of local democracy. At bottom, however, the issue was less local democracy than local political power. Especially in the rural areas (where roads were often the supreme public question), the commissioners were the key men in county politics, their influence resting on their control of road funds. In challenging the commissioners, the executive was challenging nothing less than the entire network of power in the courthouses and the legislature—the same legislature that must pass on his proposals.

At the peak of the struggle, the governor employed public appeals to refresh his badly tarnished mandate and resorted to the crudest instrument of executive power—patronage. In late April, Joe Cannon, who had resigned the directorship of the Public Safety Commission to become the administration's untitled hatchetman, boldly announced the

---

[28] Jones, *Oklahoma Politics,* p. 167.

[29] Bertil L. Hanson, "County Commissioners of Oklahoma," *Midwest Journal of Political Science* 9 (1965):388-400. These allegations culminated in the scandal that surfaced two decades later. In 1981, federal investigators revealed a systematic kickback racket in which contractors routinely bribed commissioners, the costs born by local taxpayers. No recent invention, the practice was expected to lead to criminal charges against as many as two-thirds of the state's 231 sitting county commissioners. See *The Wall Street Journal,* September 22, 1981.

firing of the appointees of the governor's principal opponents, Senators Ray Fine, Clem McSpadden, Everett Collins, Frank Mahan, and Joe Bailey Cobb. Among the dismissed was Senator Fine's brother-in-law.[30] In addition, the governor withheld critical appointments, including the state warden, state highway director, and members of the state election board, hoping to retain a club over the legislature's head. The legislators refused to bow, however, and met the governor's challenge with one of their own—the threat to recess rather than adjourn, a potentially disastrous move that would have resulted in no program at all but would leave open the constant threat of impeachment.[31]

Exhaustion, not compromise, finally resolved the impasse. Unable to move the legislature, the governor attended the burial of his highway proposals, and the assembly approved the necessary appropriation bills. The final budget figure—$218 million—was well above Edmondson's initial recommendation; nonetheless, it also testified to the growing financial squeeze on state government. The tax system had seen no substantial change since the Turner administration, and the 1941 budget-balancing amendment limited yearly appropriations to the average revenue collected over the previous three years. The result was that state spending lagged ever farther behind state needs. The solution that the governor and legislative leaders wearily accepted in 1959 was to approve a decent program for state functions but leave much of the funding to the subsequent legislature. The 1959 common school code, for example, provided for a $94 million program for the next two years, but the actual biennial appropriation was set at $82 million, $47 million in the first year and $35 million in the second. The $12 million difference for the latter year was left to the 1961 assembly. It would have to make a supplemental appropriation, either by drawing upon the projected surplus or by raising taxes. Similarly, the $54 million commitment to higher education would demand a supplemental appropriation in 1961 of $4 million. That solution, awkward at best, finally allowed the Twenty-seventh Legislature to adjourn in early July. Their 179-day session had been the longest and one of the most bitter in the history of the state.[32]

That bitterness did not subside with adjournment. The truce was temporary. Following adjournment, Edmondson prepared an initiative campaign to bypass the legislative blockade and appeal directly to the voters to adopt three petitions: legislative reapportionment, the constitutional highway commission, and the transfer of county road funds.

Meanwhile, Lloyd Benefield's resignation as Democratic state chairman touched off a fresh struggle for control of the party. Fully expecting the customary privilege of naming the party's head, Edmondson asked Tulsa attorney Pat Malloy to complete the remainder of Benefield's term.

[30] *Oklahoma City Daily Oklahoman,* April 23, 1959. The merit system, of course, was not yet in effect.
[31] Ibid., May 17, 1959.
[32] Ibid., June 23, July 4, 1959.

In September the party's executive committee rejected Malloy, however, and named Alva's Gene McGill, an ally of the legislative Old Guard and a bitter Edmondson foe, as interim state chairman. The committee's unprecedented rebuke of the governor was only magnified when a majority of its members next refused to meet with him to plan future party affairs.[33]

The battle between Edmondson and the legislature began to exact heavy casualties. The administration accelerated its dismissal of the patronage appointees of its legislative foes. Several of Edmondson's supporters in the previous assembly moved to dissociate themselves from the governor. Robert Lollar of Miami, one of Edmondson's 1959 floor leaders, displayed as much ill-tempered wit as political acumen when he announced his future allegiance to the Old Guard against what he called Edmondson's "all-out effort to centralize our government in one family, two cities, and three beatniks."[34] Sallisaw's Noble Stewart, another floor leader, also broke his ties with the governor, who retaliated by ordering the closing of the Highway Department's engineering office at Sallisaw, costing the town an institution that was thirty-two years old and had an annual payroll of more than $127,000.[35]

The climax of the struggle for party control came in the precinct and county conventions of early 1960. Although Edmondson tried to coordinate his forces in the local conventions, he was decidedly handicapped, for those forces tended to be inexperienced and idealistic amateurs, no match for the well-organized professionals arrayed against him.[36] Any doubt about the outcome was removed with the returns from the county conventions of February. Sixty-two counties elected delegations to the state convention pledged to McGill as permanent party chairman. It was the worst defeat ever suffered by an Oklahoma governor in a party organizational fight.[37]

The subsequent state convention became the forum for antiadministration spite. The convention whooped through a resolution declaring the party's official intent to oppose its own governor's pending reform initiatives "with all possible vigor." The otherwise routine commendation of Senators Kerr and Monroney and the Democrats in the state congressional delegation pointedly made no mention at all of the governor. Selecting the state's delegation to the national convention, the state assembly grudgingly honored Edmondson—or, at least, his office—by naming him a delegate. It was, however, a limited gesture: Edmondson would have exactly one-half vote at Los Angeles, and he could not control even that because the entire delegation was bound by the unit rule, which required that its entire twenty-nine votes be cast according to the dictates of its majority.[38]

[33] Ibid., September 23, December 27, 1959.
[34] Ibid., November 12, 1959.
[35] Ibid.
[36] Ibid., January 22, 1960.
[37] Ibid., February 21, 1960.

Edmondson's utter loss of party control became nationally apparent at the Los Angeles Democratic National Convention in July. In the absence of gubernatorial leadership, Senator Kerr took control of the Oklahoma delegation and turned its support to the presidential ambitions of his Senate ally from Texas, Lyndon Johnson. Edmondson, however, announced his support of Massachusetts Senator John Kennedy, whose youth, Catholicism, and liberal reputation left him exceptionally unpopular with the other Oklahomans. When Edmondson rose to deliver one of Kennedy's five seconding speeches before the convention, a portion of the Oklahoma delegation booed their own chief executive, an act of uncommon rudeness that was lost on neither Edmondson nor television's national audience. In the subsequent balloting, the Sooners' votes went to Johnson. Edmondson watched the proceedings while sitting with the more hospitable Kennedy forces.[39]

Events back home in the same month testified less visibly but more importantly to Edmondson's misfortunes. The governor had hoped to force an election on his initiative proposals before the July 5 primary elections in order to remove them as campaign issues in the legislative races. The initiatives' opponents, however, managed to tie up the petitions with repeated contests of their validity, keeping the governor's program in the foreground of the local races. The effect was disastrous for Edmondson, particularly in the senate contests. Only Wagoner County's Tom Payne ran as a candidate backing the proposals. The great majority of the Democratic aspirants campaigned as vigorous foes, and even the governor's supporters in the previous assembly hastened to separate themselves from his program rather than risk a pro-Edmondson label. Those who delayed their conversion too long or attacked the governor with insufficient vigor faced serious threats from more adamant anti-Edmondson candidates.[40]

The July primaries eliminated any hope that the governor might face a friendly Twenty-eighth Legislature. With rare exceptions, it was the most determined Edmondson foes who won Democratic nomination. The unprecedented rebuke was compounded by the premature organization of both incoming chambers, even as sixteen legislative seats still awaited runoff contests. House Democrats chose J. D. McCarty, Oklahoma City's trenchant Edmondson critic, for the speakership. In the senate, the rout of the governor was even more complete. The jubilant Old Guard named Everett Collins president pro tempore and pledged to write a program independent of the governor.[41] Not since the scandalous impeachment era had both chambers been organized with so much hostility to the governor. Ray Fine could barely conceal his glee. The Gore veteran and intended victim of an Edmondson purge chortled that

[38] Ibid., March 20, 1960; Anne Hodges Morgan, *Robert S. Kerr: The Senate Years* (Norman: University of Oklahoma Press, 1977), p. 203.

[39] *Oklahoma City Daily Oklahoman,* July 4, 1960; Morgan, *Robert S. Kerr,* pp. 203-204.

[40] *Oklahoma City Daily Oklahoman,* February 28, April 10, 1960.

[41] Ibid., July 7, July 14, 1960.

he would rather serve in the 1961 sessions than in "all of the past ones put together."[42] With his triumphant colleagues, Fine was fully prepared to make war upon the young governor, whom he described as standing with "a yo-yo in one hand and hula hoop in the other."[43] Neither would be an adequate weapon in the struggle certain to come.

Unceremoniously stripped of party authority, his legislative influence diminished to abject ridicule, Edmondson had but one card left to play. After long delays, his initiative petitions were finally certified, and he ordered them placed on a special election ballot for September 20, 1960. The trio of state questions became the focus of one of the state's most brutal conflicts, with the governor's fate and the legislature's power resting on the outcome.

The three proposed constitutional amendments—State Questions 396, 397, and 398—called respectively for the constitutional highway commission, legislative reapportionment, and the transfer of county road funds to the State Highway Commission. Although the major metropolitan newspapers gave each a ringing endorsement, the ratification campaign was essentially the governor's own show. It was reminiscent both of his stunning gubernatorial race and the successful drive to repeal prohibition. As in the 1958 contest, Edmondson relied on polished television appeals to persuade voters of the simple justice of his position. The *Prairie Fire News,* the gubernatorial campaign newsletter, was revived and circulated in tens of thousands of copies.[44] At the same time, Joe Cannon worked assiduously to dredge up scandals to discredit the present system. A McClain County grand jury investigation of that county's commissioners became the focus of some attention, and Cannon attempted to use it as he had used his much publicized pre-repeal raids: to demonstrate the corruption of the existing road system and, in this case, its principal defenders.[45]

The opponents to the governor's proposals constituted a formidable array of powerful groups, including the Farmers' Union, the Rural Electric Administration Cooperatives, the state Farm Bureau, the County Commissioners' Association, and the preponderance of state legislators. United under the heading of "Oklahomans for Local Government," they emphasized the dangers of centralization of authority in the state government and the transfer of legislative influence to the metropolitan areas. Predictably, their strength was greatest in the rural centers, where the local legislators and county commissioners were generally respected and

---

[42] Ibid., July 28, 1960. Edmondson's firing of Fine's appointees had been directed at blocking his reelection. Even more direct was the governor's order placing State Crime Bureau agents in charge of the ballot boxes in Fine's district during the primary.

[43] Ibid., April 10, 1960.

[44] Ibid., August 31, 1960.

[45] Hauan, *He Buys Organs for Churches,* p. 100. Hauan served as a public relations specialist for the initiatives' opponents. As he reports, the effort to "Cannonize" the campaign generally backfired. In the McClain County case, the grand jury fully exonerated the commissioners, in fact, commended their behavior.

politically potent figures, and where reapportionment would exact its greatest toll.

In their final form, the Edmondson proposals were much less extreme than they might have been. The reapportionment proposal, for example, would have eliminated rural domination of the state senate, but it would have barely affected rural strength in the house because the amendment guaranteed each county at least one legislative seat regardless of population. In that regard, it was even more generous than the existing—but never enforced—constitutional formula, which would have denied the twenty-six least populous counties any representation at all.[46] The county road transfer proposal was similarly diluted to make transfer subject to local option, by allowing each county to vote for continuing the commissioners' road authority or turning it to the State Highway Commission. In the latter event, provision was made for preference in buying road materials locally and for immediate supervision under a resident county road director.

A tactical complication was the inclusion of all three measures on a single special election ballot. Knowing that success would largely depend on the size of voter turnout, the governor had rejected the option of placing the issues before the electorate at the November, 1960, general election. Although the turnout for the presidential election would have increased the vote, he dared not risk the negative effect of the silent vote. Thus he gambled on consolidating all three in a single special election, where there would be no silent vote and the reapportionment proposal presumably would attract a large enough urban turnout to carry all three. To his opponents, however, that decision was their blessing. Calculating that a negative vote on one proposal would become a negative vote on all three, they concentrated their fire on the specific question that seemed most objectionable in each locality. For most of the state, that was the county road issue, around which they unfurled the standard of local self-government. In the hinterland, it was reapportionment, which they portrayed as establishing legislative dictatorships from Tulsa and Oklahoma City at the expense of small towns like Sayre, Stilwell, and Madill.[47]

The election results confirmed the opposition's strategy. Each question failed by nearly identical margins of roughly two to one. Only three

---

[46] The *Daily Oklahoman*, which endorsed the initiatives, calculated the effect of Edmondson's reapportionment formula, comparing it to the current apportionment as well as that authorized by the constitution. According to those calculations, the Edmondson proposal would allot 48.8 percent of the state's population a majority of senate seats, compared to the 29.4 percent that actually elected a senate majority at the time. Under the unenforced constitutional formula, 41.5 percent of the population would elect a senate majority. In the lower house, the Edmondson formula would still allow 37.8 percent of the population to elect a majority, compared to 37.7 percent under the constitutional formula and 33.2 percent under the existing apportionment. *Oklahoma City Daily Oklahoman*, April 3, 1960.

[47] For the fullest account of the opponents' campaign, see Hauan, *He Buys Organs for Churches*, pp. 99-105.

urban counties—Oklahoma, Tulsa, and Washington—showed up in the affirmative column, and their support was washed away in a flood of rural opposition.[48] Even the opponents were astounded at the magnitude of the rural sweep, for in some counties the negative vote was virtually unanimous. In Beaver County, for example, reapportionment lost by a count of 2,349 to 56.[49] The governor was publicly philosophical, saying that the measures had lost because the voters simply did not want the reforms.[50] But he also knew what *he* had lost. In less than two years he had lost party control, legislative command, and his faintly remembered mandate, as well.

Edmondson's prestige dropped still further with the results of the presidential race two months later. Despite the governor's early enthusiasm for Kennedy, few doubted that the GOP would win Oklahoma for the third consecutive time. The Republican nominee, Richard Nixon, was able to campaign as heir to the Eisenhower tradition, while the Democratic nominee suffered, above all else, for his religion. Kennedy's Catholic religion became the subject of debate and certain defeat. Public discourse was not so frenzied nor so ignorant as in the Hoover-Smith campaign of 1928, but the fear of intolerance silenced Democratic partisans from open affiliation with their presidential nominee. Weak and belated endorsements were made by candidates for lesser office, who feared the effect of Kennedy at the heart of the ticket. Even Senator Kerr, theretofore a reliable spokesman for the "unterrified Democracy of Oklahoma," generally separated his own reelection campaign from the presidential contest. His support of the ticket always emphasized the presence of Lyndon Johnson, Kerr's neighbor and trusted Senate ally, as the vice-presidential nominee. Eventually he grew outraged by the ugly spirit of Know-Nothingism and boldly presented Kennedy to an Oklahoma City campaign audience as "a patriotic Catholic Democrat for President."[51]

The Democrats' misgivings were not misplaced. Carrying a total of sixty counties, including some that had never appeared in a Republican column, Nixon doubled Eisenhower's previous majorities and drew more votes from Oklahomans than any candidate had ever received. The impact of the religious issue was measured in the fact that this was then one of only two elections in which Oklahoma's Democratic percentage was less than the national average—the other was in 1928, when Catholic Al Smith headed the ticket.[52]

State Republicans clearly benefited from the Nixon landslide. B. Hayden Crawford, the GOP's nominee for Kerr's Senate seat, lost by 88,000

---

[48] *Directory of Oklahoma, 1977*, p. 662.
[49] *Oklahoma City Daily Oklahoman*, September 21, 1950.
[50] Ibid., September 22, 1960.
[51] Morgan, *Robert S. Kerr*, pp. 204-207, quotation from p. 206.
[52] Benson et al., *Oklahoma Votes*, p. 68. Despite his commanding majority, Nixon failed to receive all eight of Oklahoma's electoral college votes. Henry D. Irwin, a Republican elector from Bartlesville, surprisingly cast his official vote for his self-made ticket of Harry

votes but still gave the party its strongest senatorial race in a decade. Kerr's endorsement of Kennedy cost him dearly in 1960, but strengthened his influence with the young JFK in the White House. Clyde Wheeler came within 76 votes of defeating Sixth District Congressman Victor Wickersham, and Page Belcher was easily returned from the First. Republican candidates polled just over 45 percent of the total congressional vote, their best performance in thirty-two years. The GOP's state legislative gains were marginal—a net increase of six seats—but among their victors were two representatives from Oklahoma County and a state senator from Washington County, the best performance in those urban areas in nearly forty years.[53]

Despite Republican urban victories, the state legislature remained overwhelmingly Democratic and rural. Beyond steadfast opposition to the governor, it lacked both purpose and direction. At the same time, Edmondson's authority had been reduced to the threat to veto especially objectionable legislation. In no sense could he exert much influence over the legislative process. The result was that the Twenty-eighth Legislature once again smashed the existing record for length and ill-temper.

Hostility between Edmondson and the lords of the legislature set the tone of the session. Long weeks were consumed in trivial exchanges. In the end, appropriating money was the assembly's only achievement of substance. The legislators had no choice but to provide the supplemental appropriations mandated by the previous session's deliberate short-budgeting. The use of the accrued surplus only made it more difficult to match the state's pressing needs with the limited revenue immediately available.

One consequence of the dilemma was that it salvaged at least a portion of the governor's original program. Desperate for money, the legislature approved an income tax withholding measure, complete with the emergency clause. Central purchasing survived, the legislators not daring to tamper with a system that had proved itself by saving eight million desperately needed dollars through coordinated buying.

As with central purchasing, the governor's most notable victory in the 1961 session was one of survival, not achievement. Hostile senators wasted no time in opening the campaign to revive their patronage prerogatives by destroying the merit system. Ray Fine, the governor's most implacable foe, spoke for the Old Guard in vowing to "treat that thing just like a rattlesnake. Whenever it sticks its head up I'll hit it."[54] Only the certainty of gubernatorial veto and the resolve of House Speaker J. D. McCarty to preserve the system's integrity prevented outright repeal. A

Byrd and Barry Goldwater. For that reason, an act of the subsequent legislature required electors to swear support of their party's nominees and levied a $1,000 fine for such independence in the future.

The Oklahoma Democratic showing also failed to attain the party's national average in the four subsequent presidential elections, 1964, 1968, 1972, and 1976.

[53] *Directory of Oklahoma, 1977,* pp. 596–97; Jones, *Oklahoma Politics,* p. 77.

[54] *Oklahoma City Daily Oklahoman,* March 3, 1961.

measure finally did pass both houses that would have weakened the system irreparably by allowing administrators to dismiss otherwise able employees for undefined "incompatibility." The governor vetoed the bill, although he did approve a subsequent measure that exempted certain temporary and unskilled employees and those who worked directly under elected officials from the system's guarantees. Despite the change, the merit system emerged, somewhat surprisingly, virtually intact.[55]

Late in the session, Edmondson tried to break the fiscal logjam by endorsing a measure to increase the state sales tax to 3 percent, the increment going to the battered general fund. With the tax measure pending approval in the lower house, the governor considered signing the first (and drastic) revision of the merit program as the legislative price for the tax increase. Only when the house shelved the measure was he able to assert the critical veto. But if one result was the merit system's survival, another was no abatement in the financial crisis.[56]

That crisis was finally postponed, though not resolved, by resort to the previous biennium's expedient: deliberate short-budgeting. More than $13 million of supplemental appropriations would be necessary from the succeeding legislature to fund the commitments made by the 1961 assembly. Even when met, those commitments testified to the financial strain. Education suffered perhaps the most grievously.[57]

On the eve of the 1961 session, Otis Sullivant, the acknowledged dean of Oklahoma's political observers, wrote that a long, wrangling session between the governor and the legislative Old Guard would enhance the future candidacy of an outsider, identified neither with the Old Guard nor Edmondson's "New Guard." Such a candidate, Sullivant predicted, could steer clear of the powerful enmity of each side and position himself as able to avoid the paralysis of executive-legislative hostility.[58] At its eventual adjournment, the Twenty-eighth Legislature had fulfilled half that prophecy. The next year's gubernatorial contest fulfilled the second half.

An act of the 1961 legislature had moved the primary election date to May, and a large field crowded into the Democratic primary, with at least three candidates hoping to replicate J. Howard Edmondson's 1958 appeal as the "fresh face" above the recent political feuding.[59] George Nigh, Fred Harris, and Preston Moore each mounted campaigns reminiscent in one way or another of the Edmondson "prairie fire." Nigh, the lieutenant governor and the incumbent administration's favorite, emphasized his youth. His campaign scrupulously avoided current controversy. Harris, a second-term state senator from Lawton, shared Nigh's youth—at thirty-one, Harris was the youngest candidate in the field—but he did not avoid

[55] Ibid., June 29, 1961.

[56] Ibid., June 21, 27, 1961.

[57] Ibid., June 29, July 14, 1961.

[58] Ibid., December 4, 1960.

[59] A full account of the 1962 Democratic primary and the source for the following paragraphs is Young, "Oklahoma Politics," pp. 212-57.

controversy. An Edmondson ally in the merit system battle and the attempt to control the county commissioners, Harris advanced a series of proposals that varied only slightly from the governor's, including reapportionment and reform of the county commissioners' spending. Moore was the most distant outsider. Politically inexperienced and poorly informed, he had served as national commander of the American Legion and based his campaign on that organization. His very inexperience was, itself, an asset in 1962, and so too was his aggressive style of campaigning and adroit use of television, especially in the campaign's closing days.

W. P. Bill Atkinson, the surprised victim of Edmondson's 1958 ambush, entered once more, determined to avoid the errors of his previous race. Under the tutelage of H. W. McNeill and former Governor William J. Holloway, Atkinson delayed a formal announcement until six weeks before the election date to force the other candidates to spend their fire on each other rather than him. Once in the race, he used a media blitz that demonstrated his painstaking preparations for improved television appearances, and his desire to reduce the excessive spending that had harmed his cause four years earlier. In one last, critical respect Atkinson reversed his earlier strategy. In 1958, Atkinson had been fatally evasive. No so in 1962: Atkinson boldly endorsed a one-cent increase in the sales tax to meet the state's financial burden.

Unlike the others, the final serious Democratic aspirant could not pose as an outsider. Raymond Gary made a bid to return to power, and he made it as the candidate and the champion of the legislative Old Guard. His campaign organization relied upon his veteran legislative allies, and his platform embraced their version of good government. Predictably, its emphasis was upon roads—$581 million for them, financed by a bond issue with no increase in state taxes. If the sales tax increase was Atkinson's distinctive issue and financial panacea, then the massive road bond was Gary's, for he had already established his record as a road builder and now he claimed that the bond sale would free general revenue funds for adequate support of schools and other services. Gary stood alone in his defense of rural interests, however. He pledged continuance of local road operations by county commissioners, and he championed a legislative apportionment that secured the rural counties' domination.

Gary's participation in the Democratic primary shaped its conduct, for all the other candidates were polarized. At one extreme was Gary, the certain front-runner whose hold upon rural Oklahoma could not be contested. At the other extreme were the ABG ("Anybody But Gary") candidates, forced to counter Gary's appeal with campaigns that separated them from rural interests. For that reason, the primary kept fresh the wounds that the dominant party had suffered in Edmondson's battles against the legislature's patronage and highway powers, its rural domination, and its potent alliances with the county commissioners. Each had divided Democrats into rural and antirural elements.

Renewed squabbling over the apportionment issue embittered the conflict. Over Edmondson's vetoes, the 1961 legislature had approved acts reapportioning both chambers and submitted a constitutional referendum to freeze rural domination under the new formulas. In September, 1961, voters had decisively rejected enshrining the new formulas as a constitutional amendment. In the next month, the State Supreme Court voided the senate reapportionment statute.[60] The State Election Board then threw itself into the fray when a majority, consisting of Clee Fitzgerald, an Edmondson appointee, and Jack Hewett, the Republican member, announced that they would refuse to accept filings for 1962's legislative contests on grounds that both 1961 apportionment statutes were in direct conflict with the state constitution. Their purpose was to force the supreme court to redistrict the legislature on the basis of the never enforced formula. In a curious decision, a divided (six to three) state court declared the 1961 house apportionment to be unconstitutional but, nonetheless, ordered the board to accept filings under it and senate filings on the basis of the 1951 apportionment.[61] Undaunted, reapportionment advocates turned to the federal courts, where a case was pending at the time of the 1962 primaries.

Bewildering legislative and judicial battles over reapportionment, enough to tax any constitutional scholar, contributed to the notable ill-temper of the Democratic primary. It also helped mobilize Gary's rural supporters into a massive show of strength in the first primary. The former governor led the field in no less than sixty counties and ran second in another eleven in rolling up 176,525 votes. Only Atkinson could even approach Gary's statewide strength. Although he carried only Oklahoma County, he ran either second or third in fifty-seven counties to earn a runoff spot. None of the other contenders did well outside their own home areas, and Atkinson entered the runoff with an 85,000-vote disadvantage.[62]

The three-week campaign that separated the two primaries became one of the state's most divisive. The single issue became one man, for Atkinson desperately made "Garyism" his target and pressed the attack with daily allegations of alleged improprieties in the Gary administration. Among the defeated contenders, Harris proclaimed his neutrality, but both Moore and Nigh took the stump for Atkinson or, more accurately, against Gary.[63] Moore was particularly venomous with his oft-repeated characterization of Raymond Gary calling up his associates: "Soeeeee! Pig, Pig, Pig, Pig!"[64]

More circumspect than the aggressive Moore were two other newly found Atkinson allies. Governor Edmondson quietly gave Atkinson as

[60] *Directory of Oklahoma, 1977,* p. 663; *Oklahoma City Daily Oklahoman,* May 12, September 13, October 4, 1961.
[61] Ibid., June 10, December 20, 1961.
[62] Benson et al., *Oklahoma Votes,* p. 104; Young, "Oklahoma Politics," pp. 227-28, 256-57.
[63] Young, "Oklahoma Politics," pp. 276-82.
[64] Hauan, *He Buys Organs for Churches,* p. 108.

much support as his administration could bestow, though it was not much. Senator Kerr could offer a lot. His faithful local allies went to work for Atkinson, and Gary began to find it difficult to raise campaign money, especially from the oil interests.[65]

By the time of the second primary, therefore, virtually every faction of the badly fractured Democratic party had been mobilized in a campaign of singular bitterness. The final balloting only added to that bitterness, for Atkinson defeated Gary by a razor-thin margin of 449 votes. Gary confirmed his hold upon most of rural Oklahoma, but Atkinson won by carrying each of the nine most populous counties and gaining 50,000 votes over his first primary performance in Oklahoma and Tulsa counties alone.[66] Not surprisingly, Gary announced that he could not support the Democratic nominee in November. The question was whether his supporters would.

Although that question had arisen with past party bolts, two new elements made it particularly pertinent in 1962. Atkinson's strength had been in those areas—the northwest and the metropolitan counties—that often appeared in Republican columns in November. The reliably Democratic bastions of southern Oklahoma had been Gary's prime territory, and their voters might follow Gary's lead in sitting out the general election. Even more important, the state's GOP heretofore had been powerless at the state and local levels. But in 1962, a Democratic bolt would only strengthen a party that was prepared to stand on its own.

That preparation had begun in late 1960, when Henry Bellmon, a Noble County farmer and one-term state legislator, assumed the previously thankless task of Republican state chairman. Bellmon's abilities transcended both his own modest background and his party's dismal record. With the expert aid of an Oklahoma City advertising agency, Bellmon launched "Operation Countdown," a carefully conceived project aimed to revitalize the party for the 1962 governor's race.[67] Its formal beginning was in 1961 when the party held an unusual off-year convention to reveal Bellmon's plan and create interest in the party's fortunes. After the convention, a much-publicized reregistration campaign was proclaimed to register as Republicans those "300,000 Democrats who voted for Republican candidates in the last three presidential elections." While the number of Democratic shifts did not approach 300,000, Republican registration did grow by 20 percent, and most of the gain came from the critical metropolitan areas. At the same time, the renewed interest also improved the party's financing, particularly with small, grass-roots contributions. The consequences of that, in turn, were to give increased numbers of voters a stake in Republican fortunes and to allow the party to maintain, for the first time, a permanent staff and headquarters. The

[65] Ibid., pp. 109-10; Young, "Oklahoma Politics," pp. 169-71, 282-84.
[66] Benson et al., *Oklahoma Votes,* p. 105; Young, "Oklahoma Politics," pp. 285-88.
[67] On "Operation Countdown" see Jones, *Oklahoma Politics,* pp. 78-83; Young, "Oklahoma Politics," pp. 151-53.

party was also able to break its past dependence upon the reactionary Tulsa oil interests.

A second stage of preparation involved the invigoration of the party organization. Upon taking the GOP's chairmanship, Bellmon replaced more than two hundred of its three hundred state committeemen. The necessity of that purge, as well as its effect, was demonstrated by one consequence: the average age of the party's leadership dropped overnight to the mid-thirties, roughly thirty years below the previous average.[68] In addition, the state headquarters established functioning committees in each of the state's counties, including the seven that had none at all in 1960. Fifteen regional task forces coordinated their work; and special county task forces, responsible to the state leadership, were dispatched to those areas where the regular county organizations proved to be ineffective.

Operation Countdown's final stage was the development of candidates. State headquarters targeted the offices thought to be particularly vulnerable to Republican campaigns, actively recruited suitable candidates, and organized special "leadership seminars" to train their contenders for campaigning. By 1962, the final result was that the GOP had come a long way from just two years earlier, when the Oklahoma County chairman had attracted national attention by running a *Daily Oklahoman* ad begging for someone to run for office as a Republican.

The earnest young wheat farmer who put it all together, Henry Bellmon, predictably became the party's gubernatorial nominee for the long-awaited 1962 showdown.[69] No candidate was more appropriate for the Republican effort, and none was better suited to capitalize upon Democratic discontent. To many who had flocked to Edmondson in 1958, it was Bellmon, the untarnished newcomer, who promised the fresh breeze of an honest citizen removed from the corruptions of Old Guard politics. To Gary's sullen legions, it was Bellmon, the simple and often poor-spoken farm boy, who stood opposed to Atkinson's expensive and slick campaigning. To voters across the state, it was Bellmon, the Republican moderate, who stood above the turmoil of recent Democratic politics. It was also Bellmon who promised no new taxes out of the conviction, publicly shared by every recent Democratic contender except Atkinson, that the state had ample revenue if only the "waste, graft, and corruption" were eliminated.[70]

All these assets Bellmon parlayed into victory as the state's first Republican governor. Beating Atkinson by a decisive count of 392,316 to 315,357, Bellmon showed surprising statewide strength, running equally

[68] Jones, *Oklahoma Politics,* p. 67.

[69] Bellmon, without a formal primary campaign, took the GOP's gubernatorial nomination with 91 percent of the vote over Leslie C. Skoien, the 51-year-old founder of Tulsa's Sunshine Gospel Tabernacle.

[70] Complete analyses of the general election campaign are available in Jones, *Oklahoma Politics,* pp. 231-52; Young, "Oklahoma Politics," pp. 296-351; and Harry Holloway, "Oklahoma Goes Republican," *Oklahoma Government Bulletin* 1:2 (June, 1963).

well in both rural and urban areas, sweeping the traditionally Republican northwest, and taking lopsided majorities out of Tulsa and Oklahoma counties. He even made serious dents in the heretofore reliable Democratic bailiwicks of Little Dixie, where he carried Raymond Gary's Marshall County with 61 percent of the vote and otherwise ran a full 14 percentage points above the usual Republican share.[71] His victory was, however, largely personal, for though Republicans picked up thirteen legislative seats, they were still a decided minority in the legislature. No other Republican was successful in a statewide race. For example, B. Hayden Crawford, the party's senatorial nominee against Mike Monroney, did slightly better than he had against Senator Kerr in 1960, but he still lost by 46,000 votes and trailed Bellmon by 84,000.[72] The difference was instructive. Crawford had run a militantly conservative campaign, while Bellmon had offered no printed platform at all and carefully repudiated the most conservative planks of his party's official program.

If hardly of revolutionary proportions, Bellmon's inauguration in 1963 helped mark the end of one era of Oklahoma politics, for it demonstrated that many things would never be the same again. In the person of a sagacious but modest Billings farmer, the GOP had shed its image as a millionaire's party and broken with its thirty-year record of inflexible conservatism. In whatever measure the Republicans learned the lesson of their success, they would be able to build upon it. As they did so, Democrats would never again be able to ignore the threat of vigorous opposition. Democrats would also have to reckon with their own internal affairs, for every observer agreed that Bellmon's success was indebted in some degree to the ferocious bloodlettings that had shattered Edmondson's administration and split the party into warring rural and urban wings.

Almost overlooked during the exciting partisan races was a second event equally auspicious for change. In August, 1962, a special three-judge federal court panel ruled that the "invidious [antiurban] discrimination" of both the existing apportionment statutes and Oklahoma's constitutional formula were in violation of the equal protection clause of the Fourteenth Amendment. The court order gave state authorities until March 8, 1963, to devise a suitable districting plan for both houses based upon "substantial numerical equality." Should they fail to do so, the court pledged to order equitable redistricting under its own plan.[73] Whatever the subsequent legislature's response, it seemed certain that the half century of rural domination of state politics would end, one way or another, in 1963. It was certain that the change would be accompanied by struggle.

In the crisis, Oklahoma Democrats would sorely miss the one man

---

[71] Benson et al., *Oklahoma Votes,* p. 106.
[72] Ibid., p. 49; *Directory of Oklahoma, 1977,* pp. 598-99.
[73] *Oklahoma City Daily Oklahoman,* August 4, 1962.

Henry Bellmon, The GOP's first Oklahoma governor and the father of modern Sooner Republicanism. Courtesy Oklahoma Historical Society.

who had proved capable of bridging the gap between farm and city. On January 1, 1963, Senator Robert S. Kerr died unexpectedly at Washington's Bethesda Naval Hospital. Kerr's death robbed the state of its most effective agent in Washington and his beloved party of the singular influence of his settled leadership. The void left by Kerr would be long felt, but never more so than in 1963, when Governor Edmondson, with only nine days remaining in his term, resigned his office and accepted George Nigh's appointment to the senatorial vacancy. For Edmondson, the move was the one way to salvage a political career seemingly ended at age thirty-seven. For his party, the opportunistic maneuver added poison to the swirling waters of discord.[74]

The inauguration of a Republican governor, the impending destruction of rural legislative supremacy, the death of a legendary leader, and the temporary ascension to the United States Senate of the state's most controversial man—all this signaled 1963 as the beginning of the contemporary era of Oklahoma politics. For all its differences, however, that era would not be altogether unlike the past periods. Oklahoma's political experience, like its weather, would continue to be occasionally violent, often confusing, and yet always answerable to its own rough logic.[75]

[74] Morgan, *Robert S. Kerr*, pp. 236–38.

[75] This appropriate analogy is borrowed from H. Wayne Morgan and Anne Hodges Morgan, *Oklahoma: A Bicentennial History*, States and the Nation Series (New York: W. W. Norton for the American Association for State and Local History, 1977), p. 72.

CHAPTER 17

The Contours of Contemporary Politics

R OBERT S. KERR'S death on New Year's Day, 1963, was a blow
to the Democratic party. Observers sensitive to political trends
prophesied that the death of the most powerful figure in recent Oklahoma history foretold change, the shape of which no one could descry.
It happened that Kerr's death marked the end of a long period of Democratic supremacy; the first Republican governor was about to be installed
in the executive mansion.

After fifty-six years of unbroken Democratic dominance in the statistics, a strong Republican opposition emerged and not in a single
protest vote. A sizable number came to adhere to the contemporary
neo-conservative doctrines of the "party of business." In an age of afflu-
ence, many a survivor of the Great Depression changed from populist-
style agitator to conservator of substantial assets.

Even as the two-party system became entrenched, the usages of the
political system were stabilized. Old practices were confirmed or modified so that, in many jurisdictions, there seemed to be no change at all
in the habitual way of doing things. The paradox of change contending
with continuity, modernity confronting tradition—this has been the puz-
zle for political scientists studying contemporary Oklahoma government.

The 1960s and 1970s brought about a rough equality between the rival
parties: the Republicans were highly visible in the glamour races at the
top of the ballot, and the Democrats continued to win most courthouses
and secondary state races. At the presidential level, Sooner Republicans
moved beyond mere equality to capture a commanding edge. Dwight D.
Eisenhower's victories of 1952 and 1956, followed by Nixon's success
(in Oklahoma, if not in the country) in 1960, ended a long drought of
presidential republicanism. Since statehood, only two previous GOP

nominees, Warren Harding in 1920 and Herbert Hoover in 1928, had taken Oklahoma's electoral votes. Their successes, however, had been aberrant; they were erased by the New Deal and slow-fading memories of the depression.

Since Harry Truman confounded the experts in 1948, only one Democratic nominee has earned Oklahoma's electoral college votes.[1] Lyndon Johnson's 1964 landslide over hapless Barry Goldwater carried into the Sooner State, but not nearly so emphatically as a Texas neighbor could wish. Johnson's success only temporarily checked the tide; it did not reverse the Democratic erosion. Four years later, Richard Nixon won a decisive plurality over Hubert Humphrey and George Wallace, the presidential candidate of the short-lived American party. Nixon beat Humphrey by 147,000 votes, almost half again Johnson's margin over Goldwater. In the tarnished glitter of 1972, the GOP again carried Oklahoma, and Nixon smashed the presumably untouchable record set by Franklin Roosevelt in 1932. Against the unpopular George McGovern, the incumbent carried all 77 counties and took a stunning 73.7 percent of the state's ballots. Even the subsequent ruin of Nixon's presidency failed to end Oklahoma's Republican preference. Although Gerald Ford ran a lackluster campaign and suffered the coolness of state Republican leaders, he nonetheless carried Oklahoma by a 13,000-vote margin over Jimmy Carter in 1976.

That record of Republican success would be remarkable for almost any state, but especially for one as traditionally Democratic as Oklahoma. Between statehood and 1960, Sooners had accorded Republican nominees less than 46 percent of the two-party vote. Between 1960 and 1976, however, Republican candidates drew an average of 57.5 percent of the state's two-party total. For all its Democratic tradition, Oklahoma in the 1960s and 1970s was, in fact, considerably more Republican than the nation. The national Republican presidential average was exactly 50 percent over the same years.

Meanwhile, events in those decades demonstrated that Henry Bellmon's surprisingly easy gubernatorial victory of 1962 was no accident. On the contrary, it signaled the beginnings of a lively Republican challenge at the state level. In 1966, Dewey Bartlett, a relatively obscure state senator from Tulsa, duplicated Bellmon's campaign to win a second governorship for the GOP. The first chief executive constitutionally eligible for a successive term, Bartlett came within a hair's breadth of reelection. In 1970 he lost to Democrat David Hall by 2,000 votes in more than 700,000 cast. It was the closest gubernatorial contest in Oklahoma history. The Republican's defeat was widely credited to his overconfidence.

In the 1970s only David Boren was able to roll up Democratic vote

---

[1] Statewide election totals for the elections discussed in this chapter are available in the Oklahoma State Election Board's *Directory of Oklahoma, 1979* (Oklahoma City, 1979), pp. 599-615.

totals with anything like the old regularity. The son of depression-era Congressman Lyle Boren and himself a four-term state representative from Seminole, Boren was the surprise victor in the 1974 Democratic primary, which included incumbent Governor David Hall and Second District Congressman Clem McSpadden. Boren ran as a virtual independent against the seasoned vote-getters. Not only did he promise a "clean sweep" of alleged Democratic corruption, he also embraced a platform not unlike that of recent Republicans. A persistent campaign rumor accused the ambitious young politician of an earlier apostasy, entertaining the idea of switching his party registration to the Republican side. Whatever the truth of that, Boren won a victory more personal than partisan when he subsequently took 64 percent of the vote over James Inhofe in the general election.

The 1978 governor's race between George Nigh and Ron Shotts was probably a more accurate gauge of relative party strength in the 1970s. Nigh was a veteran Democrat who had served as lieutenant governor for sixteen of the previous twenty years. Scarcely anyone in either party disliked him. Shotts was a comparative political amateur. Although he earlier had served two terms in the lower house, most Oklahomans knew him as a University of Oklahoma football player a decade before. His campaign was hardly as lavishly financed as recent Republican efforts, and it never seemed to catch fire. Nonetheless, Nigh barely won with 51.7 percent of the ballots. Nigh's margin was the smallest for any Democrat in state history except for Robert Williams in 1914, Johnston Murray in 1950, and Davis Hall's upset of Governor Bartlett in 1970.

The pattern of recent United States Senate contests has paralleled the Republican emergence in presidential and gubernatorial races. Between 1964 and 1978, Sooner voters went to the polls six times to select their senators.[2] Three times, Republicans defeated veteran Democrats. In 1968, Henry Bellmon ran more than 20,000 votes ahead of Richard Nixon to end Senator A. S. Mike Monroney's thirty years of congressional service. Bellmon's was the first Republican senatorial victory since Ed Moore's nominally bipartisan effort in 1942. In 1972, Bellmon's successor in Oklahoma City joined him in Washington. Dewey Bartlett won by a comfortable margin over the Second District's ten-term congressman, Ed Edmondson. In a much closer contest, decided after a challenge suit, Bellmon also beat Edmondson to earn a second term in 1974.

In sum, Sooner Republicans have won nine top-level (presidential, gubernatorial, or senatorial) contests since 1960, compared to a total of seven in the first half century of statehood. The Republican renaissance has brought victory in exactly half of all those races held since 1960.

---

[2]The 1964 senatorial election was to complete the remaining two years of the term originally won by the late Senator Robert S. Kerr. Fred Harris, who enjoyed the backing of the old Kerr organization, won the election over token Republican opposition after defeating the appointed incumbent, J. Howard Edmondson, in the Democratic primary. Harris won a full term in 1966.

Whatever the future holds for Oklahoma politics, the era of certain Democratic supremacy appears to be over.

Gone with it is the character of the state legislature, disproportionately rural in personalities, theories, and values during its first five and one-half decades of statehood. The issue that helped shatter the administration of J. Howard Edmondson and added to his party's woes in the 1962 gubernatorial race came to a head in the following year, when the legislature met under a federal court ultimatum to reapportion itself equitably by March 8, 1963.[3] Futile oratory against the impending federal intervention prevented consideration of a serious plan of compliance, so the assembly barely met the deadline with a reapportionment more cosmetic than real. Under it, about 30 percent of the state's population would continue to elect a majority in the lower house. The populations of the proposed senate districts varied by almost five to one.

That plan clearly evaded the court's initial mandate of a new apportionment based upon "substantial numerical equality." Not surprisingly, the federal court panel ruled the legislature's scheme unacceptable. Consequently, the judges ordered both chambers apportioned on a population basis; the plan therefore was designed by the Bureau of Government Research of the University of Oklahoma.

Reapportionment's steadfast foes answered with a lawsuit that resulted in yet another apportionment plan, this one issued by the state supreme court. It was largely a modification of the original legislative effort. Still adamantly opposed, reapportionment's foes also won a stay of the federal court's order on appeal to the United States Supreme Court. It was the refashioned legislative plan as issued by the Oklahoma Supreme Court that defined legislative districts when the 1964 primaries were held in May.

In the next month, however, the United States Supreme Court upheld the district court's authority over reapportionment, thus vacating the results of the first primary. Oklahoma authorities finally accepted the inevitable. Attorney General Charles Nesbitt pleaded with the federal judges for a compromise order that only slightly modified their first plan for the rural areas but maintained the electoral integrity of the counties by creating multimember districts for the major urban counties. The court accepted Nesbitt's minor revisions for rural apportionment but insisted upon dividing populous Oklahoma and Tulsa counties into substantially equal separate districts that totaled 34 in the house and 16 in the senate.

Under the final court order, new legislative elections were hastily scheduled for September. A massive turnover in the legislature's make-

[3]The denouement of the reapportionment struggle of the 1960s is covered in Richard D. Bingham, "Reapportionment of the Oklahoma House of Representatives: Politics and Process," Legislative Research Series, no. 2 (Norman: Bureau of Government Research, University of Oklahoma, 1972), pp. 4-6. See also Samuel A. Kirkpatrick, *The Legislative Process in Oklahoma: Policy Making, People and Politics* (Norman: University of Oklahoma Press, 1978), pp. 40-49.

up was the immediate consequence. More than half the incumbents of 1963 failed to return to their seats after the final 1964 balloting. The losers included many of Governor Edmondson's old foes whose comfortable boundaries had been enlarged to include many strangers. The winners were the new urban electorates, who finally won representation commensurate with their numbers.

Moreover, that population was steadily growing. It was 1950 before the state's urban population equaled the rural, but the movement from countryside to city accelerated swiftly thereafter. Between 1960 and 1970, thirty-nine predominantly rural counties suffered population losses, while the metropolitan regions surrounding Oklahoma City and Tulsa grew by 207,000 people, or 20 percent. In the latter year, roughly 40 percent of the state's total population lived in those two metropolitan areas. By 1975, half of all Oklahomans lived in the areas surrounding the two giants.[4] The hinterlands had lost exactly half their power base in the third quarter of the twentieth century.

The contemporary population shift was much greater, if less noticeable, than that of the Dust Bowl era or World War II. It was influenced also by profound changes in the Sooner economy, some of which reached back into the Great Depression or beyond. The most impressive was an accelerating economic maturation that finally freed the state from its traditional dependency on agriculture and petroleum. The national image of the Sooner State as a land of poor farmers and rich oilmen lingered, but the facts contradicted the stereotype.

Changes in agriculture were the more visible. They were rooted in continuing mechanization that demanded ever more land, ever more capital, and ever fewer people. Between 1950 and the end of the 1960s, the total number of farms declined by 42 percent, from 142,000 to 83,000. The number of farm workers dropped even faster, by 51 percent, as 131,000 farmers left agriculture. Those who remained were more prosperous: real farm earnings per worker grew by 260 percent over that period. Farmers earned their prosperity less with their labor than with their capital. Average farm size increased by nearly three-quarters, from 252 acres to 434, and the average investment in land and buildings alone soared by 584 percent between 1950 and 1969. In addition, the use of fertilizers increased by 429 percent, and the number of acres subject to irrigation doubled nearly four times over.[5]

In the last quarter of the century, the typical Oklahoma farmer is no

[4]Gerald M. Lage, Ronald L. Moomaw, and Larkin Warner, *A Profile of Oklahoma Economic Development: 1950-1975* (Oklahoma City: Frontiers of Science Foundation of Oklahoma, 1977), pp. 27-30. The definition of "metropolitan area" follows that of the United States Census Bureau for a "Standard Metropolitan Statistical Area": the counties which include the central cities as well as certain counties contiguous to those. The metropolitan area of Oklahoma City thus embraces Oklahoma, Canadian, Cleveland, McClain, and Pottawatomie counties. Osage, Tulsa, Washington, Rogers, Mayes, Creek, and Wagoner counties define the Tulsa metropolitan area.

[5]Ibid., pp. 49-54.

longer Alfalfa Bill Murray's agrarian sage or the Socialists' desperate toiler. He is a businessman, an entrepreneur who has survived the shift to "agribusiness" to the extent that he has had the good fortune to partake of it. Those survivors are few: little more than 5 percent of Oklahoma's work force made their living from agriculture in 1975. Farming accounted for only 4.6 percent of the state's income, down from 13.8 percent a quarter century earlier.[6]

A parallel decline in the relative importance of oil received less notice but was no less significant. Between 1950 and 1970, the state's share of its total income derived from mineral production, mostly oil and gas, dropped from 9.6 to 5.6 percent. By the start of the 1970s, only agriculture and contract construction contributed less to Sooner incomes. The proportion of total state employment engaged in mineral production dropped from 5.2 percent to 3.3, leaving it the smallest of the state's major sources of employment. Despite the continuing mythical importance of oil to Oklahoma, the reality is that the state's petroleum production peaked at 277 million barrels a half-century ago—in 1927. By 1976, Oklahoma's production of crude oil had fallen to 151 million barrels, the lowest figure for at least a quarter century.[7]

Petroleum refining, which helped build Tulsa, Ponca City, and Bartlesville, declined even faster. Between 1954 and 1972, the number of oil refinery workers dropped by a third, to fewer than 6,000. The total value added by refining barely increased over the same years. In constant dollars, it fell by 27 percent.[8] Worldwide convulsions in oil pricing would add enormously to dollar volume after the OPEC forced a steep rise in the value of domestic or "old," oil.

The steady decline in agriculture and oil lasted more than four decades. Historically, it produced the population exodus that began in 1930 and continued over the next thirty years. Even as late as the 1950s, Oklahoma suffered a net out-migration of 219,000 persons, the largest share of them squeezed-out, marginal farmers. Only in the 1960s did the flow of population reverse itself, as migration into the state slightly exceeded (by 13,000 people) the movement out of Oklahoma. By the 1970s, the reversal was well under way. Between 1970 and 1976, Oklahoma gained an estimated net in-migration of 107,000.[9]

The demographic turnabout that began tenuously in the 1960s and gained momentum in the next decade testified to the diversification of the Sooner economy. For the first time since the Great Depression, the losses in Oklahoma's farmlands and oil fields were outpaced by increases

---

[6]Ibid., pp. 40, 43. As used throughout this chapter, "state income" when referring to Oklahoma's population includes all income derived from labor and proprietorships. It excludes that small fraction of total personal income derived from property ownership (such as rents or stock earnings) or resulting from transfer payments (such as welfare benefits).

[7]Ibid., pp. 64-73.

[8]Ibid., p. 96; calculated from pp. 94, 97.

[9]Ibid., pp. 24-25.

in other centers of the economy. Between 1960 and 1970, the state's
manufacturing employment increased by 36 percent, its government
workers (not including those in health or education) by 21 percent.
In the same decade, workers in wholesale and retail trade increased
by 18 percent; those in finance, insurance, and real estate by 39 percent; and service employees (including health and education workers)
by 41 percent. In 1950 those fields had accounted for 61 percent of the
state's total income. By 1975, they provided just under 75 percent of a
much larger income.[10]

Each of these social and economic changes was crucial in its political
effect. The flight of natives from the state, the later migrations into it,
the population movement toward the booming cities—each would mark-
edly alter the fortunes of the two political parties.

Since statehood, the bedrock of Democratic party strength had rested
in the broad stretch of the state that lies south of the Canadian River.
It was that region that suffered most from the recent economic changes,
particularly the displacement of marginal farmers. Twenty-four of the
thirty-two counties lying south of the river lost population between 1950
and 1975. Their losses ranged upward to 43 percent and averaged more
than one-fifth.[11] An indeterminable but major portion of the voters who
left the state took with them their Democratic voting habits. They left
behind them a weaker party.[12]

The same economic and demographic changes that distressed state
Democrats worked to the advantage of Sooner Republicans. The in-
migration, which increased so dramatically after 1970, was one source
of the reversal of party strength. Some 35 percent of the contemporary
Sooner electors were born outside Oklahoma, the greater part of them in
the northern or border states. According to plausible surveys, these immigrants show a slight but noticeable political preference for the GOP,
especially in comparison with the voting habits of the natives.[13] The net
effect of the streams of migration both into and out of the state was,
therefore, to exchange Democratic loyalists for Republican.

A larger source of Republican gain was the movement to the cities.
Both major metropolitan counties had been Democratic in the early
decades of statehood, but by the end of World War II the white sections of Oklahoma City and Tulsa had become bulwarks of Republican
strength. The tendency to Republicanism was visible in the cities of the
Deep South as well as in the Southwest: the "Solid South" was not
threatened until large numbers of prosperous and influential people,
concentrated in the larger cities, reacted against the economic liberalism of the New Deal. It is a curious paradox that as northern agricul-

[10] Ibid., pp. 40, 43.
[11] Ibid., p. 29.
[12] Samuel A. Kirkpatrick, David R. Morgan, and Thomas G. Kielhorn, *The Oklahoma
Voter: Politics, Elections, and Parties in the Sooner State* (Norman: University of Oklahoma Press, 1977), pp. 130, 139.
[13] Ibid., p. 140.

tural states became urban, people from Republican backgrounds were likely to become more open to Democratic appeals. Thus, while Dallas, Memphis, Birmingham, and Charlotte elected more and more Republicans, the great Democratic centers in the north became powerful enough to turn rock-ribbed Republican states into Democratic strongholds: e.g., New York, Chicago, Philadelphia, Cleveland, and Detroit.

No Democratic presidential candidate, not even Lyndon Johnson in 1964, carried metropolitan Oklahoma in the five presidential elections from 1960 to 1976. In gubernatorial and senatorial races, moreover, only two Democrats were able to take majorities from Oklahoma and Tulsa counties. Robert S. Kerr in his last Senate campaign (1960) was one; David Boren, in the 1974 governor's race and 1978 Senate election, was the other. On four occasions, the steadfast Republicanism of the two urban counties was decisive as the GOP won three Senate victories as well as Gerald Ford's capture of the Oklahoma electors in 1976. All overcame decided deficits from the other 75 counties to place the top of the ticket in the Republican column.[14]

Ordinary citizens did not regard changes in the party label as questions of great significance. Political differences are much more perceptible in "hard times." The net impression of the years since the watershed election of 1962, recorded by many a political observer, is *plus ça change, plus le même chose*. No governmental change seemed really earthshaking. The elements of continuity—those things that do not change—brought about a stable society unaffected by the electoral and legislative battles that attracted only routine interest in the years of plenty after World War II.

Legislative reapportionment is a ready example of the unchanging nature of our politics. For all the furor that surrounded the question in the 1960s, for all the hopes of one side and the fears of the other, the final fact of reapportionment turned out to make surprisingly little difference. It certainly had little effect upon partisan divisions in the two chambers. Since reapportionment, the Republicans have constituted only 23.2 percent of the members of the lower house, just five points higher than their average share over the long period from 1907 to 1963. In the upper house, the Republican percentage has averaged 18.8, not appreciably greater than their 18.2 percent average over the first fifty-six years of statehood.[15] Moreover, recent studies of legislative voting

[14] Ibid., pp. 89-91. Although the differences between the metropolitan vote and that of the remainder of the state were decisive only in the presidential and senatorial contests, they were the greatest in the governors' races. Oklahoma and Tulsa counties combined to give Republican gubernatorial aspirants an average of 56.8 percent of their ballots between 1962 and 1978. The rest of the state cast an average Republican percentage of 44.4. The difference, though one of 12.4 percentage points, was never decisive because the two winning Republican gubernatorial candidates carried both the metropolitan and the nonmetropolitan areas, the latter by very small margins.

[15] Oliver Benson et al., *Oklahoma Votes: 1907-1962* (Norman: Bureau of Government Research, University of Oklahoma, 1964), p. 49; *Directory of Oklahoma, 1979,* pp. 138-41, 195-202.

behavior agree that, with few exceptions, partisanship remains a poor
guide to legislative performance. Election from metropolitan versus nonmetropolitan districts makes even less difference.[16] More important still,
the change in the legislature's composition produced very little change
in its leadership, which was usually exercised, as in earlier sessions,
by rural and small-town veterans. As the most exhaustive analysis of
the legislative operations concludes, "the generally increased legislative
power for large urban areas . . . was not realized by the early 1970s,
and significant changes have not occurred since that time."[17]

Even the electoral reinvigoration of the GOP, so impressive at first
glance, begins to diminish. Recent presidential victories become less
imposing when one recalls some of the victims—John F. Kennedy, whose
religion was a stumbling block to many an otherwise loyal Democrat;
Hubert Humphrey, whose candidacy was irreparably tarnished with the
disorder of the convention that nominated him; and George McGovern,
surely the weakest Democratic contender of this century. Similarly, the
two Republican gubernatorial triumphs were both taken over Democratic candidates who were bloodied in unusually divisive party primaries. W. P. Bill Atkinson, whom Bellmon defeated in 1962, suffered
the fatal bolt of Raymond Gary's angry followers after Atkinson won
the nomination with "anti-Garyism" his chief weapon. Preston Moore,
Atkinson's irascible ally, experienced the same fate in 1966. He, too,
won Democratic nomination in a close contest with the former governor,
only to see Gary and his troops desert before the final battle with Dewey
Bartlett.

More striking is the fact that every Republican success though the
1970s ended campaigns waged by exactly two men: Henry Bellmon and
Dewey Bartlett. Successively elected to the governor's chair, it was they
who won the three Senate victories of 1968, 1972, and 1974. Without
them, their party fumbled for leadership. State Senator James Inhofe
could not provide it in the 1974 governor's race. In subsequent elections, the GOP had to turn to unskilled amateurs—Ron Shotts, the 1978
gubernatorial nominee whose laurels were won on the football field, and
Robert Kamm, the former president of Oklahoma State University, who
was drafted by his desperate party to make his maiden race for the Senate
in that year. To an unusual degree, Henry Bellmon and Dewey Bartlett
were the Republican party of the sixties and seventies. The latter's death
in 1979 and the former's announcement that he would retire from the
Senate in 1980 closed out those two decades, and left unclear whether
the resurgence of their party would continue.

One final fact marred the Republican electoral accomplishments since
1960: they seldom reached beyond the top of the ticket. When Warren
Harding took Oklahoma's electoral college vote in 1920, he took with
him one United States senator and five of the state's eight congressmen.

---

[16] Kirkpatrick, *Legislative Process in Oklahoma,* pp. 138–40
[17] Ibid., pp. 35–40, quotation from p. 40.

He left behind Republican winners in every statewide race on the ballot and a Republican majority in the state house of representatives. When Herbert Hoover won in 1928, the GOP also elected three of eight congressmen, again swept every state office on the ballot, and took de facto control of the legislature's lower chamber.

Compare the record of the 1960s and 1970s. Only once did a Republican victory at the top of the ticket produce a Republican's election to a secondary state office.[18] In half the elections over that period, the GOP failed even to nominate full statewide tickets. Indeed, the party neglected to contest at least one-third of the lesser state offices on those five occasions. The congressional delegation rarely varied from a five-to-one Democratic split.[19] And, of course, the Republican performance in legislative contests was not much better than it had been over the long decades of unquestioned Democratic dominance.

The Republican resurgence in top-level races amid continuing Democratic supremacy at every other level nicely illustrates the paradoxical mixture of change and continuity in recent state politics. The resolution to the paradox lay in the fact that the most decisive change in partisan attitudes was not the substitution of Republican immigrants for lost Democrats. Even less was it a massive conversion of individual Democrats to Republicanism. Rather, it was the steady erosion of loyalties in favor of independence, if not indifference, to both parties.

The old armies of "yellow-dog" Democrats and "rock-ribbed" Republicans have passed. In their places are a decisive bloc of voters unattached to either party. In a systematic survey of the Oklahoma electorate in 1972, a team of political scientists discovered that only 29 percent of the voters still identified themselves as "strong" followers of any political party. Twenty percent were "strong Democrats"; 9 percent were "strong Republicans." Nearly as many—a total of 26 percent of the electorate—considered their politics to be independent of party. Similarly, when asked to score each party upon its handling of thirteen general qualities of government, 18 percent of the voters found equal or nearly equal merit in each. Only 19 percent assigned decided virtue to either.[20]

The diminution of partisanship and of the intensity of voter loyalties did not eliminate the Democrats as the state's normal majority party.[21]

---

[18] That instance came in 1966, when G. T. Blankenship won election as attorney general to accompany Bartlett's win in the governor's race. Otherwise, the only successful Republican candidate for secondary state office since 1948 was Tom Daxon, who was elected auditor and inspector in 1978. Daxon defeated John Rogers, who had held secondary office since 1926.

[19] *Directory of Oklahoma, 1979*, pp. 597-615.

[20] Kirkpatrick, Morgan, and Kielhorn, *The Oklahoma Voter*, pp. 103, 117-20. The authors' discussion of partisanship, pp. 95-125, is easily the most informed contemporary analysis.

[21] Kirkpatrick, Morgan, and Kielhorn estimate (ibid., p. 125) that the "normal" partisan distribution—"the hypothetical vote that would develop when both parties nominate equally attractive candidates and all other short-term forces (religion, issues, etc.) are balanced"—remains 55-45 Democratic.

In routine races, they still prevailed. Nonetheless, party regularity was a negligible virtue when popular passions were strongly aroused by issues (as in the Nixon-McGovern presidential race) or when an especially attractive candidate was matched with a controversial opponent (as in Bellmon's and Bartlett's gubernatorial campaigns). Sooner Republicans had unlocked the secret of electoral victory. Republicans could win elections, and they did.

In that respect, the Oklahoma electorate was not becoming so much more Republican as it was becoming more modern. Indeed, the erosion of traditional loyalties was only one element in what is a much larger theme in recent state politics: the continuous modernization of government. Modernization[22]—government's increasing reliance upon professional and efficient techniques, along with the steady expansion of its scope—integrated the elements of both change and continuity in contemporary Sooner politics.

Other than the decline of predictable voting habits, the most compelling evidence of modernization and its effects came from the state legislature. The biennial legislative session, as late as the early 1960s, was a forum for politics of the old school. Though always poorly paid[23] and often poorly educated,[24] the legislators included in their number the foremost of the state's traditional politicos. A shrewd chief executive, like Bob Kerr or Raymond Gary, knew better than to meddle with their jealously guarded patronage, their potent alliances with the county courthouses, or their zealous determination to retain influence and appropriations for their tiny bailiwicks. Inexperienced or idealistic governors like J. Howard Edmondson eventually learned the same lesson.

The adoption of a state merit system in 1959 and the realization of court-ordered reapportionment five years later toppled two of the pillars of legislative tradition. Another fell when a 1968 constitutional amendment cleared the path to professional salaries.[25] A constitutional

---

[22]The concept of modernization, central to much of contemporary social science, is introduced and developed in the following: Jason Finkle and Richard Gable, eds., *Political Development and Social Change* (New York: John Wiley & Sons, 1971); Myron Weiner, ed., *Modernization: The Dynamics of Growth* (New York: Basic Books, 1966); and Samuel P. Hayes, "Modernizing Values in the History of the United States," *Peasant Studies* 6 (1977):68-79.

The fruits of political modernization, which varies in its timing and its intensity, include the abandonment of blind party loyalty, the substitution of merit appointment for patronage or popular election, the growth of government's responsibilities, and a spreading popular apathy that is often measured in declining turnout rates. Each is characteristic of modern Oklahoma politics, some for a full generation, more during the recent past, most with an accelerating intensity.

[23]Legislative pay, fixed by a constitutional amendment of 1948, was $15 per day for up to seventy-five days when the legislature was in session, $100 per month when out of session. Three times over the next sixteen years voters rejected decisively attempts to raise or remove the constitutional limit.

[24]In the 1963 session, nearly a third of the lower house members had high school educations or less. Barely half were college graduates. Kirkpatrick, *Legislative Process in Oklahoma,* p. 27.

[25]The 1968 amendment eliminated any constitutional figure to provide for indefinite salaries as established by a legislative compensation board. After that change, legislative

amendment of 1966 authorized annual sessions. After that, a new breed of legislators appeared. Three-piece suits began to outrank cowboy hats; meerschaum pipes became as common as cigars. Strikingly better educated,[26] these legislators were also inclined to take broader, less parochial views of their responsibilities. For example, few regretted that the earlier adoption of the merit system had deprived them of the patronage prerogatives that had been traditional to their offices. With rare exceptions, most were pleased to have been relieved of such risks.[27]

Changes in the legislative machinery accompanied the changes in personalities. Structural modifications brought a streamlined committee system, including the creation of joint committees responsible for the interim between sessions. A revitalized legislative council with an expanded and more capable staff brought a new measure of professionalism to the work of lawmaking. In the early 1970s, the prestigious Citizens Conference Committee on State Legislatures ranked the fifty state assemblies on the basis of such modern practices. By their calculations, the Oklahoma legislature had an overall rank of fourteenth, well above any southern or border state except Florida.[28]

When the reapportionment issue reappeared after the 1970 census, Oklahomans had an opportunity to witness the difference in legislative behavior. A decade before, the legislators had used every weapon to avoid change. On the latter occasion, they wasted no energy in futile resistance. Instead, they contracted for expert assistance from the University of Oklahoma's political scientists and employed the computer to redraw district lines. Although they carefully protected most incumbents (including most of the Republican incumbents), the session calmly and dispassionately drew new district lines that left both houses among the most equitably apportioned in the nation.[29] It was a far cry from the

---

salaries soared by about 850 percent over the next decade. At an annual total of $12,948 in 1978, Oklahoma's legislative pay was exceeded by only eight states. Council of State Governments, *The Book of the States*, vol. 22 (Lexington, Kentucky: The Council, 1978), p. 21.

[26] Only 10 percent of the membership of the 1975 legislature had high school educations or less. Nearly two-thirds were college graduates. Kirkpatrick, *Legislative Process in Oklahoma*, p. 27.

[27] Jean G. McDonald, "Legislators and Patronage in Oklahoma," Legislative Research Series, no. 10 (Norman: Bureau of Government Research, University of Oklahoma, 1975), pp. 35-40, especially p. 35; Kirkpatrick, *Legislative Process in Oklahoma*, pp. 59-67, 199-211.

[28] Citizens Conference on State Legislatures, *The Sometime Governments: A Critical Study of the 50 American State Legislatures* (New York: Bantam Books, 1971), pp. 52-53. Of Oklahoma's neighbors, only New Mexico, ranked eleventh, rated more favorably. The remainder were far down the list: Texas (thirty-eighth), Arkansas (forty-sixth), Missouri (thirty-fifth), Colorado (twenty-eighth), and Kansas (twenty-third).

[29] Bingham, "Reapportionment of the Oklahoma House of Representatives," pp. 6-24; Kirkpatrick, *Legislative Process in Oklahoma*, pp. 48-49. After the 1970 reapportionments, only four states permitted smaller population variances in their senate districts, only thirteen in their house districts. David R. Morgan, *Handbook of State Policy Indicators*, 3rd ed. (Norman: Bureau of Government Research, University of Oklahoma, 1978), pp. 32-33.

stormy scenes of the previous decade, when only three state legislatures exceeded Oklahoma's in malapportionment, and few, if any, matched its resistance to modernization.

The most conspicuous change within the executive branch neatly tracked the evolution of the legislature. A shortened ballot, long sought by reformers as a step toward achieving more professional administrative expertise, was finally realized. As late as 1966, Oklahoma voters still chose twenty-one executive officers, including such functionaries as the mining inspector and his four assistants, in popular elections. By 1978, they elected only eight. The remaining thirteen by then had become subject to appointment, consolidation, or outright abolition.

The judiciary was not exempt. In fact, the winds of change reached storm strength in the third branch. Partisan election of state judges was a lingering and outmoded legacy of the populist sentiments of 1907. In the modern era, most states ended popular elections to their judiciaries. By the early 1960s, Oklahoma was one of only seventeen states that retained the practice. Various groups, most notably the state bar association, repeatedly urged reform, arguing that partisan elections served little public purpose and subjected judges to unseemly influences. After a series of rebuffs, they found their argument seemingly confirmed when a judicial scandal erupted in 1965. A retired justice of the state supreme court, N. S. Corn, was convicted of federal bribery charges that involved his collection of campaign contributions. Corn subsequently implicated two sitting justices, Earl Welch and N. B. Johnson, in his misdeeds. Welch was impeached and removed from office. Johnson escaped that certain fate by his last-minute resignation, only to be convicted on related criminal charges.[30]

The scandal cleared the way to reform of the judicial selection process. Two constitutional amendments, both approved in 1967, ended partisan election of state judges in favor of a plan based largely upon Missouri's successful plan of 1940. Justices of the appellate courts thereafter were initially named by gubernatorial appointment from a list of nominees selected by a bipartisan judicial nominating commission. Incumbents were retained periodically upon receiving majorities favorable to retention. Lower judges continued to be elected, but on a nonpartisan basis.

While state government in every branch grew steadily more professional, it also grew in size. As Oklahoma grew more complex, demands for state services kept pace. In fact, they raced ahead, for the state was called upon not only to provide more of its traditional services but also to add new ones, like vocational-technical training schools and a comprehensive system of state junior colleges. The state budget is the most direct form of measurement. Including emergency appropriations and

---

[30] John W. Wood, "Reform of Judicial Selection Procedures in Oklahoma," *Oklahoma Government Bulletin* 2, no. 1 (February, 1964); Alan Durbin, "Popular Election of the Oklahoma Supreme Court," *Oklahoma Government Bulletin* 4, no. 1 (Spring, 1966); Arrell M. Gibson, *Oklahoma: A History of Five Centuries* (Norman: Harlow Publishing Corp., 1965), pp. 435-36.

allocations from dedicated funds, the 1959 legislature authorized a total of $293.4 million. Twenty years later, the 1979 legislature approved the state's first billion-dollar budget, and the 1980 session was expected to add another $217 million to that. The one-year increment alone was roughly equal to total state spending as late as 1955.[31]

One consequence of government's growth was its enlarged significance to the state's economic vitality. By the mid-1970s, government employment (at the federal, state, and local levels) was the largest single source of personal income. Just over a fifth of Oklahomans' total income came to them as government paychecks. Government's contribution to state income was more than four times that derived from agriculture and about triple that from oil and gas production.[32]

As government grew in size and significance, it also became more centralized. Power steadily shifted from the city halls and county courthouses to the state capitol. It also moved from Oklahoma City to Washington. The major cause for the relocations was probably financial. Dependent upon the decrepit property tax system, local school boards and municipal and county governments perforce looked to the state treasury. Even more impressive was the state's growing financial dependency upon Washington. By the late 1970s, eighty separate agencies, almost half of those operated by the state, relied upon federal allocations for part or, in some cases, all of their revenues. In 1977 those federal grants totaled $668.4 million, having increased by nearly $39.5 million per year over the previous nine years. Through the late 1960s and the 1970s, federal grants accounted for more than a third of the state's total revenue. That share was not much less than that contributed by all state taxes combined: about 43 percent. It was this flow of money from Washington to Oklahoma City that largely explained the fact that for every dollar that Sooners paid in federal taxes, the national government was spending $1.22 in Oklahoma.[33]

The swelling federal contribution to the state's spending also helped obscure the fact that its own tax collections, though increasing, failed to keep pace with those of other states. Most states increased their tax rates to tap the unprecedented prosperity of recent years, but Oklahoma generally held fast to a steady tax line. The only substantial increase in the state's tax levies since World War II came in 1971, when Democratic Governor David Hall won a bloody battle to raise income and

[31] State of Oklahoma, Oklahoma Tax Commission, *Budget for the Fiscal Year Ending June 30, 1968* (Oklahoma City, 1967), p. 176; *Directory of Oklahoma, 1979*, pp. 481-89; *Tulsa Tribune*, January 8, 1980.

[32] Lage, Moomaw, and Warner, *Profile of Oklahoma Economic Development*, p. 40.

[33] Ibid., pp. 110-11; Larry Walker, "State Legislative Control of Federal Aid Funds: The Case of Oklahoma," Legislative Research Series, no. 13 (Norman: Bureau of Government Research, University of Oklahoma, 1978), pp. 16, 13; David R. Morgan and Joan O'Brien, *Oklahoma State Finance: A Longitudinal and Comparative Overview* (Norman: Bureau of Government Research, University of Oklahoma, 1977), pp. 7, 11; Kirkpatrick, Morgan, and Kielhorn, *The Oklahoma Voter*, p. 22.

gross production taxes.[34] For all the uproar that surrounded (and continues to surround) that tax increase,[35] the adjustment did not reverse Oklahoma's decline in taxes relative to the rest of the nation. In 1960, Oklahoma's state and local tax collections per $1,000 of its personal income was $120.87. The state ranked twentieth of the fifty states on that score, about 10 percent above the national average. In 1976, Oklahoma's absolute figure had increased, but relatively the state had dropped to thirty-fifth place, and its total ($144.80) was nearly 10 percent *below* the national average.[36] When political scientists measured Oklahoma's tax effort for 1960, they ranked it twenty-eighth nationally. When they calculated it for 1971 and 1975, the state had drifted to the lowest in the nation—for both years.[37]

Not even the federal subsidy could check the relative decline in services that resulted from the bipartisan hatred of taxes. In 1960 only thirteen states had invested more in public elementary and secondary education in relation to personal income. In 1976 only four invested less. Nineteen states had paid their public schoolteachers higher average salaries in 1960. Forty-seven did so in 1976. In 1960 only ten states had given more aid to their needy old people. In 1976 only four gave less.[38] In some aspects, the decline was more than relative. In constant dollars, the state spent 10 percent less for higher education in 1975 than it had in 1968. General welfare and highway spending slid even faster, by 24 and 25 percent respectively.[39]

Whatever these figures meant, they did not demonstrate that Oklahomans greeted the modern era with open pocketbooks. Despite their

[34] E. Lee Bernick, "Legislative Decision-Making and the Politics of Tax Reform: The Oklahoma Senate," Legislative Research Series, no. 9 (Norman: Bureau of Government Research, University of Oklahoma, 1975).

[35] The 1971 tax increase has been raised in every subsequent gubernatorial contest. Every Republican aspirant has attacked it; hardly any Democrat has dared to defend it. Indeed, both David Boren and George Nigh pledged to repeal at least a portion of the income tax increase. Both Democratic governors won slight tax reductions from the legislature, though, in both cases, less than they had requested. The long-smouldering controversy finally came to a head (and presumably an end) in the fall of 1979 when voters decided a Republican-sponsored initiative to undo most of the tax's effects. They narrowly defeated it, the distribution of votes closely following those of recent partisan contests.

[36] Morgan, *Handbook of State Policy Indicators,* p. 39.

[37] Ibid., p. 40. A state's tax effort, though difficult to compute, is simple in concept. It involves comparison of a state's total tax collections under its actual tax structure with the collections hypothetically possible had the state levied its taxes at the average rates for all states. Division of the actual figure by the hypothetical figure yields an index number that allows relative ranking. Moreover, any quotient less than 1.00 indicates that the state's overall tax rates lagged behind the national average. In 1960, Oklahoma's index figure was .94. Because its rates did not increase in the 1960s while those of most states (and, thus, the average) did, the index had dropped to .68 in 1970. Despite the 1971 tax changes, the state was still in last place in 1975, although its index figure had increased to .79. That figure indicated that Oklahoma's overall rate was still just 79 percent of that of the average state.

[38] Ibid., pp. 48, 50, 67.

[39] Lage, Moomaw, and Warner, *Profile of Oklahoma Economic Development,* p. 123.

acceptance of new techniques. Oklahomans retained a stubbornly traditional attitude toward governmental policies. Taxing and spending were the focal points.

On an objective base, state and local taxes remained among the nation's lowest. The one step to increase them did no more than slow the retreat relative to the rest of the country. Objectively, the state was losing ground, especially in the most modern of government's functions—education, particularly higher education, and public welfare. Objectively, the federal contribution, both to individual pocketbooks and to the state treasury, was a vital source of economic growth and of solvency itself. All the while, frugality served as a public shibboleth, dutifully pronounced by politicians of both parties. Few dared question the subjective consensus that state taxes were climbing beyond control, that government was too expensive and growing too fast, or that Oklahomans' federal tax dollars were squandered by liberal bureaucrats on giveaway programs in the East.

There was a bridge that united the objective to the subjective and linked circumstance to belief. It was built of irony, an irony that testified to the tensions within the steady modernization of state government. In the life-spans of two generations, Oklahomans had settled a frontier, built a state, and fought a depression and two world wars. Their children inherited a world in which the pace of change, always quick, became all the swifter. They found themselves in a modern, urban state charged with modern, urban responsibilities. Yet they struggled to retain the political values that sprang from an older tradition, a bucolic tradition that distrusted government and exalted individual rights at the expense of social obligations. As Oklahomans faced the future, they struggled with their own past.

History can record the sources of a state's tradition and of its contemporary forms. History can note the tensions that linger between the two. History will not, however, resolve them. That task is history's legacy to the future.

Bibliography

Special Sources for Oklahoma Politics

OUR study of Oklahoma political history was full of challenges for research. We were covering an unusually long period of time, much of which had not been subject to previous scholarly investigation. Although all of the secondary literature consulted for this book is listed herein, the purpose of this essay is a brief description and evaluation of the resources, especially the primary materials, that are available to future students of Oklahoma's political experience.

The chief depositories of primary materials for the study of Oklahoma politics are located within a few miles of each other. In the capitol complex at Oklahoma City are the Oklahoma Historical Society and the Oklahoma State Archives, the latter a branch of the Oklahoma Department of Libraries. At Norman, the University of Oklahoma Library maintains its impressive Western History Collections, the repository of personal papers of many of the state's most active public men.

The Historical Society has traditionally emphasized preservation of records relating to the long early period of Indian occupation. The poststatehood era has been neglected. Even so, its massive newspaper collection of virtually all extant microfilm copies of Oklahoma newspapers from territorial days is invaluable. Several score newspapers were perused for this book. There was special concentration on the election years to assess campaigns and to sample editorial opinion. Particularly for the latest years, the authors relied heavily upon the *Oklahoma City Daily Oklahoman*. Easily the most powerful newspaper in Oklahoma, and one of the most powerful in the Southwest, the *Oklahoman* itself has been important to the political history of the state. Its editorial views were undisguised. More important, however, was the

Oklahoman's integrity in reporting political news, particularly through the reporting of Otis Sullivant. Sullivant was the newspaper's statehouse reporter and political analyst from the 1920s through the 1960s. Whatever the predilections of his publisher and editor, the legendary E. K. Gaylord, Sullivant was scrupulously dependable with his facts and remarkably keen in his analyses. Moreover, the *Oklahoman* offers the researcher an inestimable advantage: detailed indexing for the years between the late 1940s and the mid-1960s. Understandably, the *Daily Oklahoman* was used as the newspaper of record for this book.

Equally valuable for the years between 1912 and 1940 are the files of *Harlow's Weekly,* which are available at each of the major depositories. During those years, *Harlow's* was a veritable encyclopedia of political news. No election campaign, no governor, and no legislative assembly escaped its incisive reporting. Its coverage was both thorough and straightforward. Its analyses usually proved to be correct.

Aside from its invaluable journalistic collections, the Historical Society also maintains manuscript collections of a few early political figures. Those of Peter Hanraty, Robert L. Williams, and William H. Murray were most pertinent to the interests of the authors.

For much too long, Oklahoma's official records were preserved in a haphazard fashion. As late as 1969, the state's archives were piled into a poorly constructed metal warehouse behind the State Armory. Happily, that state of affairs has been corrected. A well-organized State Archives, staffed by competent professionals, is now housed in the Allen Wright Building as a branch of the Oklahoma Department of Libraries. In addition to its collection of official records, the Archives maintains the papers of various officials, most notably those of recent governors.

Otherwise unavailable state documents were usually held somewhere in the Archives. Through them, it was possible to trace the major actions of public servants. On matters of special interest for particular problems—e.g., relief during the Great Depression—the unpublished records of appropriate agencies were examined. Among the governors' papers studied were those spanning the administrations of Roy J. Turner through J. Howard Edmondson. Much of the material in those collections is routine bureaucratic paperwork, with the relevant information gleaned by use of the exceedingly detailed listings, which describe box-by-box and folder-by-folder the material in those uncommonly well-organized collections. Even before visiting the Archives, the researcher should take advantage of the good descriptive guide to its major holdings, as well as those of the Oklahoma Historical Society: Kenny Franks and John Stewart, comps., *A Guide to Research at the Oklahoma Historical Society and the Oklahoma State Archives* (Oklahoma City: Central Printing Co., 1975). Serious future students of state politics would do well to start with that.

The University of Oklahoma's Western History Collections has long assumed the mission of preserving the private papers of individuals and institutions of importance for the state's modern history. Neither the

Archives nor the Historical Society can match its collection of manuscript materials, particularly from a host of political figures that range from the utterly obscure to governors and senators. A somewhat dated guide to these holdings exists: Arrell Morgan Gibson, *A Guide to Regional Manuscript Collections in the Division of Manuscripts, University of Oklahoma Library* (Norman: University of Oklahoma Press, 1960). Lack of funds and staffing unfortunately has prevented greatly detailed shelf listings for all except the largest collections, such as that from Senator Robert S. Kerr. The researcher must, therefore, rely upon the incomparable knowledge of archivist Jack Haley and, ultimately, personally work through the materials.

More than two dozen of the university's manuscript collections from the political figures most central to the story were examined. In some measure, it was discovered that the quality of the material varied inversely to its quantity. With time comes complexity: the size of collections increases almost geometrically. Most of the increment is, however, incidental: form letters to voters and constituents, disorganized personal grievances from citizens, official commendations, and the like. Undoubtedly, use of the telephone has reduced to near extinction the reflective political observations that earlier politicians incorporated in personal letters. For a project of this scope, the manuscript collections turned out to be surprisingly disappointing. Their value would be considerably greater, of course, for more narrowly defined studies.

The following list of secondary sources is as complete as possible. As a whole, the literature on Oklahoma's politics tends to be most uneven. It is most impressive in the field of biography. The finest examples are Keith Bryant's work on William H. Murray, Monroe Billington's on Thomas P. Gore, and Anne Hodges Morgan's treatment of Robert S. Kerr. Only a few periods or specific problems have received scholarly treatment that can be described as first-class. Charles Alexander's history of the Klan era is one. The phenomenon of early socialism as analyzed by Garin Burbank, James Green, and Ellen Rosen is another. In contrast, no single, good account of the collapse of the Democrats' early progressive consensus nor of the complex maneuverings unleashed by the Great Depression and the New Deal can be singled out for its quality.

A special form of secondary literature invaluable for the study of the recent past is the work of political scientists. The reference notes for the final chapters confirms our indebtedness to the University of Oklahoma's Bureau of Government Research. In addition to the large number of works provided by the Bureau of Government Research, the school's political science professors and their graduate students have written informative monographs involving particular elections and more general problems of public affairs.

Two general reference works stand out as indispensable. Since 1917 the State Election Board has issued biennially its *Directory of Oklahoma.* Especially in its most recent editions, the *Directory* is the authoritative encyclopedia of politics. Its compilation of statistics for every election, as well as all state questions voted upon, since 1907 was used at length. County election figures for the gubernatorial, presidential, and senatorial contests were taken from the study made by Oliver L. Benson and his associates under the title of *Oklahoma Votes, 1907-1962.* Researchers may also consult a companion volume under Benson's direction, *Oklahoma Votes for Congress,* which provides county-by-county totals for the congressional races through 1964. More recent county election figures are available in published form from the State Election Board.

Secondary Sources

Books

Aldrich, Gene. *The Okie Jesus Congressman (The Life of Manuel Herrick).* Oklahoma City: Times-Journal Publishing Co., 1974.

Alexander, Charles C. *The Ku Klux Klan in the Southwest.* Lexington: University of Kentucky Press, Kentucky Paperbacks, 1966.

Allen, Clinton M. *The Sequoyah Movement.* Oklahoma City: Harlow Publishing Co., 1925.

Alley, John. *City Beginnings in Oklahoma Territory.* Norman: University of Oklahoma Press, 1939.

Ameringer, Oscar. *If You Don't Weaken: The Autobiography of Oscar Ameringer.* New York: Henry Holt & Co., 1940.

Bartley, Numan V. *The Rise of Massive Resistance: Race and Politics in the South During the 1950s.* Baton Rouge: Louisiana State University Press, 1969.

Barrett, Charles F., ed. *Oklahoma After Fifty Years.* 4 vols. Hopkinsville, Kentucky, and Oklahoma City: Historical Records Association, 1941.

Beckett, A. L. *Know Your Oklahoma.* Oklahoma City: Harlow Publishing Co., 1930.

Benson, Oliver, et al. *Oklahoma Votes, 1907-1962.* Norman: University of Oklahoma, Bureau of Government Research, 1964.

————. *Oklahoma Votes for Congress, 1907-1964.* Norman: University of Oklahoma, Bureau of Government Research, 1965.

Bernick, Emil Lee. *Legislative Voting Patterns and Partisan Cohesion in a One-Party Dominant Legislature.* Norman: University of Oklahoma, Bureau of Government Research, 1973.

Billington, Monroe Lee. *Thomas Pryor Gore: The Blind Senator from Oklahoma.* Lawrence: University of Kansas Press, 1967.

Bitterman, Henry J. *State and Federal Grants-in-Aid.* New York and Chicago: Mentzer, Bush & Co., 1938.

Blachly, Frederick F., and Oatman, Miriam Eulalie. *The Government of Oklahoma.* Oklahoma City: Harlow Publishing Co., 1924.

Blum, John Morton. *V Was for Victory: Politics and American Culture During World War II.* New York: Harcourt, Brace, Jovanovich, 1976.

Boren, Lyle H., and Boren, Dale. *Who is Who in Oklahoma.* Guthrie: Co-operative Publishing Co., 1935.

Brookings Institution. Institute for Government Research. *Report on a Survey of the Organization and Administration of Oklahoma.* Oklahoma City: Harlow Publishing Co., 1935.

Brooks, John S., comp. *First Administration of Oklahoma.* Oklahoma City: Oklahoma Engraving & Printing Co., 1908.

Bryant, Keith L. *Alfalfa Bill Murray.* Norman: University of Oklahoma Press, 1968.

Buchanan, James Shannon, and Dale, Edward Everett. *History of Oklahoma.* rev. ed. Evanston, Illinois: Row, Peterson & Co., 1935.

Burbank, Garin. *When Farmers Voted Red: The Gospel of Socialism in the Oklahoma Countryside, 1910-1924.* Contributions in American History, no. 53. Westport, Conn.: Greenwood Press, 1976.

Burns, James McGregor. *Roosevelt: The Lion and the Fox.* New York: Harcourt, Brace & World, Harvest Books, 1956.

Bynum, E. T. *Personal Recollections of Ex-Governor Walton: A Record of Inside Observations.* Oklahoma City: The Author, 1924.

Campbell, Angus, et al. *The American Voter: An Abridgement.* New York: John Wiley & Sons, 1964.

Citizens Conference on State Legislatures. *The Sometime Governments: A Critical Study of the 50 American State Legislatures.* New York: Bantam Books, 1971.

Council of State Governments. *The Book of the States.* 22 vols. Lexington, Kentucky: The Council, 1935-.

Cross, George Lynn. *Blacks in White Colleges: Oklahoma's Landmark Cases.* Norman: University of Oklahoma Press, 1975.

Dale, Edward Everett, and Aldrich, Gene. *History of Oklahoma.* Edmond: Thompson Book & Supply Co., 1972.

———, and Morrison, James D. *Pioneer Judge: The Life of Robert L. Williams.* Cedar Rapids, Iowa: Torch Press, 1958.

———, and Rader, Jesse Lee. *Readings in Oklahoma History.* Evanston, Illinois: Row, Peterson & Co., 1930.

Daniels, Josephus. *Editor in Politics.* Chapel Hill: University of North Carolina Press, 1941.

David, Paul T.; Moos, Malcolm; and Goldman, Ralph M. *Presidential Nominating Politics in 1952.* Vol. 3. *The South.* Baltimore: Johns Hopkins University Press, 1954.

Debo, Angie. *And Still the Waters Run: The Betrayal of the Five Civilized Tribes.* Princeton, New Jersey: Princeton University Press, 1940.

———. *Prairie City.* New York: Alfred A. Knopf, 1944.

———. *Tulsa: From Creek Town to Oil Capital.* Norman: University of Oklahoma Press, 1943.

Dubofsky, Melvin. *We Shall Be All: A History of the Industrial Workers of the World.* Chicago: Quadrangle Books, 1969.

Ellis, A. H. *History of the Constitutional Convention of the State of Oklahoma.* Muskogee: N. A. Ellis, 1923.

Finkle, Jason, and Gable, Richard, eds. *Political Development and Social Change.* New York: John Wiley & Sons, 1971.

Fischer, LeRoy H., ed. *The Territorial Governors of Oklahoma.* The Oklahoma Series, vol. 1. Oklahoma City: Oklahoma Historical Society, 1975.

Fowler, Oscar Priestly. *The Haskell Regime: The Intimate Life of Charles Nathaniel Haskell.* Oklahoma City: Boles Printing Co., 1933.

Franklin, Jimmie Lewis. *Born Sober: Prohibition in Oklahoma, 1907-1959.* Norman: University of Oklahoma Press, 1971.

Gallup, George H. *The Gallup Poll: Public Opinion, 1935-1971.* 3 vols. New

York: Random House, 1972.

Gibson, Arrell M. *Oklahoma: A History of Five Centuries.* Norman: Harlow Publishing Corp., 1965.

Goble, Danney. *Progressive Oklahoma: The Making of a New Kind of State.* Norman: University of Oklahoma Press, 1980.

Goodwyn, Lawrence. *Democratic Promise: The Populist Moment in America.* New York: Oxford University Press, 1976.

Graves, Richard S. *Oklahoma Outlaws.* Oklahoma City: State Printing & Publishing Co., 1915.

Green, James R. *Grass-Roots Socialism: Radical Movements in the Southwest, 1895-1943.* Baton Rouge: Louisiana State University Press, 1978.

Gittinger, Roy M. *The Formation of the State of Oklahoma, 1803-1906.* Norman: University of Oklahoma Press, 1939.

Gunther, John. *Inside U.S.A.* rev. ed. New York: Harper and Brothers, 1951.

Harlow, Rex F., comp. *Makers of Government in Oklahoma.* Oklahoma City: Harlow Publishing Co., 1930.

————. *Oklahoma Leaders.* Oklahoma City: Harlow Publishing Co., 1928.

————. *Successful Oklahomans.* Oklahoma City: Harlow Publishing Co., 1927.

Harlow, Victor E. *Oklahoma.* Oklahoma City: Harlow Publishing Co., 1934.

Hauan, Martin. *He Buys Organs for Churches, Pianos for Bawdy Houses.* Oklahoma City: Midwest Political Publications, 1976.

Hill, Luther B. *A History of the State of Oklahoma.* 2 vols. Chicago and New York: Lewis Historical Publishing Co., 1908.

Hines, Gordon. *Alfalfa Bill: An Intimate Biography.* Oklahoma City: Oklahoma Press, 1932.

Hodge, Oliver. *The Administration and Development of the Oklahoma School Land Department.* Tulsa: Prompt Printing Co., 1937.

Hurst, Irvin. *The 46th Star: A History of Oklahoma's Constitutional Convention and Early Statehood.* Oklahoma City: Semco Color Press, 1957.

Johnson, Roy M., comp. *Oklahoma History South of the Canadian.* 3 vols. Edited by John P. Gilday and Mark H. Sait. Chicago: S. J. Clarke Publishing Co., 1925.

Jones, Stephen. *Oklahoma Politics in State and Nation: The Democratic Years.* Enid, Oklahoma: Haymaker Press, 1974.

Kerr, Robert S. *Land, Wood, and Water.* New York: Fleet Publishing Corp., 1960.

Key, V. O., Jr. *Southern Politics in State and Nation.* New York: Random House, Vintage Books, 1949.

Kirkpatrick, Samuel A. *The Legislative Process in Oklahoma: Policy-Making, People, and Politics.* Norman: University of Oklahoma Press, 1978.

————, and Morgan, David R. *Oklahoma Voting Patterns: Presidential, Senatorial, and Gubernatorial Elections.* Norman: University of Oklahoma, Bureau of Government Research, 1970.

————; ————; and Kielhorn, Thomas G. *The Oklahoma Voter: Politics, Elections, and Parties in the Sooner State.* Norman: University of Oklahoma Press, 1977.

Klein, John J., et al. *The Oklahoma Economy.* OSU College of Business Economic Research Series, no. 1. Stillwater: Oklahoma State University, 1963.

Kluger, Richard. *Simple Justice: The History of Brown v. Board of Education and Black America's Struggle for Equality.* New York: Random House, Vintage Books, 1977.

Lage, Gerald M.; Moomaw, Ronald L.; and Warner, Larkin. *A Profile of Okla-*

homa *Economic Development, 1950-1975.* Oklahoma City: Frontiers of Science Foundation of Oklahoma, 1977.

Lampe, William T. *Tulsa County in the World War.* Tulsa: Tulsa County Historical Society, 1919.

Logan, D. M. *Structure of Oklahoma Government.* Oklahoma City: Harlow Publishing Co., 1931.

Luthin, Reinhard H. *American Demagogues: Twentieth Century.* Boston: Beacon Press, 1954.

Mathews, John Joseph. *Life and Death of an Oilman: The Career of E. W. Marland.* Norman: University of Oklahoma Press, 1951.

Meyer, Leo, comp. *Oklahoma State Manual.* Guthrie: Leader Publishing Co., 1909.

Morgan, Anne Hodges. *Robert S. Kerr: The Senate Years.* Norman: University of Oklahoma Press, 1977.

Morgan, David R. *Demographic Correlates of Suburban Voting: The Oklahoma City Metropolitan Area.* Norman: University of Oklahoma, Bureau of Government Research, 1970.

———. *Handbook of State Policy Indicators.* 3rd ed. Norman: University of Oklahoma, Bureau of Government Research, 1978.

———; Kirkpatrick, Samuel A.; and Edwards, Larry G. *Oklahoma Voting Patterns: Congressional Elections.* Norman: University of Oklahoma, Bureau of Government Research, 1970.

———. and O'Brien, Joan. *Oklahoma State Finance: A Longitudinal and Comparative Overview.* Norman: University of Oklahoma, Bureau of Government Research, 1977.

Morgan, H. Wayne, and Morgan, Anne Hodges. *Oklahoma: A Bicentennial History.* States and the Nation Series. New York: W. W. Norton for the American Association for State and Local History, 1977.

Morris, Lerona Rossmond. *Oklahoma—Yesterday—Today—Tomorrow.* 2 vols. rev. ed. Guthrie: Co-operative Publishing Co., 1931.

Murray, William Henry. *Memoirs of Governor Murray and True History of Oklahoma.* 3 vols. Boston: Meador Publishing Co., 1945.

Oklahoma Publishing Company. *Oklahoma Almanac.* 2 vols. Oklahoma City: Oklahoma Publishing Co., 1930, 1931.

Patterson, James T. *The New Deal and the States: Federalism in Transition.* Princeton, New Jersey: Princeton University Press, 1969.

Peterson, H. C., and Fite, Gilbert. *Opponents of War, 1917-1918.* Madison: University of Wisconsin Press, 1957.

Porter, Glenn W. *The Rise of Big Business, 1860-1910.* New York: Thomas Y. Crowell, 1973.

Poole, Richard W., and Traver, James D. *Oklahoma Population Trends.* Economic Resources Series, no. 4. Stillwater: Oklahoma State University, 1968.

Proceedings of the Constitutional Convention of the Proposed State of Sequoyah. Muskogee, Oklahoma: Muskogee Printing Co., 1907.

Pruiett, Moman. *Moman Pruiett, Criminal Lawyer.* Oklahoma City: Harlow Publishing Co., 1944.

Richards, W. B., comp. *Oklahoma Red Book.* 2 vols. Tulsa: Leader Printing Co., 1912.

Ryan, Frederick Lynne. *A History of Labor Legislation in Oklahoma.* Norman: University of Oklahoma Press, 1932.

———. *Rehabilitation of Oklahoma Coal Mining Communities.* Norman: University of Oklahoma Press, 1935.

Saloutos, Theodore. *Farmer Movements in the South, 1865-1933.* Lincoln: University of Nebraska Press, 1964.

Shannon, David A. *The Socialist Party in America: A History.* Chicago: Quadrangle Books, 1967.

Shirley, Glenn. *West of Hell's Fringe: Crime, Criminals, and the Federal Peace Officer in Oklahoma Territory, 1889-1907.* Norman: University of Oklahoma Press, 1978.

Settle, William A. *The Dawning, A New Day for the Southwest: A History of the Tulsa District Corps of Engineers, 1939-1971.* Tulsa: United States Army Corps of Engineers, Tulsa District, 1975.

Sinclair, H. M. *Making Oklahoma Safe for the Democratic Party, or How the Williams Machine Stole the Election of 1916.* Oklahoma City: The Author, 1917.

Stein, Walter J. *California and the Dust Bowl Migration.* Contributions in American History, no. 21. Westport, Conn.: Greenwood Press, 1973.

Stewart, Dora Ann. *Government and Development of Oklahoma Territory.* Oklahoma City: Harlow Publishing Co., 1933.

Teall, Kaye M., ed. *Black History in Oklahoma: A Resource Book.* Oklahoma City: Oklahoma City Public Schools, 1971.

Thelen, David P. *Robert M. LaFollette and the Insurgent Spirit.* Boston: Little, Brown & Co., 1976.

Thoburn, Joseph B., and Wright, Muriel H. *Oklahoma: A History of the State and its People.* 4 vols. Chicago and New York: Lewis Historical Publishing Co., 1929.

Tindall, George B. *The Emergence of the New South, 1913-1945.* History of the South, vol. 10. Baton Rouge: Louisiana State University Press, 1967.

Tindell, John H. N., ed. *Makers of Oklahoma.* Guthrie: State Capital Co., 1905.

Tolson, Arthur L. *The Black Oklahomans, 1541-1972.* New Orleans: Edwards Printing Co., 1974.

Truman, Margaret. *Women of Courage.* New York: William Morrow & Co., 1976.

Tucker, Howard A. *History of Governor Walton's War on the Ku Klux Klan, the Invisible Empire.* Oklahoma City: Southwest Publishing Co., 1923.

Waldby, H. O. *The Patronage System in Oklahoma.* Norman: Transcript Co., 1950.

Wardell, Morris L. *Political History of the Cherokee Nation, 1838-1907.* Norman: University of Oklahoma Press, 1938.

Weaver, Findley. *Oklahoma's Deficit.* Norman: University of Oklahoma Press, 1940.

Weiner, Myron, ed. *Modernization: The Dynamics of Growth.* New York: Basic Books, 1966.

Woodward, C. Vann. *Origins of the New South, 1877-1913.* History of the South, vol. 9. Baton Rouge: Louisiana State University Press, 1951.

Articles and Short Monographs

Albert, Carl. "Reflections on My Early Life." *Chronicles of Oklahoma* 52 (1974): 30-37.

Amidon, Beulah Elizabeth. "Sooners in Security: What is Happening in Oklahoma?" *Survey Graphic,* April 1938, pp. 203-207.

"Aroma in Oklahoma." *Time,* July 19, 1954, p. 18.

Basu, A. K. "Socio-Economic and Demographic Correlates in Voting in Oklahoma's 1960 Presidential Election." *Oklahoma Government Bulletin* 2, no. 4 (1964).

Bernick, E. Lee. "Legislative Decision-Making and the Politics of Tax Reform: The Oklahoma Senate." Legislative Research Series, no. 9. Norman: University of Oklahoma, Bureau of Government Research, 1975.

Bilger, Eddie. "The Oklahoma Vorwarts: The Voice of German-Americans in Oklahoma During World War I." *Chronicles of Oklahoma* 54 (1976):245-60.

Billington, Monroe. "Public School Integration in Oklahoma, 1954-1963." *Historian* 26 (1964):521-37.

Bingham, Richard D. "Reapportionment of the Oklahoma House of Representatives: Politics and Process." Legislative Research Series, no. 2. Norman: University of Oklahoma, Bureau of Government Research, 1972.

Blackburn, Bob L. "Law Enforcement in Transition: From Decentralized County Sheriffs to the Highway Patrol." *Chronicles of Oklahoma* 56 (1978):194-207.

Beard, Charles A. "The Constitution of Oklahoma." *Political Science Quarterly* 24 (1909):95-114.

Blake, Aldrich. "Oklahoma Goes Rosicrucian." *Nation,* September 14, 1927, pp. 247-48.

————. "Oklahoma's Klan Fighting Governor." *Nation,* October 3, 1923, p. 353.

Bliven, Bruce. "From the Oklahoma Front." *New Republic,* October 17, 1923, pp. 202-205.

Boles, David C. "Effect of the Ku Klux Klan on the Oklahoma Gubernatorial Election of 1926." *Chronicles of Oklahoma* 55 (1977):424-32.

Brinker, Paul Albert, and Sangha, Kehar S. "Manufacturing, Value-Added, and Wages in Oklahoma, 1899-1953." *Southwestern Social Science Quarterly* 38 (1957):111-23.

Bryant, Keith L. "The Juvenile Court Movement: Oklahoma as a Case Study." *Social Science Quarterly* 49 (1968):368-76.

————. "Kate Barnard, Organized Labor, and Social Justice in Oklahoma During the Progressive Era." *Journal of Southern History* 35 (1969):145-64.

————. "Labor in Politics: The Oklahoma State Federation of Labor During the Age of Reform." *Labor History* 11 (1970):259-76.

Buck, Solon J. "The Settlement of Oklahoma." *Transactions of the Wisconsin Academy of Sciences, Arts, and Letters* 15 (1907):385-90.

Candee, Helen Churchill. "Oklahoma." *Atlantic Monthly,* September 1900, p. 328.

Casey, Orben J. "Governor Lee Cruce." *Chronicles of Oklahoma* 52 (1974): 456-75.

————. "Governor Lee Cruce and Law Enforcement, 1911-1915." *Chronicles of Oklahoma* 54 (1976):435-60.

Celarier, Michelle. "Public Opinion on Desegregation in Oklahoma." *Chronicles of Oklahoma* 47 (1969):268-81.

Chandler, Alfred D. "The Beginnings of 'Big Business' in American Industry." *Business History Review* 33 (1959):1-31.

Childs, Marquis. "The Big Boom from Oklahoma." *Saturday Evening Post.* April 9, 1949, pp. 22-23, 118-20.

Clark, Blue. "Beginning of Oil and Gas Conservation, 1907-1933." *Chronicles of Oklahoma* 55 (1977):375-91.

Clark, J. Stanley. "The Career of John R. Thomas." *Chronicles of Oklahoma* 52 (1974):152-79.

Cochran, Louis. "Imperial Alfalfa Bill." *Outlook,* December 30, 1931, pp. 555-56.

Cooke, Thornton. "Collapse of Bank-Deposit Guaranty in Oklahoma and Its Position in Other States." *Quarterly Journal of Economics* 38 (1923):108-39.

———. "Insurance of Bank Deposits in the West." *Review of Reviews,* May 1910, pp. 625-26.

Creel, Von Russell. "Court in Peril." *Chronicles of Oklahoma* 52 (1974): 220-36.

Dangerfield, Royden J., and Flynn, Richard H. "Voter Motivation in the 1936 Oklahoma Democratic Primary." *Southwestern Social Science Quarterly* 17 (1936):97-100.

Detweiler, John S. "The Negro Teacher and the Fourteenth Amendment." *Journal of Negro Education* 36 (1967):403-409.

Dillard, Irving. "Oklahoma Makes Ready for 1944." *New Republic,* August 9, 1943, p. 194.

Doyle, Thomas H. "Single Statehood Versus Double Statehood." *Chronicles of Oklahoma* 5 (1927):18-41, 117-48, 266-86.

———. "Supreme Court—Territory of Oklahoma." *Chronicles of Oklahoma* 13 (1935):214-18.

Durbin, Alan C. "Oklahoma Congressional Elections and Presidential Coattails." *Oklahoma Government Bulletin* 3, no. 2 (1965).

———. "Popular Election of the Oklahoma Supreme Court." *Oklahoma Government Bulletin* 4, no. 1 (1966).

Ewing, Cortez A. M. "Impeachment of Oklahoma Governors." *American Political Science Review* 25 (1930):648-52.

———. "Sufficiency Certification of Initiative Signatures in Oklahoma." *American Political Science Review* 31 (1937):65-70.

Fassey, W. Richard. "'Talkin' Dust Bowl Blues': A Study of Oklahoma's Cultural Identity During the Great Depression." *Chronicles of Oklahoma* 55 (1977):12-33.

Fite, Gilbert C. "Oklahoma's Reconstruction League: An Experiment in Farmer-Labor Politics." *Journal of Southern History* 12 (1947):535-55.

Forbes, Gerald. "Shaffer County—A Southwestern Boom Episode." *Southwest Social Science Quarterly* 21 (1940):23-29.

Foreman, Grant. "Oklahoma." *State Government* 19 (1946):127-32.

———. "Oklahoma and Indian Territory." *Outlook,* October 5, 1907, p. 550.

———. "Trusts and the People Get Together." *Independent,* December 11, 1916, p. 454.

Frost, Stanley. "Behind the White Hoods: The Regeneration of Oklahoma." *Outlook,* November 21, 1923, pp. 492-95.

———. "Klan, the King, and a Revolution." *Outlook,* November 28, 1923, pp. 530-31.

———. "Night-Riding Reformers." *Outlook,* November 14, 1923, pp. 438-40.

Gage, Duane. "Al Jennings, The People's Choice." *Chronicles of Oklahoma* 46 (1968):242-48.

Gard, Wayne. "Alfalfa Bill." *New Republic,* February 17, 1932, pp. 11-12.

Gary, Raymond. "I Say Oklahoma's OK." *Saturday Evening Post,* July 9, 1955, pp. 27, 67-68, 70.

———. "The South Can Integrate Its Schools." *Look,* March 31, 1959, pp. 119-21.

"Governor Murray on Crime—Excerpts." *Journal of Criminal Law* 24 (1933): 454.

"Grandfather Clause in Oklahoma." *Outlook,* August 20, 1910, pp. 853-54.

Hanson, Bertil L. "County Commissioners of Oklahoma." *Midwest Journal of*

Political Science 9 (1965):388-400.

———. "Oklahoma's Experience with Direct Legislation." *Southwestern Social Science Quarterly* 47 (1966):263-73.

Harger, Charles Moreau. "Oklahoma and the Indian Territories as They Are Today." *American Review of Reviews,* February 25, 1902, p. 177.

———. "The Next Commonwealth: Oklahoma." *Outlook,* January 5, 1901, p. 273.

Harrison, Walter M. "Oklahoma, Bounty Bought." *Review of Reviews,* April 1936, p. 54.

Haskell, Henry Joseph. "Martial Law in Oklahoma." *Outlook,* September 26, 1923, p. 133.

Hayes, Samuel P. "Modernizing Values in the History of the United States." *Peasant Studies* 6 (1977):68-79.

"Head Hunting in Oklahoma." *Independent,* December 31, 1927, pp. 642-43.

Hill, Mozell C. "All-Negro Communities of Oklahoma: The Natural History of a Social Movement." *Journal of Negro History* 11 (1946):254-68.

Hilton, O. A. "The Oklahoma Council of Defense and the First World War." *Chronicles of Oklahoma* 20 (1942):18-42.

Holland, Reid. "CCC [Civilian Conservation Corps] in the City." *Chronicles of Oklahoma* 53 (1975):367-75.

———. "Oklahoma's CCC." *Chronicles of Oklahoma* 48 (1970):224-34.

Holloway, Harry. "Oklahoma Goes Republican." *Oklahoma Government Bulletin* 1, no. 2 (1963).

"Homeric America." *Nation,* January 24, 1923, p. 86.

Hubbell, John T. "The Desegregation of the University of Oklahoma, 1946-1950." *Journal of Negro History* 62 (1972):370-84.

"Incorrigible Enemy of Academic Freedom." *New Republic,* May 18, 1932, pp. 3-4.

James, Louise B. "Alice Mary Robertson: Anti-Feminist Congresswoman." *Chronicles of Oklahoma* 55 (1977):454-62.

Kerr, Robert Samuel. "Aims and Purposes: Democratic Keynote Address." *Vital Speeches,* August 1, 1944, pp. 611-16.

"Latest Developments." *Publishers Weekly,* June 12, 1943, p. 2240.

Lilienthal, David E. "Oklahoma, A Test of Our Theory of Constitutional Government." *Outlook,* October 10, 1923, pp. 216-17.

McDonald, Jean G. "Legislators and Patronage in Oklahoma." Legislative Research Series, no. 10. Norman: University of Oklahoma, Bureau of Government Research, 1975.

McDonald, Stephen L. "Some Factors in the Recent Economic Development of the Southwest." *Southwestern Social Science Quarterly* 45 (1965):329-39.

Mackaye, Milton. "The Shame of Oklahoma." *Saturday Evening Post,* April 24, 1948, p. 16.

Mason, Jerome. "Oklahoma's Fuller Life Salesmen." *American Mercury,* January 1938, pp. 68-76.

Matson, Clarence H. "Oklahoma, a Vigorous Western Commonwealth." *American Review of Reviews,* September 1905, pp. 310-19.

Melcher, Frederick Gershom. "Radical Books in Oklahoma." *Publishers Weekly,* January 23, 1941, p. 521.

Mellinger, Phillip. "Discrimination and Statehood in Oklahoma." *Chronicles of Oklahoma* 49 (1971):340-78.

Melton, L. D. "Design for Taxing: Oklahoma's Novel System of Sales Tax Administration." *State Government* 8 (1935):235-36.

Meredith, H. L. "The Agrarian Reform Press in Oklahoma." *Chronicles of Oklahoma* 50 (1972):82-94.

———. "Agrarian Socialism and the Negro in Oklahoma, 1900-1918." *Labor History* 11 (1970):277-84.

———. "Oscar Ameringer and the Concept of Agrarian Socialism." *Chronicles of Oklahoma* 45 (1967):77-83.

Meserve, John Bartlett. "The Plea of Crazy Snake." *Chronicles of Oklahoma* 9 (1931):126-38.

Milburn, George. "Oklahoma." *Yale Review* 35 (1946):515-26.

———. "Sage of Tishomingo." *American Mercury,* May 1931, pp. 11-21.

Moore, Jessie Randolph. "A Tribute to Mrs. Mabel Bassett." *Chronicles of Oklahoma* 32 (1954):359-63.

Morgan, David R. "Legislative Reapportionment and Urban Influence on the Oklahoma Legislature." *Oklahoma Business Bulletin* 40, no. 3 (1972):5-9.

———. "The Urban Impact on Oklahoma Voting Patterns." *Oklahoma Business Bulletin* 40, no. 2 (1972):10-15.

———. "Urban-Rural Divisions within the Oklahoma Legislature." *Oklahoma Business Bulletin* 40, no. 4 (1972):5-9.

———. "Urbanism and Oklahoma Politics." *Oklahoma Business Bulletin* 40, no. 1 (1972):10-14.

Murphy, Lionel D. "Alfalfa Bill Murray's Initiative Program Defeated in Oklahoma." *National Municipal Review* 21 (1932):203.

———. "Two Trials of Oklahoma's Runoff Primary." *Southwest Social Science Quarterly* 14 (1933):156-74.

Murray, Johnston. "Oklahoma's in a Mess." *Saturday Evening Post,* April 30, 1955, pp. 20-21, 92, 96-97.

Murray, William Henry. "The Constitutional Convention." *Chronicles of Oklahoma* 9 (1931):126-38.

Nelson, Llewellyn. "KKK for Boredom." *New Republic,* January 14, 1925, pp. 196-98.

Nesbitt, Paul, ed. "Governor Haskell Tells of Two Conventions." *Chronicles of Oklahoma* 14 (1936):189-217.

Neuringer, Sheldon. "The War on the Ku Klux Klan in Oklahoma." *Chronicles of Oklahoma* 45 (1967):153-79.

"A New State's New Ideas." *Nation,* April 4, 1907, pp. 304-305.

Oatman, Miriam Eulalie. "Oklahoma's Dramatic Year." *Southwest Political and Social Science Quarterly* 4 (1924):319-32.

"Oklahoma Bookstore Owner's Conviction Reversed." *Publishers Weekly,* October 2, 1943, p. 1337.

"The Oklahoma Kid." *Saturday Evening Post,* May 16, 1959, pp. 36-37, 70-75.

"Oklahoma's Impeachment Muddle." *Literary Digest,* January 14, 1928, p. 11.

"Oklahoma's Radical Constitution." *Outlook,* October 5, 1907, pp. 229-31.

Patterson, Samuel C. "Dimensions of Voting Behavior in a One-Party State Legislature." *Public Opinion Quarterly* 26 (1962):185-200.

Peterson, Samuel C. "The Role of the Lobbyist: The Case of Oklahoma." *Journal of Politics* 25 (1963):72-92.

Phillips, Leon C. "A Southern Democrat Renounces the New Deal Party." *Manufacturers' Record,* August 1943, pp. 32-33, 60.

Pickens, Donald K. "The Sterilization Movement: The Search for Purity of Mind and State." *Phylon* 28 (1967):78-94.

Schruben, Francis W. "The Return of Alfalfa Bill Murray." *Chronicles of Oklahoma* 41 (1963):38-65.

Shepherd, William Gunn. "King of the Prairie: Alfalfa Bill." *Collier's,* November 28, 1931, pp. 12-13.

"Sooner Strongboy." *Time,* January 22, 1940, pp. 20-21.

Stanley, Ruth Moore. "Alice M. Robertson, Oklahoma's First Congresswoman." *Chronicles of Oklahoma* 45 (1967):259-89.

Sullivant, Otis. "Rich Man's Race." *Nation,* June 26, 1954, p. 542.

Taylor, Robert Lewis. "Dear Constituent: Go Fly a Kite." *Saturday Evening Post,* July 17, 1943, pp. 9-10, 78-80.

Thoburn, Joseph B. "Frank H. Greer." *Chronicles of Oklahoma* 14 (1936): 265-94.

Travis, Paul D. "Gore, Bristow, and Taft." *Chronicles of Oklahoma* 53 (1975): 212-24.

Troper, Harold Martin. "The Creek-Negroes of Oklahoma and Canadian Immigration, 1909-1911." *Canadian Historical Review* 53 (1972):272-88.

Tweeter, Luther, and Shaffer, Ron. "Measuring Net Economic Changes from Rural Industrial Development in Oklahoma." *Land Economics* 50 (1974): 261-70.

Vestal, Stanley. "First Families of Oklahoma." *American Mercury,* August 1925, pp. 489-94.

"The Victory for Popular Government in Oklahoma and Its Political Significance." *Arena,* June 1907, pp. 642-43.

Walker, Larry. "State Legislative Control of Federal Aid Funds: The Case of Oklahoma." Legislative Research Series, no. 13. Norman: University of Oklahoma, Bureau of Government Research, 1978.

Ware, James. "The Sooner NRA: New Deal Recovery in Oklahoma." *Chronicles of Oklahoma* 54 (1976):339-51.

Warrick, Sherry. "The Working Class Union." *Chronicles of Oklahoma* 52 (1974): 180-95.

Watson, Elbert L. "Oklahoma and the Anti-Evolution Movement." *Chronicles of Oklahoma* 42 (1964):396-407.

Wood, John W. "Reform of Judicial Selection Procedures in Oklahoma." *Oklahoma Government Bulletin* 2, no. 1 (1964).

Woodburn, Joseph Albert. "Western Radicalism in American Politics." *Mississippi Valley Historical Review* 13 (1926):143-68.

"WPA in Oklahoma an Administration Handicap." *New Republic,* July 13, 1938, p. 279.

Wright, James R. "The Assiduous Wedge: Woman Suffrage and the Oklahoma Constitutional Convention." *Chronicles of Oklahoma* 51 (1973):421-31.

Wright, Muriel H. "William Shaffer Key." *Chronicles of Oklahoma* 37 (1959), 138-48.

Unpublished Works

Benson, June Tompkins. "Election Practices in Oklahoma." Master's thesis, University of Oklahoma, 1954.

Bish, Robert Arthur. "Leon C. Phillips and the Anti-New Deal Agitation in Oklahoma, 1935-1944." Master's thesis, University of Oklahoma, 1966.

Booth, Edward John. "Economic Development in Eastern Oklahoma until 1950: The Impact of a Rigid Settlement Pattern, Meager Industrialization and Agricultural Adjustment in a Low-Income Rural Area." Ph.D. dissertation, Vanderbilt University, 1961.

Briscoe, Hermione B. "The 1938 Oklahoma Gubernatorial Campaign." Master's thesis, University of Oklahoma, 1939.

Brown, Thomas E. "Bible-Belt Catholicism: A History of the Roman Catholic Church in Oklahoma, 1905-1945." Ph.D. dissertation, Oklahoma State University, 1974.

Bush, Charles C. "The Green Corn Rebellion." Master's thesis, University of Oklahoma, 1932.

Carney, Champ Clark. "The Historical Geography of the Chickasaw Lands of Oklahoma." Ph.D. dissertation, University of Indiana, 1961.

Carney, George Olney. "Oklahoma's U.S. House Delegation and Progressivism, 1901-1917." Ph.D. dissertation, Oklahoma State University, 1972.

Clark, Carter Blue. "A History of the Ku Klux Klan in Oklahoma." Ph.D. dissertation, University of Oklahoma, 1976.

Conley, John. "A History of the Oklahoma Penal System, 1907-1967." Ph.D. dissertation, Michigan State University, 1977.

Crim, Ed Franklin, Jr. "The Effect of Regional Public Expenditures on the Level of Regional Income as Illustrated by the State of Oklahoma." Ph.D. dissertation, University of Illinois, 1960.

Durbin, Alan C. "The Election of the Oklahoma Supreme Court Justices, 1907-1964." Master's thesis, University of Oklahoma, 1961.

Fraker, Elmer L. "The Spread of Populism into Oklahoma Territory." Master's thesis, University of Oklahoma, 1938.

Forbes, Charles Gerald. "The Origin and Early Development of the Oil Industry in Oklahoma." Ph.D. dissertation, University of Oklahoma, 1939.

Furr, Carolyn Joan. "The Voting Habits of the People of Oklahoma's Sixth Congressional District from 1952 to 1966." Master's thesis, University of Oklahoma, 1971.

Gray, Walter L. "The Long Ballot in Oklahoma." Master's thesis, University of Oklahoma, 1952.

Harmon, William S. "Oklahoma's Constitutional Amendments: A Study of the Use of the Initiative and Referendum." Ph.D. dissertation, University of Oklahoma, 1951.

Hubbell, John T. "Racial Desegregation at the University of Oklahoma, 1946-1950." Master's thesis, University of Oklahoma, 1961.

Humphrey, Charles Allen. "Socio-Economic Study of Six All-Black Towns in Oklahoma." Ph.D. dissertation, Oklahoma State University, 1973.

McCool, Elizabeth. "Impeachments in Oklahoma in 1913." Master's thesis, University of Oklahoma, 1935.

McDonald, Jean Graves. "Oklahoma Patronage, the Political Parties, and State Elective Officials." Ph.D. dissertation, Michigan State University, 1972.

Manheimer, Eric. "The Public Career of Elmer Thomas." Ph.D. dissertation, University of Oklahoma, 1953.

Marland, E. W. "My Experience with the Money Trust." Typescript in authors' possession.

Mauer, George J. "Political Equality and Legislative Apportionment in Oklahoma, 1907-1964." Ph.D. dissertation, University of Oklahoma, 1964.

Meredith, Howard L. "A History of the Socialist Party in Oklahoma." Ph.D. dissertation, University of Oklahoma, 1970.

National Youth Administration. "Proceedings and Debates of the Oklahoma Constitutional Convention." 4 vols. Typescript, n.d.

Parkhurst, Guy Harold. "Uses and Legal Questions of Martial Law in Oklahoma." Master's thesis, University of Oklahoma, 1935.

Paulin, Bernard H. "The Presidential Election of 1912 in Oklahoma." Master's thesis, University of Oklahoma, 1965.

Robinson, James Arthur. "Anti-Sedition Legislation and Loyalty Investigations in Oklahoma." Master's thesis, University of Oklahoma, 1955.

Rosen, Ellen I. "Peasant Socialism in America? The Socialist Party in Oklahoma Before the First World War." Ph.D. dissertation, City University of New York, 1976.

Saxe, Allan. "Protest and Reform: The Desegregation of Oklahoma City." Ph.D. dissertation, University of Oklahoma, 1969.

Short, Julia. "Kate Barnard: Liberated Woman." Master's thesis, University of Oklahoma, 1970.

Sims, Bobbie C. "The Oklahoma Farmer-Labor Reconstruction League." Master's thesis, University of Oklahoma, 1966.

Singleton, Julius Allen. "The Effects of Reapportionment on the Oklahoma House of Representatives." Ph.D. dissertation, Texas Tech University, 1970.

Solomon, Lewis Elma. "The Personnel of the Oklahoma Constitutional Convention." Master's thesis, University of Oklahoma, 1924.

Spears, Earnestine B. "Social Forces in the Admittance of Negroes to the University of Oklahoma." Master's thesis, University of Oklahoma, 1951.

Stacey, Karl. "Petroleum and Gas in the Economy of Oklahoma, 1900–1954." Ph.D. dissertation, Clark University, 1955.

Stephenson, Malvina. "Covering the Oklahoma House of Representatives." Master's thesis, University of Oklahoma, 1936.

Swearingen, Eugene. "The Political Economy of Petroleum Conservation: A Case Study of Oklahoma." Ph.D. dissertation, Stanford University, 1955.

Thornton, Hurschel Vern. "Oklahoma Municipal History: Indian Territory." Master's thesis, University of Oklahoma, 1929.

Thorpe, Claude R. "Robert S. Kerr's 1948 Senatorial Campaign." Master's thesis, University of Oklahoma, 1967.

Turner, Cecil L. "Oklahoma's New Deal: Program and Reaction." Master's thesis, University of Oklahoma, 1963.

Vaught, Edgar S. "A New Chapter in an Old Story." Manuscript in Oklahoma Historical Society, Oklahoma City.

Wallace, Elton Harvey. "Alfred E. Smith, The Religious Issue: Oklahoma City, September 20, 1928." Ph.D. dissertation, Michigan State University, 1965.

Welborn, Claude Alson. "The Red River as a Boundary Between Texas and Oklahoma." Ph.D. dissertation, University of Texas, 1957.

Womack, John, Jr. "The Green Corn Rebellion." Manuscript in authors' possession.

Young, Wayne F. "Oklahoma Politics with Special Reference to the Election of Oklahoma's First Republican Governor." Ph.D. dissertation, University of Oklahoma, 1964.

Index